Her Cold War

This book was published with the assistance of the Greensboro Women's Fund of the University of North Carolina Press.
Founding Contributors: Linda Arnold Carlisle, Sally Schindel Cone, Anne Faircloth, Bonnie McElveen Hunter, Linda Bullard Jennings, Janice J. Kerley (in honor of Margaret Supplee Smith), Nancy Rouzer May, and Betty Hughes Nichols.

© 2021 Tanya L. Roth
All rights reserved
Set in Charis by Westchester Publishing Services
Manufactured in the United States of America

The University of North Carolina Press has been a member of the Green Press Initiative since 2003.

Library of Congress Cataloging-in-Publication Data
Names: Roth, Tanya L., author.
Title: Her cold war : women in the U.S. military, 1945–1980 / Tanya L. Roth.
Other titles: Women in the U.S. military, 1945–1980
Description: Chapel Hill : University of North Carolina Press, [2021] | Includes bibliographical references and index.
Identifiers: LCCN 2020056874 | ISBN 9781469664422 (cloth ; alk. paper) | ISBN 9781469664439 (paperback ; alk. paper) | ISBN 9781469664446 (ebook)
Subjects: LCSH: Women soldiers—United States—History—20th century. | Sex role—United States—History—20th century. | Sex discrimination against women—United States.
Classification: LCC UB418.W65 R68 2021 | DDC 355.0082/0973—dc23
LC record available at https://lccn.loc.gov/2020056874

Cover illustration: Cover page of *Women Marines* (NAID 26323300). Department of Defense, Department of the Navy, U.S. Marine Corps, Division of Information; Records Relating to the Commemoration of the Year of the Women Marines, and to Subsequent Women Marine Activities, 1/1968–4/1972; Records of the U.S. Marine Corps, 1775–, Record Group 127; National Archives at College Park, College Park, MD.

Excerpt from "What Makes a Wave?" (written by Ralph Blane, music by Harry Warren) from *Skirts Ahoy!* (directed by Sidney Lanfield [Beverly Hills, California: MGM Studios, 1952]) is used by permission of Four Jays Music.

Her Cold War

Women in the U.S. Military, 1945–1980

....

TANYA L. ROTH

The University of North Carolina Press Chapel Hill

For women in uniform—past, present, and future

Contents

Acknowledgments, xi

Abbreviations in the Text, xv

Introduction, 1
Constructing Womanpower

Part I
A Shared Responsibility
Defining Sexual Integration in the Early Cold War

1 A Nucleus of Women in a Nuclear Age, 21

2 The Real Miss America, 40
   Recruiting Womanpower

3 You in the Service, 60
   Training Uncle Sam's Nieces

Part II
The Possibilities and Problems of Wielding Womanpower

4 Unequaled in the Civilian World, 81
   Working for Uncle Sam

5 The Possibility of Maternity, 100
   Motherhood and Military Service

6 Top Secret and Obscene, 119
   Sex and the American Servicewoman

Part III
Integration Is Not Enough
Changes from Within and Without

7 Catalysts for Womanpower, 141
The Defense Advisory Committee on Women in the Services

8 Battling for Equality, 159
Challenging Military Limitations

9 Reimagining Equality, 179

10 Second-Class Soldiers, 199

Conclusion, 215

Key Dates in Women's Military History, 227

Women Military Leaders, 229

Notes, 231

Bibliography, 277

Index, 291

Illustrations

1.1 Colonel Mary Hallaren portrait, 26
2.1 "Proud Parents" recruiting poster, 47
2.2 "Mother . . . Dad . . . and Grandma," in *Somebody Special* pamphlet, 49
2.3 "A Brand-new Beauty," in *Somebody Special* pamphlet, 52
2.4 "Great myths about The Women's Army Corps," 58
3.1 Navy recruit training, 65
3.2 Waves sewing badges, 68
4.1 "Serving You in Air Force Blue!" recruiting ad, 83
4.2 "Food service, machine accounting, and information," in *Somebody Special* pamphlet, 87
8.1 Brigadier General Mildred Bailey, 167
8.2 General Elizabeth Hoisington portrait, 169
8.3 Major General Jeanne Holm portrait, 171

Acknowledgments

Books begin with questions. This book began with one question two decades ago in an undergraduate seminar, grew into an honors thesis with new questions, and those questions led me to my PhD ten years later. Being able to ask these questions, explore them, and find new ones has been one of the greatest privileges of my adult life. It's been an even greater privilege to be surrounded by people along the way who have indulged me as I asked questions, pushed me to rethink my questions, challenged me to go further than I might ever have imagined, and helped me find answers—often, answers I didn't know I needed.

As an undergraduate at the University of Missouri–Columbia, Linda Reeder and the late Mary Neth introduced me to women's history and changed my life. I'm grateful to both of them, and for Professor Reeder introducing me to the study of gender and war. Thank you for assigning Vera Brittain's *Testament of Youth*, which became the foundation for everything since, and thank you for all the time you invested in me and my work.

At Washington University in St. Louis, I got to learn from and study with people who opened my world further. I cannot express just how fundamentally my graduate experience shaped both my writing and my professional career as a teacher. In my final year of graduate school, a generous American Fellowship from the American Association of University Women allowed me to devote my time to writing and polishing off my research. I would never have been able to apply for that fellowship without the support of the Department of History faculty, and all the things I learned in my time there. First and foremost, I thank Andrea Friedman, my advisor. Your voice echoed in my head every step of the way in writing this book. Even when I wasn't sure if my writing was making sense, you always had a way of seeing what I was after and helping me figure out how to say it better. Thank you for putting up with me and for all you have taught me. Two others shaped this project and my writing in significant ways, too. First, the relative scarcity of semicolons in this manuscript is because of Peter Kastor: thank you for your advice and mentorship over the years. Tim Parsons, years ago you challenged me to meet veterans and hear their stories. I didn't think I could be an oral historian and the idea scared me to death, but I didn't want to let you down. Also, you have always insisted on one crucial question—"so what?"—and while that could be infuriating, you were also right that it is *the* question to ask. Now I make my own students ask that question.

Research is an adventure, and while researching what became this book, I got to have so many adventures across the country. Some days, I felt giddy with the prospect of uncovering fascinating documents; others were full of long drives and D.C. Beltway traffic, but doing research in archives is like nothing else. I'll never forget hiking the University of Texas–Austin campus with my friend Seth Offenbach as we both pursued our research at the towering Lyndon B. Johnson Presidential Library. In Abilene, Kansas, before and after long hours bent over old papers, I discovered chocolate tea at a bed and breakfast where President Eisenhower played as a child and saw my first (and to date, only) combine tractor derby. While researching at the Kennedy Presidential Library, I trekked in the falling snow on the waterside path from my hotel to the library. Thanks to a few days at the National Archives in D.C., I will always get to say that I've done research in the same building that houses the Declaration of Independence, and what's cooler than that? I'm grateful to the John F. Kennedy, Lyndon B. Johnson, and Gerald Ford presidential libraries, who helped fund research adventures that led to important information for this book. I hope I contained my squeals of glee in your reading rooms and didn't disturb the other researchers too much when I discovered particularly interesting items. Staff at these libraries, as well as the Dwight Eisenhower and Harry Truman presidential libraries, all graciously helped me refine queries and sift through materials to find obscure information on women's military service. Staff at the National Archives in College Park and Washington, D.C., the U.S. Army Women's Museum, the Navy Historical Center's Operational Archives, the Marine Corps Archives, the Air Force Historical Research Agency, Schlesinger Library, the Library of Congress, and the Smithsonian were indispensable in helping me navigate their systems and find what I needed. In particular, though, I am grateful for Britta Granrud at the Women in Military Service for America Memorial in Arlington, Virginia, and Beth Ann Koelsch at the Betty H. Carter Women Veterans Historical Project at the University of North Carolina–Greensboro. These collections are remarkable and are a must for anyone who wants to know more about women's military service. Thank you to the Women's Memorial, the Smithsonian, and Four Jays Music Company for permission to use materials in this book.

While archival research is important, I discovered that my project came to life as I began interviewing women veterans. Tori Vernau and members of American Legion Post 404 St. Louis Women Veterans shared their time and experiences with me, including Rose Wuellner, Carol Wheeler, Wilma Nations, LaDonna Darks, Kathy Sutphen, Marge Menke, Melanie Gregory, Shirley Walz, Bernadette Stapleton, Margie Jacob, Thelma Blumberg, and Esther Ellspermann. Friends introduced me to their mothers who had served, and veterans across the country answered my calls to talk to them about their time in the armed forces. I learned so much in speaking to these women, and I am grateful for their time. I thank Gloria Clifford, Carol Schoon, Sarah Langley, Cheryl Bucy, Carol Poynor, Judy and John Campbell, Polly Hazelwood, Barbara Ann Wilson, and MaryAnne Haarhaus. Not every story made it to these pages, but all of your stories made this book possible. This book is not only about you, but for you and in honor of your service.

Over the years, countless people in my life have helped me grow, encouraged me, and read my work. Amy Minella gave me a push years ago that set me off on these discoveries and didn't laugh when I told her I wanted to be a writer. So many scholars have been generous with me, sharing their time, resources, and helping me think through ideas, including Jackie Whitt, Kara Vuic, Heather Stur, Margot Canaday, Sarah Myers, and Michael Doidge. My cohort and instructors in the 2010 West Point Summer Seminar in Military History helped me understand the military in new ways. Jane and Nate Green, your friendship and your encouragement to keep working on this book, even when I doubted anyone would actually read it, has made such a difference in my life. Bryna Campbell, I miss our regular Skype sessions that weren't really about writing but kept us accountable and inspired and moved us on to many good things. At MICDS, I get to work with so many wonderful people who inspire and encourage me regularly: thank you to my colleagues and friends. You know who you are, and I hope you know how important you are to me.

A few years ago, I had almost given up on this book, and thought I'd try one more time. I submitted a version of this manuscript to the Society for Military History's Coffman Prize and was honored to receive the award in 2019. I'm so glad the committee believed in this book's potential. That award led me to UNC Press, and the people there have been wonderful in this process, which has included finishing a book in the midst of a global pandemic. Thank you to everyone at UNC Press, particularly Debbie Gershenowitz, an incredible editor, whose thoughtful comments made this work better, and Dylan White, who has had to deal with my newbie emails time and again. The copyediting team was indispensable in helping me fine-tune the text: because of you, I was able to read the manuscript with new eyes. Thank you to the anonymous reviewers, whose comments at times made me eat more chocolate than I should admit and may have had me pull out my hair as I tried to write something that would meet their expectations. If I could give you each a box of chocolates in return, I would: your feedback helped me become a stronger writer and find the heart of this book.

Years ago, I promised myself that I would finish this book. It's just taken longer than I planned. Through it all, my family members have been some of my biggest cheerleaders. Growing up, my parents not only survived my incessant stream of questions, but also listened patiently, pointed me toward books and libraries, and now get to laugh because my son asks me many questions, too. I hope I can help my son cultivate a lifetime of asking questions.

This book would have never gotten finished if not for my husband Nick, and my son Andrew. I wouldn't have had time to write if not for Nick and Andrew's marathon Minecraft sessions and other father-son adventures that took them out of the house so I could get a little writing done around lesson plans and grading. Nick has patiently tolerated years of hearing me think aloud about my research, and at key moments his insights helped push me in directions I hadn't yet explored. Right now, Andrew is only vaguely aware that I've been writing a book and has expressed disappointment that it's not about dragons. I like to think that someday he'll feel proud. I'm good with that. I'm so lucky to have such a wonderful family: thank you, Nick, for growing with me through the years. I love exploring the world with you.

Abbreviations in the Text

DACOWITS	Defense Advisory Committee on Women in the Services, an organization of civilian women, founded in 1951 to advise the Department of Defense on all matters pertaining to the use of women in the military
DOD	The Department of Defense; created in 1947 to combine earlier defense groups such as the War Department, Department of the Army, and Department of the Navy
WAAC	Women's Army Auxiliary Corps, created in 1942
WAC	Women's Army Corps; succeeded the WAAC in 1943 and lasted until 1978
Wac	Refers to a woman in the WAC
WAF	Women in the Air Force; informal term used to designate women's element of the air force. Unlike the WAC, did not exist as a formal, separate institution within the air force.
Waf	Refers to a woman in the WAF
WAVES	Acronym for "Women Accepted for Volunteer Emergency Service" in the navy. Created in World War II. Although it was not a formal institution after the war, the WAVES moniker persisted.
Wave	Refers to a woman in the navy
WM	Women Marines; also used to refer to a woman in the marine corps

Her Cold War

Introduction

Constructing Womanpower

∙∙

In 1976, one of the first female American generals proclaimed that women in the military "were pioneering the women's movement long before many of those who have been pushing for women's rights in recent years ever realized they didn't have them . . . we have fought the battle for equality and have it almost won."[1] Major General Jeanne Holm's announcement specifically identified the U.S. military as a site of social change, something few Americans tend to think about when they consider the role of the armed forces. Holm's opinion also contrasts with the better-known history of women's fights for equality through second-wave feminism in the 1960s and 1970s, suggesting a new chronology for understanding women's efforts to gain equality with men. Well before the second-wave movement emerged, military service offered American women an avenue to equality through careers in national defense. In the years immediately following World War II, Congress passed new legislation that permitted women to serve permanently in women's components of the army, navy, air force, and marine corps. In the aftermath of this legislation, the United States military initiated a pivotal transition process as servicewomen began their "battle for equality." That transition continues today.

The story of integrating womanpower into the U.S. military is one of simultaneous institutional and social change. After World War II, military leaders eyed preparedness for future conflict, which prompted them to evaluate growing personnel needs. Finding solutions to meet those needs meant not just continuing the draft, which began in World War II, but also reconsidering who served in the armed forces and in what roles. Sexual integration became one of the main consequences of these reconsiderations. Using the term "womanpower" to specify the use of women personnel, in contrast to the more commonly used "manpower," defense officials promoted this change not as a radical shift in military organization but to maximize access to potential personnel and improve utilization efficiency.[2] Although officials cast womanpower as a matter of efficiency and need, the military's postwar sexual integration efforts began a process of redefining equality. While leaders intended to uphold existing conceptualizations of women's social and economic roles, over time that approach increasingly came under fire.

During the first thirty years of the Cold War, equality for women in the armed forces shifted from a narrow definition to a broader one. In the 1940s, defense officials structured women's military roles on the basis of gender difference philosophy, the idea that women's and men's biological differences made it necessary to create distinct opportunities—and limitations—for servicewomen. Classified as noncombatants, servicewomen filled roles Americans would perceive as socially acceptable for women, jobs they might also perform in civilian life such as communications, clerical, or office administration positions. Furthermore, defense officials created regulations that prohibited mothers of minor children from staying in the military and made allowances that encouraged many women to end their service commitment early if they married. Today, such regulations do not seem to represent a commitment to women's equality, but in the mid-twentieth-century military, government leaders and many servicewomen did not view these limitations as obstacles to equality. The fact that women had an opportunity to serve at all seemed enough. Instead, by basing their definition of equality on assumptions that innate gender differences meant men and women should have different roles and functions, officials could and did claim they offered equality because they sought to respect those differences. During World War II, the necessities of fighting total war taught military leaders that there were tasks women did as well or better than men. Consequently, equality for servicewomen centered on the idea that women deserved the same pay for that work, a standard that women had also begun seeking in the private sector.

Servicewomen's experiences, however, demonstrate the problematic nature of regulating women's military careers using a gender difference vision of equality. Women in the military found themselves negotiating such limitations to keep their jobs or secure important benefits, or leaving military service because their efforts failed. As long as gender difference remained the guiding principle of military and government policy, servicewomen and their allies faced many obstacles in their efforts and struggled to secure lasting change. In the 1960s, however, this definition of equality became increasingly unpopular and a newer definition began to develop, one that left no room for assumptions about women's capabilities. The new definition of equality, based on gender sameness philosophy, recognized that gender is socially constructed. It called into question existing ideas about women's roles in national defense, highlighting the ways in which limits on those roles, such as excluding mothers, relied on assumptions or expectations about what women should do, rather than women's actual mental or physical capabilities. As this broader understanding of equality emerged, government leaders eliminated protective labor laws based on sex difference. By the 1970s, many servicewomen, civilian second-wave feminists, and members of Congress called on military leaders to remove gender-based service restrictions and instead structure women's service based on the new definition of equality.

The gender difference approach to defining equality persisted into the 1960s because Americans had long idealized distinctly separate gender spheres for men and women. The most iconic images of women in the early Cold War focus on women in the home—white, middle-class, caring for their children and husband. These are the women that feminist icon Betty Friedan wrote about in *The Feminine Mystique*, drawing attention to what she called "the problem that has no name," the malaise women felt as they went through their daily lives as wives and mothers because, Friedan claimed, they had been taught that this was what they should want from life.[3] When Friedan began writing her book in the late 1950s, most women married at the age of twenty, and the marriage age was trending downward. The number of women going to college had decreased, and more than half of women left college without their degrees because they worried a degree might stop them from marrying. The birthrate rose, and by the 1950s, Friedan explained, "the suburban housewife—she was the dream image of the young American women and the envy, it was said, of women all over the world."[4] Friedan's portrait of the American housewife, cast today as the stay-at-home mom, remains familiar to Americans more than half a century later.

Despite the cultural resonance of the stay-at-home mom, the integration of women into the military in 1948 illustrates that Friedan's portrayal of postwar culture does not tell the whole story of opportunities for and limitations on American women in the early Cold War. While marrying and having children was a common path for American women at that time, it was not the only option. In the early Cold War years, domesticity might have loomed large, but historians have helped provide important context for Friedan's understanding of her own times. In particular, historian Elaine Tyler May argues that the suburban housewife was a phenomenon specific to the immediate postwar years, a period when recent national trauma made family immensely important to Americans. After the instability of the Great Depression and World War II, May argues, Americans sought security and comfort in families that emphasized "traditional gender roles"—namely, with the father as breadwinner and mother as homemaker.[5] May emphasizes that these trends were short-lived, but they were powerful ideas for many Americans. Not only are such ideas still entrenched in American popular culture, but during the Cold War these trends shaped politics and law in numerous ways, such as defining women's military service. Joanne Meyerowitz builds on Friedan's earlier research to look at mass culture in the 1940s and 1950s, reviewing nonfiction magazine articles. She discovered that mass culture, based on her review of nearly five hundred pieces from magazines with a combined circulation of about 22 million readers "did not simply glorify domesticity," but also "celebrated nondomestic activity" as well.[6] That is, while the dominant images of women in the mid-twentieth century often appear centered on the home, the Cold War was also a time when new opportunities opened for women.

May and Meyerowitz's studies help us better understand Friedan's vantage point, as well as those of world military and government officials and potential women recruits. While demographics reflect the significance of the domestic ideal, it is also important to remember that the men and women who constructed women's military opportunities drew from this ideal self-consciously. For example, as chapter 2 demonstrates, military officials knew that family mattered, creating enlistment standards and recruiting methods that required parents to actively endorse their daughter's choice to join the armed forces. Additionally, military leaders formulated women's service on the assumption that the women coming into the armed forces would be the best of the best, proper future wives and mothers. In their view, military service would help turn these women into better citizens (and then better wives and mothers). Women's military service did not compete with the domestic ideal; it complemented it.

Even if military and government leaders paid close attention to women's roles as potential wives and mothers, joining the military gave a woman a job—an economic role with patriotic purpose. This was true during World War II as well, but during the war patriotism was a powerful motivator for many women, leading them to enlist so they could help fight the war, too, along with the promise of a steady job and paycheck. During the war, however, women's service was temporary: government officials assumed that women would help until the war ended, just like women working in manufacturing and other jobs on the homefront. But in 1948, members of Congress decided to give women a permanent place in the armed forces, a decision based on perceived need. They hoped that women would patriotically answer the call to service as they had in World War II, but also created policies that gave women a measure of the equality they continued to fight for in the private sector. Although women elsewhere had been fighting for years to earn pay equal to their male counterparts, the military became one of the first employers to offer women equal pay.

Women's military integration represents an important arena of women's postwar labor because of the ways in which military service offered women unprecedented equality with men as workers. In the armed forces, women and men earned the same pay if they held the same rank. The system was not perfect, and there were ways in which servicemen could acquire greater pay and benefits compared to women at the same rank. Additionally, the U.S. military is not known for high salaries. Yet even with these caveats, military equal pay policies enabled servicewomen to claim a greater share of what historian Alice Kessler-Harris calls "economic citizenship," or the ways in which an individual's wage-earning ability helps them achieve the independence and autonomy associated with full citizenship. That is, when an individual can earn enough money to be self-sustaining, they need not depend on someone else for support and thus can participate fully in the economy, politics, and society. Because true economic citizenship presumes one need not be financially dependent on someone else, Kessler-Harris argues that men historically have been the ones most likely to gain full economic citizenship.[7] One of the most remarkable things about the military's postwar sexual integration process is that military service became a means for American women to also acquire economic citizenship. By establishing women's service on a foundation of equal pay for equal work, military leaders ostensibly offered American women—particularly young single women—access to economic citizenship unavailable in the civilian world. In the 1960s and 1970s, second-wave feminists took up the fight for economic citizenship, led by Betty Friedan and other women. As indicated earlier, however, some people—such as Major General Jeanne Holm—felt that servicewomen seemed perhaps a little closer to equality than their civilian sisters because of the opportunities the military already offered. Equal pay was a major element of those opportunities.

Tracing the genesis and evolution of American women's fights for social and economic equality has been central to understanding how American women's social and economic roles changed in the Cold War, but the military remains largely invisible in that effort. While Kessler-Harris, for example, credits feminist activism of the 1970s for women's access to economic citizenship, the 1970s represent a turning point in women's fight for

Constructing Womanpower 5

equality, not the beginning. Second-wave feminism is important, but the successes of the movement and the focus on gender sameness approaches to equality mean that earlier efforts and other avenues of the struggle for equality sometimes disappear. In her work on labor union women's activism, for example, historian Dorothy Sue Cobble points out that key struggles for equal pay emerged among labor women before World War II and continued during and after the conflict. Like military leaders, labor union women based their arguments on the same gender difference definition of equality that military leaders used.

Because gender difference visions of equality fell out of favor by the 1970s, important voices have become absent in the history of women's rights in the twentieth century. As women who embraced gender difference, the labor feminists Cobble studies do not readily appear to be feminists.[8] The same is true of military women, particularly the highest-ranking women who led the Cold War women's service components. Cobble's work shows the diverse ways in which women fought for and defined equality. The histories of labor women and servicewomen both underscore that second-wave feminism is not the only site for understanding changes in women's status. While second-wave feminism brought questions of women's rights and equality into the mainstream, servicewomen—like labor women—had long navigated such issues. The military was a rare employment opportunity that combined equal pay with protective regulation based on gender difference: analyzing women's military integration helps explain how and why the definition of gender equality evolved in the twentieth century, and why that changing definition of equality matters.

Between 1948 and the early 1970s, servicewomen did not immediately see gender-based limitations on their service as discrimination or inequality, although this does not mean that women always accepted limitations without question. Many servicewomen perceived themselves equal with men because they too participated in national defense, but when sex-based restrictions affected their careers, women were quick to push for change—even if change was not always quick to occur. A few years before Major General Jeanne Holm pronounced servicewomen's battle for equality as "almost won," she reflected in her retirement interview that pushes for change often came internally, as shown in 1960s' efforts to remove rank limitations. As Holm explains, "Pressures were building from women themselves . . . women who were eligible for promotion to full colonel suddenly coming against that blank wall. Here we'd had integration, and equal competitive promotions for all [rank] grades [in the air force], and we bragged about it, and then all of a sudden you were right up against that blank wall for full colonel."[9] The key to such changes, according to Holm, was that women had to identify something as a problem to advocate change.[10] This is exactly what they did over and over again in the Cold War: as servicewomen identified and negotiated obstacles, they redefined equality on their terms. Gender difference equality was intended to account for biological differences and the ways in which those differences affected men and women's roles as workers. The reality, as servicewomen experienced it, was that gender difference equality relied on deeply embedded cultural assumptions about the work women could perform. The assumptions, however, were not fixed: they changed as circumstances required.

During World War II, military need created an environment in which cultural assumptions about women's work capabilities lifted, but only temporarily. The war did not create an in-depth reconsideration of these assumptions, but women's wartime military successes were enough to convince some that womanpower might be even more useful than previously imagined. Individuals like General Dwight Eisenhower argued to members of Congress in 1947 and 1948 that the experiences of World War II indicated that utilizing all Americans—regardless of sex—would be crucial to future military success. Postwar occupation missions in Europe and Asia, Cold War peacekeeping missions, and efforts to combat communism ensured the military remained an important institution in American lives, but the military would also need people.

This growth in national defense meant that militarization continued even after the war's end, although the assumptions about what women could and should do in military service shifted. Historian Michael Sherry argues that militarism became a significant part of American life as far back as the 1930s, noting that the postwar continuation of militarism has affected every facet of American life. He argues that military service constrained women's rights, rather than expanded them, because their participation in the masculine-dominated defense system induced charges that servicewomen subverted the natural gender order and could be dangerous, not supportive, to national defense.[11] In this formulation, according to Sherry, what is important is the fact that military service is masculine in nature. But this concern about women's place in national defense was not new after World War II, and until the early 1970s all service branches actively worked to counter this narrative by placing women in roles deemed particularly suitable for women. By applying a gender difference approach to the definition of equality, military leaders ensured that the military remained a fundamentally masculine institution. The United States military has always been a male-dominated institution, and its traditions, structures, regulations, and masculine culture derive from that experience.

Even after women's integration, the default military body continued to be assumed male. This meant that job opportunities, training, benefits, and regulations all developed from assumptions about what men could or should be able to do, as well as their needs based on their position in society. The question, then, is whether equality is possible for women at all in such an institution. While Sherry argues that military service has been bad for women's rights, political scientist Cynthia Enloe has argued that the masculine military establishment is inherently antithetical to women's equality. Writing in the 1980s, she relies on a gender sameness definition of equality just as Sherry does, the one military and government leaders began to use a decade earlier. According to Enloe, the military is "so fundamentally masculinized that no woman has a chance of transforming that military into a place where women and men can be equal."[12] She and Sherry both suggest that unless and until the fundamentally male-oriented nature of military service in the United States changes, women will never achieve equality as defined with a gender sameness lens.

While the military has historically been and still is a masculinized institution, that does not mean it cannot become otherwise. Both Sherry's and Enloe's works provide important frameworks for understanding women's military integration, but they obscure the significant fact that the military is an institution made up of people. These people hold values that reflect the times they live in, but those values change over time. In her study of Army Nurse Corps (ANC) officers during the Vietnam War, historian Kara Vuic stresses that the military cannot be separated from the society in which it is found. While military leaders might try to regulate service based on a set of specific rules and requirements, sometimes those rules and requirements fall short of lived experiences. In Vietnam, Vuic argues, this meant that military officials tried "both to appeal to individuals with evolving ideas about the proper roles for women and men, and to meet wartime needs."[13] Military policies are created to help officials run an important institution, but sometimes those policies inhibit more than they help. This was one of the challenges that military leaders and servicewomen encountered in the Cold War. Gender difference philosophy led military leaders to rely on key assumptions to structure women's military service in a way that they felt would be respectable and attractive. There was little to no room for evolving gender ideals: military policies tend to reflect what officials believe they will need, not what service members might want.

Yet policy cannot account for lived experiences, and women's individual lived experiences became catalysts for change, often despite military leaders' wishes. This happened throughout the Cold War in the women's service components, as the chapters ahead demonstrate. Vuic illustrates this as well, arguing that gendered assumptions shaped nurses' service experiences in key ways. Viewed by soldiers as simultaneously the girl next door, a sister, or a medical professional, Vuic argues that nurses—primarily women, the majority of the ANC—confronted such stereotypes alongside their own ideas of what it meant to be a member of the military, and during their service "defined and redefined what it meant to be women and men, nurses, and members of the military."[14] Servicemembers were actively and perhaps constantly agents of changes, navigating expectations, opportunities, and limitations that did not always reflect what they expected. In particular, Vuic emphasizes that in the Vietnam-era ANC we see that gender expectations are fluid in time. "Femininity and masculinity were not fixed entities in either the military or society at large, despite claims to the contrary. What it meant to be feminine and masculine varied and changed, contingent upon each person's experiences and expectations."[15] The ANC was particularly burdened with gendered assumptions about personnel, given the historically feminine nature of nursing. Women serving elsewhere in the military also negotiated gendered assumptions about women's work but did so as participants in a historically masculine larger military institution. For servicewomen outside the ANC, assumptions about women's capacity to do work, including cultural norms of women's work, created tensions. By the 1970s, women fought to eliminate most assumptions that limited their military participation, although combat remained firmly gendered as something only men did.

Historian Charissa Threat builds on Vuic's study of the ANC, specifically arguing that the ANC was part of the larger fight for civil rights in the postwar United States. Her study of African American women's and white men's integration into the ANC helps contextualize the changes Vuic observes in the Vietnam War ANC, highlighting the idea that even though we do not think of the military as a site of social change, we cannot separate American social and cultural values from military service. Instead, as she argues, "the U.S. military, especially in the period between World War II and the Vietnam War, was a reflection of the social and cultural values of American society, not divided from them."¹⁶ Her work further demonstrates that policy and lived experiences do not always line up, asserting that even though the ANC embraced racial and gender inclusive policies after World War II, "changes in policy did not alter practices of discrimination and inequality."¹⁷ In short, the ANC reveals that the U.S. military evolves not simply when military leaders authorize it. Sometimes, changes happen despite leaders' best intentions. *Her Cold War* demonstrates this phenomenon in the larger military, illustrating the important part that service members at all levels play in shaping the armed forces.

The history of the Cold War military underscores that the U.S. military is a social institution: while officials may focus on abstract terms like "effective utilization," that phrase fundamentally refers to the question of how military leaders might use people. As leaders considered effective utilization of personnel in the Cold War, effective utilization and equal opportunity increasingly became interconnected. As Threat explains, "the ANC and the U.S. army often found themselves at the very center of the conversation, if not shaping the conversation" about social change.¹⁸ This happened, in part, because the armed forces needed people, and that need led officials to reconsider practices such as racial segregation and the possibility of womanpower in order to accomplish national defense goals. Vuic's study in particular shows how wartime needs for professional nurses further created gender change in the armed forces, even though that was not the intention of ANC or other military leaders. In both instances, and with women outside of the nursing corps, such as those in *Her Cold War*, it is evident that Cold War military and government officials found themselves engaging with impacts of wider social change in many ways.

Ironically, given military and government leaders' insistence that the military is not a laboratory for social change, both the sexual and racial integration of the military began in the summer of 1948. Recognizing that desegregation would be difficult to achieve through legislation, President Truman and members of the President's Committee on Civil Rights began to tie effective utilization to equal opportunity in the armed forces. In the committee's 1947 "To Secure These Rights" report, members argued that racial segregation practices negatively affected both minority servicemen and the military as an institution. "Any discrimination which, while imposing an obligation, prevents members of minority groups from rendering full military service in defense of their country is for them a peculiarly humiliating badge of inferiority. The nation also suffers a loss of manpower and is unable to marshal maximum strength at a moment when such strength is most needed."[19] In July 1948, President Truman used executive order to begin desegregating all service branches, a process that would make the military a laboratory for social change while promoting more effective utilization options.[20] Thus, in the first few decades of the Cold War, military and government leaders specifically engaged in the idea that the U.S. military is not just a defense organization but a social institution. "Effective utilization" may sound like an abstraction, but at its root it requires understanding the people in the organization and what they bring to the defense team.

Executive Order 9981, which came just six weeks after President Truman signed the Women's Armed Services Integration Act into law, effectively meant that women's Cold War military service was racially integrated nearly from the beginning. As African American men increasingly witnessed the removal of such institutional practices as all-Black combat units, the racially integrated women's components became the only remaining segregated systems in the military, now segregated due to sex. Despite being in the vanguard of the military's integration efforts, this fact has largely been ignored aside from Threat's study of the postwar ANC. Studies of the social aspects of the Cold War military focus primarily on racial integration and the role of race, but what is striking about the military's racial integration efforts are the ways in which women disappear from these areas of understanding policy. This does not mean that military officials accomplished desegregation and racial integration completely: racial discrimination and race-based inequities persisted for decades.

Racial discrimination and inequities persisted in part because military leaders believed that changing policy—and enforcing this by controlling behavior, but not attitudes—was all they needed to do. It took years for all the military branches, particularly the army, to desegregate, with the exception of the women's service components. According to political scientist Ronald Krebs, desegregation mattered, but he suggests that the military's larger desegregation efforts "did not have the reverberations that some foresaw and desired. It was . . . a relatively weak signal."[21] But Krebs and others study desegregation by focusing on servicemen and do not consider servicewomen's racial integration experiences. Sherie Mershon and Steven Schlossman's work on the military's desegregation process provides important analysis of how desegregation happened and the challenges African American servicemen faced, but they assume that the default military body is male.[22] Mershon and Schlossman's work is important for understanding race in the military, but renders African American servicewomen invisible.

The official military history of racial integration by Morris MacGregor in 1980 does a more effective job identifying how racial desegregation affected men and women, yet MacGregor acknowledges that the work is an "administrative history," describing what happened but offering little to no analysis.[23] Significantly, by focusing primarily on male service members, studies of the military's racial desegregation efforts have missed the fact that as race-based restrictions disappeared, sex-based restrictions took their place in shaping the military.

The postwar institutional racial desegregation efforts made military service an important site of economic opportunity for African American women—if they could get into the armed forces. Racial desegregation policies, put in place in the women's services by the early 1950s, meant that on an official level, servicewomen's sex mattered more than their race. Some servicewomen's experiences illustrate that race-blind policies did seem to work. However, recruiting standards for women made it difficult for African American women to participate in national defense. Black women remained underrepresented in the women's components—particularly in the officer corps—until the 1970s, when their numbers in the services grew disproportionately. Sociologist Brenda Moore observes that the growth of African American women's presence in the military began after 1974. For example, she notes that enlisted Black women were 14.4 percent of all enlisted women on active duty in 1971, while Black officers were 3.3 percent of all female officers on active duty that year. For context, consider that by June 30, 1972, the total number of women—all races—in the army, navy, air force, and marines was 44,256 (12,639 officers, 31,617 enlisted).[24] While overall numbers of servicewomen, regardless of race, remained low in the first few decades of the Cold War, the numbers of African American women in the armed forces were particularly low.

According to a 1974 history of African American servicewomen, between 1948 and 1963, only 6.6 percent of all Women's Army Corps (WAC) officers were Black, a total of forty-three women. By 1972, however, the number had grown to 176 Black WAC officers and just over 2,000 Black enlisted WAC members. That same year, the air force counted 180 Black women officers out of more than 4,000 women officers. The percentages remained even lower in the navy and marines: by 1974, the seventy-five Black female officers of the navy's WAVES accounted for 1.2 percent of their total officer strength, while the Women Marines had only fourteen Black officers.[25] One retired officer argued that several factors accounted for the growth in Black women officers' numbers in the 1970s, including "overall intensive recruitment of women," at times accompanied by diversity initiatives.[26] Their erasure from military desegregation studies means that historians have yet to fully understand Black women's military service. As Moore points out, their dual status as women and African Americans in the military "placed black women at a greater disadvantage than black males because the military, albeit racist, was socially and politically a 'masculine' institution."[27] When it came to women, however, military leaders acted colorblind: regulations only limited women because they were women, so officials did not think that race mattered in the women's services.

Race absolutely mattered when constructing womanpower, however. Through enlistment and commissioning standards and recruitment and training efforts, leaders of the women's services projected an emphasis on whiteness in an environment that supposedly welcomed women of all races and a very class-conscious image designed to appeal to members of the middle class and above. Relying on white, middle-class formulations of femininity and women's appropriate gender roles offered leaders of the women's services a connection to the idea that military service offered women a career that could help them prepare for marriage. Since white, middle-class values—particularly in the 1950s—emphasized women's primary calling as a wife and mother, leaders of the women's services drew on these class values to suggest that military service did not usurp these roles. Until the 1960s, this strategy created a pattern of short military careers and made it difficult for Black women to meet recruiting standards that were established based on assumptions of white women's educational background. For example, all women recruits had to have a high school diploma, but through the 1950s, approximately 40 percent of white women completed high school, while only 20 percent of African American women had high school diplomas.[28] Furthermore, while military leaders devoted attention to questions of racial equality for male service members through the years, their studies did not include women. Because women's sex, rather than their race, regulated their military service, officials did not consider that African American servicewomen might be facing discrimination because of their skin color. In theory, the women's service components operated on a colorblind basis for much of the Cold War, but that does not account for the fact that three of the four women's services conducted basic training in Southern states. This meant that no matter what their experiences on base, Black women who wanted to leave base during their recruit training for WAC, women in the air force (WAF), or Women Marines (WM) would be visiting, living, and training in communities in the segregated

Constructing Womanpower 13

South. At an official level, however, equal opportunity in the Cold War military always focused on sex alone when it came to servicewomen.

Servicewomen and civilian women associated with the military pushed the Department of Defense (DOD) and Congress to reassess women's place in national security continually, often by reevaluating the relevance of sex-based limitations. This process of negotiation led military and government officials toward the gender sameness definition of equality most supported by second-wave feminists by the late 1970s. Servicewomen and their allies fought against gender difference equality and in doing so, servicewomen achieved major gains: rank limitations disappeared, women received entry to the military academies, and husbands could obtain dependent benefits. Mothers could stay in the service after giving birth. In the navy, women won the right to serve on ships. While servicewomen pushed for many of these changes themselves in the 1950s and 1960s, new ideas about women's roles as mothers and workers, as well as the additional support of civilian women, increasingly made the difference in improving servicewomen's status and access to opportunities.

By the 1970s feminists, members of Congress, and some military leaders began to believe that sexual integration remained incomplete, based on the new mainstream definition of equality that relied on eliminating gender differences and any barriers that limited women's ability to pursue opportunities equally with men. Women continued to experience formal and informal discrimination that prevented military leaders from utilizing women fully, according to their capabilities. While most military branches experimented with the types of jobs that women could perform, by and large women found themselves limited to jobs historically defined as "feminine," while too few women received opportunities to move into more nontraditional career fields. Using language and ideas from the civil rights and women's rights movements, women inside and outside of the military argued vociferously that there were still steps to take to make women fully integrated—and equal—as members of the armed services. These arguments appeared rarely in the 1950s and 1960s: more than two decades after the Women's Armed Services Integration Act laid the foundation for women's military service, it became clear that equal pay did not equal full integration and equality. Servicewomen and their advocates had successfully negotiated a new definition of equality.

Her Cold War encompasses the years 1945 to 1980, beginning with the postwar efforts to admit women to the armed forces permanently and concluding with the first graduation of women from the service academies. Women's permanent military integration began with the efforts to pass the

Women's Armed Services Integration Act after World War II, legislation that focused on the army, navy, air force, and marine corps. In 1947, the Army-Navy Nurse Act made the ANC and Navy Nurse Corps (NNC) permanent institutions as well, but these organizations began in the early twentieth century. This means that they have much longer histories of integration and a distinct perspective on women's military service due to the all-female orientation of those corps until the early Cold War. Further, both corps are comprised only of officers, women with professional nursing degrees. Significantly, *Her Cold War* focuses on the transition toward military utilization of women beyond the well-defined medical fields. At times, women in medical military jobs make an appearance in these pages, because medical jobs constituted one of the top three occupations for military women up through the 1960s. Women who held jobs as medics or hospital corpsmen were enlisted women who did not belong to the more specialized nurse corps, meaning that their experiences more closely resembled those of servicewomen in their own components. Additionally, restricting this project to the four primary military service branches included in the Women's Armed Services Integration Act of 1948 excludes the coast guard. Women served in the coast guard during World War II, and they also received permanent integration through separate legislation in the late 1940s. Except for times of war, the Department of Commerce maintains the coast guard. While defined as a military organization, this status is somewhat different from that of the other four branches.

Her Cold War follows a thematic trajectory, beginning with the question of women's integration immediately following World War II and ending with the effects of redefining servicewomen's equality in the 1970s. The three chapters of Part I, "A Shared Responsibility," examine how government and military leaders defined women's service in the 1940s, 1950s, and 1960s and how understandings of women's equality shaped the boundaries of women's military participation. Chapter 1 provides the history of the Women's Armed Services Integration Act and the fight to admit women to the military permanently. Once that law passed, military officials had to convince women to join: chapter 2 analyzes Cold War recruiting practices and their impacts. After women joined the services, they had to learn what it meant to be in the military: chapter 3 explains military training practices. These three chapters offer top-down history to explain how military and government leaders established and constructed womanpower.

Part II, "The Possibilities and Problems of Wielding Womanpower," shifts the narrative to servicewomen's experiences, with attention to how they experienced the limitations placed on them and how they negotiated those limitations according to their individual needs and desires. While not always successful, their efforts are important to understanding the evolution of how gender equality has been defined in the armed forces. Because officials emphasized military service as a career opportunity for women, chapter 4 focuses on women's work experiences. But women could only serve if they were not mothers, as chapter 5 explains, detailing how women fought against motherhood regulations and how those policies affected their service. Likewise, none of the military services permitted homosexual men and women in the ranks: chapter 6 illustrates the lengths to which military officials went to ensure lesbians did not participate in national defense.

Together, Parts I and II highlight the structure and impact of gender difference equality that government and military leaders established after World War II. While Part II shows how some women pushed back against this definition of equality, Part III, "Integration Is Not Enough," analyzes the ways in which servicewomen and their allies challenged limitations and fought for equality—not equality as defined by policy makers, but equality as they defined it for themselves. Chapter 7 follows the women of the Defense Advisory Committee on Women in the Services (DACOWITS), a civilian organization authorized to guide the DOD on all matters related to womanpower. In the 1960s, as chapter 8 shows, DACOWITS members teamed with other prominent civilians and female military leaders to revise key regulations on women's service. Chapter 9 explores how the second-wave feminist movement of the 1970s and momentum over the Equal Rights Amendment contributed to a broader definition of equality based on gender sameness rather than cultural assumptions. Finally, chapter 10 explains how women gained access to the service academies and service aboard ships, two significant changes that relied on the new vision of equality.

Within a thirty-year period following World War II, women went from winning a place in national defense based on their ability to perform some jobs better than men, to securing the military's promise that servicewomen deserved equal opportunity as members of the armed forces. The experiences of women in the armed forces from the end of World War II through the 1970s reflect ongoing struggles and uncertainty over how to best utilize women, how to make women's military roles acceptable to the American public, and how to operate a sexually integrated military. Ultimately, how the armed forces handled women's integration in these decades laid the groundwork for women's current status in the military. In recent years, women in the U.S. military have become increasingly visible, first in Operation Desert Storm in the 1990s and more recently in Operation Iraqi Freedom and Operation Enduring Freedom. The American media draws attention to servicewomen and their roles in national defense routinely, considering such topics as sexual and gender harassment of servicewomen, women and combat, women as prisoners of war, or servicewomen leaving families behind when they deploy.

Today, the barriers that restricted women's service in decades past are gone. In December 2015, Secretary of Defense Ashton Carter specified that women could "drive tanks, fire mortars and lead infantry soldiers into combat. They'll be able to serve as army Rangers and Green Berets, navy SEALS, marine corps infantry, air force parajumpers, and everything else that was previously open only to men."[29] Carter's announcement reignited debates over women's defense roles, from legislation that proposed drafting women, to harassment of some of the first female marine infantry personnel by posting nude photos of them online.[30] The change was supposed to be for the better. "Fully integrating women into all military positions will make the U.S. armed forces better and stronger . . . The military has long prided itself on being a meritocracy, where those who serve are judged only on what they have to offer to help defend the country."[31] When it comes to job assignment, gender no longer trumps ability—at least in theory, as new questions have emerged about the rights of transgender Americans to serve in the armed forces. Consequently, all servicemembers continue to face the legacies of Cold War efforts to integrate women into the military. Forty years after the last of the women's services disappeared, military service continues to be a crucial arena for understanding what it means for women to be equal with men, an unfinished process that continually evolves.

Part I **A Shared Responsibility**
Defining Sexual Integration
in the Early Cold War

1   A Nucleus of Women in a Nuclear Age

In February 1948, General Dwight D. Eisenhower visited Capitol Hill just twelve days after leaving his post as army chief of staff. Moments after the House Subcommittee on Organization and Mobilization was called to order, Eisenhower addressed the group man to man. Of course, he suggested, it was only natural that they were skeptical of the idea of keeping women in defense roles. The military was a man's world, an institution of strong men who fought and protected the country. General Eisenhower planned to change that: not for the first time, the question of womanpower was at the center of his testimony. Several years before, Eisenhower explained, he himself had been against women's service, as he expected the representatives would be. In fact, "like most old soldiers, I was violently against it. I thought a tremendous number of difficulties would occur . . . that maybe we were exposing people to various types of temptation and other things that would get us into trouble. None of that occurred."[1] General Eisenhower was a man on a mission: the war was over, and he had just taken on a new role as the president of Columbia University, but the five-star general still had a fight to finish. The converted skeptic was determined to convince a roomful of men that womanpower mattered.

World War II catapulted the nation into a new global leadership role; the United States was powerful, running military occupations on two continents and assuming position as a key player in the young United Nations. But power cannot guarantee safety. If Pearl Harbor taught American leaders one thing, it was this: better overprepared than caught off guard. At the time Eisenhower testified, the United States might have been the world's only nuclear power, but that knowledge held little comfort for the nation's leaders, who kept a wary eye on the Soviet Union. Preparedness had become the watchword in the halls of Congress and the newly constructed Pentagon across the Potomac. The draft continued into early 1947, although fewer men were being called up and assignments seemed generally safer than they had been when the war was being fought.[2] As the victor, the United States now had defense obligations around the world. Uncle Sam still needed some of his citizens to maintain a military presence in both Germany and Japan.

Meanwhile, U.S. officials worried about Stalin and the Soviet Union and how to prevent the spread of communism. New policy approaches emerged; President Truman's advisor Clark Clifford began arguing in 1946 that the Soviet Union would only ever understand military strength. A year later, the so-called Long Telegram furthered this perspective. The document, by diplomat George Kennan of the American embassy in the Soviet Union, argued that dealing with the Soviet Union—and communism in particular—would be "undoubtedly [the] greatest task our diplomacy has ever faced and probably greatest it will ever have to face."[3] Ironically, though, the Soviets had shown no outward signs of aggression against the United States. Instead, early concerns emerged in other parts of the world, such as the growing Soviet presence in Eastern Europe, a civil war in Greece, and the resumption of the Chinese civil war. The Soviets wouldn't explode their first atomic weapon until 1949, but the American government was already beginning to prepare for what they increasingly worried would be a massive showdown.[4]

By 1947, armed with both fears of communism and expectations of continuing postwar occupations around the world, civilian and military leaders developed a new vision of national defense in a nuclear era.[5] It was clear that keeping American military personnel stationed around the world would require keeping at least some number of people in the armed forces. The nation's defense team had never been as large as it was in World War II, with more than 16 million personnel serving worldwide over the course of the war.[6] Demobilization took time: although begun as early as VE Day in 1945, in 1946 the army had to slow down the process of bringing its soldiers home to keep from losing so many personnel. Yet by 1947, staffing needs were not as pressing, and President Truman let the Selective Service Act expire. By the end of June, the army considered its demobilization process complete, nearly two years after Japan's surrender.[7] American troops remained stationed at home and abroad, but their mission was new, forward focused and no longer aimed at wrapping up the war. Fewer in number, their presence still mattered, and military officials knew they had to keep that presence constant, especially considering ongoing world events. Some, like General Eisenhower, believed it was time to capitalize on all the organizational and technological military advancements of the past conflict. The central question was how to best weigh preparedness for the future against the voices of thousands of servicemen and women who were ready to go home.

Amidst these considerations, a group of high-ranking male military allies and women in uniform focused on the possibility of continuing a controversial wartime experiment: womanpower. Approximately 350,000 women joined every service branch over the course of the war, in the process making Americans more used to women in uniform.[8] If many Americans still did not love the idea of women in defense, the sight was no longer shocking. Moreover, womanpower had worked so well during the war that by 1945 former skeptics like General Dwight D. Eisenhower were talking about the benefits of women in national defense.[9] Not everyone agreed about continuing women's service, however. Even the highest-ranking wartime female officers believed that "the women should serve only during the war, and . . . should be disbanded as fast as possible after the war."[10] Originally, the use of womanpower in World War II had been designed as an emergency response, meant to be neither permanent nor normal. Consequently, the wartime leaders of the Women's Army Corps (WAC) and the Women Marines (WMs), Colonel Oveta Culp Hobby (Director of the WAC) and Colonel Ruth Streeter (Director of the Women Marines) did not believe women's service should continue. They were content to see women return to their homes or to more appropriate careers, believing that women's military service should be an exception rather than the rule. Accordingly, Colonel Streeter resigned in December 1945. After Colonel Hobby resigned for health reasons in the summer of 1945, her successor, Colonel Westray Battle Boyce, initially followed Hobby's plan to disband the wartime WAC as soon as possible.[11] But as Colonel Boyce worked through demobilization plans, she soon discovered that not all servicewomen wanted women's military service to end. Many senior WAC officers in Europe, along with other up-and-coming female military leaders, felt otherwise: Colonel Joy Bright Hancock, Director of the WAVES (Women Accepted for Volunteer Emergency Service in the Navy), expressed interest in permanent integration, as did the WAC Deputy Director, then-Lieutenant Colonel Mary Hallaren.

Before the end of 1945, Eisenhower made it clear that he saw a sexually integrated military as a key part of preparedness. His experiences in World War II convinced him that womanpower had a place in modern warfare and would be essential in the future, but the wartime legislation that created the WAC specified that it was to be eliminated six months after the end of the war.[12] Acting as the new army chief of staff, in early 1946 Eisenhower directed his Assistant Chief of Staff General Willard S. Paul to draft legislation to keep women in the army permanently. Paul assembled his team in February and stressed the urgency of the effort as he understood it from the boss: "Ike says we have to have a permanent WAC . . . I'd like you to come up with a plan and a bill within the next ten days. The entire resources of the War Department are at your disposal."¹³ The group consisted of Lieutenant Colonel Allan Leonard, Lieutenant Colonel Emily Davis, and Colonel Mary Hallaren, supported by nine part-time military consultants from general and special staff divisions and major commands: Lieutenant Colonels John F. Cassidy, James C. Herberg, Elizabeth H. Strayhorn, Dorothea Coleman, Kathleen McClure; Majors Selma Herbert, Jere Knight, Elizabeth Smith, and Elizabeth Hardesty. The group moved quickly, and on February 25, a copy of "A Tentative Plan and Proposed Bill on Establishing the Women's Army Corps in the Regular Army and Organized Reserve" appeared on Paul's desk.¹⁴

Meanwhile, naval leaders pursued their own efforts to retain womanpower. As the WAC draft legislation circulated internally that March, Secretary of the Navy James Forrestal had already used his influence to place draft legislation for womanpower in front of the House Naval Affairs Committee. The proposal focused on the navy and marine corps reserves, with small numbers of women on regular status. This established a recurring theme in the battle for womanpower: whether to use women on active duty or keep them primarily in the reserves as a sort of backup generator plan. For many people within the military and Congress, limiting womanpower to the reserves made the most sense for preparedness, because that implied they were there in case of an emergency, nothing more. Marine corps Commandant General Alexander Vandegrift, for example, did not want to see women continue in the marines, but insisted that if it happened, he would support no more than ten women on active duty in the Women Marines during peacetime, officers who would manage planning, training, recruiting, and administering WMs in the event of an emergency.¹⁵

It took nearly a year for these early legislation proposals to get any hearing, even though the army and navy had moved so quickly because their wartime womanpower authorizations would end soon. The navy's legislation made it out of committee in May, but no further, while the WAC Integration Act of 1946 did not even see the committee stage. Instead of viewing the lack of momentum as an obstacle, advocates looked ahead to when the 80th Congress would convene in January 1947. However, the opening of the 80th Congress, the first with a Republican majority since 1930, ushered in several structural changes that sent both the army and the navy back to the drawing board. The old military and naval affairs committees in the House and Senate disappeared, replaced by armed services committees.¹⁶ Not losing any momentum, by April 1947 the WAC Integration Act of 1947 arrived in both the House and Senate armed services committees; that month, Congress passed separate legislation that made the Army Nurse Corps and Navy Nurse Corps permanent. This was not unexpected, given that nursing was seen as a decidedly feminine career path and because nurses had a longer history of serving alongside and within the armed forces.[17] Nevertheless, introducing the WAC Integration Act at the same time kept womanpower on legislators' minds. By late June, navy and marine corps legislation also materialized. Just five days later, a Senate armed services subcommittee convened hearings to consider both.

At the early hearings, Senate Armed Services Committee members wanted to know whether womanpower was even an advisable defense strategy. Yes, Eisenhower and his colleagues insisted: it was time for Americans to stop thinking of women primarily as people to be protected. During World War II, practicality had been paramount: in total war, the key was to be able to win the war by using all available citizens in some capacity. In *Crusade in Europe*, Eisenhower's 1948 account of his role in the war, Eisenhower detailed how he and other leaders had become convinced that the military needed servicewomen. Citing what he called, "the changing requirements of war," Eisenhower explained: "The simple headquarters of a Grant or a Lee were gone forever. An army of filing clerks, stenographers, office managers, telephone operators, and chauffeurs had become essential, and it was scarcely less than criminal to recruit these from needed manpower when great numbers of highly qualified women were available."[18] For Eisenhower, women's integration was a matter of military necessity: the armed services needed qualified personnel to help in wartime, and women had demonstrated they could do the work, often in jobs they already held in the civilian world. The myth that women could be protected well behind the front lines, even an ocean away from the fighting, no longer made sense. The destruction of Europe by the Allies and Axis powers made it clear that war could touch *any* life. The American decision to firebomb Japan and drop two atomic weapons made that message even clearer. While the Americans might be the only ones holding the bomb, it was just a matter of time before someone else might fire back.

Colonel Mary Hallaren, who joined the WAC early in the war, argued it was time to recognize that defense was no longer just about combat (figure 1.1). War was no longer something that might happen only on the other side of the world. "Experts tell us that modern warfare makes us vulnerable in our own backyard," Hallaren emphasized. "In the future, we won't have to worry about recruiting the women or convincing the men. When the house is on fire, we don't talk about a woman's place in the home. And

FIGURE 1.1 Colonel Mary Hallaren was an early advocate of women's permanent military integration in the years following World War II. National Archives, College Park, Maryland.

we don't send her a gilt-edged invitation to help put the fire out."[19] Instead, Hallaren explained, future Americans would focus more on how to best utilize all citizens and would not question womanpower at all. The modern military extended far beyond battle zones and hospital wards, into administrative sectors, logistics, human resources, and other venues. In a military establishment, a bureaucracy in which women provided essential support in diverse roles, the nation needed to reconsider the relationship between women and national defense.

While the senators seemed to understand the practical merits of womanpower, they worried what Americans would think. Connecticut Republican Raymond Baldwin fretted about whether the military was appropriate for women, regardless of their recent wartime service. He called on General Paul to address Americans' potential fears, noting, "there may be a reluctance on the part of some of our people to put women in places of danger, because the whole instinct of mankind is to preserve what we used to call, but no longer dare call now, the weaker sex."[20] Even as he made this request, Baldwin acknowledged that ideas about women were changing. Like Hallaren, Paul stressed that distinctions between civilians and military personnel in total war were impractical. "The women have worked in every war. Women suffer more than men in any war, no matter what their status is. Whether they are waiting for their loved ones or whether they are actively participating, I think the women takes [sic] the beating on it."[21] If women already suffered because of war, no matter how they experienced it, then it was senseless to invoke or rely on a need to "protect" women, in his opinion. Women always played some role in national defense, no matter where they were; this legislation offered an effective way to make use of that reality.

Within two weeks, the subcommittee streamlined the efforts to secure womanpower permanently, combining the two separate bills into the Women's Armed Services Integration Act of 1947, or S. 1641. Only a day later, the Senate Armed Services Committee agreed to move forward; by July 23, the full Senate approved, and the legislation moved to the House. The momentum was promising; Eisenhower remained convinced of the bill's importance and reached out proactively to voice his support to the House Armed Services Committee. Eisenhower wanted to see the legislation pass quickly. "My experience in the use of Wacs . . . has convinced me that a modern army must have [women] . . . the women of America must share the responsibility for the security of their country in a future emergency . . . I heartily support, and urge speedy Congressional approval of, the bill to integrate women."[22] Things were looking good, especially when a House subcommittee held a hearing the very day they got the legislation from the Senate. Justifying womanpower on the basis of military preparedness seemed to make sense to those who needed to be convinced.

In a sudden, problematic turn of events, that summer the House Subcommittee postponed any further discussion of the legislation until January 1948, a move that looked like it might kill the bill entirely. The legislation that established the WAC in 1943 specified that the WAC must disband six months after the war ended. Although Americans recognize September 2, 1945, as the day the war ended when the Japanese surrendered to American troops, Truman did not declare the end of formal hostilities of World War II until December 31, 1946.[23] When the House subcommittee decided to postpone further hearings due to the House recess from July 28 to November 16, 1947, the women's services were practically out of time, and losing personnel quickly as a result.[24] Fortunately, if members of Congress didn't want to take up the legislation right away, they at least offered some hope: before the end of July 1947, Congress passed legislation continuing some wartime measures. Public Law 239 extended authorization for the WAC, WAVES, and Women Marines until July 1, 1948.[25] There was still time after all—but not much.

Seven long months later, hearings resumed on February 18, 1948, and the debates that followed in the next few months laid bare all the possibilities and problems members of Congress might imagine. The delay was not a total loss, because the National Security Act of 1947 went into effect that September. The National Security Act strengthened and centralized the nation's defense system, creating the Secretary of Defense, and the Departments of the Army, Navy, and Air Force (along with other new groups like the National Security Council).[26] Within two years, the organization assumed its more familiar name: the Department of Defense.[27] Significantly, the National Security Act created the air force as a separate military organization. Previously, the air force had been part of the army, but now it was a full-fledged military branch all on its own—one that would need both manpower *and* womanpower. In the meantime, news continued to spread within the armed services about the pending womanpower legislation. In October 1947, the *Army-Navy Journal* (a publication for military officers and leaders) reprinted Hallaren's statement to Congress. Her comments emphasized from the start that women's integration was about preparedness. "The War Department's decision to ask Congress for a permanent Women's Army Corps was not the result of snap judgement. It was the conclusion of twenty-five years' progressive thinking."[28] Hallaren made this same point many times in 1947 and 1948, always stressing that womanpower was not radical, but practical. As she said to a meeting of WAC staff directors and senior officers in early 1947, "we are not a bunch of feminists looking for jobs in the army at all."[29] For Hallaren and other supporters of women's integration, permanent use of womanpower was simply pragmatic, patriotic business. Even so, the fight for the Women's Armed Services Integration Act illustrates the ways in which military need and efficiency intersected with some opportunities for gender equity.

Representing a civilian woman's viewpoint, Mary Pillsbury Lord, chair of the WAC's National Civilian Advisory Committee, testified before the 1948 House Armed Services Committee in support of women's integration. During the war, she and her committee advised the War Department on the use of womanpower and liaised with the American public "to guarantee . . . that the well-being of the women in the army was in line with the high standards that the American public has the right to expect."[30] Echoing military leaders, she endorsed the legislation because she had seen firsthand how women could benefit the military and how the military could benefit women. She suggested that integrating women would be "invaluable" to the military, but also argued that womanpower would be good for the nation in broader ways. Military service, she explained, would make women better citizens, which would only help the nation moving forward. Noting that military life imbued servicemembers with "immeasurable" characteristics, she emphasized that military service would teach women "tolerance, respect for the Nation, an awareness of the benefits of democracy, an understanding of the functions of government, a keen appreciation of the value of time and money and the building of interest in self-improvement . . . Women in the services is a natural . . . chapter in American history. It is today's acceptance of the responsibilities as well as the privileges of democracy by American women."[31]

Eisenhower took his stand in these February 1948 hearings, even though he was no longer actively in the military. He argued that the army's central problem at that very moment was a lack of manpower: now that the draft had ended, volunteers were hard to come by.[32] While he had previously attested to women's invaluable service during the war, Eisenhower reminded members of Congress that the military's mission continued on a new global scale in the postwar world, and the military still needed women just as it had during the war. Citing women's efficiency and ability to do some jobs better than men, Eisenhower pointed out that the military had occupying forces around the world. Consequently, the army required people—and that included women. Without this legislation, the army would lose a group of Americans who had proven to be willing volunteers. "If we cut down our basis for volunteer enlistment by removing women from [service] we are merely making an already difficult job an impossible one to solve."[33] There were no longer any valid arguments against retaining women, Eisenhower argued, but a plethora of reasons to strengthen the nation's use of womanpower.

If the subcommittee members had bought Eisenhower's testimony, the story would end there, but this audience pushed back hard, initiating what became a months-long negotiation over womanpower. Representative Walter Andrews (R-NY) explained that he understood the army's personnel needs and the past record of women's wartime service. "That being true, first, I would like you to assume that there is considerable, not antagonism, but antipathy to the thought of women generally being brought into the regular services . . . to them being brought in on exactly the same basis as men permanently."³⁴ Instead, Andrews proposed bringing women into the reserves only, perhaps a more palatable arrangement that might solve the personnel problem. In those opening moments of the subcommittee session, Andrews changed the agenda, shifting the focus away from Eisenhower's and his allies' support for permanent, regular use of womanpower. As Representative Carl Vinson (D-GA) noted, "We all recognize we should have [women in the services]. It is only a question of whether it should come in the Regulars or in the Reserves."³⁵ Womanpower might be necessary for preparedness, the representatives agreed, but giving women both regular and reserve status went too far.

Full service, both in regular and reserve capacities, was radical because it seemed to place women on an essentially equal footing with men. Reserve personnel were part-time defense support, called up only when need arose. Keeping women in the reserves would ensure that the military remained an all-male domain except in case of emergency. More to the point, reserve status would preserve the armed forces the way they had been for a century and a half, just as limiting women to the nursing corps essentially kept the military all male. In that sense, if preparedness alone was the goal, reserve status should have been enough. From a practical standpoint, both Secretary of Defense James Forrestal and General Eisenhower understood the matter differently.³⁶ They saw it as a matter of equity, because regular military status offered full-time employment and access to important benefits, including retirement. While defense officials readily admitted that incorporating women into national defense would mean making some allowances for sex, admitting women to the reserves seemed discriminatory and problematic in the long run. Secretary Forrestal argued that reserve-only status would be like when women were only given auxiliary status early in World War II: it might work for a little while, but would cause more problems than solutions.³⁷ Women had already proved their worth, he argued, thus they deserved the same military status and privileges.

Forrestal maintained that there must be some foundational similarities for women's integration to be effective. "No business, no governmental organization, and especially no military force, can accomplish its objectives where individuals working side by side, doing identical work with equal degrees of responsibility are classified differently as to status, prerogatives, or emoluments." Forrestal again invoked preparedness, noting that if Americans wanted to be ready to win the next war, "preparedness requires trained skeleton staffs. These skeleton staffs are composed of Regular personnel who form the nucleus which can be expanded in time of war." If members of Congress wanted to keep that nucleus small, that was fine, but regular status was a must. "If we are going to use women in the armed forces, we should go the whole way and give them identical status and benefits as men."[38]

While Forrestal's arguments implied that some amount of equality between the sexes might be a by-product of womanpower, he did not mean that women could take on just *any* defense role. Forrestal believed that it was possible to give a measure of equality, defined in terms of pay and benefits, yet limit women from "unsuitable" roles—combat and combat-related assignments. None of the subcommittee members questioned Forrestal about women's equality in terms of pay and benefit equity, nor General Omar Bradley's assertion that women deserved benefit equity with men. Bradley pointed out that only "a very small percentage of the men in the army ever hear a hostile shot fired" because the military required so much more manpower than just on the battlefield.[39] The modern military was more than guns and ammunition: it was also an intricate network and bureaucracy with many layers and roles. If Congress denied women equal benefits and status with men because they would be noncombatants, then they should also deny noncombatant men the same.

The other argument against reserve-only status held that building a successful nucleus of womanpower would depend on recruiting career-minded women with an innate drive for success and career excellence. The war was over, Forrestal reminded the representatives; preparedness was certainly central to the philosophy behind womanpower, but it was also important to realize that the average American women might not understand the larger need. During the war, recruiting women had been relatively painless: military service was patriotic and a way to help the war. Now that there was no war, Forrestal reminded committee members that they would have to imagine other ways to recruit women. If women got reserve status only, without the same equality of service as men, recruiting might be a harder sell. "In peacetime, without the same status [as men], the same pride of being in an organization, which is an intangible thing, [recruiting] is difficult to do."[40] By authorizing women for both regular and reserve status, the U.S. military could offer women attractive jobs and careers. Using womanpower was about practicality for the armed forces, but military recruiters, Forrestal suggested, would also have to sell women on the practical opportunities service careers offered them.

Letting women serve as reserves for a couple of years would only reinforce a sense that they were "backup" to the "true" military. In contrast, enlisting as regulars would be very different: "by including [women] in the Regular Establishment first you show that they are valuable, that you are perfectly delighted to get hold of them."[41] Vice Admiral Radford, Vice Chief of Naval Operations, took things further, arguing that Congress must understand the importance of a regular military structure, otherwise regular status would not exist at all. "Some, who admit that WAVES will be essential in war, argue that in time of peace they should be retained in the reserve and not in the regular navy. If that argument were valid, all the armed services could be maintained in a reserve status only."[42] Twenty years earlier, Congress might have taken that route, but since the war's end, members of Congress did not seem to be moving toward keeping men as reserves alone. A small military, like the one that existed in 1939, no longer seemed appropriate. Subcommittee member and future president Lyndon B. Johnson (D-TX) asked Forrestal, "if we are to prepare to wage war, it is very important that we authorize you to train these women and at least have a nucleus that can provide leadership?" Absolutely, Forrestal replied. Such a nucleus would be essential to further wartime expansion of womanpower: "they [servicewomen on regular status] have the know-how, they have the record, they have the method of recruiting, and above all else, they have the morale, and a spirit which attracts people immediately to the service."[43] Put women on regular and reserve duty now, and they would pave the way for finding additional women when the nation needed them even more.

Despite military leaders' efforts, the bill moved to the House Armed Services Committee in March with a new twist: reserve status *only*. Revising the act entirely, the new version removed all provisions for active duty, and restricted women to permanent inclusion in the military reserves. Once revised, twenty-six members of the House Armed Services Committee embraced the changes wholeheartedly. Only one committee member stood opposed: Margaret Chase Smith, a Republican from Maine. Smith had been an active supporter of women's military service for more than half a decade and had followed the women's integration legislation closely. According to one biographer, Smith was livid when the House Armed Services Committee decided to change the core of the legislation. As Smith later reflected, she was consistently against reserve-only status for women and told military leaders she would only support legislation for permanent women's integration if she could be convinced that the services needed women. She believed that the military "either needs these women or they do not," seeing reserve-only status as "unfair and dishonest . . . a contradiction in terms."[44] When the House subcommittee altered the legislation for reserve status only, Smith became the most outspoken advocate to negotiate restoration of the original wording—and the only member of the House Armed Services Committee to vote against reserve-only status for women that spring.

If Representative Vinson and his supporters thought their edits were the end of it, they were wrong: the battle was just beginning. Even the *New York Times* criticized the shift in an editorial on March 31. "Nobody has yet offered a credible reason to explain the sudden decision of the House Armed Services Committee to exclude women from our national defense forces" by giving them reserve status only. Considering everything women had done in World War II, where they "undertook tasks they could perform better than men, such as clerking, typing, telephoning, nursing and message delivery," the editors at the *New York Times* argued that women deserved more than just token recognition by being shuttled into the reserves. After all, the editors pointed out, women were still serving in many important functions. "To dispense with their services would be a sorry blunder."[45] Women had demonstrated that they deserved access to military service and the benefits that came with it at any time, not only during a national crisis.

By April 1948, American support for womanpower included individuals and groups within and outside of the military. Nine organizations had passed resolutions supporting the original 1947 act, such as the American Legion, the Reserve Officers' Association, the National Council of Young Men's Christian Associations, and several women's organizations, including the General Federation of Women's Clubs, the Daughters of the American Revolution, the American Association of University Women, National Federation of Business and Professional Women's Clubs, and the Junior Leagues. Colonel Hallaren noted that further support had come from many other places, as well.[46] Mayrell Johnson, President of the Murray, Kentucky, Federated Women's Club, wrote directly to Senator Chan Gurney (R-SD), Chair of the Armed Services Committee, to support regular and reserve status for women. "At this time, just as we are all going 'all out' to convince the public of the need for increasing our defense forces . . . this decision by the House appears most inconsistent with what the general need is believed to be." Reminding Senator Gurney of women's work in World War II and testimony in Congress regarding the need for women, she argued that "if women are to be asked to serve in reserve status in periods of national emergency, they should be given equal privileges of training and of permanent tenure in order to keep a minimum nucleus of trained people."[47]

Representative Smith's opposition may have made her a minority in the House, but she persisted and convinced other members of the House to question whether reserve status was enough. When the full House considered the bill in April, those who had pushed reserve-only status argued that they had created the revision because they did not think the original bill could make it to a vote. Missouri Representative Dewey Short (R) noted that "from a realistic point of view the gentleman must know that it would have been very difficult if not impossible to ever to have gotten a rule to consider this measure had we put [women] into the Regular Establishment." And yet, as Representative Lyndon Johnson pointed out, "We have it here now," in the original legislation proposed. Representative George Bates of Massachusetts (R) went a step further, saying "We have no right to abrogate our right and authority on the floor of this House. If we believe [women] ought to become a part of the Regular organization, then we ought to have courage enough to come out on the floor of the House and be given an opportunity to speak our piece."[48] One voice of opposition slowly gave way to several more.

Smith remained instrumental in the regular versus reserve debate on the House floor, offering her own amendment to revert the bill to its original format. While she didn't get House members to revise the bill as she wanted, she did force her colleagues to think about the implications of such a limited bill. Smith got her colleagues to debate the legislation and to recognize the fact that the Senate had already approved both regular *and* reserve status for women. The House might be nervous about granting women regular military status, but the Senate clearly felt otherwise, and their influence held as the legislation went to joint conference between the House and Senate Armed Services Committees for further negotiations that May. When the final version of the bill came back to the House on June 2 after the joint conference, the proposed Women's Armed Services Act of 1948 included both regular and reserve status, as Eisenhower, Forrestal, Hallaren, Smith, and so many other advocates had wanted.

The Senate position must have been influential, but by the spring of 1948, members of Congress also could not help but notice that the world was getting a little more chaotic. Internationally, a Communist government took over in Czechoslovakia in February 1948, and by March the Soviets had started controlling traffic into Berlin; the first Arab-Israeli War began on May 15 when Israel declared independence.[49] The Marshall Plan to help rebuild Europe went into effect in April as the first incarnation of the 1947 Truman Doctrine. With all of this happening, it was not surprising that Congress was also debating whether to reinstate the draft and renewing discussion of Universal Military Training.[50] Womanpower seemed more important than ever with increased manpower on the line. Many representatives may have found it hypocritical to enforce male service obligation while declining an entire pool of voluntary personnel strength. On June 2, the House of Representatives passed S. 1641 by a vote of 206 to 133.[51] On June 12, President Truman signed the Women's Armed Service Integration Act of 1948 into law, only nineteen days before the original World War II authorization for women's military service would have expired.

The Women's Armed Services Integration Act always focused on military need, not women's rights, but the battle for womanpower highlights the ways in which nonfeminists inadvertently advocated for women's equality. Women's efforts to secure citizenship rights, such as voting, historically hinged on women's protests of being excluded. The Women's Armed Services Integration Act, however, did not come about because a large group of women protested their exclusion but because a group predominantly made up of men believed that womanpower would benefit the country. Proponents of the law had argued that granting women regular military status was about military need, not women's rights, and the final version of the law reflected this position through specific limits on women's service. The fight to convince members of Congress that women should be integrated into the military involved carefully negotiating what women would and would not do, how they fit into the defense system, and why the military needed noncombatants. In the process, advocates of a sexually integrated military promoted a new vision of national defense and its role in American life. The debates over the Women's Armed Services Integration Act created new questions about the nature of modern warfare by considering questions about who should defend the nation, and offer an early glimpse into what would become the Cold War military-industrial complex—ironically, something Eisenhower would warn against when he left the presidency in 1961. The integration of womanpower underscored growing recognition that preparation for total war affected everyone. Total war had not ended with the Japanese surrender in 1945: it had simply been reincarnated.

The Women's Armed Services Integration Act was forward-thinking because it gave life to the proposition that gender no longer prevented Americans from defending their nation. At the same time, provisions of the act ensured that gender shaped the terms of military service, fundamentally restructuring military service into male and female arenas by defining women solely as noncombatants. While not every man would ever see combat, men's service continued to be shaped around the idea that any man *could* be sent into combat; women could not. Although Eisenhower and Forrestal emphasized the importance of granting women regular military status in order to maintain equality between men and women's services, defining military personnel as combatants or noncombatants primarily on the basis of their gender created an unequal military structure. Military service ultimately would offer women a greater degree of equality with men than they might find in other careers, but there were very specific limitations as well. The Women's Armed Services Integration Act itself created a distinct organizational plan for womanpower and limited women's service based on assumptions about women's places in society and their status or potential status as daughters, wives, and mothers.

Due to fears of making men report to women who outranked them, the Women's Armed Services Integration Act established a separate administrative support structure for women's service, utilizing the organizational scheme begun in World War II. As a result, women's decision-making authority and policy influence began and ended in the women's service components. Strictly speaking, only the WAC was officially a separate corps, although women in the navy continued to be known informally as WAVES, and WAF and WM were used to designate women in the air force and marines, respectively. The creation of a women's director in each service branch, to guide and support women, often made it look like there were separate women's services. The top permanent grade of lieutenant colonel or commander allowed women to lead the women's components, but also ensured that men made the most important military decisions. This simultaneously limited the influence that higher-ranking women might have on lower-ranking men, since women officers were primarily tasked with leading other women. In accordance with that thinking, the highest officer grades allotted to women until the 1960s were administrative roles designed to make the WAC, WAF, WAVES, and WMs function smoothly.

Promotion is an important element of almost any career path, signifying professional growth and success; but in the military, officer promotion often connects with combat leadership. In the armed forces, the highest rank any officer can hold is general (in the army, air force, and marine corps) or admiral (in the navy). It takes years to get to one of these positions, and few service members achieve such a high-level rank. According to the Women's Armed Services Integration Act, women would never be eligible for that status: instead, the highest rank possible for women would be colonel or captain, the rank just below general or admiral. This would be the most elusive rank for any woman, though: not only was it the top possible rank, but only four women could ever hold those positions at one time, and even then, the ranks were temporary. Only the director of the WAC, director of the WAF, director of the Women Marines, and director of the WAVES (formally known as the Assistant Chief of Naval Personnel for Women) could hold that highest-level rank, and only while they served as the director of their service component. Once they retired, their official rank reverted to lieutenant colonel or commander for the purposes of their permanent retirement pay and benefits.

At the same time, the authors of the Women's Armed Services Integration Act tried to ensure promotion equity by establishing separate male and female officer promotion lists in the army, navy, and marine corps. Only the air force integrated its promotion lists, presumably because the branch was so new that women would not be at a disadvantage with men when it came to rank promotions. In general, separate promotion lists allowed the services to minimize the number of female officers by prioritizing men's promotions. Separate lists prevented women from taking promotions from men, but in theory also meant that women would not have to compete with men for promotions. Colonel Hallaren argued that such protection was important: in officer promotions, "men have combat experience and training, in which the women would not compete."[52] Since the military categorized women as noncombatants, separate promotion lists would presumably protect both men and women based on their unique defense roles.

Although supporters argued against seeing women as a class of Americans who needed protection, the Women's Armed Services Integration Act nonetheless assumed that women were a protected class, insisting that women under age twenty-one have parental permission to enlist. At age eighteen, women could enlist, but between ages eighteen and twenty-one, parents had to provide written consent for a woman to enlist or receive an officer's commission. This rule recognized cultural ideas of parents as young women's protectors in a way that men did not need: men only needed parental consent if they were under the age of eighteen when they enlisted.[53] Setting different enlistment ages for men and women and requiring parental signatures for women under twenty-one suggested that unlike men, women lacked the autonomy to make such career choices for themselves until a later age and needed guidance to ensure they made the correct life decisions. Although men could make a personal decision to enter the armed forces, military service essentially became a family issue for women under age twenty-one.

If military leaders saw women under age twenty-one as their parents' dependents, yet another provision underscored both prevailing popular opinion of women as dependents and the need to ensure women did not control men. One of the hallmarks in American gender hierarchies in the mid-twentieth century was the belief in husbands as the head of households, with wives and children as dependents. Thus, the Women's Armed Services Integration Act included a provision that would prevent women from claiming husbands and children as dependents, except in rare circumstances. The regulation simultaneously prevented women from becoming heads of households while ensuring women's military service would not emasculate their husbands. According to the law, servicewomen's spouses "shall not be considered dependents unless they are in fact dependent on their wives for their chief support." In order to get dependent benefits for a male spouse, women would have to jump through many hoops to demonstrate that their husband really could not work, perhaps because of a disability.[54]

The law assumed some women would marry, as the benefit restriction indicated, and as such, one final limitation emerged specifically because members of Congress presumed women would eventually become mothers. The Women's Armed Services Integration Act gave the secretaries of each branch the authority to end women's military service at will. "The Secretary of the Army . . . may terminate the enlistment of any enlisted woman in the Women's Army Corps [WAC], and each person whose enlistment is so terminated shall be discharged from the army."[55] Hallaren explained during the legislative hearings that the termination clause was a way to remove pregnant women, because the act also rendered women with children under age eighteen ineligible for duty. The termination clause was a way to discharge pregnant women while avoiding a lengthy legal process and remained in place until the 1970s. To further ensure that mothers would not wind up in the ranks, the law also excluded married women with no prior military service, assuming they would soon become mothers anyway.

Even with these limitations, womanpower supporters believed that regular and reserve status offered women equality with men. Not only did the Women's Armed Services Integration Act grant women permanent access to a previously all-male arena, but women also gained access to equal pay and benefits and opportunities often unavailable to women in civilian careers. The restrictions in the act, military leaders insisted, were not designed to make women inferior to men, but to maintain existing gender ideologies by prescribing appropriate activities for men and women. In part, they believed this strategy would help make military service attractive to women and their families. Gender difference thus became the hallmark of defining equality in the Cold War defense system: leaders would utilize women based on their alleged special capabilities as women—doing things they did as well or better than men. Likewise, men would be utilized based on their special capabilities as men, filling any number of roles that women might fill, but also masculine duties like combat.

The Women's Armed Services Integration Act of 1948 expanded and solidified the burgeoning women's world within the U.S. military. Just like in World War II, each of the women's components would have a permanent female director.[56] As in the war, women would work alongside servicemen and often report to male supervisors. However, servicewomen would also have female superiors and would never be the sole woman assigned to a specific military location. Consequently, when women gained permanent access to national defense roles in 1948, they also became part of a segregated system that delegated womanpower as something women should primarily manage. Ironically, this "separate but equal" system of organizing women's service persisted into the 1970s, even as the armed forces worked to eliminate racial segregation beginning in July of 1948. Rather than complete integration, the Women's Armed Services Integration Act more accurately incorporated women into the defense structure by giving military leaders the means to develop separate spaces for women.

The legislation established a vision of military service divided into separate spheres for men and for women. While sex no longer constituted a barrier to military participation, the Women's Armed Services Integration Act defined gender identification as an important part of understanding men's and women's defense roles. Maintaining a separate administrative structure designed to lead women's service, manage women's issues, and generally support servicewomen helped perpetuate the sense of women's separateness from men. Initially conceived as a way to help support women's integration, the female-based support systems instead reinforced women's differences. The modern military was about far more than just sending men into battle, but the Women's Armed Services Integration Act brought women into a historically all-male institution, where a service member's (male) sex and combat had always defined participation. The new law underscored the significance of gender in the military more than ever.

2 The Real Miss America
Recruiting Womanpower

....

Four years after the Women's Armed Services Integration Act passed, someone in recruiting decided that the first all-out campaign for womanpower should take place with the 1952 Miss America pageant. It must have seemed like the perfect pairing: the pageant highlighted the best young American women from around the nation, perfectly poised, beautiful, talented, and educated. Recruiters dreamed of signing just these types of young ladies for service in the armed forces. Military publicity officers secured a presence for servicewomen throughout the pageant, ensuring visibility whenever possible. The goal was simple: get Americans to associate servicewomen with the excellent reputation Miss America contestants had at that time and to impart a sense of glamour into Americans' ideas of women in uniform. Yet the pageant offered another publicity opportunity when an up-and-coming starlet named Marilyn Monroe, the first celebrity marshal of the Miss America pageant, posed with several servicewomen. But the photo shoot planned by military officials created a much different kind of buzz than intended.

The photo generated immediate concerns that Monroe's presence might send the wrong message. Only three hours after the image went out, the *New York Journal-American* reported, "an embarrassed army official requested the picture 'killed.' A spokesman here who saw a print of the picture said it might give parents of potential women recruits a wrong conception of life in the service." An interview with Monroe revealed that the budding actress was "surprised and hurt," over the debacle, prompting the army to reverse its position. According to the *Journal-American*, the problem lay with Monroe's attire, as her dress was "cut square in front and exposed about half of [Marilyn's] bosom."[1] Even so, the *Philadelphia Inquirer* pointed out that Marilyn "has posed in less." Perhaps that "embarrassed" army official worried about leaving too little to viewers' imaginations. The *Inquirer* certainly seemed to think so: "male recruits also might get the wrong impression of life in the service, although the spokesman didn't say so."[2]

The photograph got enough attention that even four years later, Monroe recalled the moment in an interview with *The Saturday Evening Post*. Reflecting on her experience, Monroe said she was "surprised and hurt," even suggesting that military officials might have reacted the same way if *she* had been in uniform. Monroe came to believe that the concern wasn't about her exposed chest, but a deeper fear of her reputation as a sex symbol. Only a year after the photo incident, an image of Monroe in her grand marshal attire in the Miss America Pageant Parade acquired even greater fame. The cover of the very first issue of *Playboy* magazine in 1953 shows a smiling, waving Monroe seated atop a car—an image taken directly from the 1952 Miss America parade.[3] By that point, however, it was unclear whether most Americans remembered she had ever shown her "meat and potatoes" while posing with four servicewomen.[4]

From the beginning, such concerns about appearances framed womanpower recruiting efforts. Recruiters followed the philosophy that familiarity and femininity would be the most practical and effective ways to entice women to military careers. Military service became advertised as an avenue by which women could become not just ideal American women, but respectable *ladies*. This approach helped make women's service acceptable to Americans both inside and outside the armed forces. If military service—especially in wartime—could transform boys into men, then military service could also turn girls into proper ladies. Women belonged in national defense in part because military and government officials saw them as partners in service with men, doing things women did best and capitalizing on their identities as women to do so. In these regards, staging the women's recruiting drive in conjunction with the 1952 Miss America pageant made sense. The pageant was about thirty years old, and community service was—and still is—an important element of holding the title "Miss America." During World War II, the crowned Miss Americas all performed war service activities such as visiting troops and selling war bonds, their version of supporting national defense.[5] Scholar Mary Anne Schofield argues that during wartime, such efforts "supported the propaganda machine that said that femininity and war work went together."[6] In the process, the pageant itself solidified the image of Miss America as "the ideal American woman."[7] By 1952, if military leaders wanted a venue that would showcase servicewomen as the very best of American womanhood *and* service, the Miss America pageant was the place to be.

The women's recruiting drive at the 1952 Miss America pageant served as the first coordinated, public effort linking femininity and glamour to emphasize that women belonged in national defense in very specific, genderappropriate ways. Along with the Monroe photo, pageant officials teamed with military recruiters to include four servicewomen in pageant-related publicity efforts throughout the event. Advertising copy proclaimed that "Womanpower is Humanpower" and stressed the importance that men and women "Share Service for Freedom." The tagline on print ads included messages such as "America's Finest Women stand beside her Finest Men." One full-page ad put four servicewomen in a drawing with the Statue of Liberty and the caption "Four more pedestals, please!"[8] Had Monroe been draped as carefully as the Statue of Liberty, her attire clearly wouldn't have been a problem.

The plan was to brand servicewomen as the "real Miss America," forging a connection in Americans' minds between the prestige and glamour that accompanied Miss America contestants, to the work that women could do in national defense. If service to one's community remained a key component of being Miss America, then why not emphasize service to one's own country as an option? Not *everyone* could be Miss America, and not every woman would meet the military's high standards, but military service offered more possibilities for young women than a pageant and a short-lived title. Forget about wearing the crown—reach for the uniform, the real hallmark of service and pride. "'The Real Miss America' of today [is] the woman who wears the uniform of the army, navy, air force or marine corps—the woman who has accepted her full share of responsibility in the preservation of peace and the protection of the privileges which we all share as Americans."[9] Pageant participants had beauty, talent, poise, and wholesomeness, but servicewomen took part in the ultimate form of community service: defending the nation. Martial citizenship had acquired a feminine look.

Martial citizenship had long centered on men, because they were the only Americans who could be drafted and because military service was something only permissible for men until the twentieth century. This meant that the idea of military service had a long connection with masculinity. Military service is often thought of as a citizenship obligation, particularly in times of war. Martial citizenship, then, refers specifically to the idea that when a person fulfills that obligation by engaging in military service, that person should receive some benefit. In historian Amy Rutenberg's words, "martial citizenship . . . is the concept that since soldiers serve the state the state therefore owes something back."[10] While this is not inherently masculine, she notes, beginning in the mid-nineteenth century "a type of masculinity that emphasized duty, honor, patriotism, and strength consistently infused cultural representations of military service."[11] In this formulation, those who objected to military service became feminized due to their opposition, but the "Real Miss America" campaign strategically linked femininity and military service in a positive way, recalling similar campaigns in World War II. Historian Melissa McEuen points out that wartime propaganda set the foundation for an idealized, feminine servicewoman. Posters such as 1944's "Mine eyes have seen the glory," and 1943's "Are you a girl with a Star-Spangled Heart?" also linked femininity and military service. In these images, McEuen argues, "a 'woman's place in war' was occupied by figures whose femininity, properly overseen, remained intact. The military could then be viewed not only as a safe place for women, but perhaps more importantly . . . a haven for white American womanhood."[12] No longer were duty, honor, and patriotism solely reserved for men: in wartime, women had proven themselves the embodiment of these ideals. Because of the Women's Armed Services Integration Act, women who served would also be eligible for the same tangible benefits as men, not just in wartime but at any time.

For a little over twenty years, femininity and familiarity remained the rule for recruiting women to military service. The leaders of the women's military services consistently tried to construct the public face of women's military service around femininity and glamour well into the Cold War. Until the mid-1970s, women's military service contrasted heavily with men's and was based consistently on white, middle-class norms of what women should and should not do as workers. This strategy emerged during World War II, where early WAC leaders focused on the need for "good" women, meaning sexually moral, white, and middle to upper class. According to historian Leisa Meyer, "white women were assumed to have greater sexual restraint as well as greater protection by men of their group, thereby emphasizing their nonavailability and therefore, respectability."[13] In the earliest days of the women's wartime services, creating a definition of "good" women provided a way to counter negativity and fears about women in the armed forces.[14] Defining servicewomen as "ladies" in the Cold War years continued this effort, negotiating concerns that military service would masculinize women or encourage lesbianism. This strategy also kept the underlying intention of combat as a male-only zone intact: as ladies, servicewomen could certainly not be expected to go into combat. A lady would stay as far away from combat as possible.

However, designating women as "ladies" also suggested that national defense efforts did not actually require women, a drawback to this recruiting scheme. When most Americans thought about military service, they imagined combat, not servicemen and women sitting at desks and handling administrative tasks. It seemed like men did the "real work" of national defense, defined by their valor in combat. Furthermore, shortly after the Women's Armed Services Integration Act passed in 1948, Congress reinstated the draft. If any military branch needed manpower, the draft ensured access to adequate personnel.[15] From the beginning then, despite rhetoric to the contrary, there was never a demonstrated need for womanpower to fill peacetime personnel shortages. Consequently, during the Cold War military officials consistently struggled in their efforts to recruit women. Servicewomen's numbers remained low, never truly hitting recruitment targets as long as the draft continued. When the Korean War started in 1950, all military branches combined had 22,000 women on active duty; of these, 15,000 served outside of the medical fields. The Women's Armed Services Integration Act had authorized women to serve as up to 2 percent of the total military strength; by 1950, they were less than 1 percent.[16]

Recruiting campaigns and materials like those from 1952 reveal that leaders of the women's services consistently imagined the American servicewoman as the nation's finest ladies in and out of uniform. Such materials had a very defined goal of selling women's service as a career opportunity, portraying idealized versions of military life to attract young women. While these documents do not give insights into servicewomen's actual experiences in the military, they highlight the crucial role gender played in creating a specific cultural conception of womanpower. These documents offered many women their first glimpse into the armed forces and helped shape servicewomen's initial perceptions about military careers.[17] Sales pitches targeted two audiences: women themselves, and their parents, who had to give permission if their daughters were under age twenty-one. Through a dizzying array of pamphlets—large and small, some printed in color or with photographs—prospective recruits and their families learned about what kinds of young women were the best candidates and how military service could transform recruits into the ideal American woman. In recruiting materials, images of white, middle-class femininity functioned as something aspirational, a status servicewomen would want to attain and embrace themselves. These paralleled recruiting materials for men, which also emphasized martial masculinity as something to attain, as seen in the 1951 "The Mark of a Man" campaign and the 1960s marine corps brochure, "The Marine Corps Builds Men."[18]

The official image of the American servicewoman seemed virtually unchanging in her first two decades of postwar service. While each branch offered its own spin on why a woman would want to be a Wac, Wave, Waf, or

Woman Marine, the colloquial ways of referring to women in the WAC, navy (still known as WAVES from their World War II days), and Women in the Air Force (WAF), recruiting materials also emphasized service benefits such as job opportunities, education, and travel. The image of the ideal American servicewoman remained consistent, but her environment changed with the times: by the late 1960s, recruiting materials depicted more images of men and women working and playing together, as well as images of Black and white servicewomen to appeal to a broader audience. These adjustments reflected new recruiting strategies, such as drawing attention to the lifestyle benefits military service offered—a key message during the Vietnam War and national dissatisfaction with the military due to the conflict and the draft.

The image of the American servicewoman changed little for nearly two decades because of generally static policies and consistent inabilities to reach recruiting goals. After the Women's Armed Services Integration Act of 1948, no substantial policy changes in women's military roles occurred until 1967. During the Korean War, none of the aggressive womanpower recruiting goals ever reached their targets, a trend that continued through the 1960s with the Vietnam War. Patriotism no longer compelled women in the same way it had during World War II. The Women's Armed Services Integration Act established that the military might at times rely on women to meet manpower needs, but defense officials largely did not feel that necessity in the 1950s and 1960s. In those decades, the military needed fighting men: officials cared little that womanpower recruiting remained low. Women filled vital support roles, yet the draft also supplied men for those same units—wars would still be fought and the nation would still be defended, even if few women stepped up to serve.

Lack of need meant that recruiters could be selective and improve the caliber of womanpower altogether, and from the beginning, standards for women were high. The image of the ideal servicewoman began with basic ground rules of who could participate in military service. Age, education, and family status qualifications remained fairly uniform across all branches, although minimum age ranges could and did vary slightly within the limits set by the Women's Armed Services Integration Act.[19] Common criteria included:

- Age: minimum of eighteen years (enlisted) or twenty-one (officers); no older than thirty-five.[20]
- Education: high school graduate (enlisted) or college graduate (officer).

- Relationships: no dependents under eighteen, parental permission if recruit was under twenty-one, and unmarried (unless applicant had prior service record).[21]

With these guidelines, recruiters primarily sought young, smart, single, and unattached women. The regulations also showed respect and recognition for authority figures: any recruit between the ages of eighteen and twenty needed parental consent to join up. Once Mom and Dad signed off on enlistment (or officer commissioning), the act of signing over permission gave the military the masculine role of protecting a young woman on her parents' behalf. Men did not need such permission: their position as men in national defense designated them as *de facto* protectors; women were not—they neither carried weapons nor did they fight.[22] Additionally, with the creation of the Universal Military Training and Service Act on June 19, 1951, all American men had to register with Selective Service when they turned eighteen and could be drafted starting six months later. Parents had no choice in the matter when it came to their sons' relationship to military service.[23]

A few recruiting materials targeted parents, reassuring Mom and Dad that their daughter would be in good hands in the service. A 1956 poster exclaiming "Proud Parents" suggested that being in the WAC was a career path that would make them happy about their daughter's choices in life.[24] Seated at a piano, the servicewoman presents a neat figure, well-coiffed and smartly dressed in a tailored WAC uniform. Mom and Dad, obviously happy based on the smiles on their faces, watch and listen to their accomplished daughter. A photograph of the daughter in her graduation attire offers a nod to her intelligence (figure 2.1). Although serving her country might require a young woman to leave her family for a time, her parents would be nothing but proud when she returned. Even more, the image suggests, the family unit would become even stronger.

"Proud Parents" was not the first time recruiting efforts had turned toward parents, but the context looked different now when recruiting adult daughters into service. During World War II, propaganda images often used children as a way to urge support for war bonds, men's service, and other elements of total war. For example, the Electric Auto-Lite Company's 1944 advertisement, "Never too young to buy a war bond!" highlights a two-and-a-half-year-old girl as she purchases a war bond.[25] That same year, the Aluminum Company of America's ad "beyond the call of duty," showcases a mother holding her tiny baby and a Medal of Honor, arguing for the impor-

FIGURE 2.1 This 1956 poster tried to appeal to the entire family, assuring recruits that their parents would be proud of their military service, and communicating to parents that military service was a career that women should pursue. Betty H. Carter Women Veterans Historical Project, Martha Blakeney Hodges Special Collections and University Archives, University of North Carolina–Greensboro.

tance of financially supporting the war cause.[26] In 1943, Best & Co's ad in the *New York Times* put the message more simply: an image of a young girl's face appears above the words "safeguard your child's future . . . buy more war bonds."[27] In wartime, such messages pulled at the heartstrings of Americans everywhere, but perhaps in particular young parents, who could see their own children in the advertisements and think about their own family members away fighting the war.

By the late 1940s and early 1950s, the same parents who saw such images during the war as they raised their young children now found themselves the targets of a new type of advertising. Never had military recruiters had to focus on convincing parents that the armed forces would be a good career option for their children: during wartime and with a draft on, a measure of national support was certainly necessary, but the effort to secure

The Real Miss America   47

womanpower was altogether something new. One brochure in 1954 provided detailed information on "Your Daughter's Role in Today's World: What every parent should know about opportunities for women in the Armed Forces." Prefaced with "A personal message to parents . . ." from the Armed Forces Chaplains Board, the ten-page booklet assures mom and dad that "fine young women" have "rendered valuable service. At the same time, they found ample opportunity for self-advancement, and they lived normal, secure, and useful lives."[28] The pamphlet argues that military service provides a young woman with a solid path for her future in a world that had changed drastically from when her parents were young. With military service, a young woman could "prepare for her future, learn the skills to be a self-supporting or contributing partner during the early years of marriage, and at the same time have . . . congenial surroundings, good companionship, and just plain fun." One air force brochure written for parents also emphasized service to country as "responsible citizens" and stressed that not just any young woman could serve her nation. Only the best would do: "your daughter must meet very high standards to enlist."[29] These were not ads comforting parents that their child's service was a patriotic sacrifice: in war, such ads served an important purpose to reassure parents that although sons might give their lives for their country, it was for a noble cause. These ads were about service and sacrifice, but since women did not see combat, these new recruiting materials combined career counseling and reassurance for parents that their daughters were taking the right path (figure 2.2). Choosing a military career would help their daughters take an important step from childhood into adulthood—a transition in which daughters would be surrounded by responsible people, have access to education and travel opportunities, and become responsible, patriotic young women—the kind of women their parents had begun raising them to be. For patriotic parents, these brochures suggested, military service should seem like a natural progression in their daughter's transition to adult independence.

Although parental support mattered, recruiters also understood that young women themselves were the most vital audience, hence the importance of speaking to more than one audience at a time with recruiting materials. Many of the techniques used in recruiting publications addressed women and their parents and families.[30] For example, specifications that recruits must be "of good character and background" spoke to young women and their parents, emphasizing that military leaders sought to attract "high-quality" women who would be good representatives of their nation at all times.[31] The 1963 Women Marines brochure "The Woman Officer" particu-

FIGURE 2.2 The trend of enlisting young women and their families extended into the 1960s; in *Somebody Special,* a detailed pamphlet showcasing many aspects of life in the military, this page focused on parents and grandparents as important people women should consider when starting a military career. Betty H. Carter Women Veterans Historical Project, Martha Blakeney Hodges Special Collections and University Archives, University of North Carolina–Greensboro.

larly notes that candidates must "be of excellent moral character."[32] To ensure a woman's character, recruiters interviewed interested applicants and checked personal references, no matter which service a woman wanted to enter, and no matter what level (officer or enlisted). A 1955 booklet explains that the military only accepted "those who are mentally, morally, and physically qualified. Those who meet the requirements can, through military service, fulfill a responsibility of citizenship as well as help to build their own future security."[33] A 1952 document explains that women's physical examinations would be like men's, but also included pelvic exams and a thorough medical history, including women's menstrual history. According to a hospitalman tasked with supporting women naval recruits' physical examinations at that time, the physical examination of a female recruit took about thirty minutes, but about twelve male recruits could be examined in

The Real Miss America 49

the same amount of time.³⁴ Women had to take tests, be physically examined, and provide educational credentials, just as men had to do, but women also faced "special additional processing which included an investigation of the records of local police, mental hospitals, schools, former employers," along with their references. WAF applicants also had to undergo a psychiatric examination. As Major General Jeanne Holm explains it, such standards reflected "not so much . . . legitimate requirements for high quality as to cultural biases toward women, which required that they be more qualified than men for the same jobs, particularly in male-dominated fields" like the armed forces.³⁵

While the armed forces maintained standards for all recruits, the continuation of the draft beginning in 1948 meant that military officials could be more selective in recruiting women. The services wanted women, but they wanted the very best women they could find to create their nucleus of womanpower. For example, men's physical examinations included only a brief psychiatric evaluation, focused on identifying major psychiatric issues.³⁶ The services sought highly qualified women who would represent the military impeccably, in part because women's service leaders continued to worry about negative perception and the directors believed that having higher-quality women would help men accept women's presence in the military.³⁷ While the Selective Service program certainly maintained standards for men, the draft was in place specifically because of ongoing personnel needs to support the Cold War. Servicewomen contributed to that need, but their presence was capped by law at 2 percent, which meant that the military needed men.

"Excellent moral character" or "good character" typically meant that recruiters preferred virgins, or at least good girls who could pass as such. All the services refused to admit women who had previous pregnancies, even if that pregnancy ended in miscarriage or adoption. Since most applicants were single, this was a way to protect against "loose" women who might be interested in service just to meet a man. Married women who had been pregnant in the past—but had no living children—might be an exception, but the only women who could enlist if already married were women who had served previously; namely, World War II veterans. "Excellent moral character" or "good character" were also codes for "lesbians need not apply." Any woman whose background might have any chance of sullying the reputation of women in uniform was distinctly undesirable.

The emphasis on character and morality helped the women's services to maintain what military officials believed was a highly reputable profile and to root out women who might later cause poor publicity or other problems. Military leaders believed it was counterproductive to admit women who would prove "unsuitable." According to a 1955 Department of Defense (DOD)/Department of Labor brochure, "the nonconformist, the escapist, the insecure or inadequate personality are soon lost in the shuffle and have to be returned to civilian life. This is an unnecessary expense."[38] Womanpower leaders hoped to avoid such a problem by interviewing potential recruits and checking references. One 1958 joint army, navy, air force publication stresses, "the public nature of military service means that women of the Armed Forces, readily identifiable as they are by their uniforms, have an additional responsibility to adhere to high moral standards. The Armed Forces cannot tolerate any subversion of accepted criteria of sexual behavior."[39] While the military also did not tolerate "subversion of accepted criteria of sexual behavior" in men, the standards were also applied differently to them, since it was acceptable for servicemen to have sex with women, as long as the men protected themselves. The only uniform sexual standard for men and women was that homosexuality was forbidden.

Physical appearance and clothing became visual markers of servicewomen's status as ladies, thus women of good character. Tailored suits, skirts, hats, gloves, and pumps featured in many brochures, whether in line drawings, watercolor realism, or photography. The 1960s WAC brochure "Somebody Special" relies on clothing heavily, apparently assuming that civilian women would respond well to images of well-tailored, feminine uniforms. The forty-seven-page publication depicts recruit Barbara and other women nearly always in skirts, carrying gloves, and wearing dress shoes. Six pages with full-color photographs emphasize the types of servicewomen's clothing and elegance, "smartness," style, and good looks that women could hope to achieve in the military. A two-page spread entitled "A Brand-New Beauty," ends with a photo of Barbara in uniform, gloves in hand, and the caption, "There is no figure more feminine, more dashing, more trim, than that of a young woman in a tailored, smartly-styled ensemble of the Women's Army Corps!"[40] As shown in this publication, service offered young women a distinct style and the knowledge of how to project a ladylike image at all times (figure 2.3).

Recruiters, who were not always women themselves, fervently sought women who aspired to be well-dressed, "feminine . . . dashing . . . trim," the consummate ideal woman. Across the decades, recruiting materials highlight women with neat hair and attractive makeup, cultivating a seemingly perfect whole-body image for young ladies when combined with the

FIGURE 2.3 *Somebody Special* also suggested that young women would become better versions of themselves by embarking on a military career. Betty H. Carter Women Veterans Historical Project, Martha Blakeney Hodges Special Collections and University Archives, University of North Carolina–Greensboro.

uniform. A 1973 navy brochure explains that recruits could wear their hair any way they wanted, but while in uniform it could not brush the top of the collar and had to be styled so the uniform hat would sit correctly. These instructions correlated with earlier details found in brochures like "Somebody Special" in the early 1960s. The 1973 brochure even borrowed from that earlier pamphlet's wording, arguing that military service would give women "newly found poise, confidence and the extra sparkle that comes with being 'Someone Special.'"[41] Similar materials from the other women's services promise that women would gain respect, confidence, and status as the nation's finest ladies in exchange for displaying gender-appropriate behavior and appearance at all times.

The ideal servicewoman had to be smart and always seeking to improve herself both physically and mentally: appearances mattered but were not enough to ensure admission to the ranks of "The First Ladies of the Land . . . America's Finest!"[42] If military recruiters required high standards of their prospects, they expected to find women with high standards of their own, particularly in terms of education. Recruiting materials stress that military service would offer educational opportunities such as professional development, tuition assistance, or G.I. Bill benefits because female leaders wanted women who would find these opportunities valuable. Women interested in further education would likely be open-minded, malleable, and willing to expand their worldviews and consider new ideas and approaches, such as the military way of life. Such women would also be more likely to accept a goal of constant improvement. "Somebody Special" introduces Barbara as a woman who values higher education. "Barbara hoped to go on to college, where she would dig into studies and build a career, while being polished into a lovely state of poise and prestige."[43] Education, in this scenario, served as a path to feminine refinement; it would simultaneously make recruits better servicewomen and offer them better futures, a benefit for institution and individual in the long run.

The vision of womanpower portrayed in recruiting materials centered on very familiar ideas of what women should be and do because this method seemed to be the best way to negotiate contemporary expectations of what American women should be and do. By emphasizing womanpower as feminine and ladylike, military leaders constructed womanpower in a way they thought would be acceptable to Americans. This approach reflected the underlying ideology that in the military, equality for women was defined as utilizing women in roles women could do as well or better than men—femininity would never be compromised. Taken together, recruiting materials from the first twenty-five years of women's postwar service emphasize a white, middle-class, heterosexual, feminine ideal as the standard by which recruits would be measured. This standard reflected the backgrounds of the women in charge of the WAC, WAVES, WAF, and WMs, as well as male military leaders' own conceptions of what the best of American womanhood looked like. It was also a continuation of World War II practices, which focused on making women in uniform as nonthreatening as possible in a time of great uncertainty.[44] Yet the image also appealed to others, including African American women and lesbians. Despite the whitewashing in most early recruiting materials, military leaders welcomed African American women and professed that race did not matter in the women's services. Lesbians, however, were decidedly unwelcome.

The public face of the women's services, as seen in recruiting materials, did not seem to extend to Black women initially, suggesting falsely that only white women could serve in the Cold War military. Yet less than a month after the Women's Armed Services Integration Act became law, President

Truman used Executive Order 9981 to desegregate the military entirely. Because these two events happened so close together, the women's services integrated early in their lifespans. By the early 1950s, all the women's services integrated their basic training or boot camp programs and made all servicewomen's career assignments regardless of race. In theory, recruiters sought women from all backgrounds, and women of color did serve in all military branches throughout the Cold War. In reality, until the 1970s numbers of African American and other women of color remained small. In the 1960s, print recruiting materials slowly began depicting African American servicewomen, a move that paralleled broader interest in the military's—and the nation's—progress toward racial integration. Broadcast television recruiting programs, such as the *Big Picture* series on ABC-TV, also showed racially integrated women's units.[45]

African American and minority servicewomen's numbers remained low for many years, in part due to heightened service qualifications applied to all women recruits. Looking back on her time as a recruiting officer, General Mildred Bailey recalled that "considerable" numbers of African American women applied to join the WAC in the 1950s. In a time when American women's career opportunities remained limited for white women and even more limited for women of color, it makes sense that military service would be attractive to a diverse population of American women. However, the existing recruitment standards were apparently out of reach for many African American women. Many applied, and could pass the tests, but in much lower numbers than white women. "That's because of the school systems at that time," Bailey, a former teacher, realized. "Segregation, the quality of the education in the black schools was such that a very large number of black women could not qualify."[46] Some college-educated African American women enlisted because they could not meet officer standards due to systematic educational disparities.[47] While female military leaders expressed that they wanted minority women to serve, they did not fully understand the impact that their own standards had on recruits. Military leaders applied white, middle-class standards of femininity to their vision of womanpower, imagining that these standards would help them recruit and retain women, but these same standards made it more difficult for some women to join the military in ways the women's directors likely did not imagine because of their own white privilege.

Bailey claimed she exhausted every potential recruiting avenue in her time in personnel procurement in the late 1950s and 1960s, but the low numbers of Black servicewomen also indicates recruiters may not have thought about how or where to recruit African American women. There is also no evidence that military leaders ever specifically considered why they had a hard time recruiting African American women, or how their own policies created such difficulties. Statistics show that the strength of Black WAC members nearly doubled from 1951 to 1952, reaching a first postwar "high" of 1,046. In 1953, the number of African American Wacs rose to 1,332. While the numbers of African American Wacs declined after the Korean War, by 1959 and 1960 more Black servicewomen were again joining the WAC.[48] The numbers are small nonetheless: womanpower recruitment never got very large in the early Cold War, and minority women's recruitment was a negligible piece of procurement work. Certainly, no one seems to have discussed how enlistment and officer commissioning standards prevented at least some African American women from joining the armed forces.

Despite recruiters' inattention, African American publications show Black Americans' interest in military service as a career for women. In late 1962 *Ebony* magazine's featured article, "Women in Uniform," honored the twentieth anniversary of women's military service. Using much of the same language found in military recruiting brochures, the piece highlights women's military service opportunities and opens by focusing on Black servicewomen's achievements.

> Negro women have been in the forefront of the women's services and have welcomed the opportunities for travel, education and exciting service for their country. They have gained high rank—Lt. Col. Ruth A. Lucas of women in the air force, the nation's highest ranking Negro woman officer, holds a rank only one degree lower than the head of the entire 10,000 member Women's Army Corps. Negro captains and majors are found throughout the WAC, WAF and the service nursing corps. There are fewer and less high ranking Negro members of the women Marines [sic] and SPARS [Coast Guard], but these units are much smaller.[49]

The article focuses on marriage (military service is "no deterrent" to matrimony), job opportunities, and the military emphasis on femininity. The message mirrored other recruiting materials, emphasizing that military service did not masculinize young women. Since World War II, military officials had worried about the perception of servicewomen as "mannish" figures because they had joined the military at all, women who wanted to usurp men's authority. To the contrary, the authors suggested: military service would make women more desirable as women. The authors note that "life in uniform can be useful and completely feminine at the same time. While training and utilizing special skills in their recruits, the women's services never make the mistake of considering WACs as soldiers or WAVES as sailors."[50] The authors refer to print recruiting materials as "glamourous, slick-paper brochures" in which "femininity is the keynote." From the emphasis on African Americans' roles in national defense through the end of the article—including four full pages of photographs of Black women in uniform—the *Ebony* piece encourages African American women to consider a military career, even if military recruiters weren't yet tapping into that demographic as fully as they might have.[51]

Within a few years, womanpower leaders' awareness of their diverse audience improved: African American women began to appear in longer recruiting pamphlets, suggesting that some in the military recruiting structure were thinking a little more about race. As early as 1966, brochures started to include glossy photographs of Black and white women together, although such images of a racially integrated military remained rare. Into the 1970s, Black women appeared as token figures—one woman in a sea of white. Nonetheless, including African American women in a narrative that constructed servicewomen as the most feminine ideals of American womanhood is noteworthy. In contrast, the 1966 brochure's sole image of a Black woman and a white man together clearly signals that the interaction is occurring in a professional work environment, and that the man is the woman's superior.[52] While recruiting materials began to show interracial, heterosexual interaction, these documents carefully structured those images: any implication of interracial sexual activity might undermine the carefully crafted, feminine visage of womanpower. Moreover, the limited images of African American women alongside white women and men not only reflects the limited presence of minority women in the services, but also suggests an implicit bias against marketing the military's racial integration efforts too vigorously in the civil rights movement.

White heterosexuality consistently remained the most important hallmark of the military's vision of womanpower. Longer brochures that emphasized benefits of the military lifestyle often included images of women and men holding hands or dancing (in and out of uniform), signaling that in the military, a young woman could meet a suitable young man.[53] Two early 1970s navy brochures include multiple pictures of women enjoying leisure time with men. The cover of *A New World of Opportunity* showcases a white Wac and a white male companion together at the Eiffel Tower.[54] In the military, servicewomen remained attractive and desirable to men—

something that the women's services presumed every woman wanted. Highlighting servicewomen's interactions with men assured prospects that the military was a great place for a lady to meet a proper mate. By 1970, one advertisement running in *Seventeen* magazine explicitly addressed the issue of marriage, assuring potential recruits that "When one of our girls finds her man, she can get married" (figure 2.4).

The emphasis was clearly on "man" and "proper mate." Integrating images of men and women working and playing alongside each other was an important way to communicate military policy that homosexuality and military service were entirely incompatible. While U.S. military officials first began discharging homosexuals during World War II, not until 1949 did the DOD implement policies explicitly prohibiting homosexuals from serving in the military. The 1950 Uniform Code of Military Justice (UCMJ) codified these policies.[55] Recruiting materials sent these messages, explaining that military service allowed women to interact with men as they would in the civilian world, downplaying same-sex interactions in on-base housing, training, and other structures of military life.

Policy, of course, is quite different from practice, and through the years recruiters remained continually unsuccessful in their goals of preventing lesbians from joining the services. By the late 1950s, the women's components had conducted thorough searches to root out and discharge lesbians, whose very presence testified to the imperfections in the screening system.[56] The navy's 1957 Crittenden Report studied homosexuality in both men and women, noting an understanding that in the navy, "the incidence rate of homosexual activity is much higher for the female than the male."[57] The authors offered several reasons for the statistics, including the proposition that "military service may be more attractive to females with latent homosexual tendencies." Although the authors conceded that female homosexuality was "difficult to detect," they also affirmed that "homosexual activity of female members of the military has appeared to be more disruptive of morale and discipline in the past than similar male activity."[58] The board recommended that the military needed to develop a better understanding and definition of female homosexuality to better police it in the future. Military leaders remained concerned that the presence of lesbians in the armed forces undermined efforts to project womanpower as an idealized version of American womanhood.

The vision of womanpower offered in recruiting materials centered on very familiar ideas of what women should be and do. Crafting an image of feminized, heterosexual white women enabled recruiters to appeal to

FIGURE 2.4 By the end of the 1960s, recruiting advertisements appeared in young women's magazines to try to educate them about career opportunities in the military. This advertisement in *Seventeen* magazine tried to clear up rumors about military service. N. W. Ayer Advertising Agency Records, Archives Center, National Museum of American History, Smithsonian Institution.

American women—or at least cater to white women and their parents' fears. Yet the image also appealed to others who did not always fit the projection, including African American women and lesbians. Officially, military leaders welcomed African American women and professed that race did not matter. In contrast, lesbians were not welcome in uniform. Within just a few years of the Women's Armed Services Integration Act, the military became—at least on paper—a career venue where young ladies gained valuable education and job training, all while maintaining their femininity. That on-the-job training and education would ensure that new recruits understood how to become the ladies they supposedly admired in the glossy promotional materials.

3 You in the Service
Training Uncle Sam's Nieces

Military leaders weren't the only ones who connected glamour and women's military service in the early 1950s. Just as the Miss America pageant runners, the government, the cosmetic industry, and others had linked glamour and patriotism during World War II, so did Hollywood filmmakers. They realized that there was public interest in this new, uniformed American woman, and of the approximately 400 war-related films that came out in the United States during the war, scholars estimate approximately 6 percent of those included at least one uniformed woman.[1] By including servicewomen, these films highlighted the new opportunities for women in national defense even if, at the time, Americans believed these roles were only temporary. When women's military service became permanent, filmmakers continued to think about how to portray womanpower on screen. In 1952 and 1953, just as public relations officers puzzled over the best ways to attract women through recruiting brochures and events like the 1952 Miss America pageant recruiting blitz, Hollywood studios offered their own brand of recruitment by keeping the image of the American servicewoman in popular culture, and even expanding it.[2] The question, however, was whether these films would offer an accurate picture of women's lives in national defense, which might help Americans better understand womanpower and cultivate interest among potential recruits. Two particular films—1952's *Skirts Ahoy!* and 1953's *Never Wave at a Wac*—seemed promising.

Neither film was perfect, but each offered a mostly military-approved portrayal of servicewomen as feminine young ladies, as well as an inside look at basic training and military life. *Skirts Ahoy!*, a musical featuring renowned swimmer-actress Esther Williams and *Guys and Dolls*' Vivian Blaine, tells the story of three young women who enlist in the navy. One is left at the altar, another leaves her own fiancé at the altar, and the third is trying to follow a sailor. While one military official worried that the movie mostly sent the message that a woman could find a guy if she joined the WAVES, Captain Joy Hancock, Assistant Chief of Naval Personnel for Women, reportedly liked how the film portrayed women's boot camp experiences. Aside from an arguably too-revealing poster, it seemed that the film might be good for publicity, and correspondence with MGM executives indicates that the filmmakers had put a lot of attention into showing servicewomen in respectable ways.[3] RKO Pictures' *Never Wave at a Wac* offered even more publicity support, including a cameo from five-star General Omar Bradley. Like *Skirts Ahoy!* the movie uses women's military service as the backdrop for romantic comedy, but once again, officials liked the (mostly) accurate inside look at women's life in the military. The March 1953 *Recruiting Journal*, sent to recruiters' offices nationwide, covered the film's premiere and offered this editor's note: "Obviously, this film should create a bonanza of interested young women for the Women's Army Corps, and will provide the golden touch of publicity when it is shown . . . recruiters who fail to publicize the appearance of 'Never Wave at a Wac' will be passing up an excellent recruiting vehicle."[4] Although produced by large film studios, military officials invested a sizable amount of time and money into these movies because they believed film could be useful in capturing Americans' imaginations about womanpower.

These films made excellent recruiting fodder, specifically because they helped showcase what women might expect in the service.[5] Even the emphasis on romance in both movies wasn't problematic, because military leaders assumed that every servicewoman would eventually move on to marriage and family life. In fact, military officials tried to convince most people that having a career in the military before marriage and family would only help a young woman be better at both of those life plans. Basic training and boot camp began the real work of making America's girls into America's finest women, instilling qualities that would make them not only great servicewomen but also the best wives and mothers the nation had ever seen. As women filling national defense roles, servicewomen were constantly subjected to public scrutiny. Their reputations could make or break what many still perceived as an ongoing experiment of sorts, and films like *Skirts Ahoy!* and *Never Wave at a Wac* helped Americans imagine who and what a servicewoman was. The pressure was high: to make womanpower work, image development was everything. This meant that government officials paid attention to popular culture: they corresponded with filmmakers, providing feedback on both films, and when released, military recruiting journals advised recruiters that the films would likely generate interest in the women's services. RKO Pictures even brought a contingent of servicewomen from NATO countries to tour the nation and promote *Never Wave at a Wac*.[6]

From the beginning, military leaders purposefully shaped women's military experience around gender ideals, building on foundations established during World War II. In her history of the wartime WAC, Mattie Treadwell notes that when women began to serve as auxiliaries alongside the army in the early 1940s, training women at all was unprecedented in the army. The Army Nurse Corps did not train women, because nurses came into the nurse corps already knowing their job function. When women came into the Women's Army Auxiliary Corps (WAAC), the predecessor of the WAC, the expectations were similar: that women would bring in skills from the civilian world that would be applied in a military context, thus no need for job training. The only thing Waacs needed, then-Director Oveta Culp Hobby believed, was a quick course to help Waacs understand army customs and discipline before they got to work.[7] Likewise, the navy did not believe that Waves needed as much training as men because of the work they would do, but also agreed that Waves would benefit from some sort of orientation to the navy and how it worked.[8] Ultimately, the wartime services did provide some sort of initial training for women, which tended to be shorter than the training given to men, because women did not serve in combat, and the training structure varied periodically.

When womanpower became permanent in 1948, all the women's components used their wartime experiences to create postwar training expectations. As before, there were various ways in which women's training looked similar to men's. Waves took many of the same courses required of men, including History, Current Events and Citizenship; Ships, Aircraft and Weapons; Organization; Personnel; and Navy Jobs and Training. Women got something more, though, a "surprise package" that reflected long-standing navy traditions of personal and professional development: five hours of lessons titled "On Being a Lady." The officer explaining this course in 1948 assured her audience this was fully appropriate. "Do not, I ask you, look askance at this phase of the curriculum, for the germ of the idea is as old as our navy itself. It was John Paul Jones who stressed the need of the service for gentlemen—defined as men of liberal education, refined manners, punctilious courtesy, and the nicest sense of personal honor. It is less than problematical that the history of the navy is so glorious because its officers and men, were first gentlemen and secondly officers and sailors . . . May our women both continue and enrich this tradition."[9] Since women could not be gentlemen, the equivalent was simply to make them ladies. Honor, education, manners, and courtesy all folded into the idea of just what made a lady, and femininity distinguished a lady from the masculine gentlemanly counterpart. The reasoning of making servicewomen into ladies served a dual purpose: defined as ladies, women in uniform would emulate the same traits expected of women in the civilian world.

Not all parts of basic training or boot camp kept women feminine. During the weeks of boot camp and basic training, however, women performed hard labor just like men did, scrubbing floors, washing dishes, and participating in "GI Parties" to clean the barracks. For women, these chores would be in line with expectations they might have at home in cleaning the house. Both men and women experienced similar lifestyle changes in their transition to military life. For many recruits, living in a large community was a new experience. Both men and women participated in KP (kitchen) duty, made beds and packed lockers according to regulation, showered daily, and drilled, although women drilled without guns in their hands. All personnel were required to stand in the presence of a high-ranking officer and to open doors for those of higher rank. Other training events took women out of the classroom and into activities that looked more like what men might experience. Although women would not serve in combat, during the first decade of the Cold War, new women recruits engaged in physically exhausting activities such as obstacle courses and bivouacs, dressing in more masculinized uniforms for the purposes of that activity only. In the 1950s, women in all services went through these activities and learned how to fire weapons, although the WAF did not give their servicewomen weapons training. By the end of the decade these recruit training elements were all eliminated.[10]

In *Never Wave at a Wac*, Rosalind Russell's character Jo McBain finds herself in some of these training exercises, mostly for comedic purposes, including a gas attack. As they fall out into the fresh air following the simulation, the instructor yells, "All right, once more! Just to remind you, it's gas, not Chanel Number Five!" Even a routine training exercise reinforced gender identity: in this case, reminding recruits that gas was not the same as perfume suggested that female recruits lacked common sense that might be expected of men, and played to stereotypes of what might interest women. In the real world, the WMs used male drill instructors to teach some classes, and these servicemen faced gendered backlash from their peers: "when they took the recruits outside the battalion area . . . Marines taunted them with, 'Hey Sarge, your slip is showing.'" This led one drill instructor to move to the sidewalk during drills, giving the appearance that he was not leading a group of women.[11]

While Hollywood had its day in promoting women's military service, by the mid-1950s the WAC also found its own voice to educate the public. In

1954, the Signal Corps Pictorial Center's Big Picture series, which ran on ABC television weekly, produced *The Wac Is a Soldier, Too*, a twenty-eight-minute piece promoting the newly built WAC Training Center at Fort McClellan, Alabama, as well as women's lives at the facility. The film marches viewers through all steps of basic training, beginning with uniform and shoe selection (all uniforms designed by Hattie Carnegie, renowned fashion designer of the day). Marching—or drill training—takes center stage in the film, not unlike in *Skirts Ahoy!* "Primarily, drill training is aimed at improving the trainees' poise, posture, and military bearing. More familiar with the dance floor than a drill ground, a few trainees invariably find they have what behave like two left feet!"[12] However, there was no need for recruits to worry, because basic training would help them regain their footing in no time. After all, as new recruits heard upon arrival at Great Lakes Naval Training Station in *Skirts Ahoy!* "As you can see, there's quite a bit of marching."[13] With proper instruction, any recruit could exchange the rhythm of the dance floor for the rhythm of a marching cadence.

Other elements of basic training fostered women's development in a number of ways. For example, regular inspections would ensure that "great pride in personal appearance becomes second nature," and after all, "No area of human relations is overlooked in the training program."[14] Basic training, as the film emphasizes, was about developing the whole person, from physical bearing and appearance to leisure (recruits could access a golf course in off-duty hours, or day rooms for "those less athletically inclined"). Women would have plenty of time for hobbies, shopping at the PX (post exchange), getting their hair done at the base beauty shop, and even opportunities for a "rich spiritual life."[15] All this was available to servicewomen in an era when few private sector jobs available to women could boast of such benefits, as well as secretarial training at no charge, as producers kindly pointed out to viewers. By providing a range of leisure time pursuits plus additional vocational training, servicewomen could enjoy their time in the military and prepare themselves for future careers as well.

In most circumstances, femininity ruled the day, no matter what training activities might look like. The message military officials wanted to send to Americans was that military service turned girls into ladies and refined women who embraced their roles as women. One 1958 ad claimed that "even a casual glance at the Woman Marine will reveal that she is well-groomed, poised and confident of her abilities. She knows that her Marine training not only fits her for duties in the Corps, but also helps bring out all her latent qualities as a woman."[16] Whether a woman already knew how to

FIGURE 3.1 In the early 1950s, the Navy included five hours of training entitled "On being a lady." While the exercise shown above was categorized as physical fitness, it also helped women be more poised as they walked, lending support to the goals of instilling femininity within all recruits. Naval History and Heritage Command.

behave like a proper lady did not matter: basic training would teach her to assume military leaders' vision of proper American womanhood as she developed those "latent qualities" she possessed. In fact, basic training instructors assumed all female recruits needed to be kept up to speed on proper standards for physical grooming and comportment (figure 3.1). These efforts ensured all servicewomen conformed to the same expectations, while also indoctrinating these expectations into women's daily lives perhaps beyond their service years.

In the 1963 WAC training film *Strictly Personal*, the white platoon sergeant informs new recruits that her job is to help make sure they all know the proper way to do things, even if they think they already know what that way is. "My job is to teach you the army way—the army way to do everything, including many things you've been doing all your lives. Things that will help you in your future jobs, and in your army living. Things that might be called Strictly Personal." During the thirty-minute film, trainees receive instruction in everything from shaving legs and armpits regularly, how frequently to bathe or shower, deodorant use, care of undergarments, and even a stipulation not to borrow someone else's brush or comb. The predominantly white recruits are advised to use not one, but two toothbrushes, rotating them and keeping them in a cup to dry in their locker (to kill the germs); shoes should also be rotated regularly. After admonishing recruits to wash their faces "a couple of times a day," the narrator explains further just how important a woman's face is while she is in service. "What you put on it at night is your own affair, but what you put on your face in the daytime is the army's business." Put more bluntly, the narrator continues, "Wearing a lot of makeup with the WAC uniform is bad taste."[17] Left unsaid is the idea that too much makeup would make a servicewoman seem gaudy or worse, might suggest she was morally questionable. A proper lady would understand that makeup should be limited.

Nothing seems off-limits in *Strictly Personal*, from the makeup and personal hygiene guidelines to detailed recommendations on diet and exercise. Even posture and walking play an important part of the training film. Four types of walking—duck walk, debutante slouch, masculine lope, and teenage wiggle—are discouraged. "None of them looks right, or uses the muscles properly. There is only one correct way to walk in the WAC," the narrator intones as a recruit skillfully demonstrates the proper stride. After a close look at drilling, recruits learn how to properly fill their mealtime trays with appropriate amounts of all the nutritious foods available in the dining hall. Private Baker, the centerpiece of the film, gets chastised by the narrator for indulging in a candy bar between meals, since "One candy bar every day can put an extra ten to fifteen pounds on you in a year, Private Baker!" To illustrate, the film shows the consequences for another young private who has apparently eaten all the wrong things at lunch and now needs her uniform let out in the tailoring shop, much to her apparent chagrin.[18]

While *Strictly Personal* and other films specifically targeted the female recruit, the constant references to drilling in that film, *Skirts Ahoy!*, and *Never Wave at a Wac* offer reminders that a large part of basic training applied to every service member. Regardless of gender, military training adapted an individual to the military structure, created communal expectations for behavior and performance, and fostered characteristics like discipline and teamwork. While this whole-person approach to self-improvement was very useful to the military, it also offered benefits to the individual when he or she returned to civilian life. The 1950s DOD/Department of Labor "Careers for Women in the Armed Forces" promoted the long-term benefits of basic training or boot camp, explaining that the training provided "self-development that will make her more effective in life: Getting and holding a job, earning a promotion, doing interesting work at fair pay, playing a useful role in the community—these depend on more than just technical skill. And basic, while it is training rather than education in the usual academic sense, helps to develop a maturity which makes for successful living."[19] As described in this brochure, joining the military was far more than an opportunity to serve the nation: it was a career choice that would reap dividends. Military service would prepare women for a job, a way of life, and success, offering unique benefits of personal and professional development to last a lifetime. Even the feminine-focused training videos continually emphasize how military training would help recruits in their lives outside the military.

Once inducted into the armed services, American women were no longer individuals, but part of something higher: womanpower. In 1950, the training booklet "'You' in the Service" put it bluntly, noting that military service elevated a young woman to a new state of being. "When you put on a uniform you become more than the individual you have always been . . . you are now representative of a military group . . . Whatever you do while you are in uniform will be judged by the standard of what is expected of a woman in military life and not by individual measures of conduct . . . Nor does your responsibility to the Service cease when you are out-of-uniform. Your appearance and behavior when you are in civilian clothes is a reflection of your military self. You are not two persons leading separate lives, but the same individual whether on or off duty."[20] In and out of uniform, a servicewoman's identity as a woman was central, so makeup application, poise, and clothing played important parts in crafting the ladylike visage of servicewomen as representatives of the armed forces (figure 3.2). Beyond having the right look, women's invisible traits also remained important: just as during recruitment, "quality" continued to be stressed in each of the women's services. This was a standard set by moral and intellectual markers that could be assessed when a woman applied to join the military.

Although military officials acknowledged that looks weren't everything, in training and throughout a woman's service career, physical appearance evidenced a woman's quality and excellence. This was particularly true in the first two decades of women's service after World War II. Along with military protocol and citizenship classes, recruits learned to cultivate a standardized, proper feminine appearance, based on white, middle-class ideals of American femininity. A 1954 WAF handbook told new recruits "You're the girl who can do something wonderful with her looks. Do you know why? Because you're in a unique spot—as a WAF . . . You know, in the eyes of

FIGURE 3.2 Learning to live with others in a group environment was another important element of recruit training. Women new to the navy—known as Waves, a holdover from World War II—consult each other on where to sew their rating badges. Naval History and Heritage Command.

everybody else you are the real Miss America."[21] This instructional guide oriented "WAF personnel in basic principles, procedures, personal conduct, and appearance during basic training and on tour of duty." The table of contents includes information related to Basic Training, Assignment, The Future, Beauty, Fashion, and The Uniform. Features on beauty, fashion, and uniforms account for thirty-nine of the book's eighty-seven pages.[22] The authors suggest that readers evaluate their character, behavior, and beauty to learn how they can improve in all three areas. The following year, The Toilet Goods Association, Inc., produced "Good Grooming for Women in the Armed Services."[23] Offered to all servicewomen, the booklet gave advice on everything from a balanced diet, weight control, and exercise to cleanliness, makeup, skin care, and clothing.

Significantly, these manuals projected white femininity as the default model women should follow. Photographs in the 1954 WAF guide include Black women in the background on several pages, but the photographs selected on all pages related to skin care, cosmetics, and hair care all portray white women, often in close-up. The Toilet Goods Association manual's line drawings represent white women as well, and the cover includes headshots of four white women. Properly groomed servicewomen, in these publications, were white; no guidance was offered for women of color, who might have had other hair and skin care needs beyond those identified for white women. When the first Black WMs arrived at Parris Island in 1949, white hairdressers did not know how to work with Black women's hair and likely would not have been willing to style Black women's hair at all. Women Marine officers had to ask a Black maid on base to buy the products Black recruits would need. The first Black WMs had to resort to doing their own hair off duty in the lieutenant's office.[24]

Image development and women's exclusion from combat training constituted the two main differences between men's and women's initial military training programs. Until the 1970s, all enlisted men and women completed basic training or boot camp in sex-segregated programs.[25] This made it easy for women to receive image development instruction, while men pursued weapons and physical training. In 1951, for example, male recruits at Lackland Air Force Base completed 384 hours of basic training, including seventy-four hours of processing, 124 hours for orientation, 127 hours in military science and tactics, thirty-five hours for mathematics, and twenty-four hours of physical training. Air force women took the same, except that unlike men, they did not take marksmanship and weapons. Instead, women took courses in Administrative Instruction (i.e., how to use a typewriter) and Personal Appearance.[26] After basic training or boot camp, further training for specific military jobs occurred mostly in coed environments. Although these programs were not generally divided by sex, the dominance or absence of women in various career fields meant that many of these specialized training programs skewed heavily toward male or female participation.

Military publicity films from the 1960s and early 1970s showcase the specific basic training and boot camp processes that men experienced, a clear contrast from similar pieces on women's service in those decades. In 1963, the army's Big Picture series on ABC television (the same series that ran *The Wac Is a Soldier Too* in 1954) aired *This Is How It Is*, a half-hour feature that showed audiences what men could expect at basic training. Although the Vietnam War hadn't yet become the conflict most Americans remember, in 1963 the draft remained in effect. Of course, the army also wanted to recruit men voluntarily as well, so films in the Big Picture series helped Americans understand national defense and military life better.

In *This Is How It Is,* viewers follow new recruits through processing and each week of basic training, occasionally hearing from them about their experiences directly. From the beginning, men's basic training shows a different tone from women's. White instructors yell at mostly white men as they run through events. As the recruits get into order for the first time, their drill instructor shouts at them "You're sounding like a bunch of girls!" and when telling them to hurry into the bunker, the drill instructor yells, "Come on girls, let's get going!" Here, femininity is the least-desired trait a recruit can have; the reference to Chanel Number Five in *Never Wave at a Wac* would not be out of place in this context, and the insults leveled at male drill instructors tasked to oversee women make more sense given how men's training appears in this video. By the end of training, the new soldiers are told "You've grown up. Those of you who were boys when you arrived are now men, and all of you are soldiers in fact, as well as in name."[27]

As soldiers, men were gentlemen just like servicewomen were told how to be ladies, but even more, soldiers were fighters. While weapons and combat training (hand to hand, and with weapons) were central to men's boot camp or basic training experiences, the armed forces eliminated those for women. *This Is How It Is* and the 1973 *. . . And a Few Good Men,* narrated by actor Jack Webb from the television show *Dragnet,* take care to show young men how important their rifle would be and highlight the extent of their rifle training.[28] Women were never issued weapons of their own during their initial training. In the 1950s, women could opt to take a weapons familiarization course or try a firing range during bivouac week when they camped out in the woods, but guns were not standard issue for women. *Never Wave at a Wac* portrays the women trying out rifles, although Jo McBain is pathetically bad at it, partially due to distractions on the field. While other women around her shoot capably under the watch of the instructors, the overall message is that perhaps women shouldn't fire guns. The weapons familiarization course disappeared by 1963 when the military adopted new weapons deemed too heavy for women to manage, and the WAC bivouac experience vanished.[29]

The women's service components became pioneers in some areas, however: beginning in 1948, women of all races shared bunk and rooming assignments at basic training and throughout their careers. While President Truman issued Executive Order 9981 to desegregate the armed forces in summer 1948, similar integration in the men's barracks did not begin to happen until 1951. Racial integration in the women's components happened earliest in the WAF and WMs, with the WAVES and WACs also becoming racially integrated a year before men in any military branch did.[30] This contrast also appears in publicity pieces about the services: *The Wac Is a Soldier, Too* and *Strictly Personal*, along with other films about women's service, almost always include personnel of color (albeit in token numbers). As in the grooming manuals, Black women remain relegated to the background—noticeable, but not immediately identifiable. The minimal presence of Black women in training and recruiting materials reflected the small numbers of Black women in the armed services, but also downplayed their presence because they remained in the background. Keeping Black women in the background acknowledged their presence—minimally—while implicitly reinforcing white social and cultural norms as the standard servicewomen would follow.

For most white servicewomen, training alongside women of color was likely not something they expected when they arrived. Basic training or boot camp probably became the first time many women lived and worked alongside someone whose skin was a different color than theirs—and moreover, in an environment in which each recruit was at the same level as another. Here, gender mattered more than race, as evidenced by the fact that women and men did not get inducted into the military identically. In the Women Marines, leaders were very aware of the reality that their recruits likely were not used to spending time with people from different racial backgrounds. When the first Black Women Marines arrived at boot camp, WM leaders assigned bunks based on where in the United States the recruits came from, although they did not tell anyone of their plan. Ann Lamb and Annie Graham, the first Black WMs, both came from northern states, so arranging the barracks by where recruits came from meant that southern white women might have less interaction with Lamb and Graham and, women leaders hoped, less potential for conflict.[31] While gender mattered more than race when women came into the military, within the sexually segregated confines of the women's services, race once again mattered. Military leaders could assign women to live and work together regardless of race, but this did not guarantee Black women would not experience discrimination from other servicewomen, or discrimination off base. Training manuals that minimized or ignored the needs of Black servicewomen perpetuated that discrimination.

To help women further develop those invisible character traits that were so essential to being a lady and a good servicewoman, character education and citizenship programs also enhanced servicewomen's status as women. Military officials explicitly promised parents and daughters that training would make servicewomen better Americans. One letter home from a basic training commander emphasized the positive changes parents would see after their daughter finished training. "We hope that when she returns to you, you will find that her army training has made her physically fit, mentally alert, and imbued with those democratic principles upon which our whole structure of American life is based."[32] As described by naval Commander Louise Wilde in 1955, developing good citizens necessarily entailed promoting character education. In the navy, for example, she noted that such programs included discussions between chaplains and recruits on topics like "Religion in the Navy, Marriage and Family Life, Moral Principles and Citizenship."[33] With the nation's expanded role in world affairs, service members needed to be good citizens who could promote a positive American image worldwide, "exemplify[ing] the highest personal honor and integrity."[34] Regardless of sex, service members became informal ambassadors for their country no matter where they served. Personnel stationed in the Far East and Europe would give many Japanese and Germans their first—and maybe only—interactions with Americans. Servicemen and women, then, had to uphold specific standards of citizenship. Being a model woman was an essential part of this equation for servicewomen.

Image development training gained new importance as the Vietnam War drew attention to the military and, consequently, womanpower. In 1967, the Women Marines took a new approach, partnering with Pan American Airways' grooming experts in Miami to create a specialized course for WMs. These grooming experts were the same ones who helped train airline stewardesses, and the goal was to help WMs learn the same femininity skills that stewardesses embodied. In preparation for launching this training for all WMs, the marines sent six prospective instructors to cosmetology classes and training with Revlon cosmetics experts, to be followed by further instruction at Pan Am's school.[35] According to Colonel Barbara Bishop, Director of the Women Marines, the training would help promote a positive image of servicewomen. "Emphasis on the feminine aspects of service woman's life counteracts the unappealing impression of military service and will improve recruitment. It will have an equally beneficial effect on the morale of the Woman Marine whose heightened self-confidence and poise will reflect advantageously on her duty performance."[36] With proper training in how to maintain a feminine image, servicewomen would become more confident and thus better workers.

Two years later, an article in *Army Digest* drew attention to the idea that some Wacs saw image development as particularly important. The "Personal

Standards and Social Concepts" training block taught basic trainees some of the finer points of being ladies. "Essentially, it's a charm course—how to feel, be, and look your best; how to be feminine and a soldier, too. We're soldiers to be sure, but we're women too. We should take more advantage of our advantage," said Major Kuhl, an attractive redhead herself. The training includes instruction in personal hygiene, basic etiquette, personal conduct, spending money, make up, how to sit and walk, fashion basics—in short, all the things necessary to insure [sic] that the girls are watched when the music is played."[37] Little had changed in terms of what recruits were being taught, and servicewomen embraced what they learned to make themselves more attractive, in addition to the military's commitment to making them better women. By 1969, an updated version of the WAF's earlier handbook from the air force ROTC/Air University now offered more than one hundred pages of advice on how to create the proper physical, ladylike image. It also now offered tailored advice based on a servicewoman's race: while the handbook did not include images, the "Selection Guides for Rouge and Lipstick" gave specific advice for white women and for women of color.[38] Additionally, military post exchanges had begun to supply toiletries for Black personnel. Military officials were also working to get Black beauty consultants to come visit some exchanges; by the time of the conference, upcoming plans included bringing Black Revlon consultants, and Black makeup artists had already come to at least one air force base.[39]

As military officials and members of Congress began to expand servicewomen's opportunities slowly, femininity and glamour continued to dominate the discussions surrounding women's roles. These practices were well-established ways to define women apart from their male counterparts. Army men certainly were not privy to such training. Another late 1960s recruit booklet demonstrates how personal appearance received primary attention during WM boot camp. Recruits completed 227 instructional hours over forty-nine training days. Topics included drill, ceremonies and parades, history, military customs and courtesies, interior guard, discipline and military justice, personal affairs, inspections, information program, character guidance, grooming and image development, first aid, uniform regulation, defense training, physical training, swimming, training examination and critique, final field, and organized recreation. The most instruction in any one area—thirty-one hours—came in grooming and image development. Drill was the next highest category, with thirty hours.[40] By 1972, this had changed: women recruits received thirty hours in drill and twenty-six hours in image development.[41] The switch from lecture-style image development to hands-on training through the Pan Am program may explain the reduction in hours.⁴²

A quarter of a century after the end of World War II, what military leaders expected from servicewomen in terms of behavior and appearance had not changed: femininity remained center stage. In 1970, the WAC commissioned a series of three short films for new recruits on "Military Etiquette and Grooming." *Mind Your Manners, Looks Like a Winner,* and *The Pleasure of Your Company* highlight three young, modern white women as they navigate the ins and outs of vying for a new overseas assignment, navigating social situations, and determining the most appropriate (and flattering) hair, clothing, and makeup. While Black servicewomen once again appear in the background or as supporting figures, the narrative of each film centers on white women, further underscoring white, middle-class ideals as the norm servicewomen should embrace. "Grace in uniform" was still the goal for all servicewomen, as exemplified in the short film *Mind Your Manners.* In this scenario, the commanding officer tries to choose between three women for an assignment to Belgium. She looks at each Wac individually, assessing her work habits and skills—and more.

Like the story of Goldilocks and the Three Bears, only one is "just right." Just because they are white servicewomen does not mean that they all embody the ideals military leaders established for them, implicitly suggesting that the film will play an important role in training women to follow the ideals set for them. Marilyn may be beautiful, but likes to wear outrageous hairstyles and shorten her uniform skirt length. Carol seems much better at military appearance, but takes it too far, cutting her hair too short. "She confuses military bearing and behavior with male mannerisms. Well, they're not the same thing at all!" In contrast, Specialist Susan Mayfield seems to have it all together. "She's not as efficient as Carol, but she's completely feminine at all times, and let me assure you, that adds to her military effectiveness. She has all the grace and charm a young girl should have. She knows how to walk, stand, and sit in a graceful, feminine manner."⁴³ While the commanding officer leaves it to the viewer to decide just which woman should get the assignment, the message is clear: feminine grace will take you far.

In Susan's case, feminine grace propels her into a starring role in all three short training films in the series. In *Looks Like a Winner,* Wacs observing her from the side assert that she's just "lucky," but the narrator corrects this assumption quickly. "Sure, Susan Mayfield looks good, but she never won any beautiful baby contests. She had to work for it. It takes more than luck to appear bright, well-groomed, and smart-looking." Audiences also learn the importance of cleanliness (daily showers), hair care and styling (something that flatters your face—consult a professional!), and makeup, because "the right cosmetics, skillfully applied, can make a woman appear more alert and alive."[44] Like *Strictly Personal*, *Looks Like a Winner* also covers good eating habits, as well as proper wardrobe tailoring. Recruits learn that all these good habits and hard work pay off. "A lot to remember, and a fair amount to do, but they pay off in a number of important ways. They pay off in social acceptance, career advancement, and in personal popularity [insert Susan going on a date with her boyfriend]. It works all right, no question about it. It works just fine!"[45] Even after two decades of negotiating cultural norms to recruit and train the best of American women, military officials believed that crafting womanpower as a highly feminine pursuit, anchored in whiteness, continued to seem like the right approach.

For more than two decades after World War II, women's basic training or boot camp changed little from year to year, always emphasizing femininity and whole-person development and even increasing the focus on those two areas. Recruits continued to drill daily, participate in calisthenics or learn how to swim, and take classes in all the subjects that would help adapt them to modern military lives and careers. In all they did, however, their identity as women remained key. The final takeaway from the 1954 *The Wac Is a Soldier Too* television spot remained as true as ever. "Eight weeks of training will not make polished soldiers of girls straight from high school, college, or farm, but the new WAC center . . . today produces women educated and prepared for duty to a degree never before possible."[46] The song "What Makes a Wave" from *Skirts Ahoy!* would still resonate with many recruits even twenty years later: "For the last two weeks I've done enough work for a lifetime/And I shudder at the thought of continually doing it for ten/How we march and we march in the navy/Every maid on parade, it's a joy/Yes we skillfully drill in the navy/We're aboard and adored, Skirts Ahoy!"[47] If servicewomen could learn to march and behave as directed in the services, if they could do what they were told and maintain an appearance that would make them be "adored," they were doing exactly what military leaders hoped.

In the final ten minutes of *Skirts Ahoy!* the lieutenant commander offers departing recruits a final speech before they head to their assigned posts. After all the women have experienced in the past nine weeks, the speech is a moving one: "Any idea how different you look from that tacky, scared, wish-I-were-dead bunch ten weeks ago? What's more, I think you are different.

You learned what many girls don't get a chance to learn. There are other people in the world besides yourself, and women don't have to be dependent, weak sisters, yakking, back biting, or the natural enemies of each other. In other words, that women can be friends."[48] Adorned in their white dress uniforms, the three protagonists look much different from when they arrived, and the journey has not just been a military one, but a personal growth one as well. They have become not just ladies, but young women confident in their abilities. Not unexpectedly, perhaps, each woman leaves a man behind (but not for long). While military officials may have worried about the message that joining the navy would help a woman find a man, it was also not a plot point that could very well be rejected. Even *The Wac Is a Soldier Too* pointed out the marriage possibility: although no one wanted to see a recruit leave service immediately for marriage—she needed to stay for at least a year—the producers carefully noted that they valued traditional marriage and family life. "Marriage will always lead all other careers for women and the WAC graduate will be a better wife, mother, and citizen thanks to her training and education during her life in the Women's Army Corps."[49]

From 1948 into the early 1970s, womanpower training programs, like recruiting materials, emphasized women's gender above all else, constructing the public image of the American servicewoman around femininity, whiteness, and, at least at times, glamour. This ensured Americans would understand that allowing women into the military was not a radical move to undermine fundamental social roles for men and women. Instead, connecting womanpower with being a lady was a careful construction. Military publications, training programs, and policy debates invoked gender ideals and stereotypes to guide expectations of women's defense roles. With such an emphasis on turning women into ladies, military service would only help women become better at fulfilling the obligations of their gender roles. Partially as a way to recruit women, partially as a way to ensure public acceptance, for two decades female military leaders and their male superiors successfully structured military service as an avenue through which women became refined ladies who would make better wives, mothers, and citizens.

Casting servicewomen as feminine, glamorous ladies had an important long-term consequence, however. The "ladies first" strategy may have countered claims that military service would masculinize women, but it simultaneously and repeatedly highlighted the fact that servicewomen were supposed to stay as far away from combat as possible. More than two decades of defining servicewomen as ladies created a clear distinction between the roles women and men held in national defense. Specifically, by the late 1960s

Americans understood fully that servicemen fought, and servicewomen did not. This distinction continues into the twenty-first century, deeply ingrained into Americans' beliefs about what it means to be a woman in the military versus a man in the military. Portraying servicewomen as "ladies first" might have helped Americans embrace the idea of womanpower, but casting servicewomen as "ladies" also constrained womanpower for more than half a century by defining women's equality with men on the basis of gender difference. Recruit training turned girls into ladies who could capitalize on their femininity to perform jobs that were uniquely suited to women, or that women could do as well or better than men. In fulfilling these roles, officials indicated, womanpower would equal manpower.

Part II **The Possibilities and Problems of Wielding Womanpower**

4 Unequaled in the Civilian World
Working for Uncle Sam

By age twelve, Carol Poynor knew she wanted to join the military. She didn't want to stay in her hometown of Ketchikan, Alaska, where she figured she could expect a life married to a fisherman. When recruiters came to town, she pored over the brochures they offered. All through high school in the early 1950s, she kept the air force on her mind, and when her father told her he couldn't afford to send her to college, that settled things. "That's okay," she said, "I'm going to join the air force." Her brother, four years older, had done the same, and she liked what she heard from him. For one year after her high school graduation, Poynor lived with an aunt in Hayward, California, working and losing weight to meet enlistment requirements. In 1958, she took the oath of enlistment and boarded a plane to Texas the same evening. That night, Carol Poynor began a military career that would take her around the world over nearly three decades.[1]

Sixteen years earlier, Mildred Bailey joined another military branch, although for a different reason at first. It was 1942, and World War II had just begun. A recent college graduate, Bailey was teaching French at a North Carolina high school when she heard that the armed forces were admitting women. With her fiancé in the marines, Bailey took a chance and tested to join the Women's Army Auxiliary Corps (WAAC). Before she knew it, she was on her way to Des Moines, Iowa, and became part of the third group of female WAAC officers. When she and her fiancé married in 1943, they each returned quickly to their duty stations—it was wartime, and the separation, they believed, was only temporary. Bailey assumed, like most other women, that she would return home after the war. Instead, Bailey realized that working for Uncle Sam had certain benefits. "As a First Lieutenant I recall my monthly salary was about $166 . . . That was more than a school teacher could make in 1946, and so I was rather anxious to stay on in the army until the day when I could afford not to work at all."[2] In making that choice, Bailey chose what became a thirty-three-year career that would take her to the highest levels, beyond what even members of Congress and military leaders envisioned when they passed the Women's Armed Services Integration Act in 1948.

As each woman reflected on her military service, it was clear that neither expected such a career. Poynor joined the air force in part because it was a three-year enlistment; Bailey always expected she would resign her commission once her husband's career was well under way. Despite their original plans, Poynor and Bailey ended up in long-lasting careers because they found the work fulfilling and the opportunities greater than they might have had in the civilian world. Their military careers were remarkable, both in terms of service performance and the length of their service. While Uncle Sam would have loved to have more women like them during the Cold War, it was more common for women to serve shorter commitments, often leaving because they married or became pregnant. Bailey married during World War II; that fact and her wartime service exempted her from postwar regulations that only allowed single women to join. Neither Poynor nor Bailey ever had children, which enabled them to continue their careers as long as they wanted. Poynor and Bailey each represent the dream of what women's military service could be: high-quality, intelligent women who devoted a portion of their lives to make the United States safe and to enhance the military's reputation as an employer.

Although Poynor and Bailey are part of a small subset of servicewomen with long-lasting Cold War careers, their military experiences look similar to many women's, regardless of length of service. Like Poynor and Bailey, many women joined for the job opportunities available in the military, or for the educational benefits promised (figure 4.1). Even if recruiters frequently struggled to attract the number of women they wanted, those who did join generally found the opportunities attractive. Reflecting on her decision to join the navy in 1950, Rear Admiral Roberta Hazard explained that she "joined an organization that from the beginning exemplified the principle of equal pay for equal work and one that offered to me as a woman, just out of college, responsibilities and opportunities, at that time unequaled in the civilian world."[3] Serving in the military was not just an opportunity to take up the responsibilities of citizenship, but also a career experience that offered women unparalleled access to economic citizenship.[4] As *workers* in the military, women found independence and autonomy, participating even more fully in a capitalist, democratic society. For women, a military career was "a woman's world of opportunities. You'll receive *equal pay, equal rank, equal advancements with our men in service.*"[5] During the Cold War, many servicewomen learned that even if such promises didn't always hold, nonetheless servicewomen did secure greater economic equality and possibility than that available to them in the private sector.

FIGURE 4.1 This 1951 recruiting ad focused on the types of jobs women might perform in the air force. United States Air Force.

In wartime, most Americans think about military service as patriotic duty, but women's integration into the armed forces highlighted military service as economic opportunity, not just patriotic obligation. This had been true for men for centuries, but the presence of the draft in the mid-twentieth century prioritized the connection between male military service and obligation. The U.S. military had offered career opportunities for men since before the Civil War, but not many Americans embraced this career path until the twentieth century. Career military men were often officers, but not

Unequaled in the Civilian World   83

exclusively: many enlisted men opted to make careers out of military service as well, becoming noncommissioned officers as they rose through the ranks.[6] Those who served as officers trained purposefully for military careers via the service academies or in officer candidate school, providing combat and troop leadership in and out of war. Some officers even chose not to pursue long-term military careers, while most men drafted into the services generally assumed they would spend only a few years in the military. Quite often, regardless of whether a man was drafted or joined of his own accord, military service offered a brief occupation, one marked by the obligation and honor of serving one's country.

Women's military service was marketed to prospective recruits with a joint focus on economic opportunity as a type of civic duty, but this message was not one generally sent to men until after the end of the draft in the 1970s. When the military transitioned to the All-Volunteer Force in 1973 and had to find new ways to recruit men, aside from the threat of conscription, military advertising began embracing many of the themes of personal and professional benefit that the women's services had used for years.[7] During the draft, particularly in the midst of the economic boom after World War II, military leaders struggled to compete with career opportunities for men in the civilian world: for example, historian Beth Bailey notes that only about a quarter to a third of the men needed were enlisting in the army each month in the late 1940s. Additionally, Cold War military deferments allowed men attending college or in certain career fields the opportunity to pursue other economic opportunities instead of fulfilling their military obligations.[8] While some men had always understood that military service held that possibility and enlisted for financial reasons, the idea became more broadly applied with the Women's Armed Services Integration Act of 1948: military service is a job, not just a sacrifice or obligation.

One of the most remarkable things about the 1948 Women's Armed Services Integration Act was that it ensured servicewomen would make the same pay as men with the same rank. This policy helped make the U.S. military one of the first workplaces to offer equal pay nearly two decades before equal pay became a rallying cry of second-wave feminists. When the Women's Armed Services Integration Act passed in 1948, the fight for equal pay was already underway, led by labor union women, but the efforts had not been successful.[9] By the early 1960s, when the second-wave women's movement began in earnest, the lack of civilian equal pay policies meant that women's income lagged continually behind men's. The U.S. Bureau of Labor Statistics reported in 1960 that working men (full-time, year-round labor) made an average of $5,435 per year, while women with the same status made an average of $3,296 annually.[10] By 1973, men's median income for full-time, year-round employment had risen to $11,468, with women making only 57 percent of that: $6,488.[11] In contrast, equal pay was central to women's military roles beginning in 1948. Naval Captain Joy Bright Hancock asserted that equal pay was central to defining women's military service opportunities. "The terms 'equal work,' 'equal pay,' and 'equal honor' are given positions of top importance to emphasize the fact that the women and the men share equal citizenship responsibilities which can be discharged in the services with equal effort and equal pay."[12] As Mildred Bailey noted, things looked quite different in the armed services at the end of World War II, where she could make more money in uniform than as a teacher. For her, the earning power she held as a military officer was vital: it would help Bailey and her husband establish themselves in the years ahead.

While recruiters and military leaders guaranteed women equal pay with men, no one ever claimed that women could perform *any* or *all* jobs in the services because not all jobs would be appropriate for women. Instead, military leaders rallied for "effective utilization" as they tried to figure out how to best capitalize on women's skills in a way that would also help keep them womanly. Air Force Chief of Staff General Hoyt Vandenberg explained his views on the problem for the newly created air force in 1951. "I do not believe that we would be utilizing very intelligent women to the best advantage of the air force in driving a bunch of trucks. I do not believe that if we get some highly skilled women that they would be replacing a man if they put gasoline in an airplane. I think those of the men with the lower intelligence rating can do that. Therefore, part of our problem, as I see it, is what are the categories that we would put the women in."[13] While women might be able to drive trucks, and had during World War II, putting them in such a position to "replace" a man for other duty might not be the best use of their abilities, and in peacetime, probably not as necessary. During World War II, after all, General Eisenhower claimed there had been many things women could do better than men. In the Cold War, it wasn't enough to put women just anywhere: they needed to serve in roles where they could be *most* effective. In late 1951, Director of the Women Marines Colonel Katherine Towle acknowledged that the Women Marines, and conceivably all the services, had not quite figured out how women could best support national defense efforts. "There are still plenty of square pegs in round holes; but honest efforts are being made to match the pegs and the holes, and thereby prevent wastage of individual aptitudes and skills."[14] Such a problem persisted because of the challenges military leaders faced in reconciling defense needs with their sense of gender ideals.

To help eliminate the square-pegs-in-round-holes problem, in early 1951 a new report for the Military Personnel Policy Committee, entitled "Maximum Utilization of Military Womanpower," explained the framework the women's services used to determine women's military careers. Laid out by a subcommittee of six servicewomen, two of whom would later become directors of their service branch's women's component, their report identified ten criteria used to determine which jobs were most suitable for women. They included concerns related to cultural acceptability, physical capability, and even geographic location. Leaders in each of the service branches evaluated these ten factors when considering whether to open a career field to women:

1. All steps in career field on promotion ladder must be open to women.
2. Physical demands of job.
3. Psychological factors.
4. Training of enlisted women as economical as that of men.
5. Replacement of men on one-to-one basis.
6. Job in undesirable or isolated field location.
7. Culturally acceptable to American public.
8. Related civilian occupation.
9. Critical personnel needs in particular ratings.
10. Restrictions imposed by PL625 [Women's Armed Services Integration Act].[15]

Eleven career fields were entirely off-limits, the report authors noted, because the Women's Armed Services Integration Act prohibited women's service in those jobs or because defense officials deemed them inappropriate for women based on postwar gender role standards. "These areas cover jobs which occur in combat, in aircraft engaged on combat missions, and on shipboard other than transport and hospital ships, and those which appear to require extreme physical demands. Jobs in these areas include those in the fields of Infantry, Armor, Artillery, Gunnery, Fire Control, Ship Operation, and Construction Work."[16] Not only would utilizing women in these fields violate the law, which prohibited women from combat or aircraft and ships engaged in combat, but the "physical demands" associated with such labor also potentially violated criteria for cultural acceptability.

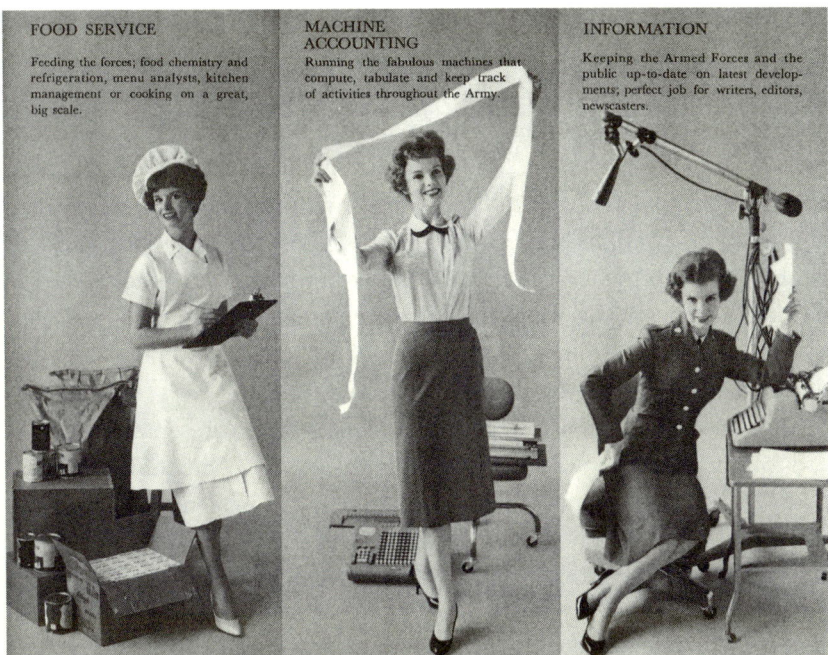

FIGURE 4.2 The 1964 *Somebody Special* recruiting brochure highlighted a number of careers women might have in the military, including those shown here. Betty H. Carter Women Veterans Historical Project, Martha Blakeney Hodges Special Collections and University Archives, University of North Carolina–Greensboro.

The list above helped determine where *not* to put women, but also helped identify the best fields for women. Given such criteria, military policymakers deemed some fields almost entirely for women, including Communications, Intelligence, Synthetic Training Devices Operation, Training, Air Traffic Control, Statistical, Budgetary, Accounting, Fiscal, Administrative, Clerical, Personnel, Education, Medical, and Supply (figure 4.2). This was a large range of career possibilities: each field included numerous specific job positions that could be filled all over the world. Just three years after integration, "all services currently utilize enlisted women in thirty out of fifty-nine occupational fields in 540 military jobs out of 930."[17] This meant that by 1951, enlisted women worked in approximately half of all career fields *and* half of all jobs within those fields. The rest presumably remained suitable for men alone.

The ten-point criteria list in the 1951 study pointed to the problems of how to maintain proper image, deal with assignment logistics, and meet military personnel needs all at once. Maintaining a positive image—so necessary to ensure successful recruitment and public acceptance of women in the military—required assessing whether certain jobs violated gender norms. In part, gender mattered because many commanders were unsure how to accommodate servicewomen in their units if they had several hundred men and only a few women. In 1950, for example, army Special Regulation 615-25-36 mandated that "Enlisted women will normally be assigned to duty only at locations where they can be quartered in groups of 50 or more . . . [except] when enlisted women perform duty with the recruiting service."[18] Concerns over logistical arrangements such as housing, proximity to resources for women, and number of other servicewomen at a location also dictated where women could serve.

Most servicewomen believed the image the services presented for career and training opportunities and joined because of such potential benefits. A 1966 WAC enlisted women survey "indicated that 25 percent joined because they believed there were advantages for individual training in various skills, 24 percent because of opportunity for additional formal education, 19 to travel. The balance included those who gave independence and security among their reasons."[19] The survey did not indicate whether women joined to pursue specific career fields, however. Regardless, the services often assigned women to "traditional" roles, such as "clerical work, record keeping. Many are in communications, including radar and traffic control towers at air bases. Some work as medical or dental technicians . . . Others may become office workers in military intelligence or photo interpreting or photo mapping."[20] But even if women wound up in "traditional" jobs like what they might find in the private sector, servicewomen received additional training, education, and travel opportunities.

Trying to balance effective utilization and culturally appropriate work roles for women sometimes created discrepancies. In theory, women were being placed where they fit best, but "best fit" could have many definitions. MaryAnne Haarhaus joined the WAF in 1969 because she liked that the air force was offering women opportunities for more education, and because she saw military service as a "semi-acceptable method of leaving home as an underage girl from the south." She was a military brat eager to get out of the house and attracted to the air force because they "really played to the idea that you were more intelligent . . . and more refined than the other three branches." During her basic training at Lackland Air Force Base in 1969, Haarhaus's occupational test results indicated that, due to her visual and tactile skills, the air force should assign her to aircraft maintenance, but that didn't happen. "They told me I couldn't do Aircraft Maintenance because I was a girl . . . they said, 'No women on the flight deck,' . . . no matter what your aptitude was." Instead, the air force assigned Haarhaus to communications, "a job that was qualified for women—the communications expert was definitely a woman's job."[21] Although the air force's own assessment tools indicated effectively utilizing Haarhaus's skills would mean putting her in aircraft maintenance, such an assignment was out of the question: the fact that she was a woman was more significant in job assignment than natural skill or talent.

When WAF Chief Master Sergeant Sharon Lee Masek enlisted in 1963 after high school, her highest score during enlisted testing was an 80 in electronics, the highest possible score. "I wanted to go into computers; I don't think it was even called computers back then; data processing or whatever . . . [the recruiter said] 'No problem! With an 80 in electronics, you are a shoe-in.'" But when she got to Lackland and told her career interviewer that she wanted to go into computer operations, she was told something very different. "There aren't any girls in that field . . . I don't care what he [your recruiter] told you. There aren't any women in that field."[22] Instead, the interviewer suggested Masek become a medic because she had three months of work experience as a doctor's receptionist. Masek protested and asked about using her other skills from high school, including four years of business administration, shorthand, and typing training—skills that helped her negotiate the path toward a military career in personnel administration.

As Masek's account shows, experience was one way that military personnel tried to determine the most effective ways to utilize women. Women who tested into jobs commonly designated as "women's work" may have achieved such results because they had been educated and trained for such roles in high school and college, or worked in similar roles previously.[23] Like Masek, though, not all women wanted to be assigned based on what they had done in their civilian life. Constance Anderson hoped to become an MP (member of the Military Police), a field that used women specifically to support the WAC. However, her father's occupation as a dentist and her own experience working for him prompted the WAC to reassign her. After a month of MP classes, "I was told I could no longer do that. 'Why?' 'Because the medical department needs you and we just found out your dad is a dentist and you've been working with him since you were a little kid.'"[24] Her personal history sealed her fate and she worked in the dental field throughout her military career from 1951 to 1955.

Women who already had experience in traditionally "feminine" fields found it easier to take on such roles when they entered the military, or even welcomed these jobs as compared to what they expected to find in civilian opportunities. Susie McArthur, an African American woman from Georgia, anticipated that her aptitude test would reflect past training in secretarial work, and she looked forward to the opportunity to continue in such a role in the WAC. When she joined the military, her only prior job experience had been some babysitting while she was in night school, and doing work around the farm she had grown up on. McArthur was just the second woman from her county to join the military, and the only person in her family to do so. When she finished night school, she couldn't find a job, and the military was enticing in part because it offered a chance to travel. "Since I had gone to school for stenographer-secretary, I knew that's what I wanted to do, so the test just proved that I would be suited for that field."[25] After basic training, Advanced Individual Training (AIT) prepared her for her job as a clerk-typist, and she went on to the job assignment she desired. Two years later, she was one of eighty-five women handpicked for a tour of duty in Vietnam. McArthur would spend twenty-six years in the military, an accomplishment even more rare at the time for African American women.

Like McArthur, WAF Major Clara Christine "Chris" Johnson's experience shaped her initial work assignments. In 1950 as a young Black woman with a college degree, she felt "there was just nothing available" to her: although she had a job as a theatre stage designer, she lacked the $500 required to join the union and was about to lose her position as a result. When she saw a sign promoting opportunities in the military, Johnson went into a recruiter's office "assuming I was going to be turned away." On the contrary, she soon began what would become a twenty-year career. Although Johnson was the only African American woman in her basic training squadron, she felt that her race did not matter. "I was always impressed with my female colleagues . . . they were readily accepting."[26] The trend continued throughout her service. With her first job in a special services unit, Johnson designed air force floats for local parades and also went to Los Angeles and Wyoming to design and build promotional floats for the Rose Bowl Parade and other events. She had the opportunity to try new roles within special services, working as a librarian, in testing services, and in service club operations.

Johnson believed that gender, more than race, shaped her military experience. After Officer Candidate School (OCS) in 1954, Johnson moved into supply-related positions as a commissioned officer. Within a few years, she received a post that required her to meet with Pentagon officials to defend budget line items. When she visited the Pentagon, "I got these looks when

I walked in the door—'A *woman*. What does she think she can tell us?' But I was able to convince them that I had the . . . information that was necessary for them to make their decisions, and they were going to have to listen to me." It was a sentiment Johnson encountered again in her next position as a special weapons officer, a position she had long wanted. Once again, she faced men who doubted whether a woman could truly have the skills to manage weapons, something usually associated with military men.

In theory—and in practice, as McArthur and Johnson's stories indicate—personnel administrators assigned both men and women "on the basis of aptitude and previous work history." This meant that three quarters of female officers worked in administrative, personnel, or information, while 70 percent of enlisted women worked in administrative and clerical roles. Even in the fields where women dominated, the small numbers of women in the military overall meant that women remained a minority in those fields. "Military women constitute a small fraction of the total occupational groups in which they are predominantly used: women occupy three percent of the total military jobs in administrative and clerical occupations; women occupy about four percent of the total military jobs in medical and dental occupations."[27] These numbers are a striking reminder of just how small a percentage women were within the larger military. Despite women's dominance in "traditional" female jobs, thousands of men also filled those roles regularly because there were so few women in the military to do that work at all.

While numbers of servicewomen remained low in the 1950s, women's military career patterns often mimicked civilian opportunities, but there were exceptions. As Johnson's experience indicates, military needs sometimes led to anomalies, such as the opportunities she had to defend budget items to Pentagon officers and to serve as a special weapons officer, where she handled duties such as making napalm. Similarly, Wac Janet Franklin completed specialty training at the army's engineering school and became a topographical draftsman in the intelligence field. Franklin believed that the WAC offered women much greater career opportunities than the private sector. "I don't think I could have landed a job like that in civilian life because there are just not as many opportunities."[28] Beginning in 1947, WAC officer Beatrice Stecher's assignment to Germany put her in charge of two prisons of displaced persons with criminal convictions. She managed repatriating prisoners from more than thirty countries, with additional responsibilities as a top-secret document courier.[29] While these represent very specialized assignments that do not necessarily reflect most women's experiences, these experiences are notable particularly because they happened at all: outside the military, they were nonexistent.

One of the things that makes women's military service remarkable in the early Cold War is that even when women held jobs stereotyped as being for women, sometimes they performed that work in unconventional venues. WM Carmen Lucas enlisted in 1954 and worked a series of "traditional" jobs for servicewomen, including subsistence supply and accounting, office support, and recruiter. But because the U.S. military was an international force after World War II, Lucas held these traditionally feminine work roles in places where few American women worked. In 1967 Lucas transferred to Japan—a place she recollected that "women didn't go." She was one of the first six WMs stationed in Iwakuni, Japan, not far from Hiroshima. In addition, once she arrived Lucas had the chance to select what job she would perform.[30] Military service offered women the ability to travel to and work in a number of places around the United States and the world. By joining the armed forces, American men and women got to see more of the world than they likely would have in civilian life. In fact, one of the justifications for having servicewomen was that the military could send a servicewoman anywhere in the world that they needed, while they could not do the same with a civilian female employee. In 1967, Colonel Elizabeth Hoisington testified to Congress that she believed mobility was "our reason for being," referring to the WAC.[31] As Cold War occupation missions continued in Europe and the Far East, American women began to serve globally, in places women generally didn't go, all because the military needed them there.

Manpower needs during the Vietnam War reflect the trend of moving women into nontraditional assignment locations. By the late 1960s, the air force began to assign women to Southeast Asia, a practice that would eventually include small numbers of women from all components except the navy. In early 1967, Barbara Dulinsky became the first WM stationed in Vietnam when she transferred to Saigon.[32] Susie McArthur also got orders to Vietnam in early 1967, and found herself working in an all-male environment for the first time in her career.[33] By the end of the year, the Southeast Asia theater also included twenty-five WAF officers and nine enlisted Wafs tasked to support the administrative command.[34] Waf Carol Poynor never served in Vietnam, although she completed a tour of duty in Thailand beginning in 1971. Later that decade, following assignments in England and Texas, she went to one of the outermost Aleutian Islands off the Alaskan coast.[35] By 1967, then-Colonel Hoisington estimated that 11 percent of all Wacs served overseas.[36]

Most servicewomen still worked in traditionally female jobs, but the 1960s became an era of experimentation not just in mobility but in job duties as well, thanks in part to the Vietnam War. Even though women's choices remained limited, Wac Carol Schoon believed that the army offered women the widest range of career opportunities. "The one thing that was real obvious was that out of what choices were available, the army had more choices for a woman than the other services did."[37] Yet women's opportunities continued to expand in other branches as well. Naval correspondence lists some of the unusual jobs navy women were doing in 1962, including a note on women serving as aerographers to prepare weather studies and research projects at the Naval Weather Research Facility; communications and electronics technicians working with "the most advanced computer systems and electronics gear," and women chairing the U.S. Delegation of the U.N. Military Staff Committee, working in the Office of the Naval Aid to the President, and supporting the Naval Advisory Group at the Air University.[38] Some women officers worked as operational programmers connected with the Pacific atomic operations; research chemist in radiation chemistry; mathematician programmer; Chief of the Technician Division; Military Liaison Committee with the AEC (Atomic Energy Commission), in charge of "interpretation, and evaluation of projects relating to nuclear weapons, nuclear power, reactor technology, and power production"; international relations instructor at the Navy Postgraduate School; head of the Judge Advocate General's Income Tax Branch; and blood preservation/blood bank technique research scientists.[39] Gale Gordon became the first woman to solo in a navy training plane in 1966 as a member of the 111th flight surgeon class. She planned to use her aviation training to help her work toward designation as an aviation experimental psychologist.[40] These weren't exactly jobs that could easily be found in the Help Wanted–Women sections of the newspaper at home, nor were they jobs that most women would have had access to training for in the outside world.

At the same time, the draft kept military leaders well-supplied in many ways, which explains why only a few women wound up in many of these new careers. While only 9 percent of all servicewomen held nontraditional roles by 1966, that figure was significant when compared to women in nontraditional civilian employment.[41] As of 1960, for example, 6 percent of all working women in the civilian workforce worked in nontraditional occupations such as factories, construction, wholesale trade, and agriculture.[42] Nearly a decade and a half later, 62 percent of women held white-collar jobs, 21 percent worked in the service sector, 16 percent had moved into blue-collar professions, and fewer than 2 percent of women workers worked in farm roles. In contrast, almost half of all working men worked in blue-collar jobs, and in fact, between 1959 and 1974, the number of women working in blue-collar jobs dropped from nearly 16.9 to 15.5 percent. In that period, women's job growth in the private sector remained concentrated in clerical roles.[43]

Beyond the influx of drafted men limiting women's access to nontraditional military jobs, there were two other major reasons why servicewomen's career opportunities continued to be limited in the 1960s: rank ceilings and policies related to marriage and motherhood. While rank ceilings affected officers only, marriage and motherhood policies frequently affected the length of service for both officers and enlisted women. These limitations and the social focus on marriage and family life for women through the 1960s meant that in practice women's military careers tended to be short and women's attrition rates high. Although some servicewomen completed twenty years of service or more, it was much more common for women to leave the military upon marriage, pregnancy, or the end of their initial service commitment, whichever came first. This mirrored trends in civilian careers. Consequently, it was often easier to put women into less specialized jobs: many leaders did not see the practicality of putting women into new, highly technical jobs if they would depart those roles quickly—whereas a drafted man would not have the ability to leave.

During the 1950s and 1960s, most women did not make long-term careers of military service. By 1967, 70 percent of all servicewomen did not complete their first term of enlistment, a trend consistent through the 1950s and 1960s altogether: on average, women spent about fourteen months in the military before leaving.[44] While this number seems high, it is worth noting that only about 20 percent of all enlisted men remained in the service after completing their first term of enlistment, perhaps because they were drafted into service.[45] Despite these high attrition numbers, then-Colonel Hoisington also pointed out that reenlistment rates were nearly double those of men's (not including male draftees). These shorter careers limited a service member's access to job and training opportunities: the longer an individual was in the armed forces, the more likely she (or he) was to receive a variety of assignments or be recommended for advanced training programs. Although women signed up for anywhere from two to six years of military service, they tended to stay in the military for even less time than male draftees.

During the first twenty years after the Women's Armed Services Integration Act, women continued to work predominantly in jobs typically done by women and remained subject to policies that assumed women did not combine careers and family lives. Despite these trends, some women found opportunities to work in unconventional jobs and workplaces thanks to the military's need. Enlisted women tended to have shorter careers, often ending their military service either upon marriage, pregnancy, or simply because they decided the military was not where they wanted to be. While some women officers left for the same reasons, women officers who elected to remain in service for longer periods of time began to find by the 1960s that the military might not offer them the long-term career opportunity available to many men. Stipulations on officer rank limits—set in 1948—meant that female officers could only move so far up the military career ladder. The military may have been "a woman's world of opportunities," but "equal pay, equal rank, equal advancements" did not mean servicewomen were completely equal with men.[46]

When the Women's Armed Services Integration Act passed in 1948, it stipulated that women could only advance to the highest permanent rank of lieutenant colonel or commander: women could not become generals or admirals. The law also created a 10 percent limit on how many women could be lieutenant colonels or commanders and a 30 percent limit on the number of naval women above lieutenant. Although similar quotas existed for male officers, it was harder for women to achieve promotions to the higher ranks because of the rank restrictions on women, the rule that women could comprise no more than 2 percent of the total force strength, and the small numbers of women in service. For example, WAC historian Bettie Morden calculated that the odds of a WAC major advancing to lieutenant colonel (the highest permanent rank for women under the 1948 law) were 1 to 14 in 1950, but 1 to 1.4 for a man. By 1960, those odds had improved to 1 to 4 for women and 1 to 1.2 for men, but by 1965 a male major still had nearly triple the chance of promotion to lieutenant colonel than a woman (1 to 3.1 for a woman, 1 to 1.2 for a man).[47]

At first, these limits may have seemed appropriate, because so few women remained in service after World War II. Mildred Bailey and a few other women were the exceptions, because many women left at war's end assuming the military no longer needed them, or because they had other family or work obligations. And, since so many women kept their length of service short, it was possible to avoid rank problems for a while. By the mid-1960s, these limits became problematic because of the number of women beginning to reach higher rank levels due to their time in service. Of the thirty-nine WAC lieutenant colonels in 1966 who were "in the promotion zone for colonel"—more than half of the total number of WAC lieutenant colonels—none of these women could hope to advance under current regulations. "Many of these officers occupied responsible positions calling for grades higher than what they were permitted by law to hold," simply because military need for individuals in those positions trumped legal restrictions. These rank limits also prevented women from attending advanced training schools such as the war colleges, since "attendance was reserved for potential generals and admirals"—ranks women could never achieve under law.[48] As long as women remained concentrated in lower officer ranks, rank ceilings seemed relatively unimportant.

Yet despite the numbers of enlisted women and officers who elected to serve only one term, growing numbers of female officers were surpassing the ten-year service mark, particularly women who began serving in World War II, like Mildred Bailey, women's component directors, and other high-level staff. Although these women had the same years in service as men of the same rank, their sex prevented them from receiving the pay and benefits they would likely have been entitled to if they were male. In the navy, for example, the cap on the number of women above lieutenant created a situation where many officers had to be discharged after thirteen years of service. This meant they could not have retirement benefits, which required twenty years of military duty. "In 1966, the navy estimated that without legislative relief, forced attrition among WAVE lieutenants would average 50 percent or more over the next five years, while promotions to commander for the next four or five years would have to be suspended."[49] A decade and a half after the Women's Armed Services Integration Act became law, the career limitations began to outweigh the opportunities for women who wanted to make a career out of serving their country.

Together, rank and jobs figured crucially in determining long-term career potential and success. The former represented privilege, advancement, and achievement relative to the overall military establishment. On the other hand, jobs mattered most immediately because the work one performed set the tone for an individual's day-to-day military experience. In addition, for some women joining the military was specifically about the opportunity to secure a job, as naval officer Judy Campbell saw it in the early 1970s after she graduated from college. Graduating with her degree in anthropology, "a very unmarketable skill," in her words, she needed a job "so I went to the recruiting office and joined the navy."[50] And, the fact that new servicewomen so soon embarked on efforts to identify the best job positions for them, speaks to the importance that job assignments held for members of the armed forces.

As MaryAnne Haarhaus also explained, in the military "rank had its privileges," meaning that the higher the rank someone held, the greater one's access to both tangible and intangible benefits.[51] Power within the military establishment was one of the key benefits that rank offered as compared with one's job. By preventing women from advancing beyond the (temporary) ranks of colonel or captain, members of Congress placed defined limits on women's power—and equality—within the military structure in 1948. Capping women's careers in the middle of the field grades meant that women would play only limited roles in shaping major military decisions. Under the Women's Armed Services Integration Act, women could theoretically devote more than twenty years of their lives to the military, but no matter how long they served, they would not have access to the highest levels of power in the armed forces: the flag ranks of general and admiral, the highest decision-makers in the nation's defense system.

Military leaders based equal pay claims on the military's established rank system. In theory, military personnel begin their service at the rank of E-1 (for enlisted) or O-1 (for officers) and progress through the ranks during their career. Like job promotions in the civilian world, rank promotions bring new job responsibilities and higher pay level. In addition, the amount of time an individual has spent in the services affects her or his base pay rate. For example, in 1949 an E-5 with more than four (but less than six) years of service made a minimum of $154.35 per month, while an E-5 with more than eight (but less than ten) years of service brought home $169.05.[52] Men and women made the same base pay according to their rank and the number of years they had served.

The rank system shaped military career opportunities because rank partially dictated what jobs would be available to someone. The higher one's rank, the more likely an individual would be to assume supervisory roles or take on greater responsibility for equipment or projects. For example, the Women's Armed Services Integration Act provided for the positions of the Director of the WAC and similar positions to oversee each of the women's components. According to that law, the Director of the WAC held the temporary rank of colonel, the highest rank available to women. As the last rank on the career ladder below the flag ranks (general/admiral and above), military leaders presumed an individual of that rank would be best prepared to lead a women's component. Thus, any woman eligible for Director of the

WAC would have already progressed through the ranks to become a lieutenant colonel, having earned both the experience required for the directorate and the time in service appropriate for someone promoted to colonel.

Generally, the U.S. military's rank system combines time in service with rewards for good work, continued training, and military need. In theory, the more time a service member spends in either the enlisted or commissioned ranks, the more likely she or he is to advance to the next rank and associated pay grade. In the process, the service member might assume expanded or new job duties. As Captain Robin Quigley advanced through the officer ranks during the 1960s, transitioning from lieutenant in 1958 to lieutenant commander in 1964, then to commander in 1970 and finally captain and Assistant Chief of Naval Personnel for Women (or Director of the WAVES) in 1971, her job roles also changed. While these assignments did not occur simultaneously with her promotions, over those years she advanced from a position as assistant guest lecture officer at the Naval War College into a recruiting job and later positions that included Secretary to the Chief of Naval Operations, Senior Aide to Deputy Commander in Chief of the U.S. European Command, and ultimately Assistant Chief of Naval Personnel for Women.[53]

Despite this apparently uniform pay system, promotion practices and supplementary pay and benefits meant that equal pay could also remain elusive for women. Military pay tables note not only base pay rates, but also the additional pay provided to personnel with dependents or those assigned to specific duties. In 1967, for example, officers and enlisted personnel received $65 in Hostile Fire Pay if assigned to a job designated in a hostile fire zone. Enlisted personnel could also receive "Special Pay Sea & Foreign Duty Pay." Additionally, Basic Allowance for Quarters (BAQ) for individuals living off-base varied depending on whether a service member had dependents or not. The Women's Armed Services Integration Act severely limited women's ability to claim dependents, and since women with children under eighteen could not serve, women remained ineligible for higher benefit rates such as these.[54] Although Mildred Bailey found her income in the military much better than what she would make as a teacher, she could not acquire housing or benefits for her husband when he returned to private sector employment after World War II. If she had been a serviceman married to a civilian, she would have been automatically entitled to those benefits.

Military career structures also helped determine who might have the potential to achieve the training and experience required for higher levels of rank. While this was true for all service members, it was particularly important for officers. For example, during World War II when naval officials established lieutenant commander as the highest rank for women, most male officers could reach that rank only after almost two decades of service (primarily at sea). Navy leaders granted women access to that rank during wartime primarily because they needed women in some higher-ranking positions, but they still lacked the training and background most officers of that level would have had, and in particular they lacked the sea duty experience required of men.[55] In her history of the WAC, Morden points out that attending Command and General Staff College was a necessary prerequisite for career progression to lieutenant colonel in the army: not until 1955 did the military begin to allow WAC officers to attend one of the prerequisite courses for attending Command and General Staff College, and then only reserved spaces for four women officers per year.[56]

Although servicewomen were theoretically "equal" to servicemen, military policies limited which jobs women could perform, the ranks they could hold, and the benefits they could receive based on their sex and relationships with men. In a 1971 hearing on the utilization of women, WAF officer Jeanne Holm explained that there were three reasons why the military continued to exclude women from certain jobs: legal, physiological, and cultural. For example, the Women's Armed Services Integration Act legally barred women from combat or combat support jobs. "We exclude [women] from jobs which are beyond their physical capabilities, such as telephone lineman, and jobs which could place them in serious physical jeopardy, such as aircraft guards. We also exclude them from jobs that are considered culturally undesirable or unsuitable, such as physical training instructors for men."[57] But these three distinctions related more to assumptions rather than fact: legal limitations emerged from beliefs about what women could or should do, rather than a clear understanding of women's physical ability. As long as women had access to jobs deemed suitable for their sex, military leaders believed they offered women equality with men, and few people questioned this conception of equality. By the late 1960s and early 1970s, however, servicewomen and their advocates would bring that definition under fire.

5 The Possibility of Maternity
Motherhood and Military Service

The belief that a mother's place is in the home remains one of the greatest myths of American history. In the twentieth century, this belief was so strong that many careers required women to leave their jobs once they married, assuming that a married woman's first job should be to take care of her husband and their home, and anticipating that motherhood would soon follow. Despite the fact that many married women worked, particularly women of color and women from lower economic backgrounds, business leaders and politicians espoused the belief that careers should not interfere with women's family lives. After World War II, the sanctity of the stay-at-home mother took on heightened prominence in American society during a time when Americans began marrying younger, in larger numbers, and having more children than ever. In the midst of this, the Women's Armed Services Integration Act and later policies all emphasized that mothers could not serve. During the Cold War, no other American belief affected women's military service as completely as the cultural norms that emphasized women's identities as potential mothers.

Keeping mothers out of military service came from earlier civilian and military policies. Because only women could bear children, early in the twentieth century protective legislation became a key element of gender difference definitions of equality, like that used by military officials during and after World War II.[1] In 1908, the landmark Supreme Court case *Muller v. Oregon* affirmed that the government could institute laws limiting women's work hours specifically because women were potential mothers. As historian Alice Kessler-Harris explains, "since the state had a fundamental interest in women's capacity to rear and nurture children, it could override their liberty and allow protections for women that it had consistently disallowed for men."[2] But more than just creating new protections for women, this decision had wider implications for women's citizenship, linking women's roles as wives and mothers in a way that often made those roles more important legally than women's rights as individuals.[3] While advocates for the Women's Armed Services Integration Act did not invoke

Muller v. Oregon, they maintained the tradition of protectionism, the use of biology and cultural norms to limit women's rights and access to employment, in their insistence that mothers would not be allowed to serve. Through their emphasis on servicewomen's identity as potential mothers, military and government officials justified institutional limitations on women's service for more than two decades and consequently made it difficult for women to create long-lasting military careers.

The fact that women could remain in the military after they married was significant in the mid-twentieth century. Outside of the military, beginning in the nineteenth century "marriage bars" required women to leave some professions when they married, and until the early 1960s persisted in several fields: teachers, flight attendants, and clerical workers commonly lost their jobs upon marriage (or in some cases, pregnancy).[4] In the armed forces, servicewomen did not have to give up their jobs when they married, but for a time, at least, there were options to do so. While married women could not enlist or become officers during the Cold War, unless they had served in World War II, the armed forces offered servicewomen marriage discharge policies, allowing them to terminate their service early, with stipulations. Policy details varied by service and changed regularly, but the trend until the late 1960s was to offer servicewomen a discharge option when they married. In general, marriage discharge options narrowed in wartime, beginning with the Korean War. In that conflict, suspending marriage discharge became one way to prevent a common form of servicewomen's attrition. During the Vietnam War, most of the services invoked marriage discharge only for cases when the military could not station a woman near her husband.[5]

Marriage discharge was voluntary, but it was so prevalent that many female veterans *believed* that women had to leave the military when they got married. "If you were married, you were discharged," which was how Joan Neuswanger left the WAF in 1953.[6] Polly Hazelwood remembered that when she was in the WAF from 1959 to 1962, "You could not get married."[7] In her experience, women left so frequently upon marriage that she accepted it as policy. "You got married, you left, which is how I left," in 1971, said Waf MaryAnne Haarhaus. Wac Cheryl Bucy (1971–73) noted that "They did not allow married women to serve in the Women's Army Corps at all."[8] Yet despite the number of women who remembered that married women could not be in the military, marriage discharge was only an option and not a requirement. The misperception may have occurred for several reasons: for example, unmarried women might have seen no need to clarify a policy that

The Possibility of Maternity

did not apply to them. It's also possible that women conflated marriage discharge with pregnancy discharge, particularly in the years before the birth control pill became available. Regardless, by the late 1970s, Carol Poynor was told she was one of the few noncommissioned officers with nearly twenty years of service. The WAF advisor over the U.S. Air Force–Europe told her, "You're one of the few that stayed in. Most of the people who came in when you did [in the late 1950s] got married and got out."[9] These servicewomen's experiences, and their sense that military service required them to leave when they married, reflect strong social pressures that discouraged married women from continuing to work, even though that standard was changing in the years after World War II.[10]

The practice of offering marriage discharge reflected widespread realities of women moving to the home. A 1955 White House Conference on Effective Uses of Womanpower noted, "The structure and the substance of the lives of most women are fundamentally determined by their functions as wives, mothers, and homemakers."[11] After World War II, the stay-at-home mother seemed ubiquitous, as all Americans began to marry younger and have larger families, contributing to the baby boom.[12] These trends were part of Cold War white, middle-class conceptions of what the American family, or the nuclear family, should look like. Even though Alfred Kinsey's research on sexuality in this period revealed that many Americans engaged in sex outside of marriage and suggested that homosexuality was more prevalent than previously believed, many Americans placed prime importance on the containment of sex within the institution of marriage.[13] Heterosexuality mattered. Sex within marriage mattered. Children mattered, and according to popular culture, they deserved to come home from school to warm, loving mothers who kept the house clean and their families as their priority. Home sales boomed; suburbs multiplied outside of cities, and the mid-century ranch home with a green lawn, a car in the driveway, and a television in the living room became the iconic portrait of postwar life. With all this in mind, if a servicewoman stayed in the military after marriage, it remained true that if she did become pregnant, she was no longer fit to serve her country because she needed to serve her family first.

This was the dominant image, but it wasn't reality for every American. Well before World War II, the concept of a mother who did not work outside the home was a salient American ideal, but not every American had such a mother. Working-class and poor families—often immigrants or African Americans—generally relied on two incomes. While the postwar economic atmosphere, combined with things like G.I. Bill housing and educational benefits, helped more Americans than ever achieve the "American Dream," women's roles in that dream were already changing. Despite the ideal of the stay-at-home mother, in the 1950s increasing numbers of women combined domestic life and paid employment. They helped enlarge the part-time job market as these mothers looked for ways to help their families increase their purchasing power, while also being able to welcome the kids home from school. Navy veteran Marge Menke, for example, got married soon after serving in World War II and focused on caring for her children until they reached school age, then took a part-time position in a local department store.[14] Although many Americans expressed ambivalence over married women's labor in the postwar years, between 1950 and 1974, the proportion of women in the work force increased while the proportion of men decreased, and within that period, women's participation in paid work nearly doubled.[15]

Even though Americans were changing their views about mothers in the workforce, pregnancy meant automatic discharge for servicewomen. This paralleled civilian workforce policies: in the decades after World War II, it was common for employers to enforce mandatory leave for pregnant women. According to legal scholar Courtni Molnar, in the mid-1960s, "pregnancy was the most frequently reported reason why married women under age 35 quit work."[16] During the 1950s, many pregnant women continued to avoid being seen in public. In the early 1950s, the WAF discharged Rose Wuellner not upon marriage (to a serviceman) but when she became pregnant. "They didn't let [women] stay in there if you were pregnant."[17] After nearly five full years of service, Waf Mary Tener Davidson Hall was discharged for pregnancy in 1956. She was three months along.[18] The navy discharged LaDonna Darks in the late 1960s when she became pregnant, even though she miscarried.[19] WM Carol Deom's military career also ended with her pregnancy in 1970. Although she was investigating a transfer to the navy so she could pursue specific career training, "I ended up being pregnant and at that time they never let you go on with your career once you was pregnant."[20] Although these women remained in the military after they married instead of taking the marriage discharge option, policy dictated that a pregnant woman's place was in the home, not with the Pentagon. Pregnancy or parenthood marked the absolute end of a woman's service until the 1970s.

The congressional debates over what became the 1948 Women's Armed Services Integration Act demonstrate this fundamental belief that motherhood was incompatible with military service. The more important question was how to best utilize womanpower while ensuring that women could (and would) still pursue such expected and normal vocations as marriage and motherhood. Every bit of planning accounted for these eventualities. No one involved in these debates imagined that military service was suitable for mothers of young children. Instead, most thought that women's military careers would help them occupy their single years before marriage and motherhood beckoned. In 1948, there was no reason to anticipate that women's career patterns would change, because the primary message being sent to Americans was that jobs should go to men returning from war, and wives should go back to the kitchen. During the debates over the Women's Armed Services Integration Act, Representative Carl Vinson (D-GA) argued that "we should not put anything in the law which should cause them [servicewomen] to hesitate getting married or to raise a family; on the contrary, we should encourage it."[21] Meanwhile, pay cuts for women workers in the private sector and the closing of wartime childcare facilities were doing just that—encouraging women to return to the home where they supposedly belonged.[22]

In 1948, no military leader advocated for allowing mothers of young children to serve in the military, a fact that is not surprising in light of cultural expectations of women at the time, as well as wartime precedent. During World War II, for example, members of Congress had generally agreed to avoid drafting fathers whenever possible, a conversation that reemerged in the Cold War as the Selective Service program developed. Ultimately, historian Amy Rutenberg explains, members of Congress established deferments for fathers because of their presumed roles as family breadwinners.[23] Likewise, in the Women's Armed Services Integration Act debates, when Representative Carl Durham (D-NC) asked WAC Colonel Mary Hallaren whether it would be possible to keep women in the services after pregnancy, Hallaren indicated that there were practical concerns, given that a mother's first responsibility was to her children, not her country.

> At this time, we do not feel it would be wise. As far as our women are concerned, they have to be a mobile group. If you have a woman with young children, she is not going to be able to move to the west coast when the army needs her on the west coast.
>
> We have to take care of that possibility, and so we eliminate on pregnancy. That, of course, is just administrative. This provision allows it, but we do not want to tie it down by law, so that, if, 20 years from now, the public thinking is quite different, and the situation for women is different, we would be excluded from so doing; in other words, allowing that maternity leave.[24]

A mother's primary responsibility to care for her children would make it difficult for the armed forces to utilize mothers because children presumably rendered them immobile. Even if military leaders could work out such problems, Hallaren's testimony suggests, the other matter was that Americans did not want to see mothers in uniform. While Hallaren insinuated that attitudes might change, for the time being, mothers had no place in the military. It wasn't a matter of discrimination: it was a matter of practicality.

In case the intent had been unclear in any way, three years later President Truman clarified motherhood discharge reasons in concrete terms. Under Executive Order 10240, the secretaries of the military branches could discharge women from service upon assuming parental duties, defined in five ways. A woman could be discharged if she:

(a) is the parent, by birth or adoption, of a child under such minimum age as the Secretary [of the branch] concerned shall determine,
(b) has personal custody of a child under such minimum age,
(c) is the step-parent of a child under such minimum age and the child is within the household of the woman for a period of more than 30 days a year,
(d) is pregnant, or
(e) has, while serving . . . given birth to a living child.[25]

Not only did this order expand the intent and language of the Women's Armed Services Integration Act, removing any ambiguity, but Executive Order 10240 expanded the definition of motherhood. Now, it was more than just pregnancy at stake, but also ways in which women could become mothers by law, such as through adoption or marriage. The message was clear: mothers did not belong in the armed forces.[26]

But the people making these policies did not consult any mothers, and not every mother agreed with these regulations. For the next two decades, although many servicewomen accepted pregnancy discharges as a matter of course, others fought back, sometimes unsuccessfully but in all instances negotiating the limitations military and government officials had placed on them without their consent. One of the earliest cases occurred in 1952, when Major Alba Martinelli Thompson decided to challenge the motherhood discharge rules. She had served in World War II and by 1951 was in the army reserves when she gave birth to her son, Loren B. Thompson Jr. After his birth, Thompson received notice she would be discharged according to the regulations prohibiting mothers of minor children from serving in the armed forces.[27] Major Thompson took her fight first to Assistant Secretary of Defense Anna Rosenberg and then to both houses of Congress. As the *New York World-Telegram and Sun* pointed out, "Mrs. Thompson didn't get all that army training without learning how to fight."[28] Thompson had nearly a decade of military experience and a range of specialized language skills; she was fluent in Japanese and could speak Chinese, Korean, and Tibetan. Given the advent of the Korean War in the early 1950s, Thompson possessed linguistic abilities valuable to military officials.

Thompson made it clear that she believed firmly that mothers could and should serve. Rosenberg agreed with Thompson's opinion that she could be a good mother *and* a good member of the reserves. But, Rosenberg asked, what if a mother in the reserves was called to active duty—what about her child then? "It is true . . . that a woman could fulfill her obligations as a member of the organized reserve without harm to her relationship with her children. I fear it is not true, however, that a mother could be called to full-time active duty with the armed forces and transferred about the U.S. or . . . overseas, without . . . jeopardizing her children's welfare."[29] Thompson particularly disagreed with the insinuation that her military service would have a negative impact on her son's welfare.

Thompson wasn't about to surrender: in her opinion, discharging mothers not only avoided the reality of motherhood as a part of most women's lives, but also penalized women on the basis of their biology. In spring 1952, Thompson testified to subcommittees of both the Senate and House Armed Services Committees as each considered whether to make exceptions for mothers in the reserves. Thompson read from her original correspondence with Rosenberg, in which Thompson argued that "it must be recognized that, women being what they are, many, in and out of service, will have children. This fundamental truth seems to have been ignored [by military planners]."[30] With that in mind, she did not think it made sense to simply discharge women because of something that was such a natural part of their lives. Instead, Thompson argued that the practice of discharging women who became mothers "is hardly a solution [to problems unique to women]. At best it is a complete avoidance of a continuing problem."[31] Men were not discharged because they had children. Thompson advocated giving servicewomen with minor children "temporary absence" just as men received in cases of illness, family problems, or travel. "To do so is recognition of the basic function of women—not penalization therefor."[32] Thompson believed that military need and motherhood need not be at odds. Where military leaders used gender difference as an excuse for limiting women's service, Thompson's testimony called their assumptions and practices into question.

Thompson became one of the first people to argue for the compatibility of motherhood and military service and assert that military policy on motherhood was fundamentally misguided. "As a mother, I find it beyond responsibility and allotted scope of the services to dictate the terms of motherhood. When has it ever been necessary to remind American mothers of their duties?"[33] Yes, Thompson agreed, home and children were a woman's first responsibility, but "I deviate from the thinking of the armed services on how that home can best be served."[34] Instead, Thompson argued, there were many, many ways in which women could best care for their children: having a career was not something that made a mother less.

> The woman who leaves her children to work for them, the woman who makes herself available for civil defense, the woman who serves in a governmental position of responsibility, as well as the woman who participates in Reserve activity, is not less a mother for having done so. Not because we love our children less, but because we love them more do we carry our energies and our hopes beyond the walls of our homes . . . Each woman serves her family who makes use of her skills and talents to bring about the greater security of her home. Some do it from within the home; some from without.[35]

It was time, Thompson argued, to reevaluate how women might embrace their maternal responsibilities. She brought a forward-thinking approach to women's military service. Unfortunately, she found herself a little alone in her position.

The limitations against mothers in military service meant that American women could pursue patriotic service either in the military as nonreproductive citizens, or at home as mothers raising the next generation of soldiers. In part, members of Congress and military leaders believed these options reflected what Americans believed more generally—few would concede Thompson's point. Colonel Hallaren's position at the same hearings aligned with military policy, which she based on her experience talking to female veterans. Women who served in World War II had told her they did not wish to join the reserves because motherhood took priority for them. "I have asked many of our people why they did not come into the Reserve, and they said they had a primary duty, and that was to take care of the children and to grow up with their children."[36] For Rosenberg's part, "strongly as I believe in women participating equally and actively in all business and professional life and military life, I am in complete sympathy with the army's regulations."[37] The difference between women in the reserves or regular service and women in industry, Rosenberg noted, was that even women who worked full time did not leave their children for long periods of time, such as a servicewoman might if deployed overseas. Motherhood simply set women apart from men in a unique way: in her reckoning, it was not practical to treat pregnancy and motherhood like a short-term health condition. Few could reconcile the idea that women might find creative solutions to keep their military careers.

While Thompson's case generated a fair amount of press, the media tended to side with Rosenberg and Hallaren, reflecting the general tenor of the period. One newspaper from Peoria, Illinois, warned Thompson that she lacked the experience with motherhood to truly understand why mothers couldn't serve. "She is obviously a new hand at this motherhood business . . . We suggest that she investigate the complications which develop in her household in the wake of one small set of tiny feet and tiny hands and tiny lungs before she climbs on to her high horse, grabs her spear, and launches herself full tilt at any five-sided windmills."[38] In the end, military policy remained what it was: separation of motherhood and military service persisted. Even though Thompson offered valuable skills that the services required, particularly during the Korean War, her new status as a mother trumped her professional abilities. The army had trained Thompson, paid for some of her education, and utilized her in Far East governmental advising roles in the years leading up to the Korean War. Thompson's language skills made her a highly skilled member of the military: it would be wasteful, she argued, for the military to turn its back on her. Although manpower shortages were a concern, motherhood won and Thompson lost.[39]

Thompson's open challenge to motherhood discharge policies makes her stand out among other servicewomen in the early Cold War who faced motherhood discharges. Most servicewomen accepted motherhood discharge, even if they would have preferred to stay in service. Joan Horton (WM 1953–57), Mary Tener Davidson Hall (WAF 1951–56) and Ruth Payne Brown (WAC 1953–55/1960–63) all received pregnancy discharges. Reflecting on their military service, they noted that they would have preferred to stay if given the option. Ann Thacker Lewis (WAVES 1961–65) thought the pregnancy discharge "was ridiculous . . . Had I been able to have the child there and stay in, I probably would have. I would have wanted to."[40] Jacquelyn Anderson (WAC 1951–54) noted that women never got the option to make a career of military service. "You either got pregnant and got out of the Service or you didn't get pregnant and stayed in if you wanted to."[41] However, none of these women openly challenged the fact that their commanders did not give them that choice.

While many women accepted the regulations, during the 1950s and early 1960s some women found a middle ground for what seemed to be, after Thompson, an unwinnable fight: they took advantage of loopholes. One small way to challenge the policies was to remain in service as long as possible during the pregnancy. Mary Salmen became pregnant soon after she married while in the WAF in 1955. In theory, women were supposed to be discharged as soon as a doctor confirmed pregnancy, but this rule was not always applied uniformly. Salmen's commanding officer let her remain on duty until the end of her pregnancy.[42] Although Salmen wasn't allowed to continue once her child was born, she did get to keep her job a little longer thanks to a sympathetic commanding officer and local base politics.

Another loophole involved women legally giving up their identities as mothers—even if temporarily—to stay in service. Ruth Brown did not just say after the fact that she would have wanted to rejoin: she used regulation loopholes that allowed women to serve if they gave up custody of their child. Brown joined the WAC in 1953 and married her first husband while in service. In 1955, she left due to pregnancy and later divorced her husband, who remained with the military. She spent a few years living with her parents and working but discovered that it was still a challenge to make ends meet. "I was having such a hard time money-wise, even living at home, because I was making $76 one two weeks and $72 the second. I just knew that I was going to have to go somewhere, so I just figured I'd rather go back in." Her sister had recently reenlisted, and she had known of a woman previously who gave custody of her children to other family members. With that example in mind, Brown's parents adopted her child and she headed off with the WAC a second time, this time winding up in Germany where she met her second husband. Brown left the WAC and her medical technician career for good in 1963, returning to the States where her husband farmed tobacco and she raised the kids. Truman's executive order said that women couldn't serve if they became mothers through adoption, but it didn't say anything about what happened if you relinquished your role as a mother by having a family member legally adopt your child.[43]

While the motherhood discharge happened most frequently due to pregnancy, leaders understood that pregnancy was not the only route to motherhood. If a woman married a man with children who would live in their home, the armed forces discharged her on the presumption that she would be the primary caregiver. During the 1960s, at least two Waves married men with young children and got around the regulations even though the children lived in their homes. Navy historians Jean Ebbert and Marie-Beth Hall note that it is unclear how these women managed to evade discharge, but speculate that the women's job performances may have been one reason, or suggest their commanders might have found the policies discriminatory.[44] Not all women were as lucky: in 1961, the Women Marines discharged Joan Gerichten when she married a widowed officer with three children. When her husband lost his first wife in 1960, the marines offered him a compassionate transfer to Philadelphia so he could be near his parents who could help with the children. Unlike women, single male parents did not receive automatic discharges for parenthood. Even if a man became the sole parent, most people believed that the father would find another female family member to help with caregiving duties. This is precisely what Gerichten's husband did when he moved to be near his parents: in close proximity to extended family, the widower would presumably be able to rely on the children's grandmother (and potentially grandfather) as caregivers.[45]

But when Gerichten married her husband, military officials did not care that her husband had a support system in place; her husband could stay in the military, but she could not. Gerichten's response to her own discharge was that "I just kind of resented it." Reflecting on her service, Gerichten recalled, "the hardest time was just having to get out of the military because I had married a man with children." Gerichten was familiar with the regulations when she met her husband, but love mattered more than military rules. However, in 1974, when her three stepchildren were much older and her own child nearly a teenager, Gerichten took advantage of more relaxed motherhood policies and rejoined the reserves "so I could finish."[46] Gerichten made peace with military policy, but clearly was not done with serving her country and returned to finish out service on her terms.

Government and military officials designed the motherhood discharge to ensure military careers would not interfere with women's "higher calling" as wives and mothers, but by the 1960s it was evident that some allowances might be made. The first accommodations came to women with long military careers, before the Vietnam War. In 1962, naval officials evaluated whether a pregnant woman who was close to retirement could remain in service to attain her full retirement benefits. The Judge Advocate General of the Navy clarified that neither the Women's Armed Services Integration Act nor Executive Order 10240 *required* the services to discharge women upon pregnancy, but merely *empowered* the services to discharge.

As naval leaders considered policy to retain pregnant women close to retirement, their research found that the army had already taken a similar step. In that branch, waivers were now an option "to lawfully married enlisted WAC personnel, who become pregnant after completing 18 years of service, in order that they may complete 20 years for retirement."[47] In his recommendation, Assistant Chief for Plans C. K. Duncan argued that the navy should adopt a similar policy, at least on an individual basis.[48] Presumably, women who become mothers of young children after eighteen years of military service would be a rare occurrence. The 1962 navy memo, for example, noted that the navy lacked such a policy because they had not yet found themselves in that situation. Granting waivers for women so close to retirement recognized a woman's many years of service and allowed the simple justice of accessing the benefits for which she had served for so long. A woman would only have to combine motherhood and military service for a couple of years to secure retirement benefits, which seemed like something the navy could work around, as the WAC was apparently starting to do.

The waiver system that emerged considered each woman's case on its individual merits: in other words, military leaders realized by 1960 that there could be exceptions to every rule. According to Major General Jeanne Holm (WAF), waivers remained rare until the late 1960s, until growing attrition from the Vietnam War and a growing trend of Americans challenging discrimination in the workplace.[49] However, the fact that the push for waivers came from women with well-established military careers is significant. It wasn't just that American society was changing, but that women were doing as the military wanted: they had established careers, and they used their records of service to negotiate change. Alba Martinelli Thompson had tried to do the same in 1952, but although she had a striking record of skills and education, she lacked the level of military experience that made waivers compelling a decade later.

In 1969, Naval Senior Chief Personnelman Winnifred Hamerlinck had also reached the eighteen-year mark and used the waiver system to negotiate retention on active duty, securing family support for childcare and agreeing not to request any special considerations because of her role as a mother.[50] Her experiences paved the way for Lieutenant Commander Jordine Von Wantoch to submit a request for retention under the waiver provision in 1970. After more than a decade of service, Lt. Commander Von Wantoch and her husband, also a naval officer, faced an unplanned pregnancy. She argued that she could combine motherhood with service, noting that she was valuable to a navy that seemed focused on a highly trained, career-oriented staff. "I believe that my retention is in the best interest of the navy since, in addition to my over fourteen years of experience with progressively greater responsibility, the quality of which is evidenced by my performance record and Joint Service Commendation Medal awarded for my work . . . I have a Master of Arts degree and have successfully completed several navy schools."[51] Like Thompson in 1952, Von Wantoch argued that the military had invested so much in her, giving her unique skills that shouldn't just be given up. Moreover, Von Wantoch argued, social ideals about the feasibility of combining work and motherhood had changed dramatically in recent years. Building off the existing waiver system, although she was several years further from retirement than the initial program offered, Von Wantoch argued that denying her the opportunity to continue would be inequitable because of her vested retirement interest.

Von Wantoch specifically invoked military need to convince navy officials that retaining her on active duty would benefit the organization. Von Wantoch suggested that her case was special because of her qualifications and experience, which included her recent appointment as Director of the Vietnamese Language School at the Naval Amphibious School in 1969.[52] The Assistant Secretary of the Navy approved her request, but specified that "this approval is based on the exceptional aspects of this matter and is not to be construed as a revision of existing policy." Two weeks later, the Chief of Naval Personnel imposed further restrictions, affirming that Von Wantoch's retention waiver applied to her current pregnancy only. Moreover, she could have the waiver only if she agreed to "submit an irrevocable request for voluntary retirement to be effective the first day of the month following the month in which you first attain retirement eligibility."[53] In other words: the Chief of Naval Personnel would grant her the waiver, but it would cost her the right to choose when to retire. The navy still expected that Von Wantoch's career as a mother would take precedence when she hit the magical point of retirement eligibility.

Von Wantoch's case was a transitional moment in changing motherhood discharge policies because of the degree of success she had in fighting for her career. Unlike earlier waivers for women with eighteen or more years of service, Von Wantoch's waiver granted her six more years of service. The length of time remaining before Von Wantoch attained retirement benefits far exceeded the standard the services generally used to grant waivers to women with long careers. Yet, it was also a compromise since the navy stipulated she must retire at her first possible eligibility date. Von Wantoch could be a mother and a member of the military, but eventually the former would have to take precedence. Her challenge to the military's clear strictures against mothers in military service was moderately successful.

By 1970, though, Von Wantoch was hardly alone as the services faced increasing challenges to such policies that limited women in particular. Rebecca Lloyd (WAVE, 1950–72), who indicated that she knew Von Wantoch, was aware of another woman who fought pregnancy discharge regulations at the same time.[54] Meanwhile, air force Assistant Staff Judge Advocate Captain Tommie Sue Smith tried to regain custody of her eight-year-old son using the same waiver system. The air force denied her request, which meant she could not take her son with her on assignment to the Philippines. But Smith was one of only seven women attorneys in the entire air force Judge Advocate Corps. The year before she submitted her waiver request, she had been Lackland Air Force Base's nominee for outstanding staff judge advocate of the year. When she joined the WAF in 1966, she gave legal custody to her parents, just like Ruth Brown did in 1960. "I was advised by my recruiter that a change of (legal) custody was only a formality and that I could keep my child with me. At no time was it mentioned that a regulation prohibited the child from being in my household more than 30 days a year."[55] This seems to have been the first time, though, that a single mother fought for the right to have her child live with her while she remained in service. Far from telling her she needed to leave the military and go home, in this case the media supported the cause of mother-and-child unity. The *Washington Post* placed Smith's case directly in the context of sex discrimination and cast the air force's regulation as one that brought "cruel and irrational hardship" to Smith, recommending that such "regulations that work special disadvantages on women in the services ought to be eliminated."[56] If men could have their children with them as they served around the world, a woman could too.

From the 1940s until the 1970s, military leaders used servicewomen's fertility as proof that women were biologically different from men and should thus be utilized and assigned accordingly. As Major General Mary Clarke, the last WAC director, noted in 1975, motherhood had become the military's excuse for limiting women's participation in national defense. Yet, by the mid-1970s, even the leaders of the women's services, like Clarke, began to accept that servicewomen could pursue both a military career and family life. The waiver system expanded during the early 1970s, but it took pushback from women like Von Wantoch and Smith to make change happen. The WAF led the way in 1971 with a more liberal waiver policy that not only allowed pregnant women to continue to serve, but also enabled previously discharged mothers of young children to rejoin the services. Two years later, Holm estimates that air force officials granted anywhere from 60 to 86 percent of waivers requested. By 1972, policies had once again changed, and Von Wantoch applied for and successfully received a reversal to the order that she retire at the earliest possible date. She remained in the services for another sixteen years, retiring as a captain after a total of thirty years with the navy.[57] By 1974, the DOD began to reevaluate the automatic motherhood discharge altogether.

Writing in 1975, Clarke examined the progress made by women in the military in recent years but cautioned Wacs that "for women in the army, the tough times have not ended. We are still going to have to confront people who do not accept us as fully participating members—soldiers—in the U.S. army."[58] While Clarke acknowledged how motherhood had limited women's careers, she also emphasized that motherhood was a unique attribute that servicewomen should embrace. "One of the differences by virtue of your sex is your possible role as a mother. The existence of this difference has often been stated as one of the key factors which limit your usefulness and productivity in a career related role—you must prove otherwise. You can be career oriented and still raise a family."[59] Women who had tried to challenge this rationale and the military's limitations against pregnancy and motherhood in earlier years threatened to upend the status quo through their insistence in trying to combine motherhood and military service. Clarke's article indicates that women who engaged in that struggle had supported a worthy cause; the armed forces had lost hundreds if not thousands of women due to the motherhood discharge, to their own loss. Women's stories of their reluctance to depart from service, their formal challenges to negotiate discharge policies, and their efforts to grant legal custody to other family members reveal that not everyone saw motherhood as something that should take precedence over their service to the nation. By 1974, military leaders had begun to agree. The DOD revised all regulations to make pregnancy and parenthood discharges voluntary as of May 1975.[60]

Now that military leaders had realized women's military service and motherhood need not be mutually exclusive, new arguments erupted over women's ability to control their biological functions. In particular, through changing abortion policies, the President, members of Congress, and DOD personnel continued to assert control over women's reproductive capacities. Abortion had long been included in the motherhood discharge, along with stillbirth and miscarriage. Information regarding servicewomen's access to abortion in the 1940s through 1960s is difficult to obtain because there are few official records about military policy on abortions. During World War II, any Wac who obtained an illegal abortion was discharged dishonorably, regardless of marital status, and the policy remained in place following the passage of the Women's Armed Services Integration Act.[61] Until 1949, women who obtained therapeutic abortions—the legal version of the procedure— were discharged, regardless of marital status. Only the air force maintained any statistics on servicewomen who aborted pregnancies in the pre-*Roe* years: twenty-five women obtained abortions in 1968, forty-four in 1969, and 275 in 1970.[62] WAC records indicate at least one instance of an abortion performed for a Wac at Fort Lee in late 1950.[63] As all the services began revising motherhood discharges in the 1970s, abortion reemerged as a key issue because it represented another arena through which women could control how motherhood shaped their lives. At the same time, Americans had begun working out the problem of abortion on a national scale through such cases as *Roe v. Wade*. Prior to the *Roe* case in 1973, abortion was illegal in thirty-three states, but its practice was nonetheless widespread. The Supreme Court's decision paved the way for the liberalization of abortion laws nationwide by affirming that, in the first three months of pregnancy, women had the right to procure abortions.[64]

In 1970, the DOD issued a directive that authorized abortions in military hospitals, irrespective of local laws. The directive also clarified the circumstances in which medical personnel could perform abortions: "Pregnancies may be terminated in military medical facilities when medically indicated or for reasons involving mental health and subject to the availability of space and facilities and the capabilities of the medical staff."[65] A 1972 army memo further explains that these policies applied to married and unmarried women, even noting that abortion was the only way an unmarried servicewoman could hope to stay in the military. If she remained pregnant, military officials would discharge the servicewoman solely because of "her potential inability to perform her army duties and to take proper care of a child as a single woman."[66] It is unclear how many servicewomen received abortions after this policy went into effect.

The policy of allowing military hospital personnel to bypass local law gained new government attention. By mid-1971, President Nixon revoked the DOD abortion policy under the rationale that abortion was "so sensitive and controversial that only the President should set the policy."[67] Nixon determined that since states historically had the right to regulate abortion, local law would determine the availability of abortions in military hospitals, even though military hospitals were federal installations.[68] Now, if a state in which a military base was located permitted abortion, servicewomen and dependents could receive abortions based on that state's law. Servicewomen and military dependents could travel to military hospitals in other states, presumably at their own expense, if the one where they were stationed did not offer abortion. Within two years, the Supreme Court asserted its role in reframing abortion rights with *Roe*, and the American Civil Liberties Union (ACLU) warned the DOD that Nixon's policy conflicted with *Roe*.[69] Defense officials resolved this problem in late 1975 with a new memo stating that "service hospitals should not follow state laws that appear to be unconstitutional under the Supreme Court ruling."[70]

With the legalization of abortion, women now had more control of their own fertility and, consequently, their sexuality—at least in theory. Until 1978, the President, DOD officials, and Supreme Court justices alternately controlled women's access to abortions in government-funded facilities such as military hospitals. The DOD generally paid for abortions for eligible women (servicewomen, military wives, daughters) if they had a documented medical or psychological need, and if local laws did not prohibit abortion. Until 1973, most states criminalized abortion in most cases, but in the five years before *Roe v. Wade*, four states eliminated antiabortion laws and thirteen states reformed their laws to permit abortion in select cases.[71] A 1975 record notes that 5,400 abortions were performed in 1974, not just for servicewomen, but also servicemen's immediate family members.[72] In a one-year period from August 31, 1976, to August 31, 1977, records indicate military personnel performed about 26,000 abortions in military hospitals or through the military's insurance program, CHAMPUS.[73] Beginning in 1979, the year after the dissolution of the last of the women's military services, members of Congress also approved legislation that prohibited the use of federal funds for abortions. An initial report on the legislation noted that it contained "A prohibition on abortions in military hospitals or through Champus [military insurance] except in cases where the mother's life would be endangered by having the baby, in cases of rape or incest or ectopic pregnancy."[74] After a slight modification, the army determined women could obtain abortions in military medical facilities, if space was available and if the woman paid the fee up front and from her own funds.[75]

During the Cold War, military leaders continually created and enforced certain policies based on women's physicality and assumptions about how women's presumptive ability to become mothers affected their career potential. As a result, military leaders created enforcement practices that profoundly affected women's utilization within the military. At the same time, the ideas behind these policies caused great debate among servicewomen themselves. High-level female officers and officials, predominantly women who served in World War II and had moved beyond their childbearing years, such as Colonel Hallaren and Assistant Secretary of Defense Rosenberg, suggested a conservative image of American womanhood that provided women a unique role in the home as wife and mother. As other women entered the services in the years following World War II, women like Ruth Brown, Joan Gerichten, and Jordine Von Wantoch fought to create a more liberalized image of "America's finest women." This image was one of a well-groomed, well-trained, and well-educated servicewoman who did her duty to the utmost of her ability and lived her life according to her terms. For these servicewomen, negotiating equality meant finding ways to combine motherhood and military service, regardless of what official policies dictated.

Limiting women's service opportunities on the basis of physicality and sexuality made it impossible for the services to either utilize women effectively or to offer a sustaining, long-term career opportunity. In an oral history interview in 1978, Brigadier General Mildred Bailey reflected that family concerns played an important part in preventing women from pursuing such careers. "It had been impossible because if she was considering the possibility of a family, the minute she had children or a dependent of any kind in her household under eighteen, she was automatically forced out. So how could she consider a long-range career? And that's the key word. Until now, for the average woman, she had to be thinking of it as short-range, just a job, until she married and had children."[76] Prohibiting servicewomen from combining jobs, marriage, and motherhood—full time—created very real limitations on how the services could utilize women. Without the option to pursue career and family, the women's components lost large numbers of women annually, wasting thousands or millions of dollars on training and expertise.

In the 1940s, members of Congress and military leaders thought they were creating a socially acceptable place for women in the armed forces by carefully constructing servicewomen's military opportunities around what they saw as the biological realities of women's bodies. For decades, women's reproductive capacities and moral ideas about women's sexual behavior drove the terms of policy related to women's service. By the late 1970s, however, norms about women's capabilities and their morality shifted in civilian society. Women increasingly proved that combining motherhood and military service was not impossible and convinced defense officials that ensuring equality for women in the military would mean removing restrictions against mothers in the armed forces. Servicewomen consistently challenged deeply held assumptions about women's appropriate behaviors and their place in national defense. Yet the policies regulating women's bodies remained so influential for so long precisely because women came to their military service with myriad opinions about women's physical capabilities and the relationship between women and work. As women pushed against the assumptions that guided military policy, it became clear that the military's definition of equality, based on gender difference, meant that leaders had not yet begun to explore how women could best serve their country.

6 Top Secret and Obscene

Sex and the American Servicewoman

In 1958, the services jointly published a new pamphlet for women officers to help them better do their job as leaders of enlisted women: "Hygiene Educational Guide for Women Officers and Women Officer Candidates of the Armed Forces." Today it would be more clearly labeled as a sex education manual, and it was part of larger military efforts to educate men and women about sexuality. In this booklet, officers learned about women's reproductive processes, why humans need sex, the "unique stresses" women faced in the military, and how officers could prevent (and identify) sexual problems and venereal disease. These topics resembled similar educational pamphlets and films given to servicemen. In the Cold War, sex education for military personnel was not new: nearly half a century earlier during World War I, military leaders had seen the negative impact sexually transmitted diseases could have on troop readiness, and this led to concerted campaigns to educate servicemen and women in hopes of avoiding future problems. These efforts expanded in World War II. For example, the 1942 "Sex Hygiene and Venereal Disease" pamphlet from the War Department educated men about their sex organs and the problems of sexually transmitted diseases.[1] That same year, the War Department also released a training film for male recruits called "Sex Hygiene," and directed by John Ford, who would later become most famous for his western films. By the time the war ended, most servicemen would have viewed "Sex Hygiene" multiple times.[2]

World War II military sex education campaigns focused on sexual health to ensure servicemen did not contract diseases that would remove them from their wartime roles, but in the Cold War, sex education for servicewomen focused more specifically on keeping women moral. To that end, the 1958 "Hygiene Education" manual included an entire chapter on "characteristics" and "management" of homosexuality. The introduction specifically exhorted readers to avoid the "conspiracy of silence, an effort to suppress any recognition or discussion of sexuality in women through associating fear or guilt with this forbidden subject." Instead, the authors noted, military leaders had learned that "dealing frankly and objectively with the sexual aspects of the personality is a much more effective way of preventing and managing sexual misbehavior." Through the education this pamphlet provided, women officers would become the first line of defense to help prevent sexual problems in the ranks. Ultimately, this was the most important reason for such training. "The public nature of military service," officers read, "means that women of the Armed Forces . . . have an additional responsibility to adhere to high moral standards. The Armed Forces cannot tolerate any subversion of accepted criteria of sexual behavior."[3] Military leaders believed that women's sexual misbehavior undermined womanpower altogether.

This publication and earlier ones demonstrate that military leaders believed that sex was a problem. Sex was a problem for servicemen when it interfered with their health and their ability to fight. Sex was a problem when women married quickly after joining the services and sought marriage discharges in the early 1950s, because sexual desire overcame patriotic commitment. When servicewomen became pregnant, sex was clearly a problem, even when the expectant mother was properly married. Once again, sex interfered with a woman's service. Considering that men comprised more than 98 percent of the Cold War military, none of this should be surprising: women found more prospects for male companionship while working for Uncle Sam than they might otherwise encounter in an entire lifetime. Military life was an "overwhelmingly masculine environment," and it wasn't uncommon that "most women assigned to isolated stations will find themselves sexually sought after with much greater intensity than would be true in a heterosexually-balanced situation."[4] This reality, however, did not mean that servicewomen had *carte blanche* to sleep with every man they saw. True, there was a double standard "under which men are permitted greater overt sexual expression without penalty than are women." This did not matter. "While the predominantly male values of the services are pervasive and strong, the women of the Armed Forces must continue to adhere to the same standards of feminine deportment expected to women in the civilian community if they wish to retain the respect and affection of the men in the services and of the American people."[5] Sex was a problem when it came to having women in the military, because there were so few of them and so many men.

The "standards of feminine deportment" emerge quite clearly in the officer manual: servicewomen needed to be chaste outside of marriage and heterosexuality was the norm. "In Western culture generally sexual relations outside of marriage are discouraged by legal, religious, and moral sanctions."⁶ Given the desire to recruit the best women possible, and the focus on training women to be ideal, feminine ladies—proper future wives and mothers—it made sense that the services would adhere to this norm. However, enforcing abstinence outside of marriage was not easy, and officers had to be trained to watch for specific types of activities and behaviors that might suggest something was wrong. The message to be sent was that servicewomen should wait on sex until marriage, ideally after they finished their enlistment term. To maintain the all-important image of the American servicewoman that leaders so badly wanted to project, no other standard would do.

But this was a standard over which military officials had only limited control. After all, Americans in and out of the armed forces had their own ideas of what an American servicewoman was, as Chief Master Sergeant Sharon Masek reflected. When she joined the WAF in the 1960s, Masek's friends told her quite clearly that a woman who sought a military career was one of three things: "a whore, a lesbian, or looking for a husband."⁷ None of these stereotypes were new: in World War II, the same message had emerged in popular culture, much to the chagrin of those in charge. Twenty years later, not much had changed. None of the leaders of the women's services would object to the third charge of "looking for a husband," although such women could prove problematic in their own way, seeking marriage discharges or getting pregnant as soon as they could after marriage to give Uncle Sam the boot. Promiscuity certainly wasn't favored, but it could be dealt with, as the officers' manual indicated. There was a bigger problem, according to the highest-ranking women in the military: lesbians.

Concerns over women's sexual behavior began during World War II, largely because of the need to make women's military service acceptable to Americans. In that context, concerns over the possibility of lesbians in the armed forces arose alongside more general fears of servicewomen's sexual behavior. According to historian Leisa Meyer, World War II WAC leaders focused on controlling all of servicewomen's sexual behavior because they believed that "only chaste women could retain public legitimacy for the corps."⁸ Any servicewoman who engaged in sexual activity might be seen as violating norms that defined women as passive sexual actors, and such behavior might only heighten the slander campaign that haunted the wartime WAC for years.⁹ Despite fears of homosexuality among servicewomen, military leaders devoted relatively small attention to their concerns during the war. In training lectures, officer candidates learned about the importance of friendships between women and were warned that sometimes, those friendships might go a step further in intimacy. Yet the lectures "minimized the differences between women who participated in homosexual expression and 'normal' women," and cautioned officers to avoid creating witch hunts that would focus on identifying and removing women suspected of engaging in homosexual activity.[10]

Mattie Treadwell's official history of the World War II WAC highlights concerns over homosexuality only once, recounting a brief investigation in 1944. It began when a Wac's mother wrote to the Judge Advocate General of the War Department after reading some of her daughter's letters. After pushing her daughter for more details, the mother wrote her letter, claiming "It is no wonder women are afraid to enlist. [The Women's Army Corps] is full of homosexuals and sex maniacs." Additionally, the letter named several other Wacs who were supposedly lesbians and noted that her own daughter "has repented."[11] WAC Director Oveta Culp Hobby immediately requested an investigation, which yielded "very little evidence of homosexual practices; the incidence seemed no greater and probably less than in the civilian population."[12] Treadwell ultimately concludes that there was no problem with lesbianism in the WAC, explaining that part of the problem lay in wider assumptions that "any woman who was masculine in appearance or dress, or who did not enjoy men's company, was apt to be singled out for suspicion." Yet Hobby and other officials stressed that this was not true and further emphasized that there should be no witch hunts based on such stereotypes.[13] Despite these conclusions, the reality is that the WAC, like the armed forces as a whole, had a vested interest in minimizing the appearance of homosexuality, which meant avoiding investigations that might make it seem like there were more lesbians in military. Whether Hobby and Treadwell were accurate in their estimates that few lesbians served in World War II, the main point is that wartime leaders undertook efforts to control women's sexual activity and paid close attention to how women's relationships to other women might be perceived.[14]

After World War II, the armed forces controlled homosexuality in a more systematic way, particularly in the women's service components. In the early years of the Cold War, the United States government maintained the official position that homosexual men and women were both abnormal and threats to national security. This position came from then-current psychiatric understandings of homosexuality, as well as assumptions—founded in belief, not in scientific fact—that gays and lesbians were weak and vulnerable because of their supposed psychological abnormalities. At midcentury, the popular understanding of homosexuals as "deviant" and threats to national security also intensified the belief that homosexuals were ineligible for the privileges of performing military service. Psychiatric professionals continued to classify homosexuality as an irregular trait. By 1952, the first *Diagnostic and Statistical Manual of Mental Disorders* (DSM-1) "firmly established homosexuality as a sociopathic personality disorder." Building from this, and from wartime efforts to eliminate homosexuality within the ranks, all branches of the armed forces began to develop postwar policies against homosexuals. While historian Allan Bérubé describes World War II as a coming-out experience that fostered postwar gay life in the United States, that was a decidedly civilian postwar gay life. In the armed forces, the closet remained tightly shut.[15]

That same year, the navy created a series of lectures that new WAVE recruits would hear when they joined. Whereas the wartime WAC leaders decided there was no need for detailed instruction, and instead just had a reference to homosexuality in psychiatric lectures, the new WAVE indoctrination speeches provided recruits with much more detailed training. "Indoctrination of WAVE Recruits on Subject of Homosexuality" included three presentations—one from a line officer, followed by one from a medical officer, and concluded with a lecture by a chaplain. The line officer's presentation proposed to give "the facts concerning homosexuality and most important of all, how to avoid becoming involved with homosexuals."[16] The lecture also provided recruits with an explanation of homosexuality, as well as scenarios in which a "practicing homosexual" might try to coerce a woman into homosexual activity, including friendship, power and intimidation, or even "the 'Come-on-and-no-risk' approach," because "you can experience sexual stimulation and sexual satisfaction in a homosexual act without risk of pregnancy."[17] The line officer's speech presents homosexuality as a misguided activity that a servicewoman might engage in, emphasizing the consequences for such behavior—from undesirable discharge, future job challenges, and the personal effects of having to tell your friends and family what you did. The medical officer, a physician in the Navy Medical Corps, further detailed why homosexuality was abnormal, explaining homosexuality in medical terms of the time and dispelling misconceptions about homosexuality. Finally, the chaplain's speech, organized in three parts, emphasized that homosexuality "Destroys a Woman's Social Status and her Social Future . . . Destroys a Woman's Character . . . Destroys a Woman's Spiritual Values and Her Spiritual Life."[18] Although the chaplain finished by telling recruits the goal was not to scare them, the messages are clear: military leaders believed homosexuality was bad, and engaging in homosexual acts was a perversion that would cost women everything.

Leaders of the women's services believed fervently in enforcing policies against homosexuality. Writing to a WAC Staff Advisor in 1951 and sounding eerily similar to the 1952 navy indoctrination lectures, Colonel Mary Hallaren referred to lesbians as "human vultures who blight the lives of youngsters," arguing that "love . . . is warped and cheapened by these poor apologies for womanhood."[19] By the 1960s, WAC trainers learned that homosexuals were not welcomed in the armed forces for three reasons: "Their lack of emotional stability and personal or group loyalty, which makes them security risks. Their continual immoral efforts to seduce other individuals into their self-destructive pattern of behavior. Necessity for maintaining the good order, reputation and honor of the Armed Forces."[20] In addition, because psychiatrists defined homosexuality as a form of deviance, the presence of lesbians in the women's components, leaders believed, would only foster more negative connotations about women in national defense, which would only feed ideas such as those Masek heard when she joined the WAF. The definition of homosexuality as a sociopathic disorder meant that the presence of lesbians in the ranks appeared to undermine efforts to present military service as a respectable career opportunity for women. Lesbians, according to military leaders, participated in sexual relationships outside of marriage and subverted normal gender systems because they tried to operate outside of accepted gender hierarchies. Put another way, lesbians placed themselves outside the bounds of social control and, as a result, endangered military effectiveness.

Not only did lesbian women engage in illicit relationships with other women, but in doing so they engaged in sexual activity that could not lead to reproduction, which marked them as abnormal. Military officials took such behavior to mean that lesbians had turned their back on motherhood, which no "normal" woman would do. Motherhood, Hallaren and others believed, could be a justification for limiting women's military careers, because motherhood was a "normal" part of an American woman's life. By turning their backs on motherhood, lesbian servicewomen disrupted the system that had been so carefully designed to emphasize that military service made women more desirable wives and mothers—better women by serving the nation. Although not always consistent in their efforts to control incidents of homosexuality within the women's services, this was one key area where higher-ranking military personnel sought to control both their reputation by avoiding "undesirables" and American servicewomen.

As historian Margot Canaday argues, military leaders enforced a concept of women's citizenship based on normative heterosexual morality.[21] This concept inherently included the potential to become a mother. Thus, suggesting that any woman might not *want* to be a mother was simply seen as unnatural—proof that something was wrong with a woman.

Ideally, recruiting procedures would filter out women with pasts or who looked like they might cause problems in the future, but military records demonstrate that this was a battle the women's services never quite won. Sometimes, the investigations were small, often as the result of barracks gossip, as in the 1949 case of a Wave. A letter from an officer at the Great Lakes, Illinois, U.S. Naval Hospital detailed that Wave "D.M.J." admitted "to having participated in about ten homosexual acts in the past four months with the same individual." Before joining the WAVES, D.M.J. explained that she had engaged only in sex with men, and had lived with a man at one time. The officer examining her highlighted not only D.M.J.'s homosexual encounters, but also identified her as bisexual because she had continued to engage in sexual activity with men while engaged in a lesbian relationship. As if to account for the diagnosis "Sexual Deviate, Bisexuality, Overt," the clinician provided an entire paragraph on D.M.J.'s history as a foster child in a religious household, her rebellion from that religion, and her inability to hold a job for a long period of time. Here, the examiner found what seemed to be the cause of D.M.J.'s "abnormality," and even greater justification for why she should be discharged from the navy. According to the examiner's report, D.M.J. was a troubled woman who did not belong in the WAVES.[22] However, it was also clear that she wasn't so troubled that the WAVES caught it before she enlisted. Such documents reveal more about mid-century attitudes about homosexuality, illustrating, in this case, the ways in which medical officers tried to find reasons why servicewomen engaged in behavior deemed deviant.

Early in the Cold War, discharges for homosexuality appear almost annually in all the services, for both men and women, on top of periodic intense efforts to identify and remove suspected lesbian servicewomen. According to Canaday, the military was particularly focused on lesbianism in the early Cold War. For decades, military leaders had already worried about men engaging in homosexual acts, but the problem of lesbians drew their particular focus beginning in 1948 and into the 1950s. In that period, Canaday notes, women comprised only one percent of the total military strength, but military leaders were more concerned about the impact of lesbianism than male homosexuality, and they believed that more women than men engaged in homosexual behavior.[23] While military officials did discharge men for homosexuality, in this decade in particular the search for lesbians took on greater focus. The records of men's and women's discharges for homosexuality indicate a greater obsession with documenting suspected cases of lesbianism: most of the men's discharge files are small, perhaps a half-inch thick at the largest, while the women's files are more commonly two to three inches thick and included far larger numbers of women.[24]

Known as "witch hunts," because these investigations came intensely on the heels of the vaguest of rumors, or sought out purposefully, in the early 1950s multiple women at one time came under scrutiny due to suspected or known homosexual activity. It was a marked contrast to Colonel Hobby's insistence nearly a decade earlier that witch hunts were not an appropriate pursuit. Now, with homosexuals defined as security risks, a rash of investigations in the WAC included activities such as intercepting mail, searching women's living areas, wiretapping, physical examinations, mental evaluations, and lie detector tests.[25] Investigators often relied on what might amount to circumstantial evidence or testimony from women who lived or worked with the accused—gossip, such as the type that led to D.M.J.'s dismissal from the WAVES a few years earlier. In one case, a suspect's roommate retrieved a letter from the waste bin as evidence of the suspect's lesbian activities; a copy of the letter made its way to the final case file. Marked as "Top Secret," "Obscene," and "Confidential" in the National Archives, these files provided detailed statements from accused Wacs, reports from psychiatric professionals, and interrogation transcripts. Interrogations of suspected women or informants included questions designed to elicit detailed responses of sexual activities performed or observed. In 1951, for example, an investigator asked Private B.P. to give explicit details about observed instances of masturbation, petting, and kissing between other women in her unit. Private C.P. gave an affidavit attesting to her own engagement in similar behavior. Psychiatric reports also noted accused servicewomen's history of homosexual activity in detail.[26]

These investigations went far beyond simply corroborating evidence of women's same-sex relationships: rather, they documented what military officials believed was the systematic deviance of women identified as having homosexual tendencies. The 1951 WAC homosexuality discharge files include cases with as few as two accused women or as many as sixty-four in a single investigation, all of which centered on women's sexual behavior and relationships with men and women. While the amount of detail in the files varies, sometimes running to several hundred pages, the files tend to include descriptions of suspected or confessed activities, including references to nudity, kissing and fondling, cunnilingus, "love-making," butch behavior, a "wedding" between two women, and mutual masturbation. Psychiatric reports, written by male and female professionals, assess the accused servicewoman's "psychosexual" development and family background, often emphasizing the subject's history with men (including relationships with fathers and other male family members). Inquiry into the suspected women's past relationships with men served to establish their histories of heterosexual interactions and attitudes toward members of the opposite sex.[27]

Investigators designed many questions for the dual purposes of proving homosexuality and establishing the suspect as someone engaged in abnormal behavior, such as tendencies toward masculine behavior. Although World War II medical officials and the 1952 navy indoctrination speeches emphasized that masculine behavior did not make a woman more inclined to be a lesbian, such behaviors became even more suspect in the Cold War, demonstrating the persistence of such assumptions in Americans' minds. Investigators asked Private M.G. questions such as whether she had ever kissed one of the other women named in the case and why she had done it. They also asked M.G. to identify herself as "fem" or "butch" and to identify other women in such a manner, a question intended to assess whether women accused of lesbianism identified more with feminine or masculine behavioral traits. Regarding her experiences kissing other women, the investigator asked, "Didn't they get you aroused?" and "Didn't she get you aroused when she played with your breasts?" Other questions included "Do you get more pleasure from kissing a girl than a man?" and inquiries as to whether she had ever masturbated with another woman or performed cunnilingus, or whether she knew what "muff diving" was.[28] The detailed questions go on and on, and given their nature, seem incongruous with the type of information that might be expected in a government document or investigation. Part of the problem, as Canaday suggests, is that government officials did not really have a good grasp of what homosexuality was, and they used these investigations to build on their assumptions of lesbianism and create their own definitions.[29]

In many cases, accusations and defenses became a matter of she-said/she-said, and when that happened, military officials' fears and distaste over homosexuality led them to believe the accuser over the accused. Corporal M.H. not only argued for the opportunity to face a court-martial, rather than be discharged, but also took her complaints about the investigative process to Arkansas Senator J. William Fulbright. In a letter dated May 14, 1951, and attached to the full discharge case file, Corporal M.H. described the investigation as poorly handled. "The manner in which we were interrogated, evidence we were informed that was against us, failure of calling in character witnesses, and numerous things have contributed to my belief that we were very unfairly and unjustly used." Corporal M.H. went on to describe how, in the six months since her arrival on base, she had heard there was already "malicious gossip" circulating amongst the women and soon found herself subject to investigation. "We were not shown the accusations, and the individuals accused did not have named to them the names of the accusers, except as a group." After being told she would need to submit to a polygraph, she did so willingly, understanding at the time that it would help clear her name. Instead, even though the machine indicated her truthfulness, "I was then told that it could not be used for me. That its weight in evidence was nothing." Corporal M.H. detailed her strong military background and her suspicions about who might have been feeding lies to the military command—a woman who was quickly court-martialed after a fit in which she suggested she may have lied about some claims made in the homosexuality investigation.

Corporal M.H. maintained her innocence and her frustration that those accusing her were not subject to lie detector tests. She closed by noting how much the investigation had been designed to wear her and the others down.

> I can't understand the army's refusal to permit us to try to prove our innocence. As far as they're concerned, we're through. During the investigation we've been repeatedly told that we were beat and why not give up. But they fail to realize that we are grown people, we have liked our jobs, and worn our uniform as a member of the Armed Forces of the Greatest nation in the world and have been proud to do so . . . As far as the army is concerned they have consented to letting these filthy liars ruin our career in the army, and have not given us a chance to prove our innocence so that we may go again out in to civilian society and hold our head up.[30]

It's not clear whether her letter to the Senator was effective, but three documents at the front of the file contain conflicting recommendations on how to handle the results of the investigation of Corporal M.H. The cover memo, dated June 1, 1951, recommends discharge for homosexuality. However, the next document, a memo from the Chief of Psychiatry and Neurology—Consultants Division, dated July 13, notes insufficient evidence for a homosexuality discharge, instead recommending discharge for emotional instability. Still a third memo from the Army Personnel Board on July 23 notes that "discharge is not favorably considered."[31]

The 1950s WAC homosexuality investigations illustrate the depth of military officials' fears and distaste about homosexuality. While in some ways the investigations are an anomaly in scope, they reflect a larger military movement in the 1950s to manage homosexuality—in men and women—proactively. A witch hunt that began in 1950 at Keesler Air Force Base targeted eleven women, then expanded, with more than twenty additional women at Lackland Air Force Base and Wright-Patterson Air Force Base being discharged. The fallout of this included two of the accused women committing suicide; a third simply disappeared.[32] Records after the early 1950s suggest that homosexuality became less of a recognized problem until the 1970s, in the sense that the number of discharges for homosexuality decreased. By the early 1960s, instances of homosexual discharge were far lower, but not necessarily because fewer homosexual men and women were serving in the military. Ann Thacker Lewis notes that when she was in the WAVES from 1961 to 1965, she knew lesbians, but asserted that homosexual behavior was well-hidden.[33] During fiscal years 1961 and 1962, a total of two Wacs became discharged for homosexuality, while sixty women received pregnancy discharges.[34] Not until the late 1970s did another witch hunt occur, when the admission of naval women onto ships led to a large investigation into alleged lesbianism following this policy change that radically expanded navy women's opportunities.[35]

While it is possible that recruiters for the women's components simply got better at screening applicants and removing suspected lesbians from consideration before they could join the military, two other explanations are more likely. First, the politically conservative environment of the early 1950s created an atmosphere in which Americans such as Senator Joseph McCarthy argued that persons with abnormalities—whether political or sexual—should be proactively eliminated from positions of power. By the mid-1950s, McCarthy's approach fell out of favor in the federal government, at least, and may have very well extended to the armed forces. Second, by the late 1950s, women had served in the military for more than a decade, but their overall numbers remained small, which made them relatively unthreatening to men in military power. By that time, the same impulses that led Americans to suspect their neighbors of un-American activities no longer held sway as it had in the McCarthy years, or during the trials of Alger Hiss and Julius and Ethel Rosenberg.[36]

More likely, the decline in homosexual discharges signified an increased willingness for servicewomen to turn away discreetly when they encountered servicewomen engaging in homosexual activity. Homosexuality remained a concern for military leaders, but for a time, at least, fewer servicewomen were turning on other women. The decline in homosexual discharges after the 1950s, then, may speak to the success of the women's component leaders in establishing military service as a respectable career for women. By early 1959, WAF Director Emma Riley told participants at the Staff Director's meeting "I do not know if the incidents [of homosexuality] are greater in number than they were say two to five years ago, but I do know that homosexuality is a very serious problem among WAF. The other Directors [of the WAVES, WAC, Women Marines] also tell me it is a big problem in their services. Frankly, none of us know any easy solution." And she offered none, particularly noting that leading officers should *not* try "to become private detectives, to start witch hunts, or to interfere in any way with investigations. What we want is to emphasize the problem, to keep constantly aware of it, and to look for solutions." Further, commanders needed to know the women in their charge, and supervise them well. Echoing the ideas in the Hygiene Education manual a few years earlier, Riley concluded that "no single thing is as important as the supervision and guidance, the precept and example of the WAF squadron section commander."[37] To avoid problems, leaders needed to know their subordinates well and to earn their trust. If military leaders believed that relationships between servicewomen could lead to deviant behavior, they also believed that nurturing the right kind of relationships was key to the success of women's integration.

Even before Riley's report, military leaders had begun to keep an eagle eye out for homosexual activity, as the navy's 1957 Crittenden Report demonstrates. The Crittenden board convened in 1956 to make recommendations on handling homosexuality cases, culminating with a thorough report assessing homosexuality in the navy. The authors indicated they did not have complete faith in statistics on homosexuality in the navy, pointing out that statistics represented only "the number of homosexuals who are actually disclosed." They believed this was "a very small proportion of homosexuals in the navy." Regarding women, the authors argue it was a challenge to define homosexuality in women. "It is considered impossible to provide a fixed and concise overall definition as to all that constitutes homosexual activity in the female."[38] Part of the problem, according to the authors, was that most Americans felt it was perfectly fine for women to be in close friendships with other women—something not as acceptable between American men. When such close same-sex relationships were a large part of women's lives, it could be challenging to distinguish where friendship bled into something more intimate.

The all-male Crittenden board members' position on homosexuality in women developed from their assumptions about women's behavior and relationship patterns as compared with men's. "Homosexual activity by women is harder to detect. Women are normally more secretive, are not as promiscuous, and are more selective than the male, whereas the male is not as selective either as to partner nor as to locale as the female." The Crittenden board members believed fully in the same cultural norms detailed in the Hygiene Education manual, and both items reflected social norms of the era: because Americans presumed that women were morally better than men when it came to sex, it was that much harder to find out when women were behaving immorally. This may explain the obsession with the thick, detailed documentation in the women's discharge files: military officials believed, in these cases, that they could identify lesbians, although their accuracy rates may be debated, given Corporal M.H.'s letter detailing how her investigation was handled. Even more, the authors noted, over the previous decade "there has been much more professional discussion of the problem of homosexuality," and these changes would only help the navy—and the rest of the military—in efforts to eliminate homosexuality from national defense.[39] According to the board, the armed forces had been particularly skilled so far at identifying lesbianism: "the incidence rate of homosexual activity is much higher for the female than male as reflected in the statistics available to the Board." They surmised that this was true, despite the challenges in identifying homosexuality in women—because women were supervised more closely, some women's relationships were misunderstood as lesbian relationships, women in the military were just more susceptible because of "the abnormal military setting," or perhaps military service was just more attractive to women with "latent homosexual activities." Regardless, the board advocated for sexual equality: women identified as lesbians should be treated the same as men identified as gay. Here, at least, was one clear instance of equality for men and women.[40]

The Crittenden Report's central message is clear: homosexual men and women have no place in the military, and the navy needed to continue doing what they had been doing to eliminate it from the ranks. At the same time, however, the board suggested that perhaps that approach need not always be the case. Even while laying out strategies to identify and eliminate homosexuals from military service, the authors admit that "*there have been many known instances of individuals who have served honorably and well, despite being exclusively homosexual.*"[41] Despite acknowledging this, board members recommended enforcing existing policies. "The service should not move ahead of civilian society nor attempt to set substantially different standards in attitude toward or actions with respect to homosexual offenders." However, the board also recommended that the armed services keep an eye on social changes regarding homosexuality. While certainly not interested in breaking new ground by accepting gays and lesbians, this admission suggests that the authors were not fully convinced that homosexual citizens would always need to be excluded.[42] After its completion in 1957, the Crittenden Report remained under wraps for about two decades, even though nothing in the report was new for military leaders. By 1957, it was clear that all the services had been carefully working to eliminate gays and lesbians whenever such behavior was suspected or caught.

While many women (and men) lost their careers due to witch hunts or smaller findings, Corporal M.H. wasn't the only woman in the 1950s to challenge the results of an investigation. In the aftermath of the 1951 WAF discharges, several women reached out to the ACLU, seeking support to fight their discharges. One of the servicewomen began her letter saying, "I'm not sure whether the following is included in the absence of Civil Liberties but if it isn't I think it should be." The servicewoman, one of the Wafs targeted at Keesler, explained that she and others were told that if they confessed and incriminated others, they would receive general discharges. She explained that she did not know until too late that she could have had an attorney on base to support her, and that although she requested a court-martial instead of signing the undesirable discharge they gave her, she was "not very hopeful" that she would get one. "Perhaps it's my own amazement that such a situation [as this] exists in this country—this wasn't what we learned in school—our govt tells us how well she has done by the Indian and the foreign nation, but where is one speck of regard for the individual govt employee? . . . here was the last place I expected a rotten deal."[43] A second woman, writing in March 1951, was the fourth discharged from Wright-Patterson and worried for the other women at Wright-Patterson "who live in constant terror of the telephone. Their's [sic] is no small problem." The author pleaded for support: "I ask you, for all those girls left, is this fair?—is it in keeping with the principles we shout so loud? How efficient can our armed forces be, with this sort of psychological warfare raging within? As an individual, I'm powerless; as an organization, can you help them?"[44] At least one of the women received a response from the Staff Counsel at the ACLU in early April, expressing sympathy but explaining that "there is no violation of civil liberties involved in the policy of the army that homosexuals of either sex must be discharged from the army. So you see, there is really nothing we can do." The staff counsel concluded by recommending that the original writer seek "medical treatment if you really desire to abandon homosexual relations."[45] These women were on their own: no one would step forward to help them fight the military's policies against homosexuality.

While the ACLU did not intervene in support of these women, others found ways to fight the discharges handed to them. In 1960, Fannie Mae Clackum sued over a discharge eight years earlier when she was a WAF reservist on active duty. For at least six months, Clackum claimed, she was subjected to repeated interviews by the Office of Special Intelligence (OSI) regarding homosexual behavior. Although given a chance to resign based on the accusations against her, she refused and demanded a court-martial. Like the Wacs the same year, Clackum had to undergo a psychiatric examination, but unlike the Wacs, "No sworn evidence . . . was taken or received by OSI or by the air force, and prior to her discharge [Clackum] was not confronted with the nature of the evidence against her." Instead, the WAF demoted her to private in early 1952 just before discharging her. It took four years for the case to make it to federal court, where Judge Madden summed up Clackum's experience by saying "One's reaction to the foregoing narrative is 'What's going on here?'" He emphasized that "dishonorable discharge is, for a soldier, one of the most severe penalties which may be imposed by a court-martial," expressing concern over how the air force had handled the case. He concluded that the air force had acted wrongly. "The plaintiff being a member of the air force reserve, on active duty, the air force had the undoubted right to discharge her whenever it pleased . . . But it is unthinkable that it should have the raw power, without respect for even the most elementary notions of due process of law, to load her down with penalties."[46] Clackum won back pay and became the first woman to successfully challenge the way the military had discharged her on accusation of homosexuality.

Likewise, so did Grace Garner, Clackum's partner, who had been discharged with Clackum. Cited as a "companion case," what made Garner's case different was that she was not a reservist and had been serving in the WAF since 1949 when the WAF discharged her in January 1952. Garner also took her case to court and not only had her discharge upgraded to honorable, but won back pay from 1952 to 1961. In that period, the court pointed out, Garner had earned just over $30,000 in her civilian job, but her total pay, allowances, and medical expenses, had she been in the military during that time, amounted to more than $37,000. The court awarded Garner approximately $7,000 in back pay, representing the income she lost due to the discharge in 1952.[47] It was a momentous moment, although not a turning point in how military officials felt about homosexuality in national defense. As Canaday emphasizes, Clackum and Garner had fought and won their battles on the grounds they had been denied due process—not on the grounds they had been discharged for homosexuality.[48]

Even with the ever-present threat of being uncovered and kicked out, lesbian women routinely challenged the official position against homosexuality by pursuing military careers anyway. It is not clear how many lesbians entered the military and managed to avoid becoming the target of homosexuality investigations, or how many lesbian servicewomen eventually faced expulsion despite efforts to hide their sexuality. Loretta Coller joined the WAF in 1951 knowing that she was a lesbian, but also knowing that the services did not accept individuals who professed homosexual tendencies. She planned to have a long career in the services and performed well in the air force. However, her relationship with another woman ended her career. Through her participation in a local basketball team, she met a civilian woman who she began to see in early 1953. "I would stay with this gal over the weekend, and I figured, now, when I put on my civilian clothes and go into Sacramento, that's my weekend and what I do has no bearing on what's going on at the base."[49] The air force didn't agree with Coller's belief in the separation of work and play: all that mattered was that she was engaging in illicit relationships. Even with a great work record and her efforts to keep her relationships off-base, Coller became the subject of an investigation that she believed was a routine purge.

Coller had thought she could find a way around the system, but once targeted she felt she had no real recourse. When investigators claimed they would grant her a general discharge, Coller felt there was some promise. However, they failed to deliver, instead giving her an undesirable discharge after the air force court-martialed her. While neither was the honorable discharge granted to most service members who completed their service without incident, undesirable discharges—sometimes referred to as "Section Eight" discharges—barred an individual from veteran benefits and carried a stigma of impropriety given its original intent for discharging individuals with "undesirable habits or traits of character."[50] The experience and the discharge devastated Coller. Nearly thirty years later, Coller applied for and received an upgraded discharge. "I learned too late that had I the money, time, and the intelligence, I probably could have fought that discharge. It was illegal, totally illegal. With no defense, no reading of my rights, and the fact that I had been lied to all the way down the line, I could have won! But alas, I didn't know all of that at the time."[51] Lacking knowledge or advocates to help provide such crucial knowledge, women like Coller found themselves forced out of the institution they wanted so much to participate in.

Coller's experience is probably typical of many women discharged for homosexuality in the military given that at the time she felt helpless against the military system, and reflects the experiences of the anonymous women who sought support from the ACLU in 1951. However, Coller's ability to go two years under the radar, serving despite knowing what the services thought of lesbians, demonstrates how some women challenged military policies they disliked. Dr. Galen Grant, for example, enlisted in the WAC in 1976. Although she had been out for about seven years—and politically active in lobbying for gay rights at the state level—Grant lied on her application and said she was heterosexual. Despite her political activity, no one questioned her application, and Grant served more than thirteen years. During this time, she was recognized as Drill Sergeant of the Year for Fort Jackson (1983). "I was the first woman soldier to have earned this honor. I believed that if I was the best soldier, I would be immune to the active witch hunts of gays and lesbians that were perpetrated during those years."[52] By the time Grant joined in 1976, the Cold War was in an all-too-brief era of détente, which may have helped cool the threat of witch hunts, and the gay and lesbian rights movement had begun. Being gay in the military certainly wasn't yet accepted, but the overall environment was perhaps a little more relaxed when it came to sexuality.

While many lesbian women like Coller and Grant tried to avoid suspicion at all, by the 1970s women whose sexual orientation came to light began to try to fight the discharge process, with mixed success. In 1974, WAF Lieutenant Janet E. Cook took her complaint to federal court, seeking a temporary restraining order to prevent the air force from discharging her due to homosexuality. Although the air force went regulation—literally—noting that "homosexuality is not tolerated in the air force," something that Cook would have known, she countered with her resume, which proved a remarkable eight-year service record. "I acknowledge that I am a homosexual," Cook told her commanding officer, but "in no sense have my 'homosexual tendencies' or practices interfered with the performance of my duties as an officer of the air force." Cook knew her future was on the line and wanted to prove her reputation. The ACLU stepped up in her support this time: "because of a code used by the Air Force in her discharge, potential future employers in civilian life will be able to learn that she was discharged because she was homosexual." While Cook did not say whether she was worried about that, she was concerned that employers "might falsely infer that her activities have harmed in her performance and the interests of the air force."[53] However, the judge sided with the air force and Cook's efforts were unsuccessful.

In a slightly different case in the mid-1970s, WAC leaders encountered something they had never seen when a current Wac married a former Wac. Specialist 4 Marie Sode married Kristian Von Hoffburg, a transgender man, in an Alabama civil ceremony in November 1976. In a military-prepared press release, the judge who officiated the wedding stated that he did not know he was marrying two individuals who were assigned female at birth. But, there was nothing illegal about the wedding, either, because there was no law prohibiting two women from marrying each other. The Assistant District Attorney confirmed that in Alabama, "the law requires only that both parties be consenting adults."[54] Von Hoffburg was living as a man, taking hormones, and planning to undergo gender confirmation operation. The couple was only outed when Von Hoffburg came to base to apply for dependent benefits, which ironically had only been available to servicewomen's spouses for a few years. At that time, a current Wac recognized Von Hoffburg as a WAC veteran and officials investigated.

Although the army pursued the case as an instance of homosexuality, Sode-Von Hoffburg argued that this was not about homosexuality at all. She argued that she and her husband were a heterosexual couple, given their individual gender identifications. Despite her claims, army officials persisted in treating the marriage as a case of homosexuality. "The army position is that Bowers-Von Hoffburg was demonstratably [sic] a woman. That will be sufficient, the army believes, to make its case for the 'homosexual tendencies' of which it accuses Marie Von Hoffburg. No mention is made of the couple's contention that the relationship is now and will be heterosexual."[55] Although Judge Sawyer, who performed the marriage ceremony, ultimately agreed with the military that he believed the marriage to be invalid, the state did not take any action to nullify the marriage. What was done, in the state's eyes, appeared to be done. Only the military acted against Sode-Von Hoffburg's marriage, beginning with an end to her housing allowance.

While Sode-Von Hoffburg could not convince the WAC to retain her, she did avoid dishonorable discharge, a significant outcome for a case that hinged (for the military's part) on allegations of homosexual activity. At her court-martial, Sode-Von Hoffburg's commanding officer affirmed that she was an "above-average soldier who had not indicated any homosexual leanings on base." Dr. Paul Walker from the University of Texas-Galveston's Gender Identity Clinic also testified that Sode could not be engaged in homosexual behavior because von Hoffberg identified and lived as a man.[56] The army called their own witness, a medical officer who emphasized that von Hoffman's biology should determine his gender. The discharge board, which included two men and two women, asserted that Sode's marriage to Von Hoffburg evidenced her "'homosexual tendencies,' a trait that the army says, 'seriously impairs the discipline, good order morale and security of a military unit.'"[57] They ruled that even though Sode "relates to von Hoffburg as her male husband" and "von Hoffburg is a psychological female-to-male transsexual," von Hoffburg nonetheless was biologically female and therefore "a husband-wife relationship between 'biological females'" made Sode "unsuitable for retention."[58] Given that WAC officials brought homosexuality charges against her, Sode's honorable discharge is surprising. The case outcome suggests that the hearing panel could not determine exactly what to make of this situation; it appears to be one of the first instances of the army dealing with transgender individuals. That she was discharged suggests the panel found Sode-Von Hoffburg guilty of transgressing the military's moral code, marrying someone who was assigned female at birth but at the time of the marriage had transitioned to male. The fact that Sode-Von Hoffburg received an honorable discharge, which meant she could still obtain veterans' benefits, suggests that the panel either acknowledged her positive service record or at least partially agreed that her husband was more male than female.

Or, perhaps, the hearing panel was just confused about how to handle the case. Sode-Von Hoffburg, after all, had argued that she married a man. Marrying a man was exactly the sort of action the women's services endorsed. Sode-Von Hoffburg had a legal marriage certificate, and her husband identified as male. The part that seemed less clear was how to handle a valid marriage in which the groom had *formerly* been the same sex as the bride. While both partners claimed to be in a heterosexual relationship, at the heart of the matter the fact remained that theirs was also a nonreproductive relationship, as Sode-Von Hoffburg could not biologically become a mother through her sexual relationship with her spouse.[59] In this regard, then, it is perhaps easier to understand why the army treated Sode-Von Hoffburg's case as one of homosexuality. She may have gotten married as a normal woman would, but being married to an individual who was assigned female at birth and in the process of transitioning, certainly went against all the military's rules on marriage.

Just as pregnancy and motherhood made women physically unfit for military service, postwar military leaders classified lesbian servicewomen as morally unfit for duty. Thus, in their efforts to remove lesbians from the women's services, leaders of the armed forces hoped to send the message that only the "best" women could serve their country—that is, those who held to accepted moral standards based on heterosexuality as "normal" behavior. Military leaders used postwar regulations to enforce their vision of equality, maintaining its foundation in gender difference philosophy that relied on heterosexuality. Witch hunts and discharges of lesbian servicewomen played to the interests in controlling servicewomen and ensuring conformity. By treating homosexuality discharges administratively—usually bypassing the court-martial system in which women might be assured representation and due process—military officials created systems intended to shame women into silence and to hide the fact that the military had "undesirable" women in the ranks. Despite these efforts, during the Cold War women such as Corporal M.H., Fannie Mae Clackum, Grace Garner, Marie Sode-Von Hoffburg, and unknown others, fought sexual policies to negotiate, on their terms, what it meant to be one of "America's finest women" and a member of the military. Their successes were limited and primarily personal: none of these women managed to create larger change in the armed forces, nor was that their goal. Regardless, their efforts matter and illustrate the power a single voice may have when speaking up to right injustice.

Part III **Integration Is Not Enough**

Changes from Within and Without

7 Catalysts for Womanpower
The Defense Advisory Committee on Women in the Services

Nearly ten years after the Women's Armed Services Integration Act, in January 1958 Adelaide Kingman rose to speak to members of the Los Angeles Chapter of the Daughters of the American Revolution about women's military service. The wife of an admiral, Kingman knew a lot about the military, and that experience had led to a position on the Defense Advisory Committee on Women in the Services (DACOWITS). Beginning with a brief explanation about DACOWITS, Kingman proclaimed, "DACOWITS. A strange word! Like something out of Lewis Carroll, or, perhaps, a pre-historic monster."[1] Once the laughter subsided, Kingman explained that the committee of civilian women helped the DOD promote and improve women's military service roles, and went on to describe the career opportunities the military offered women. Kingman's speech provides an introduction into how the Cold War DOD marshaled civilian womanpower to expand it in the military, creating a group of advocates who pushed military leaders to rethink womanpower in key ways.

DACOWITS began in 1951, when Korean War personnel needs led military leaders to expand efforts to recruit women. Anna Rosenberg, the Assistant Secretary of Defense for Manpower and Personnel—the first woman to hold that position—saw that servicewomen needed advocates. The use of women to support defense planning, particularly as military or government advisory consultants, had been an important strategy to enlist women's support of national defense efforts during World War II. Agencies such as the Office of War Information, Office of Civilian Defense, and the War Manpower Commission, served as important training grounds for postwar female advisors like those in DACOWITS.[2] The goal in all these groups was to capitalize on women's long history of civic activism for government purposes.[3] Texas newspaper woman Oveta Culp Hobby became the first head of the Women's Interest Section of the War Department's Bureau of Public Relations in 1941 and created the Advisory Council of the Women's Interests, work that led to her wartime military service as the first director of the WAAC/WAC.[4] Mary Pillsbury Lord served on the National Civilian

Advisory Committee for the WAC during World War II and championed the 1948 Women's Armed Services Integration Act. Afer the war, government officials continued to enlist the support of women like Hobby and Lord. In 1950, Lord was asked to chair a conference for civilians at the Pentagon to help support the use of womanpower: the idea for DACOWITS developed there.[5] In retirement, Colonel Hobby became part of DACOWITS from 1951 to 1953, offering a unique blend of civilian and military expertise. By creating a group of women, a select group of mostly white career professionals and clubwomen, some married to prominent civilian or military men, Rosenberg established an organization of women whose voices could help legitimate women's service to the outside world. These women could use their understanding and experience of the civilian world, as well as their demonstrated ability to navigate ideal American womanhood, to help military leaders ensure women's service kept pace with changing attitudes and expectations about women's roles in society and the workplace.

DACOWITS is part of a larger narrative of opening federal government and policy-making roles to women. After World War II, women active in political organizations urged presidents to think about women appointees as they formed their administrations. For example, India Edwards, as Executive Director of the Democratic National Committee's Women's Division, pushed President Truman to include women appointees. She later became part of DACOWITS, bringing her experience and expertise to the question of womanpower. President Kennedy's administration, however, was the first to offer women more than a token role, as historian Cynthia Harrison explains, particularly with the creation of the President's Commission on the Status of Women (PCSW).[6] The PCSW, initially chaired by Eleanor Roosevelt, marked a significant moment in understanding women's position in U.S. society, politics, and economy, and helped initiate second-wave feminism, with many members becoming active in later groups such as the National Organization for Women (NOW). Significantly, DACOWITS rosters include women with federal appointments, like Oveta Culp Hobby, as well as women who served on the PCSW.[7]

DACOWITS evolved quickly into an advocacy group that suggested policy changes DOD officials did not always embrace. Rosenberg and her boss, Secretary of Defense George Marshall, hoped initially that DACOWITS members could bring the world of military opportunity into local communities, envisioning these women as the DOD's ambassadors to help the women's services improve their recruiting efforts. A committee of well-respected, influential business professionals and clubwomen from around the nation who endorsed women's national defense participation would bring an additional air of respectability to the idea of women in the military. Through publicity efforts within their own spheres of influence, DACOWITS members could help Americans understand women's military service as a reality of Cold War defense.

Although DACOWITS achieved its first success in recruiting efforts, in later years recruiting became just one of the organization's goals. In 1951, the DOD authorized the organization with three objectives: "to inform the public of the need for Women in the Services [sic] . . . to create further public acceptance of Women in the Services . . . to accelerate the recruitment of women, stressing both quality and quantity."[8] Three years later, however, a new directive stated that DACOWITS' purpose was "to provide the Department of Defense with assistance and advice on matters relating to women in the services," and assigned DACOWITS two key functions: help Americans understand why the military needed women, and advise the armed forces on anything related to women's service.[9] DACOWITS members quickly established internal groups that reflected this expanded charge to provide advisory services on a number of topics. In 1954, the new DACOWITS Operating Guide identified five subcommittees or "working groups": Training and Education; Housing, Welfare, and Recreation; Utilization and Career Planning; Health and Nutrition; and Recruiting and Public Information.[10] These groups and later ones demonstrate the seriousness with which DACOWITS members understood their purpose. Over the years, occasional restructuring in committees reflected, in part, changing ideas of what DACOWITS members saw as most important to servicewomen.[11] Members used their positions on the committee to propose policy changes that sometimes made male defense leaders uncomfortable, such as recommending draft registration for women, insisting on the removal of rank limitations, and fighting for servicewomen's rights to receive dependent benefits.

DACOWITS members believed their task of promoting women's military service required hands-on efforts to improve women's military opportunities and lives. In 1958, Kingman told southern California civic organizations that DACOWITS had four goals.

1. To advise the Department of Defense on policies relating to Women in the Services;
2. To recommend measures to bring about a more effective utilization of the capabilities of Women in the Services;

Catalysts for Womanpower   143

3. To recommend standards for the training, housing, health, recreation and general welfare of the Women in the Services;
4. To increase . . . the public acceptance of the concept of military service for women as a facet of good citizenship.[12]

Kingman's description demonstrates how members interpreted their role as an organization, describing a mission that expanded beyond the functions in the 1954 DOD directive. Nowhere did she mention that the organization provided recommendations *only* at the DOD's request. Rather, Kingman suggested that DACOWITS members believed that making recommendations was the organization's standing objective. DACOWITS records illustrate that the organization's members believed they could best advise the DOD by proactively and regularly suggesting ways to improve the role of womanpower in national defense. DACOWITS members interpreted this charge broadly, seeing a connection between improving standards in "training, housing, health, recreation, and general welfare" for servicewomen and promoting women's service.

Servicewomen helped DACOWITS members understand womanpower. High-ranking female officers served as executive secretaries and project coordinators for the organization, rotating in three-year terms and from different branches to ensure representation from across all components. The 1954 Operating Guide details the Executive Secretary and Project Coordinator roles, suggesting that these were full-time appointments for one tour of duty. The executive secretaries and project coordinators handled all administrative aspects of DACOWITS planning, liaising with members, planning the semiannual meetings and field trips, and interfacing with DOD officials. DACOWITS members visited military installations routinely to learn more about what it was like to be a woman in the military, speaking directly with select servicewomen at those locations.[13] Meeting reports and other documents suggest these trips played an important part in helping the civilian activists better understand what women's military service was. The women's components directors contributed their knowledge and expertise regularly to help support DACOWITS goals. They (or women from their staff) provided updates on their servicewomen at DACOWITS meetings, participated in panel discussions to answer member questions, and worked with the group to achieve the overall goal of assisting and advising the DOD on womanpower. In addition, it was not uncommon for DACOWITS members to call on local servicewomen in their efforts to promote women's military service, either by bringing servicewomen to speaking engagements, creating special events to highlight women in military service, or securing publicity opportunities with local and national media. Whether DACOWITS members encountered servicewomen on base or brought them into the community, servicewomen were indispensable to DACOWITS' efforts to understand women's military service, promote it, and find ways to improve military career opportunities for women.[14]

Servicewomen and DACOWITS remained the real experts on womanpower. Male military leaders, such as Rosenberg's successors, or the male chiefs of the various branches, or even the president, stepped in only occasionally, offering words of encouragement or information about issues the armed forces faced. DACOWITS members took what they learned from their fact-finding issues and regular meetings and used the information to determine policy priorities and ways to promote women's service. In the first two years, members focused on publicity, helping with recruiting campaigns like the development of a postage stamp featuring servicewomen. By 1955, committee members had expanded their interests to examining housing standards and trying new publicity methods such as taking college students to tour officer training sites.[15] By 1971, Director of the WAF and then-Brigadier General Jeanne Holm argued that DACOWITS' presence promoted cooperation, communication, and collaboration among the women's components in a time when most men in the military structure did not pay much attention to womanpower.

> I feel that if there was not a DACOWITS, and this is a very important thing I think, the Department of Defense probably would not really be as aware of the fact that we are around. As a matter of fact, the directors wouldn't get together so often to talk and exchange ideas if it weren't for the DACOWITS. You are a catalyst for us. You keep the Department of Defense on their toes and you keep us on our toes by your questions, by bringing these things out and examining them and calling attention to them.[16]

The women's services relied on DACOWITS to help them better understand themselves as organizations and to assess their place in the defense system. Because the majority of DACOWITS members were not in the military, they could look at womanpower differently than those inside the armed forces and ask new questions about what they saw. Even so, DACOWITS' efforts frequently demonstrated the difficulty of getting the DOD to pay attention. While the DOD might not always be as attentive as preferred, the leaders of the women's components recognized the significance of having a chorus of voices to help negotiate womanpower and were eager for DACOWITS' ideas and support.

These voices included women well known in their communities and, at times, nationally. The primary criterion for DACOWITS membership was "outstanding reputation in civic, business or professional fields."[17] Most members belonged to one or more prominent community or women's organizations. Because DACOWITS women were influential in their hometowns, they were well connected and could lend their presence and voices to recruiting efforts. These members offered a strong screen of legitimacy to protect servicewomen from negative stereotypes about women in uniform, such as those that had developed during World War II.[18] Additionally, DACOWITS members represented as many U.S. states as possible; since DACOWITS members should promote women's military service in their communities, geographic distribution ensured a firm reach into households nationwide. No matter where a recruit lived, she could likely find a DACOWITS woman nearby. And where a DACOWITS member was, there was usually a flurry of events each year to promote women's military service, from luncheons and fashion shows to parade or television spots.

Kingman described DACOWITS members as two types of women: career women and "civic leaders." "Professionally we might be classified as the feminine counterparts of the old nursery rhyme characters—doctor, lawyer, merchant, chief." During her tenure, she served alongside college deans and presidents, the Wisconsin Secretary of State, a physician, and magazine editors, among others. In contrast, Kingman classified herself as a "civic leader": "Others of us are used to being called housewives. For some reason this is a fighting word, so the Department of Defense sought to give us a label more flattering than the Registrar of Voters does. And thus, to everyone's surprise the prosaically-labeled housewife became overnight—guess what—a civic leader! Certainly a surprising butterfly to emerge from that dull cocoon, housewife."[19] The DOD saw both groups of women as vital to its goals. Professional women and civic leaders maintained connections with diverse organizations where DACOWITS members could reach important audiences. For example, Kingman brought six servicewomen with her for her interview at the Los Angeles Junior League Meeting on February 11, 1958, which enabled Junior League members to hear directly from servicewomen just what their careers were like.

Professional women's ties to business could help secure resources to promote servicewomen's image, such as magazine, television, or radio publicity opportunities. Typically, these efforts targeted young women and their families, but they would also reach other civilian community leaders: their goal was to make sure Americans understood the opportunities military service afforded young women. From 1959 to 1961, Evelyn Walker used her position as a television programmer and producer to create a weekly series on women in the military. Betsy Blackwell, editor of *Mademoiselle* magazine, publicized women in defense in some of her monthly editorial columns, but also included women in a fashion show in 1957. Women like Kingman with strong ties to civic groups could reach other similar women and convince them that military service offered excellent benefits to their daughters. To do this, members held events like military uniform fashion shows, scheduled television appearances, went on the radio, and spoke with young women and parents at local schools and organizations.[20] DACOWITS member Mrs. Jules Lederer—better known as advice columnist Ann Landers—used her newspaper column to promote women's military service. "I recommend the Armed Forces for the young woman who wants to see some new faces, get out of a rut, and at the same time serve her country."[21] Whether civic leaders or professional women, all DACOWITS members used their influence to promote womanpower. The extent of their messages' reach depended primarily on each DACOWITS members' own connections, but whether local or national, the publicity served an important function to help legitimize women's service.

The demographic profile of DACOWITS members remained consistent, with rosters through the 1970s continuing to reflect the somewhat elite nature of DACOWITS membership of women from upper-middle-class or upper-class backgrounds. Regardless of their political leanings or organizational affiliations, the trend was to recruit women who represented the sort of "high-quality" American woman that the armed forces hoped to attract: educated women who garnered respect for their actions. The first DACOWITS class in 1951 included high-profile women such as industrial engineer Dr. Lillian Gilbreth (of *Cheaper by the Dozen* fame), actress Helen Hayes, World War II WAC Director Oveta Culp Hobby, Mary Rockefeller, civil rights activist Dorothy Height, Democratic National Committee member India Edwards, and Mary Pillsbury Lord, who later succeeded Eleanor Roosevelt as U.S. Representative to the United Nations Human Rights Commission. Helen White, president of the American Association of University Women, Idaho Republican Party member Rose Mayes, and Lord and Taylor department store president Dorothy Shaver also counted themselves in the first membership. Other members included educators, leaders of the National Business and Professional Women's Clubs, veterans, and the directors of the World War II women's services. The Honorable Lorna Lockwood, Chief Justice of the Arizona Supreme Court, served in 1966. Journalist and White House correspondent Sarah McClendon, a World War II WAC veteran, participated from 1971 to 1973. Future U.S. Supreme Court justice Sandra Day O'Connor participated from 1976 to 1978.[22]

DACOWITS members were nearly always white, with one to two African American women serving at any time. Out of more than 400 members who served from 1951 to 1978, there were approximately a dozen Black members.[23] Dorothy Height, known for her work with the National Council for Negro Women and the YWCA, was the first African American woman on DACOWITS in 1951.[24] Zelma George replaced Height from 1955 to 1958 and later served as a goodwill ambassador and alternate U.S. delegate to the United Nations General Assembly in the early 1960s.[25] Dr. Jeanne Noble (first African American woman tenured at New York University in 1962), Rosa Gragg (National Association of Colored Women's Clubs president and prominent Detroit social activist), and Aminda Wilkins (Director of Community Relations, New York City Department of Welfare) served two-year rotations between 1960 to 1967. Neuroembryologist Dr. Geraldine Woods, who devoted much of her activism to expanding minority science education opportunities, participated on DACOWITS from 1966 to 1968 and chaired the organization in 1968.[26] From 1969 to 1971, Myrtle Ollison participated in DACOWITS while chairing the National Association of Colored Women's Clubs.[27] Additional Black members in the late 1960s and through the mid-1970s included Bernice Johnson, Mamie Reese, Dr. Vivien Davenport, Dr. Ethel Allen, Inez Kaiser, and 1976 DACOWITS chair Judith Turnbull.

During its first few decades of existence, the organization never focused on issues specifically relevant to minority servicewomen. In a 1955 article, George commented that she thought racial integration in the women's components was proceeding well but pointed out that recruiting continued to be a problem, because there were still few Black servicewomen. She also noted that continued segregation practices off-base made it difficult for Black servicewomen to pursue friendships in off-duty hours.[28] Dorothy Height later reflected that she "worked a lot on the racial situation and had any number of young women who were in the services who were discriminated against."[29] Although no formal records detail her work, she may have worked individually with Black servicewomen to learn more about their experiences, given her professional background. Having such a well-respected civilian activist pay attention to the experience of being a Black woman in the Cold War military would have offered these servicewomen the opportunity to feel their experiences were heard. The ability for Black servicewomen to interact with a Black member of DACOWITS mattered particularly in decades where Black women remained largely invisible in public images of womanpower.

Overall, little information about DACOWITS and race in women's recruitment and military service appears in meeting and activity reports. Instead, DACOWITS' attention to race remained in the hands of one to two women each year, limiting the extent of such focus and the organization's ability to help recruit and retain minority women. The December 1967 member activity report mentions that Dr. Geraldine Woods was instrumental in getting military representatives and the DACOWITS executive secretary to the National Convention of the Delta Sigma Theta Sorority to promote women's military service, but the report does not mention that this is a historically Black women's organization.[30] In 1970, Myrtle Ollison used her capacity as President of the National Association of Colored Women's Clubs to procure servicewomen and DACOWITS members to speak at the National Association of Colored Women's Clubs' 75th anniversary convention.[31] Despite these individual efforts, race was never a matter of issue in DACOWITS recommendations to the DOD. In general, it seems that DACOWITS members, being primarily white middle- and upper-class women, assumed that gendered barriers to women's service, rather than racial ones, were the most important issues.[32] Nevertheless, because DACOWITS had Black women members in the organization—even in small numbers—women like Woods and Ollison played an essential role in ensuring that young African American women could learn about the opportunities open to them in military careers.

Recruiting and public information occupied much of DACOWITS' early efforts. The November 1951 "Share Service for Freedom" campaign that developed from their initial recommendations sent materials to ten thousand newspapers nationwide and included a two-minute newsreel and ten-minute film feature. The DOD invested $170,000 in the campaign, but through partnerships with media associations and other nonprofit organizations, often leveraged through DACOWITS contacts, committee members estimated that the investment "netted time, space and materials conservatively estimated at between four and five million dollars." More importantly, the campaign netted women. "The tangible results can best be indicated in recruiting figures which show a total net increase in the number of women in the Armed Forces of almost 14 percent from 39,625 to 45,934—during the year."[33] While the response of women was smaller than anticipated, the numbers indicated

DACOWITS' success in publicizing womanpower.[34] DACOWITS noted that one of the most impressive increases was "the sharp upward trend in the monthly recruiting rate, the highest monthly input since World War II being attained in September 1952."[35] The belief that a group of influential women could promote womanpower paid off. The 1951 to 1952 successes garnered through DACOWITS' participation in the "Share Service for Freedom" campaign and related efforts in members' own communities demonstrated that there were benefits to drawing on accepted ideas of women's activism to gain support for women's changing roles as citizens and service members.

While military service offered women many opportunities, DACOWITS members began to argue very early that limitations placed on those benefits created obstacles to women's recruitment and retention. DACOWITS members and DACOWITS-created recruiting materials often highlighted the intangible benefits of military service, such as becoming better American women and citizens. But as DACOWITS representatives started to study and promote more tangible service benefits, such as career training, insurance, and living-quarters benefits, many DACOWITS women identified problems or contradictions within those benefits. As Vice-Chair Margaret Pendleton told the new 1968 DACOWITS members, the first DACOWITS members learned "recruiting's job is lessened when women are retained in service after their initial enlistment—that adequate housing, opportunities for education and advancement, a pay schedule which is realistic, a chance for duty overseas all contribute to retaining women."[36] If military leaders were serious about recruitment and retention, DACOWITS members realized, they would need to change existing provisions to women's service so that women could have the equality military service proposed to offer.

Questioning existing provisions to women's service effectively meant that DACOWITS began challenging the DOD and Congress's vision of womanpower. In 1956 DACOWITS first began to address what they saw as a major inequity: DACOWITS recommended allowing married servicewomen to live off-base and to receive basic allowance for quarters (BAQ) for spouses.[37] The 1948 integration act dictated that women could not claim any spousal benefits unless a woman could prove that her spouse was dependent on her for at least half his financial support. DACOWITS records suggest that the DOD remained silent on these issues, noting that in 1957 the group resubmitted the recommendations. Despite DACOWITS' efforts, the issue of BAQ for married women was not resolved until 1973.[38]

As early as 1963, the DACOWITS members also began suggesting that mothers could remain in service, presenting a study on the possibility of servicewomen having dependents while in service.[39] However, "only the Army Nurse Corps was in favor of having women on duty with minor children and then, only if the children were over 15. Accordingly, at this time, the study was dropped."[40] It does not appear that DACOWITS members pressed the issue further, but once again, pragmatism played an important role in how the group understood its functions. The prospect of allowing mothers to serve suggests that DACOWITS members saw pregnancy discharges as a problem for retention and were eager to find ways to alleviate that concern, even if it meant considering options that flew in the face of accepted social practices.

Throughout the 1950s, 1960s, and 1970s, DACOWITS members focused on housing standards, arguing that quality housing would offer an additional selling point for young women. In 1956, DACOWITS' first study of servicewomen's housing examined officer quarters and found that across the armed forces the status of women officers' housing exhibited "wide discrepancies . . . as to what is accepted as suitable or unsuitable." The military had no clear standards on how to determine what made officers' quarters "adequate for occupancy." In some places, civilians and women officers shared housing facilities, but paid different levels of rent. In the group's opinion, facilities that did not have private baths for senior officers or semiprivate baths for junior officers, cooking facilities on every floor, laundry in every building, and "sufficient closet space" did not qualify as quality housing.[41] Such housing recommendations were among DACOWITS' more successful proposals. By 1959, Assistant Secretary of Defense Charles Finucane directed the services to apply these recommended standards to all new construction of single-officer housing, while the DOD sent staff to Purdue University to study the use of prefabricated facilities for personnel housing.[42]

DACOWITS members also believed housing standards remained important to retention because women unhappy with their living arrangements might be more prone to decline reenlistment. Although surveys did not indicate that living conditions were a major factor in women's reenlistment decisions, living arrangements were certainly an important aspect of enlisted military service. In a 1952 survey, 21 percent of enlisted women "felt that living conditions could be a lot better . . . with one-third of them stating that living conditions could be improved considerably."[43] DACOWITS members understood that living conditions mattered because military service was more than a job: it was a comprehensive lifestyle. Living on base under military authority, close to work, and with other military members meant living conditions shaped a service member's military service experience dramatically.

One of the earliest major DACOWITS recommendations to expand women's opportunities and create a new path for recruitment came in 1952, when WAC Staff Advisor Harriet Moses suggested to Education Committee member Myrtle Austin that defense officials should open ROTC to high school and college women. Although the idea interested Austin, she voiced several concerns. "We are now encouraging college women to get a threefold education—an education which will prepare them for citizenship, for homemaking, and for the practice of a vocation, after marriage, if necessary. This vocational emphasis, we believe, is justified by present economic conditions. Women more and more are under the necessity of contributing to family income. Will it be difficult to persuade college girls to add to their programs preparation for another vocation, which must terminate (and rightly) when they have children?"[44] ROTC's primary goal at that time was to prepare an educated cadre of men to serve their country after college as an alternative to the draft. Because the government expected men to participate in the military in some fashion, ROTC did not conflict with social ideals of American manhood. However, ROTC participation could conflict with ideas of American womanhood—particularly motherhood—by adding an unnecessary burden to women's already full plate of social expectations. If women wanted to serve in the military, there were other routes available. Austin argued that ROTC would not be an effective way to recruit women who were already en route to other career and life goals. Thus, there seemed little point to pursuing a coeducational ROTC.

Yet three years later, the idea of women in ROTC gained enough acceptance to become a formal DACOWITS recommendation. At the 1955 DACOWITS meeting, the Professional Committee recommended "the exploration of the possibility of adapting the plan and policies in the ROTC training program for specialized personnel to meet the need of training women for the professional military services."[45] With its recommendation, DACOWITS members acknowledged that ROTC could offer useful benefits for both women and the military. In a shift from Austin's concerns, DACOWITS members believed that ROTC might be an effective way to recruit women at a young age. However, the recommendation did not move forward. Part of the problem lay in the fact that the air force independently pursued its own test of a coeducational ROTC program around the same time. As the newest of the service branches, the air force seemed most willing to experiment with women's roles and recruiting methods, which led them to open ROTC programs to women in a few colleges, but the Secretary of the Air Force deemed the program unsuccessful because of lack of interest and it lasted only briefly.[46]

Although recruiting, publicity, and practical matters remained important to DACOWITS every year, their vision of expanding women's roles in national defense involved testing boundaries and working to remove limitations regularly. The 1955 failed ROTC recommendation and the multiple attempts to permit married women to live off base and to collect dependent housing benefits demonstrate how DACOWITS members saw such issues as practical matters central to women's service. At the 1971 DACOWITS meeting, General Holm observed that the admission of women to ROTC programs in the air force had worked out very well. While this opening was not directly because of DACOWITS, Holm alluded to DACOWITS' early work on the matter in her speech, noting that "The results of women to this program has been exceptional. Moreover, the Commander of the air force ROTC has said that he thinks the retention of men in those universities where they have women in the ROTC program has been better. I think they're trying to tell us something . . . [and] it only took us 14 years to come to this observation."[47] By admitting women to ROTC, the military opened a new avenue through which to promote women's service by recruiting early in college, before many women started to marry—a consistent challenge, since only unmarried women could enlist. In addition, women's presence challenged men's conceptions of what it meant to be a service member. When placed alongside hardworking women, men pushed themselves, presumably to demonstrate their own excellence but perhaps also because they found the coed environment more enjoyable. More importantly, opening ROTC to women was a win for equal opportunity. As women moved into ROTC programs across the country, by the mid-1970s their foothold in such programs became an essential part of the arguments for admitting women to the military academies.

Year after year, the DOD responded selectively to the variety of recommendations DACOWITS members submitted. The DOD implemented ten out of fifteen recommendations in 1951, excluding recommendations such as the one that advocated a women's registration system. Perhaps unsurprisingly, DOD seemed to respond more positively to more minor or conservative recommendations. For example, in 1956 the DOD agreed to support a career incentive bill for nurses and medical specialists after DACOWITS' urging, as well as a bill to give military service credit to women who served in the World War II WAAC.[48] These recommendations were more benign than women's registration because they reinforced women's existing roles and the benefits of patriotism. In 1959, DACOWITS members had less luck with their recommendations: the DOD declined to support the (returning) recommendation that they propose legislation to allow BAQ benefits for married women. On the other hand, a recommendation for a quarterly DACOWITS member newsletter passed successfully.[49]

Even if the DOD did not always respond as desired, servicewomen continued to see DACOWITS as a key partner. Navy Captain Robin Quigley echoed Holm's belief in DACOWITS' importance as an advocacy body.

> I think the single most important continuing contribution is that you tell the story to people who will not listen to us. That's just human nature. It's the same thing that keeps kids from listening to mothers. Somebody else can come into the family circle and say exactly the same thing and it makes a lot of sense. So when we stand up and try to tell our story, very frequently we are not listened to because there is an immediate mental block of association. You all can reach countless of numbers of people that we can not [sic]. To my view this is something for which we are lastingly grateful and continuingly so.[50]

Although the DOD listened to DACOWITS members only sporadically, DACOWITS still had a strong voice. Quigley recognized that beyond the DOD, DACOWITS also reached many Americans, changing perceptions of what military service meant for women. This was often as important as trying to get the DOD to implement policy changes. Part of DACOWITS' stated mission was to promote women's military service to the American public. Even if the DOD made policy changes difficult, if DACOWITS continued to positively alter Americans' ideas of what military service meant for women, then the organization was a success. By the early 1970s Generals Mildred Bailey and Holm recognized the group for its "bulldog tenacity" and willingness to challenge the DOD on many issues to promote servicewomen's opportunities.[51] As it turned out, finding ways to help the military retain and utilize women effectively—the goals DACOWITS members saw themselves achieving—frequently meant devising solutions that also proposed expanding servicewomen's opportunities.

But as other voices brought attention to the status of American women in the 1960s and 1970s, critics began to charge DACOWITS for being too limited in their thinking and not doing enough to support servicewomen. In 1972, an article in *Family Magazine*, a military publication associated with the *Army/Navy/Air Force Times*, suggested that DACOWITS was a rather useless organization altogether. As part of a series on military women's progress, the article "DACOWITS: a nice little group that doesn't do very much" argued that the nature of using high-profile women as an advisory group meant that these women did not have the time to do that job properly. Author Margaret Eastman observed that thirty-one out of the fifty members made it to the 1970 meeting, and some members, like GOP national committee co-chair Anne Armstrong, were so busy with other responsibilities that they could not devote time to DACOWITS. Eastman quoted unnamed civilian media professionals covering the Pentagon, who told her, "I hope to tell you the truth about DACOWITS . . . because they don't do much at all." She also inquired into member promotional activities and noted there were no real efforts to track members' actions beyond the annual activity report. Eastman offered a negative assessment of DACOWITS, quoting journalist and DACOWITS member Sarah McClendon, who argued that the group needed to take more action.[52]

Considering the efforts DACOWITS members had undertaken in the previous two decades, the perceived decline in women's active participation in the organization became particularly problematic as many Americans began to rally for women's rights. To those outside the organization and some inside of it, it appeared that DACOWITS could no longer be counted on to provide a clear voice of leadership in matters related to womanpower. Eastman's article and McClendon's concerns over the group came at a crucial moment of transition for the military, just before the end of the draft and transition to the All-Volunteer Force and just as the Equal Rights Amendment (ERA) passed both houses of Congress. As the ERA went to the states for ratification, the anti-ERA coalition began its efforts to defeat the amendment. The issue of women and the military constituted one of its chief arguments against the ERA. Under the ERA, they argued, defense officials would draft women alongside men in future wars. Despite the end of the draft in 1973 and the fact that a future draft did not seem likely for many years—if ever—anti-ERA activists tapped into something that concerned many Americans intensely and brought servicewomen to the fore of many Americans' minds. In the process, DACOWITS attracted renewed attention and scrutiny for their role in shaping women's place in national defense.

DACOWITS meetings reflected this expanded interest in military women as civilians began to request access to the group. In October 1973, *Margaret*

Gates v. James R. Schlesinger challenged the closed nature of DACOWITS meetings and asserted that civilians outside the organization had their own interests in learning about DACOWITS and its activities.[53] A preliminary injunction opened the fall meeting to the public, but at the session, DACOWITS members affirmed their view that guests should be welcome, and nothing more happened with the suit as it no longer seemed necessary. Starting in 1974, representatives from the Women's Lobby, the ACLU, and most notably, NOW, began to present their own recommendations to DACOWITS on how to improve servicewomen's status. DACOWITS no longer had to act alone to advocate for servicewomen, but they also had to contend with a variety of opinions on how to fix things.

Although Eastman might have identified a real weakness in DACOWITS' strength as an advocacy body in 1972, the 1974 meeting notes demonstrate that DACOWITS members took their charge seriously. Organization members were all too aware of the problems the DOD had given them through the years and wanted the DOD to know that its current relationship with DACOWITS was not acceptable. DACOWITS members' critique of the DOD on its commitment to equal opportunity had good timing. The ERA had passed in Congress two years earlier and roles for women in the military were continuing to expand partially because of this change. That summer, a subcommittee of the House Armed Services Committee had considered admitting women to the academies, during which many members of Congress expressed their belief that restrictions against women serving in combat-related fields—particularly at sea or in the air—would soon need to be removed. The women of DACOWITS saw themselves as engaging in advocacy and activism and had done so for two decades. In that time, their voices had been a select few that had access to high-level military leaders. Now, a greater number of voices were speaking up and pushing military and government leaders to rethink women's military service in important new ways.

In addition, outside organizations' interest in DACOWITS suggested that the group had the opportunity to again expand its audience and effectiveness as they had done with President Kennedy's PCSW in the early 1960s. Although there is no evidence that DACOWITS ever partnered formally with feminist organizations in the 1970s, during that decade these organizations presented similar ideas to the recommendations DACOWITS made, particularly in areas of removing combat restrictions and admitting women to the service academies. Many times, it is difficult to tell who led in the efforts to create such change. NOW, for example, finally created their own internal

Committee for Women in the Military in early 1975. According to NOW member Pat Leeper, the group supported women's entrance to the service academies, addressed servicewomen's complaints, and worked to expand servicewomen's career opportunities.[54]

The added voices championing the concerns and needs of military women played an important part as the 1970s exploded in positive changes for servicewomen and servicewomen's numbers increased dramatically after the end of the Vietnam War and the transition to the All-Volunteer Force beginning in 1973. With more women in the military than ever before, in the 1970s DACOWITS' influence helped the military and the federal government move beyond many of their limitations to expand opportunities for women. DACOWITS members understood that ongoing changes to women's military status called not for an end to their committee's efforts, but for renewed commitment to understanding the new issues women faced as the military moved toward more effective utilization as well as equal opportunity. But the fact that DACOWITS pushed for these changes and played a key role in helping these changes occur illuminates how the military moved ever slowly toward equal opportunity for women. After twenty-five years of hard work, military personnel and DACOWITS members could look back on the organization's accomplishments and claim to other women's groups that they had done much to secure not just effective utilization, but also servicewomen's equal rights.

DACOWITS members continued to make annual recommendations faithfully to the DOD, despite the frequent reticence in the DOD's response or lack of response. They listened patiently to NOW and other interested parties who challenged their vision or claimed that DACOWITS was not doing all that it should. To many within the military administrative structure, however, DACOWITS had secured its reputation not only as an advocate for servicewomen, but more specifically an equal rights advocate. As military leaders anticipated changes that would come from the ERA, DACOWITS members supported such changes unwaveringly and, as in the issue of women in the service academies, prodded the DOD to revise its stance. Members continued in their efforts to convince the DOD that removing restrictions on women's service was truly the path toward effective utilization.

DACOWITS' role as a vital ambassador between the military and the civilian world, regardless of complaints, solidified the organization as a long-lasting advocate for womanpower. In a 1973 memo supporting DACOWITS' continued existence, General Bailey argued that "[DACOWITS] members evidence a strong interest in equal opportunity for women. If dissolved, the internal and external publics could perceive this as a lack of emphasis on equal opportunity by DOD or an attempt to obscure problems in this area."[55] Although some may have thought DACOWITS was out of step with mainstream ideas of equal rights, DACOWITS had helped to advance womanpower immensely in two and a half decades, leading efforts to improve servicewomen's reputations, remove rank limitations, and advocate for new opportunities. As Bailey recognized, they still had much to contribute. In 1971, Holm argued that "the day we are fully and totally integrated as full fledged members of the Armed Forces will be the day there will be . . . no need for a DACOWITS."[56] As long as formal policy continued to limit women's ability to participate in national defense, DACOWITS members would persist as women's advocates.[57]

8 Battling for Equality
Challenging Military Limitations

Changes to military regulations of women's service began from the inside, including servicewomen who sought legal relief for policies that constricted their careers, as well as women who protested policies in their day-to-day environment. The directors of the women's services also kept a close eye on matters through the years, suggesting changes of their own. The women of DACOWITS played an important part in making sure male military leaders were aware of and thinking about issues related to womanpower—whether or not DACOWITS' recommendations were taken. While DACOWITS members never questioned the overarching femininity framework that shaped women's military experiences, they consistently tried to improve women's military experience by recommending changes that expanded women's job opportunities and created a better military environment overall. Working closely with servicewomen and the directors of the women's components, DACOWITS members used their experience and influence to try to change the military's use of womanpower from within the system.

In addition to pregnancy, motherhood, and homosexuality discharges, one other crucial regulation limited women's careers in the 1948 Women's Armed Services Integration Act: rank ceilings. According to law, women could not hold a permanent rank above lieutenant colonel or commander, titles which fell approximately halfway up the promotion ladder. One woman in each of the women's services could hold the rank of colonel or captain while she served as the director of her component, but the title was temporary. Under this law, women would never advance to the "flag ranks," more commonly recognized by civilians with the title of "general" or "admiral." Some argued that this limitation would deter many women from military careers: even if military service came with better pay, benefits, and a wider range of job opportunities, promotion restrictions made it hard for military careers to compete with other opportunities young women might find.

Women interested in careers wanted opportunities, not restrictions, argued DACOWITS, the first vocal advocate for removing rank restrictions. In 1960, DACOWITS began to petition the DOD to remove rank ceilings.[1] It was a radical move for that time. The women's movement had not yet taken the prominent role it would achieve within a decade, which meant there were no outside pressures to remove rank restrictions, apart from DACOWITS. In 1960, the numbers of women approaching rank limits remained small, but projections indicated this would soon change, as the small numbers of women who began serving during World War II approached the twenty-year mark of their military careers. After all, it took years for officers to have enough time in service to even approach the ranks of colonel or captain. Additionally, Congress controls the size of the military through budgetary legislation, meaning that the number of officers across all branches at any time ties directly to finances. In wartime, budget changes can expand the officer pool, but in peacetime, this budget may contract and cause officer reductions. Because the military limited the number of officers, particularly those at the more senior grades of colonel/captain and above, opening higher ranks to women would limit promotion opportunities for men. In addition, moving above colonel or captain, officers enter the flag ranks, the highest ranks in the military forces, usually reserved for those with strong records of leadership—and historically, combat. Given these realities, the DOD did not respond favorably to DACOWITS' requests to remove rank limits.

But DACOWITS gained substantial outside support beginning in 1961, when the Committee on Federal Employment Policies and Practices, part of President Kennedy's bipartisan President's Commission on the Status of Women (PCSW) teamed with DACOWITS to study servicewomen's careers. Both Margaret Hickey, chair of the PCSW Committee on Federal Employment Policies and Practices, and committee member Dr. Esther Lloyd-Jones had served on DACOWITS in the 1950s, where they became well aware of issues surrounding military women's employment. Altogether, no fewer than seven PCSW members had past associations with DACOWITS, and two more PCSW members would join DACOWITS later in the 1960s. The Committee on Federal Employment Policies and Practices included three DACOWITS members: committee chair Hickey (DACOWITS 1955–58), Esther Lloyd-Jones (1951–54), and Dr. Jeanne Noble (1960–62), who brought with them nearly a decade of expertise on servicewomen's status and needs. Further, civil rights activist Dorothy Height (1951–54) participated on the PCSW Committee on Private Employment; Purdue University's Dean of Women Helen Schleman (1951–54) on the Committee on Education; and Rhode Island Associate Justice Florence Murray (1952–56) on the Committee on Civil and Political Rights. The Committee on Home and Community included both Elinor Guggenheimer, president of the National Committee for the Day Care of Children (1963-65) and future DACOWITS member Rosa Gragg, president of the National Association of Colored Women's Clubs (1964-66). Committee on Civil and Political Rights member Katherine Peden, past president of the National Business and Professional Women's Clubs, would serve on DACOWITS from 1966 to 1968.[2]

In the PCSW's Committee on Federal Employment Policies and Practices, the non-DACOWITS members quickly agreed with DACOWITS' recommendation to remove promotion ceilings for women officers. The groups argued that it not only made no sense to place such limitations on women, but it also limited the military's ability to recruit, retain, and utilize women effectively because women would see such restrictions as an obstacle to recognizing their full capabilities as professionals. The PCSW recommended "that separate statutory restrictions on the number of colonels/captains and lieutenant colonels/commanders in the women's components of the Armed Forces be eliminated."[3] The PCSW saw no practical reason why women should be limited to certain ranks and recommended eliminating rank ceilings so that servicewomen could compete for open rank promotions on the same basis as men. By removing promotional barriers, PCSW members argued, the military would come one step closer to creating an equal opportunity environment on the basis of sex.

DACOWITS and the PCSW's joint efforts, the first time DACOWITS partnered with another civilian women's group, demonstrate the relationship between military ideas of effective utilization and the growing importance of equal rights for women as a social ideal. Not only did the Committee on Federal Employment Policies and Practices include three DACOWITS members, but the group also heard from current servicewomen to learn more about their roles in the military. Committee members specifically thanked DACOWITS members in their final report of the Committee on Federal Employment Policies and Practices, signaling that the Committee members considered women's military service a significant part of their charge. For a full decade, DACOWITS had been servicewomen's lone advocate and the only organization with any real understanding of women's military roles. Since they reported to the DOD alone, this was the first time DACOWITS gained an ear outside of the defense structure. This partnership signifies the growing political interests in American women's changing roles as evidenced through the rise of women's organizations focused on women's rights beginning in the 1960s.[4] The overlap in membership between DACOWITS and the PCSW is less surprising when considering the emphasis on utilizing women activists for these political committees—the women who had the political and civic experience that made them "authorities" on women.

Working together, DACOWITS and the PCSW convinced the DOD that equal opportunity offered a real solution to using womanpower effectively. The PCSW specifically recommended removing restrictions on how many women could serve as colonels/captains and lieutenant colonels/commanders at any one time: according to the Women's Armed Services Integration Act, only 10 percent of female officers could be lieutenant colonels or commanders (the equivalent in the navy), and the navy had a 20 percent cap on women lieutenant commanders.[5] This was step one; it did not go as far as what DACOWITS sought, but was an improvement. By removing promotional barriers, PCSW members argued, the military would come closer to creating a true equal opportunity environment. The DOD listened and modified a bill draft in 1963 to remove the rank limitations.[6] The legislation failed to pass, in part because it was attached to an officer promotions bill that had been unsuccessful in Congress for more than a decade. Additionally, as of 1964, none of the branch leaders thought there was a need to promote the women directors, who served in the highest ranks open to women under existing law. While the navy supported ending rank limits, the air force disagreed, and the army dithered.[7]

Although DACOWITS and the PCSW had not managed to change the DOD's view on rank limitations, WAC Director Colonel Emily Gorman continued her efforts to create change. In 1963, she began by recommending an increase in the grade structure, which would have expanded the number of women at multiple levels, including colonels. The expansion was disapproved in early 1964, but the Commander of the Continental Army Command, General Hugh P. Harris, Jr., requested the ability to promote Lieutenant Colonel Elizabeth Hoisington to colonel, given her dual role as the commander of both the WAC Center and WAC School. The request was refused. In May of 1965, however, President Johnson expressed interest in promoting Lieutenant Colonel Mary Juanita D. Roberts, his executive secretary, a reservist on extended active duty. When the President bypassed the army to get Senate confirmation for Lt. Colonel Roberts's promotion, it looked like it might make it possible for Colonel Gorman to expand the number of colonels as she had long desired. Gorman requested an additional number of women colonels and began work to determine what their positions would be. In the process of making this change, however, the judge advocate general clarified that it was not possible to simply expand the number of women colonels or promote women to colonel as the president desired. The only way would be to pass a new law changing the Women's Armed Services Integration Act provisions.[8] Gorman, more determined than ever, engaged DACOWITS members to start a new campaign to remove rank limitations.

A year later, draft legislation was in front of members of Congress. Like the early versions of the Women's Armed Services Integration Act, this legislation stalled in late 1966 when Congress recessed, but in 1967 members of Congress finally began considering the issue of women's promotions. As they considered the legislation, DACOWITS members—past and present— teamed with women's groups from around the nation, wrote letters, garnered media interest, and lobbied members of Congress as individuals. Colonel Gorman, now retired (and stepped back in rank to lieutenant colonel, according to the law), continued her efforts of support, including writing bills, educating people about why the legislation was important, and gaining support from White House staff.[9] During the proceedings, all four directors of the women's services provided detailed testimony about women's military service, including Women Marines Director Colonel Barbara Bishop, Assistant Chief of Naval Personnel for Women Captain Rita Lenihan, WAC Director Colonel Elizabeth Hoisington, and WAF Director Colonel Jeanne Holm.[10] The directors provided information on women in the ranks, including numbers, enlistment and reenlistment figures, jobs performed, and a variety of other details to help members of Congress understand why the time had come to remove the artificial rank limitations put in place nearly two decades earlier.[11] The hearings for H.R. 5894, legislation focused on removing rank limitations, became the first sustained examination of womanpower since the early 1950s.

In November 1967, President Johnson signed the first law to eliminate gender difference as a basis of defining women's military service, Public Law 90–130 (PL90–130). The legislation established the largest changes in women's military status since the Women's Armed Services Integration Act of 1948, eliminating both percent limitations on women officers, as well as the 2 percent cap on total womanpower in the armed forces. The law allowed women officers to be promoted to any rank, including general or admiral. PL90–130 also helped remove inequities in men and women's retirement regulations and enabled women to enter the Air National Guard for the first time.[12] Surrounded by servicewomen in their dress uniforms as he signed the bill, President Johnson made a direct link between the new law and advancement toward equality for women. He described the legislation as "another blow for women's rights. At long last we are going to give the dedicated women of our Armed Forces the equal treatment and the equal opportunity that they should have had from the very beginning."[13] It was a bold statement, especially considering that pregnant servicewomen and lesbians were still being discharged regularly on account of sex.

At the same time, government officials were paying more attention to women as workers. The 1964 Civil Rights Act, for example, barred discrimination on the basis of sex, even though the inclusion of sex was done at the last minute and initially as a way to stop the bill's passage. According to historian Cynthia Harrison, neither Representative Howard Smith (D-VA) nor members of the National Woman's Party wanted to see the Civil Rights Act pass at all and believed that including sex in the act would make it less likely to pass, or if it did, would at least help protect white women's rights and not just black men's. Harrison explains that the PCSW members also wanted to see separate efforts to attack racial and sexual discrimination because the women of the PCSW largely wanted to preserve protective labor legislation that favored women.[14] Yet because sex was included in the 1964 Civil Rights Act, the new Equal Employment Opportunity Commission (EEOC) created as part of that legislation almost immediately began receiving (and ignoring) complaints about sex discrimination in the workplace. By 1967, President Johnson had already experienced firsthand how government regulations limited servicewomen on his own staff, and he was also pursuing executive actions to eliminate sex discrimination in federal hiring. Just a month before he signed Public Law 90–130, President Johnson also signed Executive Order 11375, which affirmed equal opportunity practices in the federal government and with federal contractors. It laid out requirements for contractors to take affirmative action in their hiring practices and also specified how complaints to the federal government would be handled.[15] PL 90–130 was part of larger trends toward ensuring equal opportunity on the basis of sex in the federal government, one that would no longer rely on protective labor laws grounded in gender.

Whether PL 90–130 offered women "equal treatment and . . . equal opportunity" was a matter of debate. Despite President Johnson's view, military lawyer Lieutenant John Wolf noted that the new law was not intended to "effect complete equality between men and women in military careers . . . This is not to say that PL 90–130 has not given to women officers equality of opportunity to the maximum extent possible in today's setting."[16] In contrast to President Johnson, Wolf argued that there was still much work to be done before servicewomen would be totally equal with men. Moreover, in her history of women's military service, Jeanne Holm emphasizes that the law still left disparities across the branches, since the army and air force could promote women as they wished, but the navy and marine corps could only promote women to rear admiral lower half (a one-star rank) and brigadier general. President Johnson was correct that the legislation was "another blow for women's rights," but he overlooked, or was unaware of, ongoing policies and utilization practices based on the idea that accounting for gender difference was the way to ensure equality between the sexes. In Holm's final analysis, although PL90–130 was "a sign of the times," she also emphasized that "the essentially masculine character of the military profession and the unequal status of women within it were never challenged." As the 1960s drew to a close, pregnancy, homosexuality discharges, and women's exclusion from combat and combat support roles perpetuated this status. Although more jobs were opening to women, many remained entirely closed because servicewomen were not men.[17]

The struggle to remove rank limitations, fought for nearly a decade by high-ranking servicewomen and their civilian allies in DACOWITS and the PCSW, reflects how womanpower was changing alongside new military needs and changes in American women's lives and careers. Two decades earlier, "equality" had meant allowing women to serve permanently alongside men, and ensuring equal pay based on rank. But "equality" had also meant recognizing that women were biologically different from men, and that this meant women should not fight and mothers should not serve. In their efforts to eliminate rank limitations for servicewomen, members of DACOWITS, the PCSW, and the directors of the women's service components all worked together to create a new idea of what equality should mean for women in national defense. Although this was not their intention, their work was invaluable in expanding opportunities for women to serve their country and develop their careers in national defense.

As changes compounded and as this new idea of equality became the foundation of women's military service through new laws like PL90–130, the directors of the women's services believed they had the best sense of how to continue to achieve positive change for military women. Each of the directors had more than two decades of military service by the late 1960s, and most had been in the armed forces since World War II. They believed that they, better than anyone, understood the military, its role in American society, the status of women in the services, and how to achieve positive change for military women. These women fought for change when most male military leaders were content to ignore their voices and their allies, not seeing a reason to disrupt the status quo. Yet the directors' definitions of equality for women in national defense sometimes made these high-ranking military women seem out of touch with the most current views on women's place as citizens, which evolved rapidly in the late 1960s and early 1970s. Consequently, the ten directors of the women's components who served between 1965 and 1978 tended to appear more conservative than women active in the burgeoning feminist movement. These leaders included Elizabeth Hoisington, Mary Clarke, and Mildred Bailey from the WAC; Jeanne Holm, Bianca Trimeloni, and Billie Bobbitt from the WAF; Margaret Brewer and Jeannette Sustad from the Women Marines; and Rita Lenihan and Robin Quigley from the navy. The amount of detail available regarding their stances on women's equality or the women's movement varies: many spoke frequently with the press and publicized their views, and several also conducted oral history interviews during their retirement. Others—particularly Bianca Trimeloni and Billie Bobbitt—are practically mysteries.

The women directors' emphasis on securing male acceptance of women in defense highlighted their beliefs that quick, radical change to women's status primarily through eliminating regulations would not foster positive long-term change. The directors drew from their own experiences when they argued that small, purposeful change would be the best way to advance womanpower. At the same time, the women's service directors also often outranked their predecessors in those positions and ardently supported the military's efforts to expand women's service opportunities.[18] Captain Robin Quigley and Brigadier General Mary Clarke, the last women to hold the director-level positions in the navy and WAC, each insisted that the military had always been about women's equality, as many of their counterparts also claimed during their time in office. According to Quigley, "since the WAVES were first established [in 1942], there have been no navy jobs relegated solely to women, except in limited areas of training and administration. The WAVE has always served equally alongside her male counterpart in many different job classifications."[19] Quigley consistently told the press that the navy and the military were ahead of much of American society in "women's liberation" issues, like equal pay.

What separated the women's directors from mainstream feminists was an insistence on defining equality on the basis of sex difference. Brigadier General Mildred Bailey (Director of the WAC 1971–75) cautioned that it was

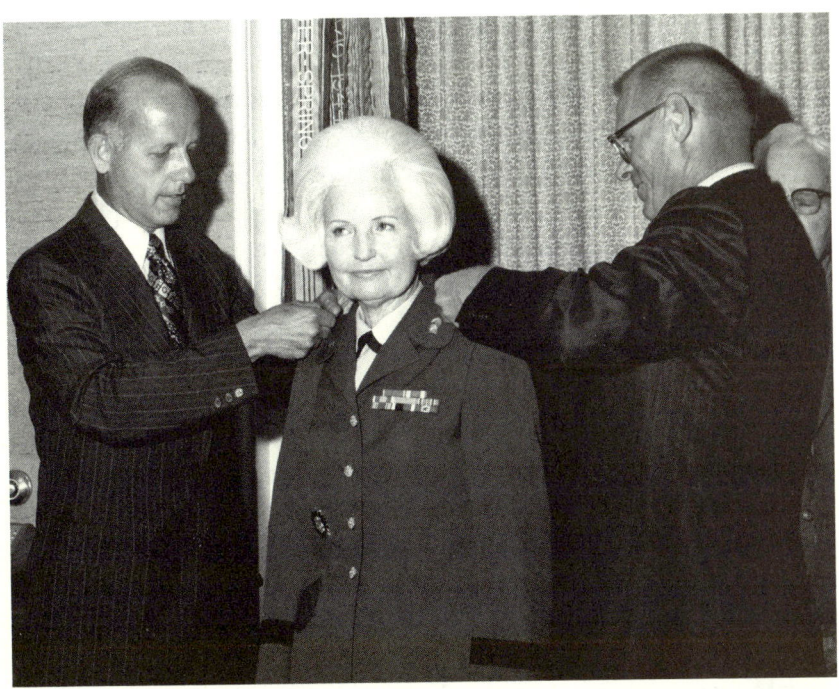

FIGURE 8.1 Brigadier General Mildred Bailey receives her stars at her promotion ceremony at the Pentagon in August 1971. Bailey served as Director of the Women's Army Corps from 1971–75. In the 1960s, Bailey was instrumental in efforts to expand recruitment of women. Photo by Frederick Hinshaw, U.S. Army Photographic Agency, Washington, D.C.

problematic to define equality as sameness (figure 8.1). "In my opinion, we get into trouble when we go on the assumption that equality means sameness. I do not feel that equal means same. I believe that we can be equal in opportunity, equal in acceptance and be different."[20] In addition, Bailey argued that accepting difference and working with it was the key to achieving equality. "True equality between groups that are different in any way can be attained only by providing for those differences. To deny or attempt to overlook such differences simply confuses the issue and creates unnecessary problems."[21] From Bailey's perspective, the military simply could not remove sex-based regulations and claim that the change offered women equality. For her, equality went deeper: achieving equality meant recognizing, respecting, and accommodating essential differences between groups. As Bailey wrote in her 1973 memo about continuing DACOWITS, "We must recognize that women can be integrated into the Armed Forces, but they

Battling for Equality 167

cannot be submerged into the whole with a subsequent loss of identity. Culturally, physically, and psychologically they are different and perceive the need for women to speak for them."[22] Her experiences with the armed forces over nearly three decades had affirmed for her that women's voices mattered in securing change and battling for equality. What she did not yet seem to acknowledge, however, was that so many of the limitations placed on women—in and outside of the military—came from assumptions about women's differences from men and how those differences affected their abilities to perform work functions.

Captain Rita Lenihan (Assistant Chief of Naval Personnel for Women 1966–70) argued that different policies for men and women were not about inequity, but recognition of men's and women's differences and different needs. "Differences," Lenihan wrote, "are not necessarily inequities."[23] But in the 1960s, this belief was increasingly called into question, and the fight over PL90–130 itself challenged this assumption. However, Colonel Jeanette Sustad (Director of the Women Marines 1969–73) also believed there were good reasons for the differences between the regulations guiding men's and women's service. According to Sustad, the military offered men and women "equal opportunities in jobs and training. Although most regulations apply equally to men and women . . . there are some differences. Most of these differences in regulations are for bona-fide reasons and cannot or should not be changed."[24] Although Sustad did not explain which differences "cannot or should not be changed," she clearly argued that such regulations were important for women's roles in national defense. Simultaneously, she suggested that changing opinions on women in American society might justify modifying some regulations. This was the issue the women's services—and the military as a whole—were beginning to face in the late 1960s.

General Elizabeth Hoisington (Director of the WAC 1966–71) thought that limits placed on servicewomen played an important role in supporting women's military integration after World War II.[25] Despite restrictions like promotion limits, Hoisington felt firmly that during her nearly three decades of military service, "I never felt I was anything but equal . . . never once in my 29 years did I feel I was being picked on or not allowed to go as fast as I could go."[26] Although Hoisington did not comment directly on whether or not the military should retain different regulations for men or women, she believed that the separate administrative structures for women, such as the WAC, were valuable and had been important to her career development (figure 8.2).[27] In the early 1970s, however, new views on gender-based differences led to even greater shifts in the military structure, and the exis-

FIGURE 8.2 Portrait of General Elizabeth Hoisington, the second woman general in the U.S. military and Director of the Women's Army Corps, 1966–71. National Archives, College Park, Maryland.

tence of the women's service directors came into question. Robin Quigley led the way in 1972 to dissolve the position of the Assistant Chief of Naval Personnel for Women, but WAC and WM leaders were much more hesitant about eliminating the administrative structures for women in their branches.

Leaders like Quigley and Hoisington argued that servicewomen had always been equal, even in spite of utilization and service limitations. Since the 1940s, the military had guaranteed women equal pay, and although women still worked primarily in female-dominated jobs by the early 1970s, the female directors felt they were living examples of the unique opportunities available to women in the armed forces. Moreover, these women had no interest in letting the rising women's movement alone take credit for the advances they and thousands of servicewomen, not to mention the women of DACOWITS, had fought for over more than two decades. In 1970, Captain Lenihan noted that the DOD had created a task force to evaluate "all differences which exist in laws, policies and directives pertaining to men and women," yet asserted that some perceived inequities, including the fact that the military held women to higher educational standards, the higher cost of women's uniforms, and different policies about men's and women's custody of children, "are differences, rather than inequities, which grow out of economic realities (e.g., uniform costs) and policies and practices which are essential to the efficient and effective management of a high quality and highly successful volunteer program for women."[28] Female military leaders believed firmly that their very presence—and persistence—in an all-male institution played an important role in changing the military. In their opinion, the military would not even be expanding women's roles if servicewomen had not proved themselves to be dependable, useful members of the military during two wars and peacetime.[29]

While some women may have chafed at the difference in standards, Hoisington's oral history suggests that some individuals did not view those standards as a problem. Yet even those directors who believed that limitations had their place also acknowledged that recent social changes meant that the military no longer needed to limit women in the same ways. The problem was to find consensus on those changes, which was not always easy. Major General Jeanne Holm (Director of the WAF 1965–73) reflected that during her time as director, her counterparts in the other services did not always share the same opinions of how to advance women's status (figure 8.3). "Sometimes we agreed, sometimes we didn't. But on policy issues, I decided to plow my own course."[30] These differences occasionally led to confrontations between Holm and her counterparts, such as on the matter of whether mothers should be allowed to remain in service. Such conflict indicates that not all women in the armed services believed some of the directors' assumptions that women's differences set them apart from men and should be regulated accordingly. Holm, significantly, worked to rethink such assumptions and how they affected women's military careers. By the time she retired in the mid-1970s, Holm's accomplishments included helping the air force work toward removing pregnancy discharge and securing dependent benefits for married servicewomen: in 1948, everyone involved in the Women's Armed Services Integration Act had assumed mothers could not be in the military, and that husbands would always be breadwinners and should not be defined as dependents. Twenty-five years later, those assumptions no longer held.

When the women's directors talked about equality for women, they were really talking about how to achieve full acceptance for women in national

FIGURE 8.3 Portrait of Major General Jeanne Holm, who served in the Women's Army Corps during World War II and joined the air force when it was created. Holm served as the Director of Women in the Air Force from 1965 to 1973 and became the first two-star female general. United States Air Force, circa 1973.

defense. Thus, they could claim that women were equal even in the face of regulations that seemed increasingly inequitable in the context of second wave feminism. Whether they used "equality" or "integration," to discuss the status of women in national defense, female military leaders were actually expressing their concerns over how men in the military responded to women in national defense. For female military leaders, servicewomen's equality in national defense hinged on whether servicemen and male military leaders fully accepted servicewomen. By the early 1970s, some of the female directors believed in the need for acceptance so much that they doubted the need for changes the women's movement proposed. In 1972, General Hoisington commented that "we have struggled for 28½ years to get people to accept women in service, and we've been accepted so well, been utilized so well that you're beating a dead horse."[31] In her opinion, the military already had a firm handle on how to achieve women's equality, and servicewomen had been steadily working toward that goal for years. She, and some of her counterparts (but not all) did not understand that the definition of "equality" was shifting, and the women's services had played an important role in creating that shift.

Given their beliefs, the women's directors feared external change and believed that the best route to women's equality lay in internal military changes. They wanted to see the military proactively make changes to improve women's status. In 1972, the military publication *Family* magazine interviewed servicewomen and the leaders of the women's components regarding changes for women in the military. In the preface to the interviews, the magazine's editors noted "all would prefer to see policy changes that improve the status of servicewomen come from within the military system, rather than see an activist in uniform force a change in the system from the outside, such as by a lawsuit."[32] These leaders saw internal change as an important component to integrating women more fully; that is, to help women achieve complete acceptance from military men. In the process, female leaders believed, integration and acceptance would pave the way for women's equality.

The female directors believed that internal change was the key to changing male attitudes about women's military roles, targeting men's personal experiences working with servicewomen. Reflecting on her own experiences, final Director of the WAC Major General Mary Clarke argued that "attitude is a big stumbling block. Majority of men think army is [a] man's world . . . you don't change overnight, legislate. But when it [change] starts from the top down and they say this is going to work [in] our army, they've got great things to contribute. You'd be surprised to how quickly attitudes change."[33] Clarke also believed that changing attitudes was important to helping servicewomen gain equality. In an interview in 1976, Clarke observed that women were not yet perceived as equals to men in the military, despite Hoisington's earlier views to the contrary. "We have a long way to go and the biggest obstacle is to overcome attitude," she said.[34] The female leaders recognized that external change might help remove regulations, but it might be perceived as women pushing their way further into the military, beyond accepted social roles. This would not help with men's perception of women's defense roles; it might cause more problems. Quigley asserted, "The only problem a woman in the military finds is attitudinal, and you can't legislate attitudes. What a woman can do is make a man respect her as a person in her own right."[35] For these women, earning men's respect had been key to their military experiences. They served and led in a time when the fight to recognize sex discrimination in the workplace was just beginning. In their efforts to remove rank limitations, the directors of the women's services had themselves participated in that effort, but they did not yet define their experiences in the context of discrimination, as other women were starting to do.

Removing sex-based regulations certainly had a place, but this was only part of the equation. In a 1975 article in *Commander's Digest*, General Bailey called the removal of sex-based rules and regulations just the "first step." In her opinion, "the greatest hurdle to overcome involves the changing of attitudes—the attitudes of women about themselves and the attitudes of those men who resist the fuller utilization of women. This is the job which lies ahead."[36] The female military leaders understood it would take far more than simply eliminating legal barriers to achieve equality for women. Although new social pressures over women's changing roles would help make it possible to remove legal barriers in the 1970s, these actions did not change the opinions of those who believed that women did not belong in every realm of national defense, such as combat. There was still a lot of work to do.

Combat, in particular, became an area in the 1970s where DACOWITS' recommendations ran contrary to the DOD's expressed interests, and perhaps contradicted the women directors' views on change. In 1975, DACOWITS members expressed their first position on women in combat, recommending that the DOD pursue efforts to repeal Title 10, Section 6015, which prohibited naval women from serving on ships or in aircraft tasked with combat missions. The recommendation came from the utilization subcommittee, an outgrowth of the group's fall 1974 recommendation that military leaders admit women to the service academies. Subcommittee member Judge Sandra Day O'Connor expressed her dissatisfaction with the reasons the DOD had given DACOWITS about why women could not be admitted to the academies, which linked back to combat. DACOWITS' support for women in the academies stemmed from members' belief that "the academies exist for the purpose and training of leaders," while the information given to the committee argued that the academies existed to "train officers for combat duty."[37] If DOD leaders were going to invoke combat for the reasons why women could not serve in the academies, DACOWITS members decided that it was time to press the DOD on just what "combat" entailed. O'Connor suggested that the subcommittee recommend that the DOD "focus attention on an analysis of 'What is combat?'" The matter of Section 6015 came up in the discussion that followed, and meeting minutes suggest that DACOWITS members' thinking on the Equal Rights Amendment (ERA) inspired them to propose the removal of these sex-based restrictions.[38] If the ERA passed, laws like Section 6015 that applied only to one sex would be invalid.

The combined emphasis on women's access to the academies, the request for a definition of combat, and the call to remove Section 6015 all indicate that the DACOWITS utilization subcommittee members were particularly concerned with how sex-based restrictions affected women's utilization. These DACOWITS members called on the DOD to further scrutinize these remaining restrictions on women, requesting justification for why women continued to face such legal limits. While Congress began pursuing this same goal that year, DACOWITS members learned in late 1975 that DOD vehemently opposed the legislation.[39] Once again, DACOWITS' efforts would not lead to the necessary change. However, DACOWITS' identification of the need to remove remaining legal limits on womanpower reflected its history of pushing the envelope. More significantly, DACOWITS' efforts illustrate that advocates of womanpower were beginning to think about women's function: if combat is key to national defense and access to combat gives service members specific privileges—recognition, rank, financial benefits—then women's exclusion from that arena of military service would only make inequality persist.

As the question of combat began to peek out repeatedly in the 1970s, the women's directors remained cautious in their views on the subject, framing their opinions in the context of military need and expanding their definition of equality to include the idea of women's capabilities. Only then, they suggested, could women and combat even remotely be a palatable change. As early as 1972, General Bailey mentioned that "she might be in favor of women in combat . . . if specific needs for them arise."[40] Testifying to the House Armed Services Committee in 1979, retired Major General Holm argued that the expansion of women's roles had begun because the military needed "quality volunteers." This need, "beginning as early as 1967, forced the services to abandon outdated, unnecessarily restrictive personnel policies and was an even more compelling reason than the pressures for sexual equality."[41] In Holm's view, military need outweighed all other considerations. While Holm did not necessarily advocate women in combat—she was particularly concerned about women in ground combat—she agreed that one day the nation might need to call on women to literally join the fight. When that happens, she argued, "The service secretaries should not be hamstrung in peacetime by laws they may not be able to live with in wartime."[42] The bottom line was that it was to the military's benefit to stop viewing women as a personnel resource defined primarily by sex.[43] While some of the directors would, in their retirement years, advocate their own personal beliefs that women should not serve at sea or in combat, in general most maintained the stance that the military should utilize women to the best of their capabilities, recognizing them as individuals first and women second. This greatly reversed the initial policies on womanpower in the 1940s, 1950s, and early 1960s, which had emphasized women's status as *women* above all else.

While the women directors left very clear opinions on how they viewed changes to women's service in the 1960s and 1970s, it is not always as clear how servicewomen responded to the women's movement growing in that period. Periodically throughout the 1970s, military and non-military publications explored "women's lib" in relation to servicewomen, asking servicewomen their thoughts about the women's movement. However, even in personal reflections of their military careers, servicewomen could be hesitant in identifying as feminists.[44] The 1972 *Family* magazine three-part series on women in the military opened with the observation that "an organized women's liberation movement hasn't reached the Armed Forces," but nonetheless, women in the military "have taken the ideals of the movement seriously. They are speaking up and, in a few cases, even fighting. Their objective: to change those policies and programs which unnecessarily treat women differently from men."[45] None of this was new; after all, Alba Martinelli Thompson's son turned twenty-one that year. Perhaps American civilian women were starting to see limits servicewomen had been fighting for years. By 1976, Major General Holm announced just that, telling an audience at the White House that women in the military "were pioneering the women's movement long before many of those who have been pushing for women's rights in recent years ever realized they didn't have them . . . we have fought the battle for equality and have it almost won."[46]

Unlike the women's leaders, who saw higher educational standards as an important means to ensure the military only enlisted or commissioned "quality" women, younger women coming through the ranks viewed such regulations as pointless and discriminatory. In contrast to the women's leaders, who saw many of the sex-based qualification differences as important to establishing acceptance for women in the military, the servicewomen interviewed for the 1972 *Family* article complained about such differences. "Aside from complaints about how their male bosses treat them, and their jobs and places of assignment, servicewomen complain about higher standards for female applicants and differences in treatment of married male and female personnel."[47] Even if many servicewomen did not participate in the women's movement or define themselves as feminists, they nonetheless shared many of the movement's ideas that women should be treated equally with men when it came to such policies. In response, the directors might have said that they lacked a sense of history to better understand why such gender-based differences had been seen as so important.

In 1973, the Supreme Court overruled twenty-five years of inequity in gender-based regulations when it ruled that the military could not deny dependent benefits to servicewomen. When WAF officer Sharron Frontiero married a male veteran and full-time college student in 1969, she soon discovered servicewomen were not entitled to either a living allowance or medical benefits for spouses. After filing a formal complaint, she initiated her suit in the district court in December 1970. Although initially unsuccessful, Frontiero appealed and the case made its way to the Supreme Court, where the ACLU's Women's Rights Project and its attorney cofounder Ruth Bader Ginsberg—in her first appearance at the Supreme Court—argued that denying dependent benefits to servicewomen constituted sex discrimination and denied women due process. In May 1973, the Supreme Court ruled for Frontiero, and in July the law officially changed to allow servicewomen equal access to dependent benefits.[48]

Sharron Frontiero's claim came alongside two decades of DACOWITS members' work to convince the DOD that married servicewomen deserved the right to dependent benefits, although the case had no direct relationship to DACOWITS. While servicemen could claim wives as dependents, even if the wife worked or had money of her own, servicewomen could claim husbands as dependents only if they were severely handicapped and unable to provide for themselves—at least, that was the intention. If a woman could demonstrate that her husband was dependent on her for more than 50 percent of his support, then she could secure dependent benefits. After all, women were not the primary breadwinners in the home—men were, or so most Americans assumed.[49] In 1968, Captain Rita Lenihan argued that it was inappropriate to classify civilian men as dependents because "the mores of our country traditionally consider the woman as a dependent and that men neither need nor desire the designation of dependent for themselves."[50] Consequently, a full year before Frontiero's first application for dependent benefits, DOD officials declined to support the first legislation that would have allowed her to claim her husband, noting that current regulations reflected existing social standards regarding men's and women's roles. Men deserved their pride, masculinity, independence, and breadwinner status: allowing women to claim a husband as dependent, in this view, unmanned her spouse by robbing him of his ability to care for her.

But members of Congress also thought about Frontiero's argument for women's access to dependent benefits even as her case made its way through the courts. In late 1970, the DOD's general counsel expressed to the House Armed Services Committee that legislation authorizing such a change was "consistent with enlightened social attitudes in regard to employment of female personnel and accordingly the Department of Defense favors enactment of legislation."[51] The "enlightened social attitudes" recognized the growing support for women's rights in the United States through second-wave feminist organizations like NOW. Although the DOD finally came out in support of the legislation, it was insufficient: members of Congress made no changes in women's ability to claim dependents that year. The all-male justices of the Supreme Court took the matter into their own hands and ruled that married servicewomen should receive the dependent benefits denied to them for twenty-five years.

The Supreme Court held that the prohibition against allowing married women to receive dependent benefits violated the Fifth Amendment's due process clause. "It is unconstitutional to differentiate in the treatment of a female member with regard to the criteria to be met in order for her civilian husband to be entitled to the basic allowance for quarters (or BAQ) and to medical care as her dependent."[52] Eleven days after the ruling, the military modified the pay manual appropriately and notified all military departments that women no longer had to prove their civilian husbands' dependency to obtain benefits. Going forward, the issue of housing and spouse benefits would follow uniform standards—those set for servicemen. Moreover, according to General Bailey, the armed forces also contacted all retired servicewomen who had been denied dependent benefits: although her husband had passed away in the mid-1960s, she applied for and received the benefits due to her.[53]

Frontiero v. Richardson was a major milestone: the highest court in the nation invalidated a key long-standing policy, and in so doing reflected a new national concern for equal rights on the basis of sex. Sharron Frontiero was not the first to discover that servicewomen could only obtain dependent benefits for individuals dependent on them for at least 50 percent of their support, but she was the first to challenge this policy successfully. At least two navy women before Frontiero had filed in claims court for dependent benefits for their spouses, but neither won. In 1966, Katherine Huber filed in claims court to obtain dependent benefits, on the grounds that the housing the navy granted her—"bachelor quarters"—was inadequate. In 1968, Sharon Lieblich unsuccessfully filed a claim for dependent benefits, alleging that her spouse was dependent on her for half his support while he studied for the bar exam.[54] What made a difference for Frontiero was that three forces outside of the military were starting to reshape the national climate in which the Supreme Court heard her case. By 1973, the draft was ending, a national women's movement was becoming increasingly influential, and the ERA was moving toward state-by-state ratification. Not only did these three elements help Frontiero achieve success in her suit, but they also helped make the 1970s a decade of major change for women within the military altogether.

Despite the women directors' efforts to distance themselves from the women's liberation movement, they could not maintain their separation for long. The interest servicewomen expressed in the movement's principles, the popularity of the movement, and the drive toward the ERA increasingly brought servicewomen closer to the women's movement. As the ERA became the central fight over women's rights in the United States during the 1970s, women in the military took center stage in national debates over women's legal status and opportunities. By the end of the decade, external changes rather than internal changes would reconfigure how the military utilized its womanpower.

9 Reimagining Equality

The end of the draft, the women's movement, and the Equal Rights Amendment created a space in which government and military leaders began imagining new ways to utilize women in defense, expanding women's roles beyond traditionally feminine jobs and increasing the number of women in national defense. But in the 1970s, gender difference no longer served as the foundation for assessing women's roles in national defense. "Equality," frequently expressed through equal opportunity strategies focused on removing sex-based limitations in military service, became the central matter in debates over women's roles in national defense. Many of the 1970s military changes grew out of a number of equality-focused social movements that reshaped the United States during the 1960s, including the civil rights movement, the antiwar movement, and the women's movement.[1] As activists in the antiwar movement pressured the U.S. government to withdraw from Vietnam and eliminate the draft, military leaders began to evaluate both options upon the president's request. In addition, as second-wave feminism gained popularity and influence starting in the late 1960s, national support for women's rights also affected how defense officials understood womanpower. By the end of the decade, the debate over women's relationship to national defense gained prominence as never before, and new definitions of "equality" moved toward a military in which very few restrictions on women's service remained. Combat remained off-limits, but in the 1970s, servicewomen's roles and opportunities expanded exponentially as old assumptions crumbled.

By 1970, the U.S. military had a public image problem, thanks to the Vietnam War and the draft. Although the United States had maintained a military presence in Vietnam since the mid-1950s, the escalation of the war against North Vietnam beginning in 1964 increased draft calls. The 1968 Tet Offensive became a turning point that marked the United States' failure in the region. Within five years, the military—and the army in particular—reached a "nervous breakdown."[2] Personnel problems abounded. Tales of rampant drug use, racial unrest, disciplinary problems, and declining morale marked all four branches. Americans inside and outside of the military expressed dissatisfaction with the state of the Vietnam War and with those fighting it. According to one survey, for example, 70 percent of army veterans said they would recommend other services instead of the army. In addition to the war not going well, Americans were also fed up with the draft, the primary source of manpower for the Vietnam War. The buildup in Vietnam after the 1964 Gulf of Tonkin incident created more demand for personnel and rising draft calls, including the lottery system and Project 100,000, which lowered draft standards so the services could acquire more men. The deferment system that young men could use to avoid the draft by staying in college or graduate school also contributed to the growth of a class-divided combat corps dominated by lower-class and nonwhite men. Reserve Officer Training Corps (ROTC) program and service academy enrollments declined as the war continued, but recruiting efforts continued to go well—in part, experts believed, because of draft-motivated enlistments.[3]

Eliminating the draft became the central strategy for improving how Americans viewed the military—and perhaps by extension, their view of the war. Fighting the war was a big enough challenge, but combating popular unrest and dissatisfaction over the war and the draft made the task even more daunting. Almost immediately after entering office in 1969, President Richard Nixon began efforts to end the draft. For the first time since before World War II, Americans faced the possibility that compulsory military service would no longer exist. This change would require extensive research and planning to determine how the military could both function without the draft and conclude the war in Vietnam. After all, for nearly three decades, the U.S. government had operated on the assumption that the draft was the best way to ensure adequate defense forces. After four years of study, the draft ended on July 1, 1973, and the All-Volunteer Force (AVF) became reality.[4] The transition to the AVF did not create equality for servicewomen, nor did AVF transition planners lead the way in really changing women's status in the military: instead, military leaders virtually ignored servicewomen as they worked toward the AVF's implementation. Despite this, shifting military needs and an awareness of outside factors helped make government and military leaders more receptive to reassessing womanpower.

The military's social status declined in the late 1960s and early 1970s just as the women's movement gained momentum, ground, and visibility. Second-wave feminists achieved success partially by capitalizing on the social, economic, and political changes of the 1960s and 1970s and the instability of the Vietnam War. By the mid-1960s, American women were beginning to question their social and economic status, even if they did not yet identify as feminists, a term that still held negative connotations for many women.[5] As the women's movement grew in numbers, it became more complex in ideas and tactics, including not just the liberal feminists of organizations like NOW who sought change through established government institutions, but also women with other approaches.[6] Media stories often conflated variations within second-wave feminism under the umbrella of "women's liberation" or "women's lib," including liberal feminism, radical feminism, and socialist feminism.[7] Through consciousness-raising groups, rap sessions, and local events, women raised awareness of social and economic problems and expressed dissatisfaction with their status as citizens, wives and mothers, and workers.[8] The growing diversity of women who identified as feminists spoke to the success of the movement in capturing the nation's attention. However, such diversity in beliefs and approaches sometimes proved problematic, often making it difficult for many Americans to clearly grasp what the women's movement was.

The Equal Rights Amendment (ERA) became one of the hallmarks of the second-wave feminist movement, even though the amendment had been contentious among women's rights advocates for more than fifty years. In the 1970s, second-wave feminists came to see the ERA as a way to combat inequities related to women's employment. Activists pointed out that women in all career fields made less money than men and tended to hold positions much lower on the career ladder. In earlier decades, however, it was precisely concerns over women's employment that led many women's rights supporters to fight against the ERA. First introduced in Congress in 1923, various advocates proposed the ERA annually but with little success until the 1950s.[9] When the PCSW concluded its efforts in 1963, the commission's official stance was that the ERA was not necessary, and that women could use the Fourteenth Amendment's equal protection clause and Fifth Amendment's due process clause to pursue sex discrimination problems.[10] Few PCSW members endorsed the ERA themselves because they did not want the ERA to eliminate protective labor legislation that existed in many states to safeguard women workers. This view reflected the ideas held by many of the directors of the women's services in the late 1960s: that protective legislation—or in the military, protective regulations—served an important function.

Attitudes toward the ERA began to change when women realized that the new Equal Employment Opportunity Commission (EEOC) had failed to respond to sex discrimination claims. Created as part of the 1964 Civil Rights

Act, the EEOC was supposed to handle employment discrimination claims. Title VII of the Civil Rights Act recognized sex discrimination existed in employment, but this apparently wasn't enough to get the EEOC to investigate women's claims. Part of the problem was that EEOC officials wanted to focus on combating racial discrimination, and members of the EEOC did not want to conflict with state protective labor laws. Despite their position, nine of the first forty-eight complaints the EEOC received had to do with sex discrimination, signaling that women took the problem seriously even if the EEOC did not. By 1966, Representative Martha Griffiths (D-MI) "accused the EEOC of a 'wholly negative attitude' toward the sex provision," citing its decision to continue to allow sex-segregated job advertisements as an example of its problematic stance.[11] In short, the EEOC's practice of ignoring sex discrimination claims made many women across the nation very unhappy. Given the EEOC's approach to sex discrimination, NOW made the ERA one of its main priorities beginning in 1967.[12] Then, in 1969, the EEOC took a stance against protective labor laws, which led many who previously opposed the ERA to reconsider their position.[13] With a legal foundation to protective legislation no longer a strong option to combat workplace discrimination, activists began to see the ERA and its removal of sex-based legal differences as the new key to achieving women's rights.

Long before the women's movement began to help advance the cause of women in the military, the women who served as the final directors of the WAC, WAVES, WM, and WAF had already worked extensively to secure women's acceptance in the military themselves. These women were not afraid of change and expansion, and they did not have a problem with equal opportunity or the concept of equality in general. Rather, the women directors worried that the politicization of women's equality would create knee-jerk changes that might seem like good ideas but would not provide what servicewomen needed at a deeper level. They worried about such changes getting in the way of real, lasting progress toward women's equality, defined as their acceptance as equal members in national defense. Ever the planners and ever the career military personnel, they preferred to determine the best action plan based on military need. These women had served through three wars and, in their experiences, positive change came only with hard work, persistence, and proving that women belonged in the military. Politics in Washington, however, had a habit of changing frequently.

Most of the women's leaders publicly distanced themselves from the women's movement, which underscored their preference for internal change but also complicated their ability to cast themselves as focused on women's rights. Instead, the directors continued to emphasize their femininity and even their own roles as secondary to men in the military, noting that they were advisors rather than actual directors. Not long after the promotions of General Elizabeth Hoisington and General Anna Hays (Director of the Army Nurse Corps) in 1970, the first women to be named as generals, one reporter made it clear that neither woman identified herself with the growing movement. "Neither woman feels any kinship toward the Women's Liberation Movement or that her elevation to general can be used as propaganda for the movement."[14] Like activists earlier in the century who eschewed the label "feminist," the women's service directors saw their work in advancing woman's rights differently than the new movement envisioned. In an article about a 1972 hearing on women's utilization, at which the four directors testified, a reporter commented that "it became quickly evident that the supporters of women's liberation in the Armed Forces were to be found more among those who did the questioning than among those who answered."[15] For example, none of the directors advocated moving women into combat, and all expressed that their services were moving forward carefully to expand women's opportunities, as General Bailey put it, "every time we feel we can, from practical viewpoints and restraints."[16] By 1972, as definitions of equality shifted around them, expanding to include the possibility that women could fill any role, including combat, the women's directors began to seem out of step with new approaches to women's rights.

Because liberal feminists did not turn their attention to servicewomen until the early 1970s, the directors of the women's services perceived feminists' efforts as a marriage of political convenience to help advance causes like the ERA. For example, NOW only began to consider servicewomen beginning in 1971, and only then in the context of the draft and the ERA. This delay in paying attention to women's status in national defense is surprising in light of the PCSW's early attention to the matter and the PCSW's influence, but the small numbers of servicewomen and popularity of the antiwar movement in the 1960s may have contributed to the oversight, causing many civilians to look askance at anything military. It wasn't until five years after its founding that NOW created its first task force on women in the military, followed by a white paper on the ERA and the draft.[17] The timing means that the organization did not begin to examine the status of military women until the ERA had already highlighted the relationship between equal rights and women in national defense. And although feminist activists began to pay attention to servicewomen as the ERA gained

Reimagining Equality 183

prominence in the 1970s, NOW did not have a clear agenda for addressing servicewomen's issues until well into the 1980s.[18]

Instead, NOW focused on responding to specific concerns as they arose. By 1976, the organization had formed a Committee for Women in the Military, "to intensify our efforts to get women admitted to the academies, process complaints from service women, and work on the general problems of sex discrimination in the military."[19] Local chapters also responded to complaints from individuals. In 1974, for example, Floridian Barbara Parise failed the army's entrance exam—at least according to the standards set for women (which were still higher than those set for men). Her mother asked the local NOW chapter to investigate, and they helped the family connect with the Center for Law and Social Policy's women's rights project in Washington, DC.[20] NOW representatives also requested information from the military regarding policies applying to women, such as when California NOW Legislative Committee member Patricia Fagan wrote to ask the assistant secretary of the navy for details about jobs available for women and those unavailable for women, including the justification for any exclusions.[21] These efforts came too late for many servicewomen who had tried over the years to combat inequities they faced, such as being discharged for homosexuality or pregnancy. What mattered was that this was changing: although DACOWITS had been and continued to be an important advocate for womanpower writ large, NOW's presence and influence made it fairly easy to link individuals to the right resources and help them find an avenue for their complaint.

While serious efforts were already underway to improve women's status in the United States, the ERA opened entirely new possibilities. It also created specific concerns, from some people, about how the ERA would affect womanpower. North Carolina Senator Sam Ervin, for example, spent the last two days of congressional debate offering ten amendments, including one that would exempt women from the draft and one that would allow Congress to make laws keeping women out of combat. None of his amendments succeeded, and on March 22, 1972, both houses of Congress passed the Equal Rights Amendment with this language:[22]

> **Section 1:** Equality of rights under the law shall not be denied or abridged by the United States or by any State on account of sex.
> **Section 2:** The Congress shall have the power to enforce, by appropriate legislation, the provisions of this article.
> **Section 3:** This amendment shall take effect two years after the date of ratification.[23]

The clock began ticking immediately: to become part of the Constitution, thirty-eight states would have to ratify the amendment within seven years. At least in the beginning, supporters felt confident they would achieve success: the same day that it passed Congress, Hawaii ratified the ERA. Delaware, Nebraska, and New Hampshire followed suit on March 23, and Idaho and Iowa on March 24. By 1973, twenty-four states had given their support to the amendment with formal ratification.[24] Then things became more challenging.

The Congressional debates over the ERA from 1970 to 1972 reveal how the broad language of the amendment could be both a positive and negative force, a challenge that carried into the ratification stage. Early analysts who assessed the ERA's potential impact focused on the amendment's gray areas. A 1975 *New York Times* article put it bluntly: "The confusion that has arisen derives from the fact that there is no way of knowing for sure how the courts would interpret the amendment in areas that are disputed."[25] Advocates argued that the ERA offered a way to end discriminatory laws nationwide, including any laws that favored or discriminated against one sex. The ERA would make it possible for women to borrow money and obtain credit on the same basis as men. It would also eliminate sex-based discrimination that affected men. For example, some existing laws did not allow widowers to claim their wife's inheritance or Social Security benefits. Additionally, while supporters affirmed that the ERA would not eliminate rape laws, it appeared that the amendment would make it possible and perhaps easier to prosecute both men and women for sexual crimes.

ERA opponents presented an alternate angle on some of these same issues, which further demonstrated the possibility of interpreting the amendment's vague language broadly. Anti-ERA groups used pro-ERA documents such as a piece in the *Yale Law Journal* to support their counterclaims about what the ERA would do; insisting, for example, that the ERA would cause divorced women to lose their right to alimony, child support, or child custody. Moreover, anti-ERA groups argued that the ERA would be problematic for working women because it would remove protective labor laws. STOP ERA, led by Phyllis Schlafly, endorsed these positions, arguing that the ERA would take away state power to legislate over abortion, force seminaries to admit women, and would "prohibit privacy based on sex in public school restrooms, hospitals, public accommodations, prisons and reform schools."[26]

One of the largest issues was the effect the ERA would have on women's military service, a topic that drew attention especially in the aftermath of a 1971 *Yale Law Journal* article on the subject.[27] The article's section on the ERA and the military began by pointing out that "the Armed Forces have always been one of the most male-dominated institutions in our society. Only men are subject to involuntary conscription . . . It is not difficult to explain why the military is structured in this way. In the past, physical strength was essential to military success."[28] The historically masculine and physical strength orientation of the armed forces made the ERA's effect on women's military service particularly important. Out of all the changes the ERA might bring, the prospect of women advancing in new ways into the military offered a particular challenge to national security. How would the legislation affect the tradition that men performed combat service and fulfilled military obligation through their conscription, if sex made women exempt from both combat and conscription? The *Yale Law Journal* article set the stage for many ERA-related controversies, offering a foundation for Phyllis Schlafly's and other opponents' fight against the ERA.[29]

The authors of the *Yale* piece argued that the ERA would break down remaining gender-based barriers to women's service, such as male-only combat units. Under the amendment, military and government officials would have to stop exempting women from the draft, admit women to the military academies, and equalize enlistment standards for men and women. Such changes would not be easy. "These changes will require a radical restructuring of the military's view of women, which until now has been a narrow and stereotypical one." The authors asserted that removing existing legal barriers would offer women the opportunity to attain the same benefits of military service that men acquired. Yes, the authors acknowledged, military service had dangers, including death in combat, or the basic idea of being trained to kill. But the modern military also provided a comprehensive whole life career package. Just like any employer, the armed forces provided benefits that many women might want or need, such as "training, medical care, and benefits for dependents . . . educational scholarships and loans, preference in government employment, pensions, insurance, and medical treatment."[30] These facts made military service similar to any other career a woman might pursue, and it was these facts that ERA advocates considered most significant in thinking about the amendment's impact on servicewomen.

On the matter of women in combat, the *Yale* article authors argued that women could physically meet the requirements and, accordingly, should fight just like men. "The effectiveness of the modern soldier is due more to equipment and training than to individual strength." Consequently, many women would be physically capable of performing combat, whether this meant "carrying loads weighing 40 to 50 pounds . . . piloting an airplane or engaging in naval operations." The question of physical capability, they insisted, was not a matter affecting women only: both women and men would be screened to assess their ability to fill combat roles, as men already were. Women's experiences in Israel and North Vietnam had already shown that women could perform combat roles alongside men. Moreover, the authors dismissed any views that it was inappropriate for women to engage in killing. "No one would suggest that combat service is pleasant . . . all combat is dangerous, degrading and dehumanizing . . . as between brutalizing our young men and brutalizing our young women there is little to choose."[31] If men had to perform such duties, then women who fit physical qualifications should also do the same: it was unfair to ask men alone to bear that burden.

Members of the D.C. Federation of Business and Professional Women's Clubs also addressed how the ERA would affect women's military service in their booklet *The Promise of Equality*, noting that even without the ERA the government could change the law to draft women. On the matter of combat, the authors wrote that "it is virtually impossible to speculate with any degree of certainty one way or the other on this question, because current laws prohibiting military women from combat duties do not apply to all military women." The authors clarified that no laws prohibited army women from combat duty assignments, for example. Although the 1948 Women's Armed Services Integration Act specifically prohibited air force and navy women from being used on air or sea vessels that could be tasked for combat, no similar prohibition existed for army women. That said, army policy was to keep women out of combat roles.[32] More importantly, the authors stressed, women—like men—would only go into combat if they possessed all the qualifications, pointing out that only a small percentage of personnel ever engaged in combat.[33]

The debates over the ERA during its ratification stage turned the nation into a battleground over equal rights on the basis of sex, and the military became an important pawn in that fight. These battles played out in national newspapers, on television, and in face-to-face encounters between ERA supporters and opponents. While NOW and other feminist organizations saw the ERA as one of the most important issues facing women, the growing anti-ERA coalition continued to step up its efforts to end ERA ratification success.[34] For the first time since World War II, Americans debated women's defense roles intensely. Even though women had served in all branches of the military since 1948, and despite the expansion of servicewomen's opportunities beginning with PL 90–130 in 1967, the ERA debates skyrocketed womanpower to national importance.

The prospect of the ERA also prompted military officials to conduct internal assessments of how the ERA might impact the utilization of women. The goal was to determine what the ERA would do once enacted and identify ways to change military policies and regulations *before* ratification, therefore alleviating the need for later changes. This strategy might also (potentially) mitigate legal assaults on the military once the ERA took effect. One resulting study, "Report of the Committee to Study the Proposed Equal Rights Amendment" (ERAC Report), in December 1972 focused on "regulations and policies that might be in conflict with the [ERA]."[35] The Committee included Director of the WAC Mildred Bailey and fifteen other members, who began by developing a list of nine assumptions based on their close study of the ERA.

These assumptions of how the ERA would affect the army, the largest of the services, guided efforts to determine what the army's action plan should be. The assumptions were:

1. That grouping of individuals in the army will be based on similar characteristics or functions but not on sex.
2. That women will be admitted for service in the army under neutral standards that apply equally to men and women.
3. That women will not be barred from any occupation in the army on the basis of sex.
4. That after entry into the army women, like men, will be assigned to duties by their commanders, depending on their qualifications and the Army's needs.
5. That admission into army training and educational facilities or activities will be based on relevant characteristics and ability rather than on the sex of the individual.
6. That a particular characteristic found only in one sex (e.g. child bearing) will not be considered a sex factor in applying the ERA to army regulations and policies.
7. That the privacy extended to men and women in army housing assignments will probably not be considered sex discrimination.
8. That Congress will treat men and women alike with respect to the current or any future draft law.
9. That deferment and exemption from the draft will be based on sex-neutral exemptions.[36]

These nine assumptions emphasized committee members' beliefs that the ERA would primarily mandate sex-neutral standards and organization. The committee members recognized some areas of difference would remain, namely in matters of personal privacy and pregnancy, but did not know how to assess combat utilization and personal privacy because they were unsure whether the ERA would be "strictly interpreted." Consequently, the committee "based its conclusions on the courts taking a balanced approach in applying the ERA to the military services, assuming consideration would be given to the services' ability to carry out their constitutional functions."[37] Or, reading between the lines, they didn't think the courts would be foolhardy enough to say that women belonged in combat or in coed living assignments.

The key to ensuring women would not move into combat was to find a reason why such a change was not good for the military. The twin issues of combat and personal privacy led the committee to its first conclusion that putting women in combat would not foster effective utilization. "The greatest efficiency in utilization of personnel in the army is achieved by assigning men to combat duties and women to all duties except those involving physical contact with the enemy . . . Privacy between the sexes could not be guaranteed by the army, if women were to be assigned to combat units."[38] It was an idea based on the assumptions that had long guided policies about women's services. No one stopped to imagine whether allowing women in combat might *improve* utilization: combat had always been for men only, and the group firmly believed there were good reasons for that.

Building from this conclusion, the group asserted that the WAC structure, the office of the Director of the WAC, and separate promotion lists for WAC officers should continue, and that the army not expand women's job roles beyond the 434 occupations already open to them. The group did advocate admitting women to West Point and all ROTC programs for noncombat roles, and supported "modified weapons and defensive combat training" in women-only basic training. Other recommendations included making men and women subject to the same moral and administrative reenlistment waivers "except those concerning pregnancy," meaning that the committee advocated letting the WAC continue to refuse reenlistment to single mothers. They also suggested applying sex-neutral entry standards, maintaining existing marriage, pregnancy, and parenthood separation policies; and extending sole survivor separation to apply to sons or daughters. Finally, if women became subject to the draft, the group argued there should be exemptions for mothers and pregnant women.[39] Uncertainty over how the

ERA might be interpreted led Deputy Chief of Staff for Personnel Lieutenant General Bernard Rogers to follow up. By early 1973, Rogers ordered studies to evaluate ERAC Report recommendations, including what might happen if women entered West Point, eliminating the WAC and separate promotion lists, creating weapons and combat training programs for women, and integrating basic training.[40] Several of these planned studies contrasted with the ERAC Report recommendations, suggesting that Rogers may not have been convinced by the committee's decision not to worry about strict interpretation of the ERA in their conclusions.

In a presentation to DACOWITS at the fall 1972 meetings, Carole Frings of the Office of the General Counsel in the Office of the Secretary of Defense stressed that no one could say for certain just how the ERA would affect servicewomen. "Any conclusions made at this point about the effects of the [ERA] on women in the military are extremely tenuous and speculative," because even legal experts disagreed over the ERA's effect and because "many of the issues created by the amendment will have to be resolved by the courts, and it is impossible to predict how the courts will handle this entirely new area of the law."[41] As she laid out the arenas of women's service that the ERA might affect—including the draft, service requirements, and assignments—Frings highlighted the complex factors involved. On combat, she explained that one reading of the ERA was that it would "require that women be allowed to enter any type of duty for which they are physically and mentally qualified, including combat duty."[42] Frings asserted that changes due to the ERA would primarily be beneficial because they would help make the U.S. military even more equitable. "These changes . . . will make our military departments among the most progressive in the world in their treatment of women, and will be an example to other branches of the government as well as to private industry of the kinds of opportunities that can be made available to women."[43]

While military leaders explored the potential impact of the ERA on servicewomen, the same matter became a weapon in the anti-ERA coalition's efforts to defeat the amendment. Led primarily by conservative activist Phyllis Schlafly, who publicized much of the anti-ERA coalition's opinions and activities in her *Phyllis Schlafly Report* newsletter, those against the ERA often drew attention to the legislation's supposed impact on women in the matter of military service. In the July 1975 edition of the newsletter, Schlafly argued that the ERA would lead to drafting women. "Nobody ever said that 'all' women will be drafted. But girls of the proper age and in good physical condition *will* be drafted and sent into combat exactly like the men. The argument that mothers will be exempted as fathers have always been exempted is wholly dishonest."⁴⁴ Schlafly further argued that the reason why ERA proponents argued that women would only have full rights when "they are treated absolutely equally with men in every job in the military" was because ERA advocates also knew that "the one thing indisputable about ERA is that it *will* require federal law and military regulations to give women and men exactly the same treatment."⁴⁵ Schlafly suggested that women who argued for women's right to fight and be drafted were themselves too old to serve in the military. With this charge, she identified her opponents as hypocrites who wanted to foist conscription and combat on young American women without feeling the effects of those duties themselves.

Schlafly was not alone in insisting that the ERA's effect on women's military service was a problem. A 1976 publication asserted that the ERA would disrupt families by requiring women to be drafted, even though the draft no longer existed. Beyond that concern, however, the article "The Equal Rights Amendment: An Attack on Personal Freedoms" drew attention to how current military policy compromised women's family roles. "Even without a draft, the volunteer armed forces presently accepts mothers with small children, an innovation that some career officers, male and female, view with trepidation." Insinuating that the current policies were problematic enough, the authors drew broad conclusions about what might happen if the military drafted mothers in the future. "Imagine the chaos, the disruption of family life in a draft situation!" The benefit of current laws, the article suggested, was that women had "equal opportunity to enlist in the military or stay at home to care for children and husbands. The ERA would leave no choice."⁴⁶ Anti-ERA rhetoric regarding women in military service transformed the ERA's impact on military service from a positive step to a problem. ERA opponents recast military service not as an opportunity or a matter of civic responsibility for women, but a liability.

At the heart of the ERA debates over women, the draft, and combat was the question of who should and can defend the nation, and whether Americans were ready to remove sex as a qualification for military obligation. But while these debates continued—and ultimately contributed to the failure of the ERA by 1982—what is ironic is that during all of this, the lines between women and combat began to blur as women secured a more expanded role in the armed forces than ever before. If the 1970s was a decade when civilian men and women hotly debated whether women should be in combat or drafted, it was also the decade when the prospect of achieving full equality of opportunity in the military, as defined by civilian feminists, became more likely than ever. In that decade, defense officials began to eliminate restrictions on the jobs women could hold in the military, do away with regulations affecting servicewomen's personal lives, and move women closer to combat than ever before as a result of these changes. NOW, STOP ERA, and other organizations fought for and against state ratification of the ERA as members of Congress continued to endorse or at least appear to support women's equal rights.

While the end of the draft, the ERA, and the women's movement all created an environment that supported improving women's military status, these factors merely accelerated changes that had in most cases already been identified by servicewomen. For example, by the time the first serious ERA debates began in Congress in 1970, servicewomen were benefiting from at least two major recent changes: PL 90–130 in 1967, removing officer rank limitations and the regulation that women could comprise no more than 2 percent of the nation's total military strength; and the admission of women to air force ROTC beginning in 1969. In June 1970, WAC Director Elizabeth Hoisington and Army Nurse Corps Director Anna Hays became the first women promoted to Brigadier General.[47] As of June 1971, a little more than 41,000 women served in all four military branches, accounting for 1.6 percent of total military strength.[48]

By 1978, however, more than 120,000 women served in the services (5.7 percent of total military strength), a numeric increase that reflected the emphasis on opening military opportunities to women over the course of the decade.[49] Each branch had at least one female general, the service academies were training women, weapons training was mandatory for *all* new recruits, and the army was beginning to try mixed-sex basic training. In 1974, the DOD announced that the military would stop discharging new mothers involuntarily.[50] Equality, particularly in terms of equal opportunity, had become the watchword of the U.S. military as a result of *both* servicewomen's pushes for internal change and the external influences of feminist activists. For the first time, it seemed that leaders in the armed forces were devoting serious consideration to how they could best utilize womanpower by largely removing gender differences as criteria for determining women's roles. The 1970s had become a dynamic era in the military, focused on improving servicewomen's status, opportunities, and utilization.

The women's movement, the ERA, and the AVF helped further justify many changes that some servicewomen already sought while also creating new conversations about the relationship between women and combat. In March 1972, just a few weeks before the Senate debated and approved the

ERA, the House Subcommittee on the Utilization of Manpower met to consider the role of women in the armed forces. In part, the hearing seems to have been motivated by the pressures for the ERA and its anticipated consideration in Congress that spring. Given this incentive, along with the approaching end of the draft, committee members appeared to pay close attention to how the armed forces were utilizing women. Chairman Otis Pike (D-NY) began by addressing some of the inconsistencies in servicewomen's roles. "For example, in the army a woman can be a cook, but not a baker. She can take still photographs, but not movies. She is told that she can both bake and make movies in times of national emergency. She cannot operate a radio or teletype machine, but she can, even in peacetime, play a tuba in the band. In the Marines, women officers may play in the band, enlisted women only in times of national emergency."[51] In wartime, as Pike indicated, women's options expanded because the military presumed there would be greater need for women in all areas of defense. In peacetime, military need did not require women in roles that men could readily fill. But more than just these inconsistencies, Pike drew attention to the fact that the army had "about one woman for every 80 men. There is one woman brigadier general for 255 male brigadier generals, one woman colonel for 500 army colonels" and so on—noting that when it came to women and rank, the army was better than the navy or the air force.[52]

Pike's larger argument was that the military reflected women's role in the nation more broadly. "We are told," he said, "that the problems in the American national service and the racial problems in the service are simply representative of the problems in America generally. I expect that the way we utilize women in the service is also representative of the way we utilize them in America."[53] In his view, the hearings were about understanding "what is right and wrong with the way we utilize our womanpower."[54] After nearly twenty-five years, Congress was taking a long, hard look at the role women played in national defense, and for the first time, the questions that arose dealt with not just the jobs women held, but also the jobs they *might* hold. To that end, representatives asked pointed questions about the possibility of putting women in combat and allowing them to train in the military academies. The 1972 hearing on manpower utilization marked the beginning of changes in how the services utilized their female personnel and new attention to other forms of sex discrimination. While the ERA had not yet passed, the specter of it, the impending end of the draft, and the women's movement had clearly prompted male civilian and military leaders' renewed attention to women, although women had been fighting for such attention for years.

Admiral Elmo Zumwalt, Chief of Naval Operations beginning in July 1970, became one of the first to expand equal opportunity to include race and sex in his efforts to use equal opportunity as a primary strategy to combat the navy's flailing image and retention rates that it experienced with the Vietnam War.[55] Addressing what he called "the navy's silent but real and persistent discrimination against minorities" of all races, as well as women, "in recruiting, in training, in job assignment, in promotion" was one of his four main plans to make naval service "more attractive and more satisfying" to Americans.[56] Although Zumwalt tasked his staff to begin studying women's status in the navy in mid-1971, he did not issue his own equal opportunity policies for women until August 1972, several months after the ERA passed.

Zumwalt's policies on equal opportunity for women reflect the first time a high-ranking military official advocated allowing women to perform sea duty, a job classified as "combat-related" in the navy and thus off-limits to women. Given the timing of his directive, Zumwalt may have been hoping to capitalize on the success of the ERA, or at least anticipating how the legislation might open further opportunities for women. Z-116, "Equal Rights and Opportunities for Women in the Navy," directed that women should move into all open billets (job assignments) in the navy, at least in limited numbers.[57] It also expressed an ultimate goal of letting women serve at sea, which was against the law at that time. Title 10 of the U.S. Code had been written in such a way following the 1948 Women's Armed Services Integration Act that it was impossible for women to serve at sea except in transport or hospital vessels.[58] Zumwalt was aware of this regulation, but saw women's service at sea as a crucial change to make naval service more attractive to women. But as ERA advocates discovered, there were many underlying fears that made people cautious about expanding women's roles.

Zumwalt found that it was often difficult to discuss his goals effectively, perceiving that the fear of expanding women's roles was a barrier not just to the ERA but also to many in the military command structures and the government. "Indeed a principal frustration connected with getting a program for female equality in the navy under way was that it was impossible to discuss the matter rationally with some people." Zumwalt noted that some individuals responded with what they believed were legitimate concerns of "unisex showers and floating orgies," but others offered little more than "locker-room jocularities on the subject." President Nixon, for example, did not seem receptive to discussing major changes to women's status in the military. Nixon was not supportive of Zumwalt's proposed sexual equality goals, reportedly telling Zumwalt that dealing with the "race thing" was one thing, but he did not want to be pushed when it came to gender. Despite these challenges, Zumwalt's efforts helped lead to the first female admiral, first woman chaplain, and a half-dozen female naval aviators by 1974.[59]

Commander Catherine Leahey was one of the women who benefited from Zumwalt's efforts to ensure equal opportunity for naval women later in the 1970s and into the early 1980s. Growing up amid the women's movement, she "wanted to do something exciting and adventurous, but I also wanted 'equal pay for equal work.' It seemed to me, at the time, that the military provided just that."[60] She became one of the first women in navy ROTC and recalled the response to Zumwalt's Z-Grams as mostly positive. "The guys were positive because many of the changes were personally beneficial to them. Many felt, however, that Zumwalt had pushed his reforms too hard, forcing too much change at once. With hindsight, we can now see that traditional reforms were too incremental to be effective and the best way to effect a 'cultural shift' in the navy was to do it wholesale."[61] After commissioning and college graduation in 1977, Leahey served in the Panama Canal Zone before being chosen as one of the first women to serve at sea in 1979.[62]

A little earlier, in 1976, Carol Wheeler became one of the first to move into a newly opened career field for WAF and experienced firsthand the struggle for male acceptance. After basic, she spent nine months in an electronics program at a military technical school, where she was the only woman training to enter a line of work nicknamed DESTE, digital switching terminal (teletype equipment).[63] As the only woman in her group, she noted that some instructors and a few classmates seemed to resent her, but by and large it went well. Her response to the resentment she perceived on occasion was simply to work as hard as she could. "Me and one other fellow were the top students in my class—and I responded [to the resentment] by saying, 'I am one of the top students, what's your complaint?'" She observed that if you wanted to be treated with respect, as she did, you learned to act in particular ways. "There were a lot of other women who behaved differently . . . they would be very flirty with the fellows, and this usually backfired on them . . . I felt it generally backfired because if you watched, they wouldn't be treated with as much respect. I wanted to be treated with respect."[64] For Wheeler, watching her behavior was one of the important things she did to ensure she got the treatment she wanted from her colleagues.

Servicewomen learned to follow certain unwritten codes to gain acceptance from male colleagues. According to Wheeler, based on her experiences, women had to adhere to a different standard. "It's not fair, but

Reimagining Equality 195

women had to behave better. If you didn't want the sexist comments and the jokes, you couldn't make them, pretty much. If you wanted to be treated not like a potential sex partner, you couldn't act like you might be a potential sex partner."[65] While formal barriers to women's opportunities eroded, informal barriers—such as attitudes and behaviors—continued to play an important role in shaping servicewomen's experiences. This was particularly true in the tumultuous state of the military in the 1970s, when so many external forces pushed to speed up the expansion of women's military roles. As female military leaders expressed consistently through the 1970s, male acceptance was crucial to women's success in these new roles: servicewomen had to prove themselves to male colleagues.

While only 35 percent of all military occupational specialties, or job classifications, were open to women by the end of 1972, within three years women could train for and serve in approximately 85 percent of all military occupational specialties.[66] Opening this range of job assignments was an important first step in the military's mission to remake itself as an equal opportunity employer. Arguably, this was what the armed forces were trying to do in the 1970s. Moreover, in 1972, only 10 percent of all servicewomen worked in "scientific, technical, or 'blue-collar' labor specialties," but three years later, more than 30 percent of all servicewomen held such jobs.[67] By 1977, women served in 356 out of the army's 389 military occupational specialties, a trend continuing throughout the services. Only combat and combat support roles were off-limits to women.

Women's situation in the military changed so much that in the 1970s, each of the services began eliminating the women's services altogether. In 1972, as Admiral Zumwalt prepared Z-116, Captain Robin Quigley began to articulate her belief that her position, Assistant Chief of Naval Personnel for Women (sometimes referred to as Director of the WAVES) should be eliminated. On February 23, 1972, she wrote to all women in the navy in her monthly newsletter, noting that she had dropped the word "Director" that usually appeared in the newsletter header. "My intent is to make it quite clear that the unofficial title which has been attached to this billet . . . the Director of the WAVES . . . is just that, unofficial, and I have stopped using it. Furthermore, it is gravely misleading in two ways. For one thing, there is no such organization as 'The WAVES'—for another, I do not *direct* it or anything else!"[68] Quigley was the first of the female directors to clarify her position, in the process critiquing the specialized administrative structures set up supposedly for women's benefits. As she noted, the WAVES had not existed formally since World War II. In theory, women had been fully integrated into the navy since 1948, but in practice, Quigley and her predecessors had been considered "Director" of the WAVES because of the DOD's tendency to view women as secondary to the military mission.

Ending the formal administrative structures for women suggested that these organizations had become barriers to integration. The other services soon followed the navy. In late 1975, the air force eliminated the Director of the WAF position, as well as its WAF squadron system and "the accompanying dual management for enlisted women."[69] By 1977, the marine corps also did away with the Director of the Women Marines position and the title "Women Marines" effective July 1, 1977. The WAC took a little longer. As the only formal corps—created in World War II and held over in the postwar era—an act of Congress would be required for the disestablishment of the Director of the WAC and the corps itself. On October 20, 1978, just like the other women's components, the WAC became nothing more than a memory and a relic of another time.[70]

In the 1940s, military and government leaders established the women's services under the idea that women would most effectively understand how to administer other women. Yet the development of these women's services— even the most informal of them—created a system that left women segregated from the military as a whole. General Bernard Rogers suggested that women were the last segregated population within the military in his speech to the members of DACOWITS at their spring 1977 meeting, Rogers remarked that in the past few decades, "[the] army progressed from treating women as *separate* (the Women's Army Auxiliary Corps) to *separate but equal* (the Women's Army Corps) and is now progressing to *equal* treatment (integration into the army's Combat Support and Combat Service Support branches the same as male soldiers)."[71] Appropriating language once applied to race in this instance is striking. The phrase "separate but equal" evokes a status set apart from the larger organization, and considered lesser in some way. Rogers' comment indicates that until the mid-1970s, women existed apart from the military as a whole. As African American men had been segregated, so had women.

The separate administrative structures for women alternately helped and hindered the acceptance of women in the armed forces. During the 1950s, such structures reassured civilians and servicemen that women were not encroaching on the most masculine domains in the military. By the 1970s, however, as social shifts led to new beliefs about the roles women could perform in the workplace and in national defense, the women's administrative structures began to appear as if they offered women special benefits and protection. These structures underscored women's differences from men, which became problematic as the ERA stressed the need for eliminating legal distinctions based on sex. As military and government leaders began to question their long-held assumptions about what women could be and do, they increasingly questioned the idea that women were the ones best equipped to manage womanpower after all.

By mid-1978, none of the administrative structures that had previously governed women's military service remained. The end of the formal women's component structures was a major milestone that signified to many, inside and outside the military, that servicewomen were finally being taken seriously as members of the military. Although they were still limited in the jobs they could do and still could not serve in combat, removing the institutional structure of a segregated component system that functioned within the main military organization was one way to force male military leaders to pay attention to their policies on female utilization. As General Holm put it in a speech in the mid-1970s, "the day of tokenism is gone."[72] Without women specifically tasked to oversee womanpower, servicewomen could no longer be taken for granted or shoehorned to the side as a matter for someone else to manage.

As the 1970s ended, equality for women in the armed forces meant removing any remaining restrictions on women's services and womanpower advocates had come to view women's absence from combat as a factor that prevented servicewomen from gaining full equality. Many of the changes that occurred to improve servicewomen's status and opportunities in the decades before the 1970s may have been small in nature. Between 1948 and 1972, the military took only baby steps when it came to women's utilization. In that light, the decade of the 1970s was an aberration in military women's history: the numerous changes in this decade occurred not in wartime, but in peacetime, not as the result of efforts to fight a foe overseas, but in an effort to soothe the beast at home. No matter what the case, when the draft ended, military leaders discovered they needed women very much. Whether the military would be good at recognizing that fact in the years to come would be another matter.

10 Second-Class Soldiers

On June 9, 1980, *Time* magazine's cover posed this question to Americans across the nation: "Who'll fight for America?" The cover story came from a seminar the *Time* editors held with five military experts, and the subtitle made the problem clear: "Manpower problems are undermining U.S. military might." Here was a portrait of a military facing problems, namely that not enough men were joining or staying in the ranks. Five pages of analysis, color photos, and two sidebars emphasized the challenge of finding enough *men* to keep the All-Volunteer Forces (AVF) going. Part of the idea behind the AVF had been that men would be attracted by military career opportunities competing with civilian ones, but the armed forces couldn't even pay many men a living wage. According to one source, servicemen could make more money working at McDonald's. The military appeared to be in a moment of crisis, and all because of men—but the article did not consider womanpower in its analysis. In fact, the word "woman" appears only five times in the entire piece. The longest statement about women comes four pages in: "Women currently account for 7.4 percent of the armed services, up from 3.5 percent in 1974. The Pentagon estimates that by mid-decade women will make up about 11 percent of the enlisted force." In the meantime, servicewomen made zero percent of the visuals accompanying the article and of the analysis.[1] While men weren't stepping up as expected, women clearly had found something they liked in national defense, even if *Time's* editorial team didn't seem to understand what was right under their noses.

According to the *Time* article, although the services were closer to meeting their recruiting goals than they'd been in the previous year, retaining people was a problem. "Today both whites and blacks are quitting at an unexpected rate." None of the services was keeping the number of personnel expected. For example, the air force wanted to retain 59 percent of pilots and 54 percent of navigators who had achieved twelve years of service, but were only achieving 27 percent and 40 percent, respectively. The problem was common in the army and the navy, too. Things simply did not appear to be going well, aside from one possibility buried in the article: the fact that women seemed comparatively eager to sign up even as their male peers looked elsewhere. It's not clear why the authors avoided the subject of womanpower and failed to ask whether women might help solve the crisis.

Someone was missing a major part of the story, part of which lay a few issues back, on May 19. Darth Vader got the cover story in that issue—*The Empire Strikes Back* had just been released—but servicewomen got their own space in the society section of that issue, with a brief piece about the upcoming graduation of the first women to attend West Point. Even there, women took second billing: the article begins and ends not with quotes from the women cadets, but from people watching them. First, a woman visitor wonders why such pretty young women would attend West Point; at the end, a male cadet notes his hope that President Carter would "not play up the woman issue" at graduation. "After all, it's our graduation too."[2] Yes—graduation for men *and* women, but it was still largely a man's military.

It is ironic that it took détente—a 1970s thaw in the Cold War—for military and government officials to acknowledge women's service as something vital to the nation. In 1948, women had been granted permanent military roles because Congress and the president agreed that all Americans, regardless of gender, would be needed for national defense in the years ahead. They made this decision with a big fear looming over their heads— uncertainty about how nuclear power and relations with the Soviet Union might escalate. In the two decades that followed, American men fought in two wars. American women filled numerous noncombat roles at military bases around the world, including support in Vietnam and Korea. But until the draft ended, military leaders did not recognize women as an essential element in national defense. Women were great to have, but few outside of the women's services cared about them because they were not crucial to mission success (aside from nurses and medical staff, arguably, since fighting wars did require skilled medical professionals). That dependable connection to manpower disappeared suddenly, just as women's voices reached a new height in American politics, and in a moment when relations between the United States and the Soviet Union were relatively calm.

It was possible to truly reimagine how the military would operate in its new draft-free reality precisely because military leaders were not preoccupied with fighting a war. This was exactly what had happened in 1948: a moment of relative peace offered clarity in rethinking strategy. Things might have looked a lot different if the women's movement had not gained national prominence, or if the ERA hadn't been so crucial an issue. As it was, these factors helped foster radical change in how Americans imagined women's roles in national defense. In the short term, the expansion to women's service that developed in the 1970s brought thousands more women into defense, helping them leverage promotions and new career paths in the process (even if the writers at *Time* magazine seemed only vaguely aware of their presence by June 1980). More importantly, however, the changes in servicewomen's possibilities in the 1970s created a foundation for long-term changes with the potential for even more radical change in the future. None of the revisions to women's military status made them completely equal with servicemen, but these changes made possible a future military in which equality could be achieved.

By the 1970s, it was clear that Americans viewed combat as a symbol of the epitome of military service. Combat experience lent servicemen a badge of honor, but that was not the concern. More importantly, combat exclusion prevented women from specific career and leadership opportunities. Until 1967, the limits on women's promotions meant that women had only very few leadership roles, generally linked to the women's services. While these roles mattered, women remained segregated outside of the leadership command structure, with very little voice in the highest echelons of defense leadership. The promotion of the first women to general and admiral in the early 1970s opened the door to a defense system with more diverse leadership. Yet men, with decades of military service, combat experience, and leadership roles, still dominated not only because of numbers but because they took priority in leadership training and had greater access to it. Many had graduated from the military academies, which set them on the path for such careers.

For the first time in the 1970s, combat became associated with questions of how to create equality for women in the armed forces. Before then, no one dared consider the idea that women might fight. By 1970, women no longer trained on how to use a weapon, and the jobs women performed theoretically kept them far away from danger. The ERA, the end of the draft, and the women's movement created a new conversation about women's military service in which combat was—for many people—very much on the table, even if contentiously so. By 1976, NOW's official position as a (civilian) feminist group was that the question of whether women "should" enter combat was not relevant. "We only need know that there are capable women who want these jobs [in combat]." If there were women who wanted to fight, then only access to combat would help secure equality for servicewomen.[3] But at the end of the decade, WAC General Elizabeth Hoisington argued that opening combat to women would not make them equal. She disagreed that such a move would help servicewomen achieve the ever-elusive "full acceptance and equality" that servicewomen and their advocates desired. Hoisington stated, "I don't think so at all—combat duty has nothing to do with discrimination against women."[4]

In the 1970s, the very definition of equality was at stake: for women to be completely equal with men in the armed forces, many people, especially feminists, began to believe that women must be allowed to serve in combat. After all, since at least World War II, combat was the be-all and end-all of military service. During the 1970s, all the changes in women's military status contributed toward eliminating job barriers so that women could fill any role men could (outside of combat and combat support), and generally trying to make sure that women's service and benefits looked as much like men's as possible. When women's military service had been defined by their difference from men, removing limitations based on those differences appeared to many people to be the solution. To make women equal, make their status equal with men's. Hoisington suggested, though, that simply removing barriers would not be enough. It turned out that she was right.

Since the 1940s, combat exclusion significantly differentiated women's service, but women had largely been barred from another important arena of military service—often, but not always, related to combat—leadership. Combat experience often led to leadership roles for career military men, paving the way for promotion as generals or admirals. Many of the men in leadership also got to such roles because they had been trained at military academies, some of the most elite schools in the nation. Since the nineteenth century, education at West Point had started impressive careers for hundreds of American men, including Robert E. Lee and Ulysses S. Grant, Douglas MacArthur, George Patton, and Dwight D. Eisenhower. The Naval Academy, too, had a long record of excellence, even if alumni names don't enter into public imagination as often, including astronauts, governors, members of Congress, and former president Jimmy Carter. The Air Force Academy, created in 1955, added a third possible military pedigree. All three institutions launched impressive military careers, and often civilian ones (all three academies have graduated many individuals who went on to serve in the federal government).[5]

Notably, these academies have also prepared many for service as chief of staff of their military branch, leaders of major commands, and more. This matters because the individuals who graduate from the military academies play a major role in shaping military institutions and policies over the course of their career. Their leadership, often forged not only at the military academies but then in battle, becomes the justification for future ideas for shaping military service. In addition to combat and combat support exclusion, keeping women out of the military academies was an important limitation women faced in the 1970s. If young women could get an education in the military academies, just like young men, then they, too, would have access to the type of leadership opportunities that could potentially bring them to the most influential levels of military leadership.

The success of the ERA in Congress prompted new scrutiny of the military academies and their male-only admission criteria. In 1974, representatives of the air force, army, navy, West Point, the Naval Academy, and the Air Force Academy responded to questions in a series of hearings before a House Armed Services subcommittee. During nine days over three months, House members pointed out that if women could attend any other educational program offered, participate in the ROTC, and hold nearly any military job, then it was unclear why women still were not allowed to attend what were considered the nation's finest military training programs: the academies. This was not the first time that the question of women and military academies had emerged. In 1955, Senate Joint Resolution 48 proposed establishing a Women's Armed Services Academy to train women officers in the same manner that West Point, the Naval Academy, and the Air Force Academy did. Given the "relatively small" requirements of female officers at the time, however, the idea died. The air force objected to the idea because they were in the midst of an early (and short-lived) experiment in WAF ROTC, which they assumed would meet their officer training needs.[6]

Four major themes dominated these discussions on women at the service academies in the 1970s: combat, women's physical abilities, logistics, and equal opportunity. The representatives from the three branches expressed that it would be wasteful to admit women because they would have to create a "noncombatant" educational track. Doing so would mean they would have to reduce the number of spaces available for men and undermine the academies' missions, which were to prepare men for combat leadership. During the June 12 hearings, Vice Admiral Mack (Superintendent, U.S. Naval Academy) argued that admitting women would require creating a "separate course of professional training and academic study, emphasizing noncombatant duties." At the June 19 hearings, the army's Vice Chief of Staff, General Fred C. Weyand, noted that he thought it would be a waste of money to use the academies to train women as noncombatants, while Secretary of the Army Howard Callaway explained that there were two images of women in the academies, including the idea that women would be on a "very separate track" from the men, which members of the subcommittee clarified was not their intention with this legislation.[7] Secretary Callaway insisted that there was no need for women in the academies, nor for a special academy for women, although he would prefer a separate academy for women over admitting them to the established institutions. Callaway and his colleagues continually asserted that the point of academy training was to prepare for combat. Whether every graduate served in combat or not was irrelevant—this was the mission, and the students needed to be prepared. Since women could not fight, they should not attend—this was the men's stance.

Women's exclusion from combat had been a justification for excluding women from the academies for a while. Several years earlier, there had been some internal defense department discussions about whether women should be admitted to the academies. At that time, Assistant Secretary of the Navy James Johnson pointed out that "the curriculum at the Naval Academy includes a considerable amount of training for combat service at sea and ashore, as well as rigorous physical performance requirements neither of which are either necessary or appropriate to women officers. Participation by women in this curriculum would be wasteful and uneconomical."[8] Given women's legal and policy status as noncombatants, navy officials saw no reason to train women in this "rigorous" physical environment since they would not be able to apply those skills in combat service. But Johnson went a step further, noting that their position was also right in line with what Americans believed the proper role of women should be. "Historically, the basic attitude in our American culture has been one of protection of women from the dangers of combat and the rigors of life at sea."[9] Speaking in 1971, it's not clear whether Johnson was unaware of the rising feminist tide around him. The claims American women were making for equal opportunity at that very moment suggest that women themselves were interested in becoming the "protectors," if that was what academy training offered. History might have said one thing, but according to American women, the future was looking different.

History is a powerful force, though: in 1974 Johnson's views were commonly held by the men who testified with him. These were some of the highest military representatives in the nation; there were no women at such levels who could provide their own testimonies because they had never had the opportunity to grow such impressive careers. The officials at the hearings repeatedly emphasized their belief that women did not belong in combat. According to Martin Hoffmann, the DOD's general counsel, women belonged in neither combat nor combat leadership roles. As a representative of the DOD, he stated that "the Department [of Defense] believes that the will of the American people, as expressed in existing laws and demonstrated by national policy in past wars, has always been and continues to be that women should not serve in combat leadership roles."[10] Heaven forbid that women should be able to lead men in fighting (since they could not participate in the fighting themselves).

Representative Patricia Schroeder (D-CO) pointed out that the "will of the people" argument did not consider recent congressional decisions about gender equality. Schroeder wryly remarked that "the Congressional Record that has the ERA results in it must not have gotten to them because I don't believe that is the belief and the will of Congress . . . when Congress passed the equal rights amendment, it did make a very clear statement as to whether this kind of exclusion should be permitted."[11] The ERA was a game-changer, prompting officials to reimagine the role of womanpower in national defense. While military leaders were busy expanding women's opportunities, the work was not done, and continuing to insist that women did not belong in the academies became problematic. Such insistence meant bowing to tradition and trying to keep one last bastion of masculinity, as if these men were worried that allowing women into the academies might undermine, rather than empower, future military leaders. Although very few women were invited to testify, those that did also threw the "will of the people" claim into question. Lt. Colonel Grace King (army) testified that she had surveyed more than 500 civilian and military men and women on the topic of women in the academies and in combat, discovering that 80 percent supported women in the academies and 73 percent supported giving women the option to volunteer for combat. She had also surveyed members of the Armed Services Committee and their staff members, learning that nearly 89 percent supported women in the academies and 81 percent supported women volunteering for combat.[12]

The "will of the people" idea might have held if there were no women interested in attending the academies, but supporters noted that *their* will mattered, too. In 1972, two congressmen had nominated women for Naval Academy appointments (unsuccessfully, since the institution only accepted men at the time).[13] At the 1974 House subcommittee hearings, Representative Donald Fraser (D-MN) testified about a female Air Force Academy nominee. That year, the Air Force Academy gave four of Fraser's top five nominees appointments. The interviewer had observed that "two had the outstanding characteristics he looks for in the people he recommends for the academies."

Fraser described the specific accomplishments of one of those noted individuals:

> The other outstanding candidate was in the top 25 percent of the class, captain of the tennis team, had three years of swimming, was a racing skier with a score of gold medals; had participated in debate and forensics, in an institute for talented youth, and a camp to learn how to survive alone in the wilderness living entirely off the land, and had been an exchange student. This was also the only applicant with a background in flying. This applicant, who became our second alternate, had a private sailplane license (and recognition as the youngest sailplane pilot in the State of Minnesota), and several hours of duo in a T-34. Along with this excellent preparation came a very specific ambition: to become a fighter pilot and to qualify for future aerospace programs.[14]

But the applicant was a woman, and consequently her nomination was "returned without action," despite the fact that she had such an excellent record *and* was the only one of the five candidates with flying experience, which tends to be useful at the Air Force Academy. Fraser further described her as the best of all their applicants, the most motivated, and the one who had put the most time and energy into preparing for military service academies. He argued that if the academy officials had judged the applicant by her capabilities instead of her sex, this candidate might have also been an outstanding asset to the Air Force Academy.

Military representatives pointed out that they were unsure whether women could meet the same physical standards applied to men who attended the academies. Some committee members found this less than compelling, suggesting it was nothing more than a bit of bluster. Sure, women would need to meet certain physical standards, but that didn't mean women should simply be excluded because of the current standards men were held to. "Some people," remarked Representative Samuel Stratton (D-NY), "seem to make a great to-do over the fact that maybe women can't chin themselves as many times as men can or do as many pushups, but again I don't think that is terribly important."[15] He pointed out that both officer candidate schools and ROTC programs had created solutions to handle the physical differences between men and women. Stratton was confident the academies could find a similar approach.[16] What Stratton was hinting at, perhaps unknowingly, was that physical standards in the military defaulted to a male standard, and no one had yet really imagined the full possibilities of rethinking that standard.

Some present at the hearings weren't worried at all because they realized women were constantly disproving assumptions about their abilities—both in and out of the military. Admiral Mack opposed the legislation primarily because of the legal restrictions against navy women in combat. However, even he had to concede, "I don't see anything a woman couldn't do that a man does now in the navy. There are some physical things, such as the SEAL's [sic] perhaps, where their physique is the key thing, being able to swim, or something of that sort, but there are women who can do that. You have only to see the Olympics."[17] Representative Charles Wilson (D-TX) agreed, and pointed out that Olympic gold medal diver Maxine King, an air force officer, had also coached men at the Air Force Academy. "She was a coach of the boys, and didn't create any problems at all. It was the greatest experience they ever had, and they came out of it with a lot better divers than they had before."[18] But while Representative Wilson was becoming convinced that women could do practically anything, U.S. Air Force Academy Superintendent General A. P. Clark emphasized the "physical, the mental, and the emotional stresses of combat" to illustrate his belief that women would simply not have the physical and mental capabilities to perform as well as men.[19]

Although the 1974 legislation moved on to the House Armed Services Committee that fall, it died there. The following year, however, Representative Stratton added an amendment, then passed within a larger appropriations bill, affirming that women could and should have the right to attend the service academies.[20] Given no choice, the three main service academies all began plans to admit women for the fall of 1976. Clearly, members of the subcommittee had not been convinced by military arguments against women in the academies. Passing women's admission as part of an appropriations bill only suggested that further debates seemed unnecessary. The defense secretaries had made their position clear in the summer of 1974, drawing on current law and their belief that women did not belong in combat. On the other hand, they were up against a Congress that seemed increasingly supportive of expanding women's opportunities and removing sex-based limitations, as indicated by the ERA. And, as representatives noted in the 1974 summer hearings, it was inconsistent for the services to bar women from the academies while admitting them to nearly every other arena of military life.

Admitting women to the military academies marked a turning point in how gender defined women's service, and a death blow to the official reliance on femininity that had reigned since the 1940s. In the academies, there would be little room for gender differences, except perhaps in terms of adapting training to meet physical capabilities. Any instances of treating women differently because of their gender—or rather, because of gender perceptions and ideals—created problems for female students because their male counterparts resented those "special favors." Physical standard variations, duty assignments, and even hair length—all would become perceived differences in treatment between men and women and, at times, problematic. At graduation, the Superintendent feted female members of the West Point class of 1980 with a reception and a gift from the Class of 1939—something male cadets did not enjoy that year.[21] (Of course, women had never enjoyed graduation from West Point until that year, so arguably, they deserved that reception, especially after four years of the harassment many of them had experienced.) In the academies, a "ladies first" mentality would set women apart even further from their male classmates. Instead, female students had to demonstrate that they could be just like the men in every way to be integrated on the same basis.

Education in the service academies slowly created major change both in terms of women's proximity to combat and to military leadership. As students in the academies, women became closer to combat because they were being trained for combat leadership, but even more, women were being trained for military leadership in a way no women had ever had access to before. In physical training and education, academy leaders modified standards based on women's physiology, but otherwise women took the same classes as men, preparing them in the same ways for combat leadership. At the Naval Academy, women competed in nearly all intercollegiate sports, although a male-only trilogy of football, lacrosse, and wrestling remained, as well as intramural football, lacrosse, wrestling, boxing, and rugby. At West Point, however, women trained with different weapons, wore protective gear (optional at times), and received other modifications to the physical education curriculum.[22] Following sexual integration, the combat mission did not change at the academies: instead, it expanded to recognize that although not *every* cadet would perform in combat, every cadet would prepare for such scenarios. Cadets had always trained in this way, but even so, not all of them saw battlefields.

The first women admitted to the academies spent four years challenging cultural assumptions of gender by joining an all-male educational system that emphasized masculinity and physical excellence. In a survey of cadets at West Point in 1975, before women's admittance, respondents had "overwhelmingly negative" comments about the prospect of women cadets.[23] These viewpoints shaped women cadets' experiences after they arrived. This was true at the Air Force Academy, as well, as cadet Janet Libby explained in her exit interview, "initially we [women] were not wanted. There is no other way to get around it. I got the distinct impression that a lot of the [men of the class of] '77 were trying to prove that the decision was wrong to let girls come to the Academy, and they set out to do that."[24] Women at all three schools showed that being biologically male was not a prerequisite to success in the service academies. Their hard work and success surviving in an environment that was more often hostile to them than not went a long way in demonstrating what women could do in the armed forces. Air Force Academy cadet June Van Horn explained that "it wasn't just accepted that because we [the women] got here we were good enough to be here. We had to go beyond that, and prove that we deserved to be here."[25] Admitting women to the service academies, to the same combat leadership training that men completed, challenged beliefs that women *should* be only noncombatants and assumptions that they *could* be only noncombatants. The women cadets encountered some of the same issues that servicewomen had been experiencing for years, such as the need to prove themselves to male colleagues and earn respect because they were women doing jobs in a man's world. Now, the stakes were higher, because women were no longer filling military roles that seemed suitable for them as women: women cadets were asserting that they belonged alongside male cadets, working toward military leadership in new ways.

While the service academies arguably offered a somewhat unique route to military service, the men's attitudes toward their female classmates illustrate the kind of military women entered. In the academies, women might bear the brunt of resentment from men who did not agree that women belonged in such elite spaces, but plenty of men throughout the military made it clear that in national defense, men mattered more. Importantly, men felt they mattered more and often struggled when women appeared to encroach on previously all-male territory. Servicewomen who held traditionally feminine jobs could get off the hook, but women who moved into jobs where few or no women had been were immediately perceived as threats. Part of the problem, according to Major General Jeanne Holm, was that many military leaders in the late 1970s saw these changes in women's status as a bit of a fluke. "The military community continued to believe that reliance on women was a temporary condition that would pass."²⁶ Only it didn't. Not only had women entered the service academies, but they were moving into airplanes and onto ships and ending up in all corners of military installations, whether the leadership wanted them there or not.

The debate over women in the military academies gave voice to concerns from the male military leadership corps and backlash from male cadets, but in the navy, another decision in the late 1970s also made many Americans upset. Admiral Elmo Zumwalt had begun making waves in the early 1970s with Z-gram 116, in which he expanded women's navy roles. When Congress decided in 1975 to allow women in the military academies, navy leaders began taking a closer look at what might limit women's full participation in the navy. The key lay in Section 6015 of the Women's Armed Services Integration Act of 1948, which specifically said "women may not be assigned to duty in aircraft that are engaged in combat missions nor may they be assigned to duty on vessels of the navy other than hospital ships and transports."²⁷ In 1948, that was fine: naval vessels could transport Waves to any assignment station, and nurses could care for patients on ships, but otherwise—and ironically enough—Waves were supposed to stay far away from the sea.

But if women could attend the military academies, it also seemed that they could serve on ships, especially since any women attending the Naval Academy in Annapolis would have to be able to go on the standard cadet summer training cruises. In 1972, the navy tried a brief experiment with the *USS Sanctuary*, an old hospital ship that became the testing ground to see if men and women could serve together. In this environment, military officials learned that the women were good at repair tasks and emergency teams, "performance on which is considered a good gauge of general naval ability."²⁸ The experiment lasted only three years and doesn't seem to have accomplished much immediate change, except providing evidence that women could serve on ships with men, doing everything from deck, supply, operations, resale, and administrative jobs (only men got to work in engineering).

As the seventies inched to a close, the navy took things even further, sponsoring legislation in Congress to partially remove Section 6015. Their goal was to have wider leverage to allow women's shipboard service while keeping them outside of the combat ships entirely. Amid all of this, though, a federal judge took things a step further and ruled in *Owens v. Brown* that Section 6015 was unconstitutional and should be entirely gone. Judge John Sirica's decision spends ample time describing the ways in which Section 6015 negatively affected women, not only during their military service, but also in the private sector. At the heart of things, he notes, "the fact remains that only so many shore-confined members are capable of being integrated" into the navy, given that its central mission is combat operations at sea. "The practical effect of this limitation is that a disproportionately small number of women will have the opportunity to embark upon a career whose successful completion carries with it numerous and economically significant veterans' benefits and preferences." But even more, Sirica notes in his decision, this law and other limitations navy women faced had no origin in science. There were no indications that women could not perform the jobs that only men held, but there were certainly indications that suggested otherwise.

Judge Sirica took issue with the fact that although the Women's Armed Services Integration Act had been heavily modified in 1967 with the removal of promotion limits and the number of women recruits, Section 6015 still stood. The result, he argued, "heightened the adverse effect of the constraint by allowing an increasing number of female members to enter the navy and advance upward through the ranks, while at the same time denying them the career opportunities that comprise the primary mission of the naval forces."[29] He applauded that the navy had worked hard in recent years to expand the use of womanpower, but in his opinion, Section 6015 persisted as the ultimate stumbling block to their efforts. The only solution, Sirica ruled, was that Section 6015 should not exist. While he understood that Congress created the clause well within their rights thirty years earlier, Sirica argued that this did not mean Congress was right. As a result, "the Court has concluded that the blanket limitation imposed by section 6015 cannot be presently justified, [thus] the effect of today's decision is to restore to the military an area of discretion that the 80th Congress unreasonably withheld." In other words, he essentially erased Section 6015 by prohibiting its enforcement, and directed that the navy move forward.

They did: naval officials declined to appeal the decision, and immediately moved to plan and implement the Women in Ships Program. Within two months, Rear Admiral John O'Connor (Chief of Chaplains) sketched out proposed methods for putting women at sea. He argued that realism was the key. O'Connor worried about statements he heard from men in the Bureau of Naval Personnel, such as "'if they're going to sea, we're going to treat them exactly like men.' To me this is very sad, and reveals underlying male chauvinism, at best, and an unwillingness to think things through for the good of the navy."[30] O'Connor recommended both a short- and long-term approach targeting multiple levels of naval command, stressing the fact that "women are welcome assets, not liabilities." To help members of the navy understand this, O'Connor emphasized the importance of recognizing obstacles to seeing women as assets. For example, naval command needed to recognize that officers lacked experience disciplining women and pointed out that navy wives might have some concerns about navy women serving at sea with their husbands.

In late February 1979, *The Washington Post* profiled the *USS Vulcan*, with its new crew of more than sixty women who would be serving alongside men on this repair ship. The crew included nineteen-year-old Christine Berringer, trained as a machinist, or "grease monkey," and doing good work according to her boss. "She does a damn good job. I'd like to have four more like her." He had overcome his initial concerns about having women on board and now realized that Berringer "works as hard as any man." On the flip side, the men were maybe not working as hard as they once did—reportedly, more than a few liked to come watch Berringer at work.[31] Executive Officer Charles L. Keithley Jr. professed to have been open-minded about women on board, but also recognized that this was something very new. The navy held human rights seminars in advance for the crew and "talks that warned against any discrimination against the women but also stressed that the men should not develop a protective attitude toward them."

While things might have been going well onboard the *Vulcan*, that month *The San Diego Union* offered an entirely different view. The writer of this article claimed that "Navy Women Deplore Life Aboard Warships," because "their male shipmates do not respect their professional capabilities and generally view them as sex objects."[32] The women in this feature served mostly shore side, supporting ships by refueling or being aboard yard tugs. In their experience, the men who worked on the boats did not seem like men who could work respectfully alongside women at sea. The senior enlisted men were no better than common sailors, according to the article. In practical terms, "most of the women were worried about their personal security aboard a warship, considering their experience on bases with a lot of ship activity and their own experiences serving on small craft." The navy hadn't protected them so far; one woman cited her experiences in Puerto Rico where the sailors frequently tried to enter the women's barracks. In their experience, "It is a bad act ashore. What will it be like at sea?"

For at least one group of women, their experiences at sea became the end of their military career. In 1980, nineteen women stationed on the USS *Norton Sound*—nearly one third of the women on board—became subjects of a lesbian investigation. The Naval Investigation Service (NIS) started out looking into accusations of drugs, loansharking, and violence, but shifted their attention when one female crew member claimed that at least twenty-three of the women serving on board were lesbians. Although the unnamed crew member did not have proof, she described ways in which some of the women on board spoke with other women, acted "very masculine," or appeared to show extra levels of interest in women. African American women, according to her, were some of the worst offenders. What followed was the same level of inquiry as found in the WAC in the early 1950s, with similar lines of questioning about women's sexual behavior and interactions between each other. One television commentator even specifically compared the investigation to the McCarthy witch hunts of the 1950s.[33] The ACLU became involved almost immediately, along with several gay rights groups, support that was not possible in the 1950s for accused Wacs or other servicewomen.

The navy dropped charges against eleven women but went forward with the remaining eight. According to *The Chicago Tribune*'s coverage on August 31, 1980, the first two women charged were acquitted. Witnesses for the women included one's fiancé and another man she had lived with previously, who both assured the board of the servicewoman's history of heterosexual behavior. In other words, she was "normal." On the other hand, the woman's mother was so upset about the charges that she tried to get custody of the servicewoman's child, who was already in the servicewoman's mother's care.[34] The next two women were not so lucky and "were recommended for general discharge under honorable conditions" because they were guilty of homosexual conduct. The remaining four hearings were canceled and the navy "abruptly dropped its charges"—apparently due to insufficient evidence.[35] One lieutenant said that in addition, "the navy felt the large amount of adverse publicity surrounding the investigation and the hearings was hurting the morale of both enlisted personnel and officers."[36] The *Norton Sound* became a public disaster for the navy, primarily because of the investigation that targeted these women. The NIS had begun investigating other problems—including a suspicious death—and had ended by putting servicewomen in the limelight in the most negative way possible.

One year after the navy began sending women shipboard, the first major story Americans saw about the new plan indicated that everything was a spectacular failure. Women's lives had been ruined and changed—they had been specifically targeted because of their status in nontraditional roles. It was easy to target them as "abnormal" because shipboard duty did not seem like something most women should want. That sort of duty, people felt, was clearly for men. One of the *"Norton Sound* Eight" noted later that there seemed to be plenty of men on board who were gay, yet no one targeted them. Of course, in 1980, the armed forces were more concerned about retaining manpower, as the article in *Time* magazine two months earlier had made clear. In that environment, targeting men who did not fit regulations did not make sense. During the *Norton Sound* Eight hearings, before the final four were canceled, one staff member at the White House noted in a memo, "Prevent future purges until after November."[37]

Within a year, the *Norton Sound* hearings had faded from public view. By 1981, ship commanders wanted more women. In response, the navy decided to aim for 5,000 women on fifty-five ships by the middle of the decade, about a quarter more than they had thought at first.[38] But the legacy of Section 6015 held firm: the navy was moving conservatively, as was the rest of the military. According to Major General Jeanne Holm, "the services were never convinced of the necessity for expanding the utilization of women since the advent of the all-volunteer force. They were especially traumatized by the forced integration of women into operational areas and the sacrosanct service academies."[39] Despite such stories as women serving on ships or occasionally moving into jobs not usually occupied by women, Holm notes that in the early 1980s most servicewomen still held stereotypically female jobs. There were more women in the military, and certainly greater visibility of women doing totally new things, but most women's experiences remained fairly similar to what they had been a decade earlier. In the 1970s, military officials reimagined womanpower in drastic ways, but it began to look as if their commitment to supporting women as they stepped into those opportunities had waned.

Conclusion

As Director of the Women's Army Corps, General Mildred Bailey (1971–75) led efforts to integrate training and headquarters staff at the WAC Center and School, as well as the staff in the Director of the WAC's office. Until that time, only women served in these roles, but as the numbers of servicewomen expanded in the 1970s, there were no longer enough women to do the work on their own. "Shades of World War II," Bailey said, only this time, the roles were reversed: the WAC needed manpower for support roles. Women commanded WAC training, and the servicemen assigned there followed women's orders. Some of the men who came volunteered, but many others did not want to be there. "They felt their manhood was downgraded, their careers were going to be ruined." When Bailey integrated her own staff, she set a high bar: any serviceman coming to the director's office would have to have the same qualifications required for servicewomen in the office, which included being at least a major or junior lieutenant colonel, and at least a graduate of the Army Staff College. Bailey also specified that any man who joined the office would need to volunteer for the position. She worried that no one would apply, but there was a fair amount of interest. The men who applied "believed in what was happening to women in the army, in the further utilization, and expanding the scope and eliminating discriminatory practices. They believed in it and wanted to be a part of it." The man hired to the position became invaluable, but when she explained the change at a deputy chief of staff for personnel staff meeting, the (male) senior officer was flabbergasted and worried for the serviceman's career path. "It didn't surprise me that that would be the attitude," Bailey reflected. "What surprised me was that this senior officer was shocked into expressing it publicly."[1]

Bailey's account of integrating men into the WAC Center highlights the challenges that persisted within the armed forces alongside all the changes that happened for servicewomen in the 1970s. As she explained, not every serviceman believed that working in the WAC was beneath him, but some did, and even high-ranking officials worried about the prospect of men doing women's work. This had been true in the 1950s, as well, when men assigned as drill instructors to the Women Marines faced gendered taunts about their positions.[2] Servicemen had certainly held plenty of office jobs in the military's history but working in an area dominated by servicewomen had a reputation as an undesirable career path because it highlighted that a job could be relegated to women. As womanpower expanded in the 1970s, both in terms of numbers and in the types of opportunities women now had the ability to pursue, these changes increased the likelihood that servicemen would work alongside or command women. In earlier decades, servicemen and women had certainly worked together in many ways, and men had commanded women as well. However, the small numbers of women and the expansion of combat roles during the Korean and Vietnam Wars had meant that many men might spend most of their years in service working with no women or very few, even perhaps only encountering women as nurses or other medical staff. By 1980, that reality was changing: at the beginning of the decade, Holm explains, fewer than one in ten service members were women, and by the end of the 1980s, women would account for 12 percent of the total military strength. In 1979, although none of the services hit their recruiting targets, 42,000 women enlisted. In 1980, the services managed to make their goals, but, as Holm points out, that was "due in large part to the enlistment of 50,000 women."[3] Reimagining womanpower in the 1970s meant that military officials and servicemen at all levels would need to confront their own assumptions and expectations about servicewomen. Speaking in 1978, Bailey emphasized, "we cannot take for granted that because laws and policies and regulations have changed, equal opportunity for women will automatically follow. It will happen only if we refuse to be complacent and we assume individual responsibility for actions to eliminate discriminatory practices and change unacceptable attitudes."[4] Integration was not complete, nor had servicewomen achieved equality: a new phase of integrating womanpower had begun, and the definition of equality began to evolve once again.

In the years immediately following World War II, military leaders and members of Congress defined women's equality in simple terms, focusing on pay equity and jobs women could perform as well as or better than men. This definition acknowledged that when women and men performed the same work, women deserved to be paid the same. It was a definition that assumed men and women were inherently different: in this formulation, American women were always, above all, ladies. Regulations reflected assumptions of gender difference, limiting women's promotion opportunities and access to jobs, and always reinforcing the idea that men came first and women second. As women entered the armed forces, their experiences complicated the use of this definition. Allies such as the women's service leaders and members of DACOWITS used their positions to advocate for a more expansive definition of equality, while some servicewomen challenged regulations that limited their careers on the basis of sex. All met with limited success for two decades. Their efforts and their experiences in the armed forces called into question the idea that military service offered women equality with men. In the 1960s and 1970s, Americans began to redefine "equality" and so did military and government officials, moving away from a definition of equality based on assumptions that men and women's biological differences must be considered when thinking about their social and economic roles. The new definition of equality centered instead on recognizing individual capability, regardless of sex. Slowly, military leaders opened more jobs, allowed women into military academies, and eventually created policy changes that put women not into combat, but in proximity to combat by the end of the century.

The definition of equality evolved due to servicewomen's experiences and Americans' changing attitudes and assumptions about sex and gender. During the 1970s, many viewed the changes and progress in women's status—particularly the elimination of the women's service components and expanded access to military jobs—as evidence that women were finally becoming equal and being integrated into the military completely. It seemed that women's roles in the military would only continue to expand and improve in the years to come, given their new opportunities. Despite a brief effort to contract women's military service from 1981 to 1982 known as "Womanpause," when some government and military officials proposed backing away from goals set by the Carter administration to recruit and retain women, by 1990 there were more women in uniform than ever before.[5] Consequently, in the 1990s the evolution of military conflicts created new questions about the roles all personnel play. Given the role that women played supporting military operations Desert Shield and Desert Storm, at the end of 1991 President Bush signed the National Defense Authorization Act with provisions allowing women to fly combat missions. The act also temporarily stopped "gender-based restrictions on sea and land combat roles" so that a new commission could study women's military roles.[6] Secretary of Defense Dick Cheney himself declared that the U.S. military "could not have won [the war] without them [women]."[7] By 1994, policy revisions permitted women to serve on combat surface ships and in air combat units.[8] Under these 1994 Aspin regulations, women could not serve in units "whose primary mission is to engage in direct combat on the ground," defined as "engaging an enemy on the ground with individual or crew served weapons, while being exposed to hostile fire and to a high probability of direct physical contact with the hostile force's personnel."[9] These policies laid the groundwork for women's participation in Afghanistan and Iraq in the early twenty-first century. Today, servicewomen both serve in and command troops in combat zones.[10] Since the 1970s, the meaning of equality has, in one way, consistently focused on eliminating barriers to women's full participation, defined in terms of whether or not women have access to all military career paths.

With that definition in mind, military leaders have continued to end regulations that prevent women from serving in combat across all branches, changes that are the result of nearly seventy years of work to integrate women into national defense. In 2015, Secretary of Defense Ash Carter announced that within one year, the armed forces would eliminate all regulations that prevented women from serving in combat roles. At that time, women remained ineligible for about 10 percent of all military jobs.[11] Earlier that year, women attended the army's Ranger School for the first time because of earlier work toward removing the combat ban. When three of the nineteen women completed the course that fall, existing regulations forbade them from filling Ranger positions. Carter's announcement a few months later meant that they could have that opportunity in the future.[12] By April 2020, fifty women had successfully completed Ranger School, and a woman was the top graduate in March 2020 for the first time.[13] Now that the combat ban is gone, these women do not have to experience what happened to servicewomen in earlier times: while servicewomen demonstrated their abilities to perform important military functions during the Cold War, regulations contradicted them because military and government leaders had assumed such a feat was either impossible or undesirable.

In the past two decades, the percentage of women in national defense and their opportunities have continued to grow with U.S. involvement in Afghanistan and Iraq. Women continue to make gains, including promotions to four-star general, increasing command responsibility, and extensive presence in combat zones. Some experts now emphasize that the armed forces could not function without women.[14] Ongoing expansion of both women's service roles and opportunities demonstrates that the definition of equality continues to evolve beyond that imagined even by 1970s activists. Both in terms of numbers and in the capacities in which women now serve, servicewomen have secured the equality sought in the 1970s, given the successful elimination of sex-based policies now understood to be discriminatory against women. Yet while women's roles have expanded, old issues continue, and new problems arise. While women no longer have to leave the services because they become mothers, regulations still punish women for childbearing and many commanding officers lack important knowledge of these regulations and pertinent exceptions for new mothers. Sexual assault of servicewomen is more visible than ever, and although it is also being addressed more, the solutions are not enough. Gender still matters in the armed forces, and military leaders continue to struggle to recognize and address this fact.

The legacy of the 1970s reconfigurations of womanpower has been that problems related to sexual integration persist in the armed forces because the culture of institutional masculinity remains largely intact. Much of the impetus for change in women's status during the 1970s resulted from the transition to the AVF and external pressures from the women's movement on both the DOD and Congress. Consequently, many of the changes seen as improvements in women's status—gains toward equality—occurred under the position that current restrictions on women's military service were discriminatory and unnecessary. At no time, it seems, did anyone suggest that the military itself might need to change because of women's participation. Rather, all changes focused on fitting women into existing military systems more fully. According to sociologist and navy veteran Darlene Iskra, in the armed forces "the male standard is presumed to be the only acceptable standard."[15] Military leaders continue to assess women's success in integrating into national defense by how well they perform against masculine, male-based standards. Setting standards any differently for women creates a perception that they do not perform as well as men, but this perception still assumes that the original standards—created for men—are the only valid ones to use.

In early 2020, the marines began to integrate boot camp at the platoon level for the first time in its history. Since the announced end of gender-based combat restrictions, the marine corps has consistently been the service branch most opposed to this shift. Little more than 200 women serve in formerly off-limits roles now, and only in 2018 did the marine corps assign a woman to head an infantry platoon for the first time in its history.[16] Women comprise about 9 percent of the marine corps, and in early 2021 the first group of women joined boot camp at Marine Corps Recruit Depot San Diego. One captain argued that although women's training in San Diego was new, "It's no different—we're going to be training essentially the same ways that we have been for years."[17] A year earlier, an April 2020 *New York Times* article about the changing boot camp experience highlighted that marine corps leaders saw no reason to change their ways. According to General Robert Neller, "We've been successful making marines, so why should we change?" Referring to gender-segregated platoons, General James Glynn, the commanding officer of Recruit Depot Parris Island (South Carolina), argued "This works."[18] Attitudes such as this create more obstacles to effective utilization, not women themselves. Relying on the way things have always been done may work, but that does not mean it's the best answer.

A moment near the end of boot camp at Parris Island in February 2020 bears this out. At that time, women and men trained in separate platoons for eleven weeks prior to the final multi-day exercise. Early in the final challenge, journalist Thomas Gibbons-Neff writes, a male recruit convinced his group that the men were strong enough to move ammo cans across a rope bridge, ignoring a female recruit's suggestion to push the load across instead. After watching the men struggle, the servicewoman in question took the lead, implementing her approach. It worked much better. Her approach was not better because she was a woman, but because she tried to tackle a problem in a new way, one that did not rely on an old stand-by like physical strength. While there are certainly many moments and instances where physical strength matters in military service and training, the female recruit's approach to problem-solving demonstrates that sometimes, there are other ways to get things done. When military leaders assume that the old way of doing things is the best way, they stand in the way of institutional growth and new possibilities for success.

The resistance servicewomen continue to encounter from men, often expressed through discounting their ideas, or aggression, sexual overtures, and discrimination, reveals the ongoing complications of integrating women into national defense and how much work remains for women to become accepted as partners with men in the military. Gender and sexuality continue to be central elements of women's military experiences, affecting how servicemen and male superiors perceive them, their assignments, and their career opportunities. Although women now serve in a greater capacity in combat zones than ever, the same questions of women's physical capability to perform combat, along with the cultural appropriateness of women in combat, remain. Opponents to women in combat accuse feminist military advocates of using the armed forces "to further social change in our society without regard for military effectiveness," a charge that suggests that women do not have the skills or abilities to be capable of serving in all aspects of combat.[19] Yet those who support women's increased combat roles continue to argue, as they did in the 1970s, that there are women who are capable of filling these roles—noting that not all men meet the physical requirements for some combat roles, either. Removing legal barriers to military jobs is only one aspect of integrating womenpower successfully. While servicewomen are now "equal" in ways that women in the 1950s, 1960s, and 1970s could only dream about, integration will remain incomplete until underlying structural issues are addressed.

Half a century after naval Lt. Commander Jordine Von Wantoch fought to stay in the military when she became pregnant with her daughter, servicewomen still encounter obstacles due to pregnancy and motherhood. In 2019, DACOWITS made extensive recommendations regarding pregnancy and parenthood policies, including the recommendation that "The Secretary of Defense should direct the Military Services to develop and implement policies that ensure a servicewoman's career is not negatively affected as a result of pregnancy."[20] This recommendation came as a part of more than 20 pages of studies and recommendations on a number of issues pertinent to military mothers, including breastfeeding, maternity uniforms, mothers reintegrating home after deployment, and stigmas pregnant servicewomen face. At the March 2020 DACOWITS meeting, Lt. Colonel Jessica Ruttenber and Major Megan Biles of the air force reasserted the importance of changing policies related to pregnancy. They argued that pregnancy remains "a long-standing and significant barrier to the career advancement of women in the Armed Forces." Through their research and experiences supporting air force women, they concluded pregnancy continues to negatively affect women's military careers. "DOD policies often convey the message that having a family and being in the military are incompatible," they explained, noting that policies also have the effect of making pregnancy seem like something women need to hide in order to protect their careers for as long as possible, even causing some women to bypass prenatal healthcare early in a pregnancy. The officers asked DACOWITS to work to further protect pregnant women through military equal opportunity policies and to continue investigating the matter.[21] In May 2020, a new study confirmed what DACOWITS, Ruttenber and Biles would have already known, as reported by *Christian Science Monitor*: "pregnancy is one of the top reasons enlisted women leave the service."[22] Servicewomen still have to fight for the right to be mothers in the military.

Although femininity no longer drives the public image of servicewomen as it did in the early Cold War, servicewomen remain subject to problematic physical standards. These standards pose challenges for many women after they give birth, and only in February 2021 did the marine corps shift their policy away from requiring servicewomen to pass physical and combat fitness tests within nine months of having a baby. The new policy specifies "No earlier than 12 months after the birth event, the marine is required to take the [physical fitness and combat fitness] test at the next regularly scheduled physical fitness evaluation in that semi-annual period," and offers exceptions for medical reasons.[23] At the end of 2020, an op-ed by female marine corps officers argued that these physical standards not only negatively affect pregnant women and new mothers, but they also rely on old standards that are no longer useful measurements of an individual's health and fitness. The authors point out that the 2002 DOD body composition standard currently in use was established in 1984, based on navy sailors.

In the three decades since then, the services adapted new physical fitness tests and the gear that servicewomen carry has changed, indicating that women now have a higher base fitness level than in earlier decades. In short, women's bodies have changed. While personnel who do not make weight requirements can be measured for body fat percentage, this alternative is highly problematic. In one case, "a female marine officer who earns very high first-class physical fitness scores, and even competed twice on American Ninja Warrior, was measured above her allowable marine corps body fat despite being 20 pounds under her maximum allowable marine corps weight and 30 lbs. below the maximum allowable DOD weight."[24] One of the authors, Major Sisbarro, took these concerns to DACOWITS for their December 2020 meeting. As with pregnancy, the issues were not new to DACOWITS members: in their 2019 report, they had already expressed concerns that "The current guidelines may contribute to . . . experience of unattainable standards for women, especially non-White women . . . unhealthy behavior to meet stringent standards . . . [and] gender bias against women." The report included feedback from focus groups run between 2015 and 2019 and concluded that the body fat guidelines relied on "outdated science" and recommended review to create new standards.[25]

In the past decade, sexual assault in the military has received increased attention. As of 2008, Pentagon studies found that approximately one-third of all servicewomen have been sexually harassed during their time in the military, a statistic that calls into question the idea that servicewomen are equal if servicemen perceive servicewomen as sexual objects to which they have the right of access at any time.[26] In 2019, the DOD reported a 3 percent increase in reports of sexual assault, a statistic that does not necessarily mean assault has increased, but that at the very least, victims are more willing to come forward. This is good, particularly since military studies indicate that sexual assault and harassment cases remain underreported—a trend that has continued since at least the mid-1970s.[27] While the armed forces began addressing sexual assault and harassment in the military at least as far back as the mid-1970s, the 1991 Tailhook scandal in Las Vegas brought the matter to national attention.[28] A 2009 CBS news story about sexual assault in the military noted that the fact that one in three military women were victims of sexual assault or harassment meant that women in the military are twice as likely as their civilian counterparts to encounter such treatment.[29] Since then, the DOD noted in 2018 that numbers of women being assaulted have fallen by half over the past decade.[30] Meanwhile, the armed forces have taken steps to address sexual assault, most recently with a study examining where most assaults happen and risk factors that might lead to assaults.[31] As of 2019, military officials also announced the criminalization of sexual harassment, in light of increases in assault and harassment reports.[32] In short, military officials are now paying more attention to sexual assault and how they address it, but the problem is far from being solved. The April 2020 murder of army Specialist Vanessa Guillen by a male soldier renewed attention to the problem of violence toward servicewomen and ignited a #MeToo moment for servicewomen and veterans.[33]

Partially in response to Guillen's murder, members of Congress began investigating Fort Hood, Texas, in fall 2020. In 2020 alone, there were almost 30 deaths at Fort Hood, "at least nine of them under unusual or suspicious circumstances," including Guillen's death.[34] According to the *New York Times*, "[T]he investigation documented a failure to properly staff and fund the sexual assault and harassment prevention program, and a culture in which women did not feel comfortable coming forward." Investigators interviewed more than 500 women. Within that group, there were "93 credible accounts of sexual assault; of those, just 59 had been reported . . . [t]hey also found 135 credible instances of sexual harassment; just 72 were reported." Even worse, investigators found, "no commanding general or subordinate senior commander proactively intervened to mitigate 'known risks.'"[35] In the aftermath of the study, military leadership removed 14 commanders from duty or suspended them in the midst of additional investigations. Army officials have promised to address the problems found—problems that are not unique to Fort Hood, or to the army alone.[36]

Both the statistics on women as sexual assault victims in the military and the tendency of such acts to go unreported indicate that neither servicemen nor servicewomen perceive servicewomen as men's equals. These statistics show that women perceive a lack of institutional support in protecting themselves from assault and suggest that the institutional culture of a lack of assault reporting protects perpetrators. Largely exempt from consequences and given the ability to behave as they wish, men continue to hold the position as the most important members of the military. Like the unquestioned assumption that existing standards must be adapted for women because the long-established standards (designed for men) are the most appropriate measure of personnel effectiveness, the persistence of sexual assault and the uneven or missing responses to it perpetuate a perception of women as second-class service members.

The mid-1990s "Don't Ask, Don't Tell" directive legally extended the Pentagon's Cold War policies against gays and lesbians in the armed forces and created new opportunities for servicemen to target servicewomen they perceived as threatening. Under this policy, ended in 2011, homosexual men and women could serve in the armed forces if they did not reveal their sexual orientation; they would not be asked about their sexual orientation, nor would they be forced out of the closet. Viewed by some as an improvement over such policies that led to the witch hunts of the 1950s, as well as studies like the Crittenden Report, the effects of Public Law (PL) 103–160 instead had particular impact on servicewomen. According to the DOD, PL103–160 accounted for at least 600 and as many as 1,273 annual personnel discharges between 1994 and 2006, with a total of more than 13,000 discharges after 1994.[37] Women were disproportionately discharged under the law, although the reasons for this remain unclear. In 2008, women comprised 34 percent of all such discharges, but made up only 14 percent of military strength.[38] The percentage of lesbian discharges under "Don't Ask, Don't Tell" begs the question of whether military officials specifically used this policy as a way to target servicewomen.[39]

The relationship between sexuality and military service continues to be contentious. In 2016, Secretary of Defense Ash Carter eliminated the military's ban on transgender service members, a move that fit with his prior announcements that ended limitations on women's service. Removing role limitations for women, ending "Don't Ask, Don't Tell," and allowing transgender Americans to serve openly in the armed forces are all shifts signaling a military in which assumptions about an individual's ability on the basis of their gender identity or sexual orientation no longer matter. For many eager to see the end of discrimination on the basis of gender identity and sexual orientation, these changes seemed positive. At the same time, these changes met pragmatic needs for an all-volunteer force seeking recruits. Military.com reported in late 2018 that "recruiters have struggled to compete in a growing U.S. economy, with low unemployment rates and private companies paying more to graduating seniors." Fewer than one-third of Americans between the ages of seventeen and twenty-four meet military enlistment requirements; "only one in eight are interested in serving."[40] However, in 2017 President Trump attempted to ban transgender Americans from joining the military; despite several legal challenges, the ban went into effect in April 2019.[41] The ban was short-lived, reversed in January 2021 with President Biden's Executive Order 14004, "Enabling All Qualified Americans To Serve Their Country in Uniform." This executive order reversed previous actions barring transgender Americans from service. "It is my conviction as Commander in Chief of the Armed Forces," President Biden wrote, "that gender identity should not be a bar to military service."[42]

When members of Congress passed the Womens' Armed Services Integration Act in 1948, they would not have imagined such a possibility as the one President Biden affirmed. But Executive Order 14004 is a legacy of the 1948 act because opening a space for women in national defense made government and military leaders redefine ideas of who defends the nation, what defense roles look like, and what it means for women to be equal with men. As servicewomen, civilians, and military leaders debated, facilitated, and lived womanpower after World War II, they often upheld cultural assumptions about women's place in society and the economy. At the same time, by acknowledging women's ability to perform defense jobs, military service became a career opportunity in which American women challenged those assumptions and slowly redefined equality. Women's history in the military exposes the evolution of persistent assumptions that drive women's military service today, such as beliefs in what women are physically capable of doing and the ways in which masculinity and combat have become the paragons of military duty. Servicewomen's persistent battles for equality, even when they seemed to fail in the short term, helped make possible a military institution where anyone can serve—not just cisgender, heterosexual individuals. Womanpower has indelibly shaped modern defense.

While military and government officials created new openings for women to pursue military careers in the 1970s, they also created new opportunities for men to treat women badly and did not consider or address these possibilities. They did not understand that there is more to equality than eliminating sex-based job limitations. Initially concerned with finding ways to alleviate charges of sex discrimination, in many ways members of

Congress and military leaders took the approach that sex no longer mattered in the military, just as race supposedly no longer mattered either. Yet in the process they failed to recognize the importance of inculcating a culture of respect regardless of sex. Many servicemen began to perceive that women had forced their way in where they did not belong, ostensibly because they were too weak to be there. Consequently, the military began to foster a culture in which many men do not respect or take servicewomen seriously. Womanpower remains problematic for military leaders because too many Americans—including high-ranking military officials—refuse to let go of their beliefs that defense is a man's job.

Today, women comprise approximately 17 percent of the nation's defense team: they are indispensable to national defense.[43] As Secretary of the Army John McHugh expressed in his confirmation hearings in 2009, "Women in uniform today are not just invaluable, they're irreplaceable."[44] In an operational sense, this may be true, but from a cultural standpoint, statistics on sexual assault, as well as women's ongoing experiences of sexual harassment and discrimination suggest that many servicemen do not see women as "necessary" to national defense, let alone equals. Rather, servicemen who participate in sexual assault, harassment, or discrimination treat servicewomen as inferiors. An environment in which servicewomen cannot find justice when they are harassed and assaulted magnifies this problem. The institutional culture that makes servicewomen feel they have to hide their pregnancies underscores the misconception that women are somehow not good enough. Once, the American rhetoric of war was built upon the idea of protecting women. Now that general convention in the United States is that women do not need protection, men treat them not as partners in defense but as prey. This is not equality: with gender-based regulations no longer in effect, government and military leaders are continuing to redefine equality, but now that definition must consider the masculinized nature of national defense and reckon with it once and for all.

Key Dates in Women's Military History

February 2, 1901	Army Nurse Corps created.
May 13, 1908	Navy Nurse Corps created.
1917–19	During World War I, women serve as Yeomen (F) in the navy and with the U.S. Army Signal Corps.
May 15, 1942	Women's Army Auxiliary Corps (WAAC) created.
July 21, 1942	U.S. Women's Naval Reserve, known as Women Accepted for Volunteer Emergency Service (WAVES) established.
July 30, 1942	Women's Marine Corps Reserve created.
July 3, 1943	WAAC becomes part of the army as the Women's Army Corps (WAC).
June 12, 1948	Women's Armed Services Integration Act makes women a permanent part of the U.S. military.
July 26, 1948	President Harry Truman signs Executive Order 9981, desegregating the military.
April 27, 1951	President Truman signs Executive Order 10240, authorizing discharge of servicewomen due to parenthood.
November 8, 1967	President Lyndon B. Johnson signs Public Law 90–130, removing rank ceilings on women officers.
June 11, 1970	Anna Hays (Army Nurse Corps) and Elizabeth Hoisington (WAC) become the first women generals in the U.S. Armed Forces.
March 22, 1972	Congress passes Equal Rights Amendment.
January 17, 1973	Supreme Court rules in *Frontiero vs. Richardson* that married servicewomen are entitled to dependent benefits on the same bases as servicemen.
Summer 1976	Women enter West Point, Air Force Academy, Naval Academy, and Coast Guard Academy for the first time.
October 20, 1978	Public Law 95–584 eliminates all elements of the WAC.
November 1, 1978	Women begin serving aboard the USS *Vulcan*, the first navy women outside of the nursing corps to serve on ships.
Summer 1980	First group of women graduates from the service academies.

Women Military Leaders

Although only the army had a separate organizational structure for women (the WAC), each service branch created offices held by women and designed to administer womanpower. The tables below identify women military leaders by their position, ending with the dissolution of the WAC in 1978. Rank designations reflect each woman's highest promotion earned on active duty.

World War II Women Military Leaders

WAAC (1942–43) and WAC	Colonel Oveta Culp Hobby (1942–45)
	Colonel Westray Battle Boyce (1945–47)
WAVES	Captain Mildred McAfee Horton
Women Marine Corps Reserves	Colonel Ruth Cheney Streeter
Women in the Coast Guard (SPARS)	Captain Dorothy C. Stratton

Source: Major General Jeanne Holm, *Women in the Military: An Unfinished Revolution.*

Director—WAC

Colonel Mary Hallaren	1947–53
Colonel Irene Galloway	1953–57
Colonel Mary Louise Milligan Rasmuson	1957–62
Colonel Emily Gorman	1962–66
Brigadier General Elizabeth Hoisington	1966–71
Brigadier General Mildred Bailey	1971–75
Brigadier General Mary Clarke	1975–78

Source: Bettie J. Morden, *The Women's Army Corps, 1945–1978.*

Director—WAF

Colonel Geraldine Pratt May	1948–51
Colonel Mary Jo Shelly	1951–54
Colonel Phyllis Gray	1954–57
Colonel Emma Riley	1957–61
Colonel Elizabeth Ray	1961–65
Major General Jeanne Holm	1965–73
Colonel Billie Bobbitt	1973–75
Colonel Bianca Trimeloni	1975–76

Source: Historical Summary, Office Directorate, WAF (July–December 1957, July–December 1961); Major General Jeanne Holm, *Women in the Military: An Unfinished Revolution.*

Director—WAVES (Assistant Chief of Personnel for Women)

Captain Joy Bright Hancock	1946–53
Captain Louise K. Wilde	1953–57
Captain Winifred Quick Collins	1957–62
Captain Viola Sanders	1962–66
Captain Rita Lenihan	1966–70
Captain Robin L. Quigley	1971–73

Source: Jeanne Ebbert and Marie-Beth Hall, *Crossed Currents: Navy Women in a Century of Change.*

Director—WM

Colonel Katherine Towle	1948–53
Colonel Julia Hamblet	1953–59
Colonel Margaret Henderson	1959–64
Colonel Barbara Bishop	1964–69
Colonel Jeanette Sustad	1969–73
Brigadier General Margaret Brewer	1973–77

Source: Mary Stremlow, *A History of the Women Marines, 1946–1977.*

Notes

Abbreviations in Notes

AFHRA	Air Force Historical Research Agency, Maxwell Air Force Base, AL
BuPersooW, Naval Historical Center	
	Records of the Bureau of Personnel Special Assistant for Women
Discharge Files	
	Decimal File 220-8 Homosexuality, Discharge Files
DOD	Department of Defense
Eisenhower Library	
	Dwight D. Eisenhower Presidential Library, Abilene, KS
Ford Library	
	Gerald R. Ford Library, Ann Arbor, MI
LBJ	Library Lyndon B. Johnson Presidential Library, Austin, TX
LOC VHP	Veterans History Project, American Folklife Center,
	Library of Congress, Washington, DC
NAB	National Archives Building, Washington, DC
NACP	National Archives, College Park, Maryland
Naval Historical Center	
	Operational Archives, Navy Historical Center, Washington, DC
PCSW	President's Commission on the Status of Women, Bethesda, MD:
	University Publications of America, 2001
RG	Record Group
Schlesinger Library	
	Schlesinger Library, Radcliffe Institute for
	Advanced Study, Harvard University
Stremlow WMs	
	Background materials to Stremlow's *History of*
	the Women Marines, 1946-1977
Truman Library	
	Truman Presidential Library, Independence, MO
USMC	United States Marine Corps
UNCG	University of North Carolina, Greensboro
WAVES	Records of the Assistant Chief of Personnel for Women 1942-1973,
	Scholarly Resources, Inc.

Introduction

1. Remarks at the White House by Major General Jeanne Holm, Special Assistant to President Ford, DACOWITS Fall 1976 meeting, O-10; Minutes: 25th Anniversary Meeting—November 14–18, 1976 Folder, Background Materials to *The Women's Army Corps, 1945–1978* (Background—WAC); Records of the Army Staff, RG319; NACP.
2. Subcommittee hearings on S. 1641, 5598.
3. Friedan, *The Feminine Mystique*, 58.
4. Friedan, 58–60.
5. May, *Homeward Bound*, xxiii.
6. Meyerowitz, *Not June Cleaver*, 231.
7. Kessler-Harris, *In Pursuit of Equity*, 5.
8. Cobble, *The Other Women's Movement*, 3.
9. Brigadier General Jeanne M. Holm interview with Captains Russel Mank, James L. Cole, Art Durand, and Joanna Vererka, United States Air Force Oral History Program, November 14, 1972, 20; K239.0512-928; AFHRA.
10. Holm interview with Mank, 22.
11. Sherry, *In the Shadow of War*, x, 150–51.
12. Enloe, *Does Khaki Become You?*, xvii.
13. Vuic, *Officer, Nurse, Woman*, 9.
14. Vuic, 9.
15. Vuic, 190.
16. Threat, *Nursing Civil Rights*, 5.
17. Threat, 5.
18. Threat, 132.
19. The Report of the President's Committee on Civil Rights, "To Secure These Rights," 1947, 8; Truman Library, https://www.trumanlibrary.gov/library/to-secure-these-rights.
20. Truman signed Executive Order No. 9981 on July 26, 1948. Executive Order 9981, "Establishing the President's Committee on Equality of Treatment and Opportunity in the Armed Services," Truman Library, https://www.trumanlibrary.gov/library/executive-orders/9981/executive-order-9981.
21. Krebs, *Fighting for Rights*, 177.
22. Mershon and Schlossman, *Foxholes and Color Lines*.
23. MacGregor Jr., *Integration of the Armed Forces*, ix. Gropman's *The Air Force Integrates*, initially published by the military, does not even contain references to women and includes data only related to men.
24. Fifteen years later, however, in 1989, Black women were 33.7 percent of all enlisted women and 13.2 percent of all female officers. For 1971, 1974, and 1989 statistics, see Moore, "African-American Women in the U.S. Military," 363. For 1972 statistics, see Office of the Deputy Assistant Secretary of Defense (Equal Opportunity), "Women in the Armed Forces: A Statistical Fact Book," August 1, 1973, chart "Strength of Women in the Armed Forces"; WAC Statistics Folder, Background—WAC; RG319; NACP.

25. Johnson, ed., *Black Women in the Armed Forces*, 7, 8, 23, 33, 41.

26. Johnson, ed., *Black Women in the Armed Forces*, 8, 41.

27. Moore, "African-American Women in the U.S. Military," 366.

28. Snyder, ed., "Figure 3," *120 Years of American Education*.

29. Cheryl Pellerin, "Carter Opens All Military Occupations, Positions to Women," U.S. DOD, DOD News, December 13, 2015, https://dod.defense.gov/News/Article/Article/632536/carter-opens-all-military-occupations-positions-to-women/.

30. Camila Domonoske, "In Defense Bill, Senate Approves Plan for Women to Register for Draft," *NPR*, The Two-Way, June 15, 2016, http://www.npr.org/sections/thetwo-way/2016/06/15/482168066/in-defense-bill-senate-approves-plan-for-women-to-register-for-draft; Jim Michaels, "Lawmakers Condemn Explicit Photos of Female Marines Posted Online," *USA Today*, March 6, 2017, http://www.usatoday.com/story/news/world/2017/03/06/lawmakers-review-marines-explicit-photos/98805710/.

31. Pellerin, "Carter Opens All Military Occupations, Positions to Women."

Chapter 1

1. Subcommittee hearings on S. 1641, 5563–64, Eisenhower statement.

2. According to historian Beth Bailey, the Joint Chiefs of Staff preferred the stability that a "professional standing force" might offer, considering postwar conditions. For a brief history of the draft, see Bailey, *America's Army*, 4–16.

3. Telegram, George Kennan to George Marshall ["Long Telegram"], February 22, 1946. Harry S. Truman Administration File, Elsey Papers. Truman Library, https://www.trumanlibrary.gov/library/research-files/telegram-george-kennan-james-byrnes-long-telegram.

4. As historian Michael Sherry has argued, the militarization of America was underway: all these events, and others in the late 1940s, gave the appearance that although the war was over, problems remained. "The Cold War in Europe," he writes, "offered Americans a clear and apparently familiar story line: as in the 1930s, their cultural cousins were in desperate straits facing a totalitarian enemy." Similar concerns emerged in east Asia, as well. For discussions of these problems and how they factored into the militarization of American life during the Cold War, see Sherry, *In the Shadow of War*, chapter 3.

5. Although the nation had emerged from the war victorious, historian Laura McEnaney notes a new emphasis on "national security" as the nation evaluated the future. "High-level civilian and military planners . . . felt confidence and fear, and an inability to resolve a new contradiction of the nuclear age: how to acclaim a postwar peace and at the same time prepare for another, certainly more destructive war?" McEnaney, *Civil Defense Begins at Home*, 4.

6. "America's Wars Fact Sheet," Department of Veteran Affairs, Washington, DC, November 2020, https://www.va.gov/opa/publications/factsheets/fs_americas_wars.pdf.

7. Sparrow, *History of Personnel Demobilization in the U.S. Army*, 357.

8. Data on women's participation available via "Their War Too: U.S. Women in the Military During WWII. Part I," The Unwritten Record, National Archives, https://unwritten-record.blogs.archives.gov/2018/03/22/their-war-too-u-s-women-in-the-military-during-wwii-part-i/.

9. Stremlow, *A History of the Women Marines*, 1.

10. Holm, *Women in the Military*, 102.

11. Stremlow, *A History of the Women Marines*, 3; Morden, *The Women's Army Corps*, 24–25.

12. Morden, 29.

13. Quoted in Morden, 39.

14. Morden, 39.

15. Stremlow, *A History of the Women Marines*, 3.

16. Morden, *The Women's Army Corps*, 55.

17. Holm argues that no one ever questioned the idea of nurses continuing permanently after the war. It was widely recognized that the military would need nurses—assumed to be women—during peacetime. Nurses had begun serving in 1901 but did not receive rank until after World War I; it wasn't until World War II that they got equal pay with their wartime commissions; the 1947 Act made these gains permanent, giving nurses rank and equal pay. See Holm, *Women in the Military*, 108. For more on the Army-Navy Nurses Act of 1947, see Vuic, *Officer, Nurse, Woman*, 53.

18. Eisenhower, *Crusade in Europe*, 220.

19. Hallaren Statement on S. 1103, 1947, 1–2. Mary Hallaren Collection, U.S. Army Women's Museum, Fort Lee, VA.

20. Senator Baldwin comment, "Hearings on S. 1103, S. 1527, and S. 1641," Senate Armed Services Committee, 80th Congress, 1st session, July 2, 1947, 21, NAB.

21. Major General Paul comment, "Hearings on S. 1103, S. 1527, and S. 1641," Senate Armed Services Committee, 80th Congress, 1st session, July 2, 1947, 21.

22. Quoted in Morden, *The Women's Army Corps*, 46.

23. Sparrow, *History of Personnel Demobilization in the U.S. Army*, 357.

24. "Session Dates of Congress, 80th to 89th Congresses (1947–1967)," History, Art, and Archives of the House of Representatives, https://history.house.gov/Institution/Session-Dates/80-89/.

25. *Termination of Certain Emergency Measures*, Public Law 239, U.S. Statutes at Large 61 (1947). Harry S. Truman, Statement by the President Upon Signing Resolution Terminating Additional Emergency Powers. Online by Gerhard Peters and John T. Woolley, The American Presidency Project, https://www.presidency.ucsb.edu/node/232104. Morden further specifies that the new law applied to the WAC; Morden, *The Women's Army Corps*, 46.

26. *The National Security Act of 1947*, Public Law 253, U.S. Statutes at Large 61 (1947), https://research.archives.gov/id/299856.

27. Morden, *The Women's Army Corps*, 43.

28. Mary Hallaren, "The Women's Army Corps," reprint of official comments, *Army-Navy Journal*, October 18, 1947. Mary Hallaren Collection, U.S. Army Women's Museum, Fort Lee, VA.

29. Conference; WAC Staff Directors and Senior WAC officers, March 26–28, 1947, 1. Mary Hallaren Collection, U.S. Army Women's Museum, Fort Lee, VA.

30. Statement by Mary Pillsbury Lord (Mrs. Oswald B. Lord), S1641 (No. 238) Subcommittee Hearings on S. 1641, To Establish the Women's Army Corps in the Regular Army etc., February 18, 1948, 5612; RG287, NAB.

31. Statement by Mary Pillsbury Lord, February 18, 1948, 5613.

32. Beth Bailey notes that they were only seeing about 12,000 men volunteer each month, only a third or a quarter of what they really needed, largely because the civilian economy was doing very well and that was competition for the army. See Bailey, *America's Army*, 11.

33. Comment of General Dwight D. Eisenhower, S. 1641 (No. 238) Subcommittee Hearings on S. 1641, To Establish the Women's Army Corps in the Regular Army etc., February 18, 1948, 5564; RG287; NAB.

34. Representative Walter G. Andrews (R-NY) Comment, S. 1641 (No. 238) Subcommittee Hearings on S. 1641, To Establish the Women's Army Corps in the Regular Army etc., February 18, 1948, 5565; RG287; NAB.

35. Representative Vinson (D-GA) Comment, S. 1641 (No. 238) Subcommittee Hearings on S. 1641, To Establish the Women's Army Corps in the Regular Army etc., February 18, 1948, 5578; RG287; NAB.

36. Forrestal had been recently named the first secretary of defense, following the implementation of the 1947 National Security Act.

37. Treadwell's history of the WAC details the myriad ways in which auxiliary status was problematic, from basic issues that meant that Army regulations did not always apply to women, and that things as basic as shopping on post exchanges, or as important as being able to obtain military life insurance, were an issue. See Treadwell, *The Women's Army Corps*, 113–15. This is perhaps best illustrated by the Women Airforce Service Pilots (WASPs) of World War II. Never classified as military, the WASPs ferried military planes and, because they were civilians, in case of death their families did not receive the death benefits regularly accorded to servicemen, as Rhonda Smith-Daugherty explains in her biography of WASP founder Jackie Cochran, *Jacqueline Cochran: Biography of a Pioneer Aviator*, 107.

38. Statement of Secretary of Defense James V. Forrestal, S. 1641 (no. 238) Subcommittee Hearings on S. 1641, 5573; RG287; NAB.

39. Statement of General Omar Bradley, S. 1641 (no. 238) Subcommittee Hearings on S. 1641, 5589, 5590; RG287; NAB.

40. Forrestal, S. 1641 (no. 238) Subcommittee Hearings on S. 1641, 5577.

41. Eisenhower, S. 1641 (no. 238) Subcommittee Hearings on S. 1641, 5566.

42. Radford, S. 1641 (no. 238) Subcommittee Hearings on S. 1641, 5585.

43. Johnson and Forrestal, S. 1641 (no. 238) Subcommittee Hearings on S. 1641, 5577.

44. Sherman, *No Place for a Woman*, 69. Smith's oft-quoted "either they need these women or they do not" phrase is included in a letter to the Honorable W. G. Andrews on February 14, 1948, reprinted in Smith, *Declaration of Conscience*, 87.

45. "Women in the Services," *New York Times*, March 31, 1948, 24.

46. Mary A. Hallaren, "Resolutions Passed by National Organizations in Favor of S. 1641," April 21, 1948. Director WAC Files, 1949–1950; Records of the Army Staff, RG319; NACP.

47. Mayrell Johnson, Letter to Senator Chan Gurney, April 4, 1948, S. 1641 Legislative Materials, NAB.

48. House Congressional Record, April 21, 1948, 4705–6. Hearings on WAC Bill—1948 Folder, Background—WAC; Records of the Army Staff, RG319; NACP.

49. Witt, Bellafaire, Granrud, and Binker, *A Defense Weapon Known to Be of Value*. Witt et al. offer additional reminders of the international context; see 28–29.

50. The Senate Armed Services Committee held hearings on Universal Military Training (UMT) in March and April 1948. Historian Amy Rutenberg examines the debates over UMT in 1947 and 1948 in more detail, noting that the Selective Service Act in 1948 ultimately did not include UMT. Marshall Testimony, Universal Military Training, Hearings before the Senate Armed Services Committee, 80th Congress, March 17, 1948, https://www.marshallfoundation.org/library/wp-content/uploads/sites/16/2014/06/48.03.17-UMT-S.pdf; Rutenberg, *Rough Draft*, chapter 2.

51. Holm, *Women in the Military*, 113.

52. Hallaren, S. 1641 (no. 238) Subcommittee Hearings on S. 1641, To Establish the Women's Army Corps in the Regular Army etc., 5648; RG287; NAB.

53. Holm, *Women in the Military*, 120.

54. Public Law 625 in *United States Statutes at Large* beginning on 361 and repeated in each title of the law. Hallaren also noted that common law gave 51 percent as the requirement for similar benefits for civilians. See S. 1641 (No. 238), Subcommittee Hearings on S. 1641, To Establish the Women's Army Corps in the Regular Army etc., 5677; RG287; NAB.

55. Public Law 625 in *United States Statutes*, 361, article (b) of Section 107. Repeated in each title of the law to apply to all service branches.

56. Only the army created a formal administrative division for its women, retaining the Women's Army Corps. The WAF did the best with incorporating women into its organizational structure, but Holm admits that even though only the WAC was a separate, formal administrative structure, women's support services in each branch, and the continued use of the director role for WAVES, WAFs, and WMs, made it look, to many people, like there were separate administrative units. See Holm, *Women in the Military*, 121. Witt et al. also explain the administrative structure, noting that the navy and marine corps continued to use World War II approaches, and noting "The prevailing attitude concerning women in the late 1940s was that women needed guidance and protection." Witt et al., *A Defense Weapon Known to Be of Value*, 35.

Chapter 2

1. "Marilyn Sad As Army Bans Low-Cut Photo," *New York Journal-American*, September 2, 1952. Image from same, with caption "She Made the Army Blush." Miss America Scrapbook, DACOWITS Scrapbooks; Record of the Office of the Secretary of Defense, RG330; NACP.

2. "Marilyn Monroe's Photo Overexposed, Army Says," *The Philadelphia Inquirer*, September 3, 1952. Miss America Scrapbook, DACOWITS Scrapbooks; RG330; NACP.

3. For footage of Marilyn Monroe as the Miss America Grand Marshall, see "Marilyn Monroe - 1952 Miss America Pageant Grand Marshall." YouTube video, 0:18. Posted April 29, 2011. https://youtu.be/l1gukHJJ9e0; cover of *Playboy* available at "What the First Issue of *Playboy* Looked Like," *Huffington Post*, https://www.huffpost.com/entry/playboy-first-issue_n_3803465.

4. Pete Martin, "The New Marilyn Monroe, Part 2," *The Saturday Evening Post*, May 12, 1956.

5. Scholars Elwood Watson and Darcy Martin have argued that the Miss America pageant "reflects the values and beliefs of the greater American society, particularly in its view of women." Quoted in Mary Anne Schofield, "Miss America, Rosie the Riveter, and World War II," in Watson and Martin, *"There She Is, Miss America,"* 55.

6. Schofield, "Miss America, Rosie the Riveter, and World War II," 56.

7. The Miss America website historical timeline emphasizes that the World War II years were important ones in which winners participated in such events. "Miss America: A History," *Miss America Online*, The Miss America Organization, https://www.missamerica.org/organization/history/#1940s.

8. "The Real Miss America" advertising draft and copies of print advertisements, n.d. Miss America Scrapbook; RG330; NACP.

9. "The Real Miss America" advertising draft, n.d. Miss America Scrapbook; RG 330; NACP.

10. Amy Rutenberg and Jacqueline E. Whitt, "The Martial Citizen," *War Room*, podcast audio, United States Army War College, https://warroom.armywarcollege.edu/podcasts/martial-citizen/

11. Rutenberg, *Rough Draft*, 4.

12. McEuen, *Making War, Making Women*, 41.

13. Meyer, *Creating GI Jane*, 63.

14. Both Leisa Meyer and Mattie Treadwell discuss the World War II "slander campaign" against the WAC. The WAVES, at least, never seemed to have had the same image problems as the WACs. Meyer says they had "minor problems with negative publicity, [but] encountered none of the extreme accusations that plagued the WAC." For detailed coverage of the World War II image problems, see "The Slander Campaign" in Treadwell, *The Women's Army Corps*, 191–218. Treadwell's account is the official Army history. For a more recent analysis, see Meyer, *Creating GI Jane*, 33–70.

15. In her study of the 1970s transition to the all-volunteer military, historian Beth Bailey notes that the resumption of the draft in 1948 was the result of the fact that a good American economy meant that American men were not signing up to join the postwar military, even though events around the world suggested an ongoing need for American military forces. Yet this concern in 1948 seems to have been overstated. Despite the reinstatement of the draft in the summer of 1948, Bailey also points out that the military began downsizing in 1949 and no men were drafted, although men continued to enlist. Bailey, *America's Army*, 11–12.

16. Holm, *Women in the Military*, 149.

17. As historians Beth Bailey and Kara Vuic argue, recruiting efforts are about appeal and attraction, which means that the image might not always match the reality. The goal is to sell a specific product to the consumer—in this case, a military career. Vuic, *Officer, Nurse, Woman*, 25; Bailey, *America's Army*, 80.

18. "The U.S. Army in the Korean War Commemorative Website," U.S. Army Center of Military History, https://history.army.mil/html/bookshelves/resmat/korea/intro/recruitment-posters.html; "The Marine Corps Builds Men," Yanker Poster Collection, Library of Congress, https://www.loc.gov/item/2015648295/

19. Age range varied. PL80–625 set eighteen as the lower age limit and thirty-one or thirty-five as the upper age limit, but the services could modify this; the WAVES, for example, required recruits to be at least twenty years old. Recruiting materials, particularly for the WAF, WAVES, and WMs, often give different upper age limits, as noted in subsequent footnotes. For details on navy enlistment standards, see Ebbert and Hall, *Crossed Currents*, 130.

20. This regulation did not change until the 1970s. In 1973, for example, Director of Women Marines Margaret Brewer recommended changing this requirement considering other recent changes in women's service policies. See Memo, "Enlistment Prerequisites," July 2, 1973; Enlistment Prerequisites Folder, Manpower and Reserve Affairs; Marine Corps Archives, Quantico, VA.

21. See Titles I, II, and III of PL80–625. Public Law 625 in *United States Statutes at Large*, Vol. 62, Part 1, 360.

22. According to Holm, men could enlist at age seventeen with parental permission, but no parental permission was needed at all once a man turned eighteen. See Holm, *Women in the Military*, 120.

23. Rutenberg, *Rough Draft*, 87.

24. "Proud Parents," U.S. Army Recruiting Publicity Bureau, 1956, Betty H. Carter Women Veterans Historical Project, Martha Blakeney Hodges Special Collections and University Archives, UNCG.

25. Electric Auto-Lite Company, "Never Too Young to Buy War Bond," 1944, Ad*Access Project, John W. Hartman Center for Sales, Advertising & Marketing History, Duke University, https://repository.duke.edu/dc/adaccess/W0225.

26. Aluminum Company of America, ". . . beyond the call of duty . . . ," 1944, Ad*Access Project, John W. Hartman Center for Sales, Advertising & Marketing History, Duke University, https://repository.duke.edu/dc/adaccess/W0372.

27. Best and Co., "Safeguard your child's future . . . buy more war bonds,"1943, Ad*Access Project, John W. Hartman Center for Sales, Advertising & Marketing History, Duke University, https://repository.duke.edu/dc/adaccess/W0127.

28. "Your Daughter's Role in Today's World," DOD, revised 1961, DOD Brochures on Women's Services—DACOWITS Folder, Background—WAC; Records of the Army Staff, RG319; NACP.

29. "Your Daughter in the U.S. Air Force," United States Air Force Recruiting Service, 1966. Sidney Keen Collection, Women's Memorial Foundation Collection, Arlington, VA.

30. "Mother . . . Dad . . . and Grandma," *Somebody Special* brochure, 9. Department of the Army Materials, Box 6. Files of the President's Commission on Equal Opportunity in the Armed Forces, LBJ Library.

31. "An Adventure in Belonging . . . a Modern Odyssey," U.S. Navy Recruiting Aids Division, June 1, 1966.

32. "The Woman Officer," 1963. Brochure 1963 The Woman Officer Folder, Women Marines 1918–1973 Files; Records of the USMC, RG127; NACP.

33. "Careers for Women in the Armed Forces," Produced by the DOD in Cooperation with the Department of Labor, 1955, 44; DOD Brochures on Women's Services—DACOWITS Folder, Background—WAC; RG319; NACP.

34. "Physical Examinations, Physical and Mental Standards and Periodic Physical Examinations for Female Members of the Armed Forces," July 8, 1952; Recruiting and Procurement Policies, 1952–1953 Folder, Reel 9; and E.R. Fiala, "Women's Physicals," U.S. Navy Recruiting Station, n.d.; Recruiting and Procurement Policies, 1947–1952; WAVES.

35. Holm, *Women in the Military*, 154–55.

36. Cardona and Ritchie, "Psychological Screening of Recruits Prior to Accession in the US Military," 303.

37. Holm, *Women in the Military*, 155.

38. "Careers for Women in the Armed Forces," 4.

39. Departments of the Army, the Navy, and the Air Force, "Hygiene Educational Guide for Women Officers and Women Officer Candidates of the Armed Forces," April 1958, 3; Hygiene Education Folder, Background—WAC; RG319; NACP.

40. "Somebody Special," 16–17.

41. "Everything You Always Wanted to Know About Navy Waves," July 1, 1973. Women in the Military Folder, Box 7, Ready Reference Files, Navy Historical Center.

42. "Take your place among the First Ladies of the Land . . . America's Finest!" Women in the Services Advertisement, c. early 1950s, Share Service Publicity Folder. Records of the United States Defense Advisory Committee on Women in the Services, 1943–1985. B-9. Schlesinger Library.

43. "Somebody Special," 5.

44. Leisa Meyer argues that in World War II, military leaders engaged in an intense balancing game, convincing the public that the military needed women, but for jobs that were appropriate for women. The emphasis was on disrupting gendered power systems as little as possible. See Meyer, *Creating G.I. Jane*, chapter 3, 51–70.

45. Signal Corps Pictorial Center, *The WAC is a Soldier Too*. Filmed in 1954 (part of the Big Picture series on ABC-TV). YouTube video, 27:58. Posted November 23, 2015. https://youtu.be/jiFyEAfJ2v4.

46. General Mildred Bailey interview with Rhoda Messer, 1978, 22–23. Mildred Bailey Collection, Women's Memorial Foundation Collection, Arlington, VA.

47. According to sociologist Brenda Moore, this is like what happened during World War II and appears to be a result of the existing racially segregated education system, which meant that African American women often "did not meet the

minimum aptitude requirements for entry." Moore, "African American Women in the US Military," 367. Data also illustrate that at midcentury, less than 10 percent of African American women nationwide completed four years of high school; only about 2.4 percent finished four years of college. Consequently, a small pool existed for African American women recruits who could meet enlistment criteria, and an even smaller pool for African American women officer candidates. Center for Education Statistics, Thomas D. Snyder, ed., "Table 4: Years of School Completed by Persons 25 Years Old and Over, by Race and Sex: April 1940 to March 1991," *120 Years of American Education: A Statistical Portrait*, https://nces.ed.gov/pubs93/93442.pdf.

48. Appendix A, Table 5: "Strength of Black Members of the Women's Army Corps, 1945–1978." No statistics on African American women's WAC service are available for 1961 to 1971. Morden, *The Women's Army Corps*, 415.

49. "Women in Uniform," *Ebony*, December 1962, 63.

50. "Women in Uniform," *Ebony*, December 1962, 64.

51. Lt. Colonel Ruth Lucas—Colonel by the time she retired in 1970—served in the military for nearly thirty years. She appears in a 1969 *Ebony* article as well, this time detailing her work creating a literacy program for servicemen. "Air Force's Education Expert," *Ebony*, November 1969, 88–91.

52. "A New World of Opportunity," 1966; WAC Brochures Folder, Background—WAC; RG319; NACP.

53. "An Adventure in Belonging . . . a modern Odyssey," "Somebody Special," and "A New World of Opportunity," offer examples of men and women engaged together in leisure activities, often with romantic undertones.

54. "A New World of Opportunity," 1966; WAC Brochures Folder, Background—WAC; RG319; NACP.

55. Historian Allan Bérubé explains how the DOD began integrating policies banning homosexual service members, which combined with the 1950 UCMJ so that by 1951, all military branches had clear systems for eliminating homosexuality in the ranks. Bérubé, *Coming Out Under Fire*, 261–62.

56. Margot Canaday builds on Bérubé's work, arguing that military officials saw lesbianism as particularly detrimental, which led to an extreme focus on the problem of homosexuality in the women's service components. See Canaday, *The Straight State*, 174–213.

57. *The Crittenden Report: Report of the Board Appointed to Prepare and Submit Recommendations to the Secretary of the Navy for the Revision of Policies, Procedures and Directives Dealing with Homosexuals*, 42.

58. *The Crittenden Report*, 43.

Chapter 3

1. Fowler and Deacon, *A Century in Uniform*, 27.

2. Fowler and Deacon have researched depictions of servicewomen in film across the twentieth century and argue that the 1950s saw an expansion in portrayals of womanpower. Half of the films they consider focus on nurses, but because

women were serving throughout the military, other films "broaden the spectrum of job assignments portrayed, highlighting the abilities of servicewomen and showcasing the possibilities of what the future could hold." Fowler and Deacon, *A Century in Uniform*, 45.

3. Memo, "MGM 'Skirts Ahoy'" April 3, 1952 and letter from Orville Crouch to Lt. Colonel Clair Towne, Office of Public Information, August 31, 1951, DOD. Office of Public Information. Pictorial Branch. (1952 - 9/22/1953); RG330; NACP.

4. *Recruiting Journal*, March 1953, 17. Procurement Division; Records of the Adjutant General's Office, RG407; NACP.

5. Finding a man was *not* a guaranteed benefit, however, even if *Skirts Ahoy!* did claim a 50-to-1 ratio of men to women at the Great Lakes Naval Training Station.

6. *Recruiting Journal*, March 1953, 17.

7. Treadwell, *The Women's Army Corps*, 631.

8. Ebbert and Hall, *Crossed Currents*, 65.

9. Lieutenant Sybil A. Grant on "Plans for the Training of Enlisted Women," 24–25; Miscellaneous District Directors Conference 1948 Folder, Reel 2; WAVES.

10. Witt et al., *A Defense Weapon Known to Be of Value*, 40–41, 103.

11. Stremlow, *A History of the Women Marines*, 30–31.

12. Signal Corps Pictorial Center, *The WAC Is a Soldier Too*. Filmed in 1954. YouTube video, 27:58. Posted November 23, 2015. https://youtu.be/HmWClQfuG4Y.

13. *Skirts Ahoy!* Directed by Sidney Lanfield. 1953. Hollywood, CA: MGM Pictures.

14. Signal Corps Pictorial Center, *The WAC Is a Soldier Too*.

15. Signal Corps Pictorial Center, *The WAC Is a Soldier Too*.

16. "Share a Proud Tradition," 1958; Rose Kirwin Collection (1019), Women's Memorial Foundation Collection, Arlington, VA.

17. The United States Army, *Strictly Personal*. Filmed in 1963. YouTube Video, 29:26. Posted July 9, 2012. https://youtu.be/pGcqXoj8MgA.

18. The United States Army, *Strictly Personal*.

19. The army and air force called enlisted personnel's initial training "basic training," while the navy and marine corps refer to it as "boot camp". Female officers new to the military also took an initial training program, referred to generally as Officer Candidate School (OCS) or even Women Officer Training Course (WOTC). "Careers for Women in the Armed Forces," produced by the DOD in Cooperation with the Department of Labor, 1955, 14; DOD Brochures on Women's Services—DACOWITS Folder, Background—WAC; Records of the Army Staff, RG319; NACP.

20. "'You' in the Service (Notes on Good Manners, Appearance, and Good Grooming Prepared for Women Recruits in the Armed Forces)," 1950, Foreword. "You in the Service" Research Evaluation 1950 Folder, Box 17, BuPers00W, Naval Historical Center.

21. "WAF: A Handbook for Air Force Women," Training Command ATRC Manual 13.2, page "You're the Girl," 1954; K220.716035-2; AFHRA.

22. "WAF: A Handbook for Air Force Women," Training Command ATRC Manual 13.2, 1954; K220.716035-2; AFHRA.

23. Myra N. Conklin, "Good Grooming for the Women in the Armed Forces," produced by The Toilet Goods Association as a public service for the DOD; Jane Sewell Collection, 168.7172; AFHRA.

24. Stremlow, *A History of the Women Marines*, 31.

25. Except for the air force, this was true of officer training, too. The air force trained all its new enlisted personnel at Lackland, but women remained separated because they were subject to "higher mental and educational standards" and shorter training periods. The air force did, however, train all male and female officers together. See Holm, *Women in the Military*, 134–36.

26. John Patrick Mora, "Historical Data of the 3700th Air Force Indoctrination Wing, Lackland Air Force Base, San Antonio, Texas, Volume Seventeen, October 1951 to December 1951," with training-specific details on multiple pages; K229.72-16; AFHRA.

27. The Big Picture: The United States Army, *This Is How It Is*. Filmed in 1963. YouTube Video, 27:59. Posted June 8, 2012, https://youtu.be/Z97domLg5RA.

28. The United States Marine Corps, . . . *And a Few Good Men*. Filmed in 1973. YouTube Video, 25:00. Posted December 16, 2011, https://youtu.be/PJCzHVzOXmw.

29. Recruiting Publicity Bureau, U.S. Army "I Will Serve," 1953. WV0002 Women Veterans General Printed Materials and Video Recordings Collection. Betty H. Carter Women Veterans Historical Project, Martha Blakeney Hodges Special Collections and University Archives, UNCG, http://libcdm1.uncg.edu/cdm/ref/collection/WVHP/id/7296; Morden, *The Women's Army Corps*, 282.

30. The WAVES did not admit African American recruits until 1944 and they were integrated immediately, although there were very few of them; Ebbert and Hall, *Crossed Currents*, 96. In the WMs, the first officially enlisted Black Women Marines arrived for training in September 1949 and were integrated immediately, in part because there were such small numbers of WMs that segregation did not make sense. Stremlow, *A History of the Women Marines*, 31. In the WAC, segregation continued until April 1950; Morden, *The Women's Army Corps*, 86. Witt et al. indicate that the WAF integrated their training system beginning in 1949; Witt et al., *A Defense Weapon Known to Be of Value*, 51–52.

31. Stremlow, *A History of the Women Marines*, 31.

32. R. G. L. Graham, "Dear 'Mother of a Soldier,'" n.d., 2; Frances Ames Collection (4348), Women's Memorial Foundation Collection, Arlington, VA.

33. Louise Wilde, "Women Are People Too—In Mufti or in Blue," Speech to Mount Holyoke Alumnae Club of Boston, March 3, 1955, 7. Mt. Holyoke Alumnae Speech Folder, Box 4, Papers of Louise Wilde, Naval Historical Center.

34. Louise Wilde, "Women Are People Too," 8.

35. "Women Marine Newsletter," Spring 1967, 3; Women Marine Newsletter, 1966–69, HQMC Folder, Records Relating to Women Marines, History and Museum Division; RG127; NACP.

36. "Development of Improved Grooming Program for Women Marines," Director of Women Marines, June 30, 1967; Major Accomplishments, 1966–1970 Folder, Stremlow WMs; RG127; NACP.

37. SP5 Richard A. Dey, Jr. "WAC: Training for Army Service," *Army Digest*, June 1969, 43; 401–07 Magazine/Newspaper Articles Folder, Background—WAC; RG319; NACP.

38. "Personal Development: A Guide for Women in the Air Force," Air Force ROTC/Air University, 1969; Joanne Rodefer Collection (4288), Women's Memorial Foundation Collection, Arlington, VA. Pages 31–32 provide guidance for servicewomen regarding rouge/lipstick with consideration for a woman's racial identification.

39. Charles F. Freburger, "Negro Hair Care Program"; WAC Staff Advisor Correspondence folder, RG 319, Box 56, WAC Staff Advisor correspondence Background—WAC; Records of the Army Staff, RG319; NACP.

40. "Woman Recruit Training Syllabus," in U.S. Marine Corps Women Marines (document with information for new recruits), dated "late 1960s"; Boot Camp Folder, Stremlow WMs; RG127; NACP.

41. "Women Marines Recruit Training," 1972, 6; Boot Camp Folder, Stremlow WMs; RG127; NACP.

42. This structure of women's training was fairly uniform across the four women's service components.

43. The United States Army, *Mind Your Military Manners*. Filmed in 1970. YouTube Video, 14:50. Posted July 18, 2013. https://youtu.be/ByIaAjXJ5_0.

44. The United States Army, *Looks Like a Winner*. Filmed in 1970. YouTube Video, 16:20. Posted May 21, 2013. https://youtu.be/pyP9WwMeuoE.

45. The United States Army, *Looks Like a Winner*.

46. Signal Corps Pictorial Center, *The WAC Is a Soldier Too*.

47. "What Makes a Wave" in *Skirts Ahoy!*

48. *Skirts Ahoy!*

49. Signal Corps Pictorial Center, *The WAC Is a Soldier Too*.

Chapter 4

1. Carol Poynor interview with Tanya Roth, May 20, 2010.

2. Lt. Col. Rhoda Messer interview with Brigadier General Mildred Inez Bailey, October 1, 1978 session, 1. U.S. Army Military History Institute Senior Officer Debriefing Program, Carlisle Barracks, PA. Copy held as File 005319, Women's Memorial Foundation Collection, Arlington, VA.

3. Rear Admiral Roberta Hazard, "Remarks before the Norfolk Women's Council Navy League of the United States," October 10, 1974, 2; Speech—Norfolk Women's Council Folder, Box 3, Papers of Rear Admiral Hazard, Naval Historical Center.

4. Kessler-Harris, *In Pursuit of Equity*, 5.

5. "Take Your Place Among the First Ladies of the Land . . . America's Finest!" advertisement, *New York Times*, April 24, 1952. Emphasis in original.

6. Skelton, *An American Profession of Arms*, 181.

7. Bailey, *America's Army*, ix. The persistence of deferment options during the draft underscores the idea of other economic opportunities having value for the country.

8. Rutenberg, *Rough Draft*, 98; Bailey notes that two-thirds of draftees tended to be deferred or ineligible in the early 1960s; Bailey, *America's Army*, 10–11, 16.

9. Cobble, *The Other Women's Movement*, 97.

10. "Background Facts on Women Workers in the United States," U.S. Department of Labor, Women's Bureau, Washington, DC; Document 39, Reel 11, PCSW.

11. Employment Standards Administration, Women's Bureau, *1975 Handbook on Women Workers*, Bulletin 297, 1975 (Washington, DC: U.S. Department of Labor, 1975), 4.

12. "Revised Copy Platform for Women in the Armed Services Information Program," 1953, 2; Recruiting and Procurement Policies, 1952–1953 Folder, Reel 9; WAVES, Records of the Asst. Chief of Personnel for Women, 1942–1973, Scholarly Resources, Inc.

13. "Minutes of WAF Meeting," January 24, 1951, 2; WAF Meeting Minutes, January 24, 1951 Folder, Box 6, Papers of Jackie Cochran, Air Force Series (1948–1971), Eisenhower Library.

14. Katherine A. Towle, "Women Today in Military Service," November 1951, 16; Speeches 1950–1951 Folder, Stremlow WMs; Records of the USMC, RG127; NACP.

15. "Criteria Used in Peacetime in Determining Jobs for Enlisted Women," in Sub-Committee Project Report Number M-7-51, "Maximum Utilization of Military Womanpower," April 9, 1951, 77; Subcommittee to the Military Personnel Policy Committee Project Report: Maximum Utilization of Military Womanpower, April 9, 1951 Folder, Military Operations, Programs, and Organizations, Marine Corps History and Museum Division; RG127; NACP.

16. "Criteria Used in Peacetime in Determining Jobs for Enlisted Women," 79 and 81.

17. "Comparison of Utilization of Womanpower by Military Services," in Sub-Committee Project Report Number M-7-51, "Maximum Utilization of Military Womanpower," April 9, 1951, 79; Subcommittee to the Military Personnel Policy Committee Project Report: Maximum Utilization of Military Womanpower, April 9, 1951 Folder, Military Operations, Programs, and Organizations, Marine Corps History and Museum Division; RG127; NACP.

18. Special Regulations, Number 615-25-36, Department of the Army, Washington, DC, 15 November 1950, 1; MOS Lists Folder, Background—WAC; Records of the Army Staff, RG319; NACP.

19. Elton Fay, "Women 'Equal' to Men in Service," July 1966 (publication not given); WAVES Miscellaneous Press Clippings, 1966—January–August Folder, Reel 16; WAVES, Records of the Asst. Chief of Personnel for Women, 1942–1973, Scholarly Resources, Inc.

20. Fay, "Women 'Equal' to Men in Service."

21. MaryAnne Haarhaus interview with Tanya Roth, September 19, 2009.

22. Hugh N. Ahmann U.S. Air Force Oral History Interview with Chief Master Sergeant Sharon L. Masek, March 1988, 8; K239.0512–1792; AFHRA.

23. "Civilian-Military Substitution and Other Utilization Programs to Increase Voluntary Manpower," report asserted that women were utilized in such roles because

of their education, which geared women toward personnel and administration, as well as administrative and clerical work (9–10); Presentations—President's Commission on the All-Volunteer Armed Forces 2; Gruenther All-Volunteer Forces Series, Alfred Gruenther Papers; Eisenhower Library.

24. Constance Anderson interview with Chris Simon. Constance Anderson Collection (AFC/2001/001/33347), LOC VHP, http://lcweb2.loc.gov/diglib/vhp/story/loc.natlib.afc2001001.33347/transcript?ID=sr0001.

25. Susie McArthur Papers, Susie (Stephens) McArthur interview with Hermann Trojanowski, 2001, WV0199.5.001; The Betty H. Carter Women Veterans Historical Project, Jackson Library, UNCG, http://library.uncg.edu/dp/wv/results5.aspx?i=2690&s=5.

26. Clara Johnson Collection (AFC/2001/001/42843), LOC VHP, http://lcweb2.loc.gov/diglib/vhp/story/loc.natlib.afc2001001.42843/.

27. "Civilian-Military Substitution and Other Utilization Programs to Increase Voluntary Manpower," circa 1969, 7–8. Gruenther Collection, All-Volunteer Forces Series. Presidential Commission on the All-Volunteer Armed Forces - 2. Eisenhower Presidential Library.

28. "Calling All Women," in *Life of the Soldier and the Airman*, June 1951, 6, Patricia Maurizi Collection (3332); Women's Memorial Foundation Collection, Arlington, VA.

29. Beatrice (Benedick) Stecher interview with Mary Jo Binker, October 3, 2000 (File 021037); Women's Memorial Foundation Collection, Arlington, VA.

30. Carmen Lucas Interview with Colonel Eleanor Wilson, June 9, 2005, 10 (Oral History File 110367); Women's Memorial Foundation Collection, Arlington, VA.

31. "Enlisted Promotion Policy Review," Subcommittee on Enlisted Promotion Policy Review, House Armed Services Committee, October 5, 1967, 1309; Pre Public Law 90–130 Hearings Folder, Military Operations, Programs, and Organization, Marine Corps History and Museum Division; RG127; NACP.

32. Barbara Dulinsky account of service in Vietnam, 1–2; Barbara Bishop File, Marine Corps Archive, Quantico, VA. Nurses would serve in the largest numbers in Vietnam out of all servicewomen. Only about thirty-six WMs, 500 to 600 WAF enlisted and officers (at least half of those were officers); and about the same number of WACs served in Vietnam during the war. No enlisted WAVES served in Vietnam and only one or two officers at any given time: WAVE exclusions from Vietnam resulted from policies that kept women from serving on ships. For a detailed account of nonmedical female personnel in Vietnam, see Holm, *Women in the Military*, chapter 16.

33. McArthur interview with Trojanowski.

34. "Historical Summary, Office of the Director, Women in the Air Force," July 1, 1967–December 31, 1967, 3; K141.33; AFHRA.

35. Carol Poynor interview with Tanya Roth, May 20, 2010.

36. "Enlisted Promotion Policy Review," Subcommittee on Enlisted Promotion Policy Review, House Armed Services Committee, October 5, 1967, 1310; Pre Public Law 90–130 Hearings, Military Operations, Programs, and Organization, Marine Corps History and Museum Division; RG127; NACP.

37. Carol Schoon interview with Tanya Roth, July 31, 2010.

38. "Unusual Jobs Performed by Navy Enlisted Women"; Non-Traditional Jobs and Education Folder, Box 1, BuPersooW, Naval Historical Center.

39. "Unusual Assignments of Women Officers, U.S. Navy"; Pers-K Bulletins Folder, Box 8, BuPersooW, Naval Historical Center.

40. "She Breaks Navy Tradition," *Navy Times*, May 18, 1966; WAVES Miscellaneous Press Clippings, 1966—January to August Folder, Reel 16; WAVES, Records of the Asst. Chief of Personnel for Women, 1942–1973, Scholarly Resources, Inc.

41. Report of the Inter-Service Working Group on Utilization of Women in the Armed Service," August 31, 1966, 9–10; K160.041-13; AFHRA.

42. "Background Facts on Women Workers in the United States," U.S. Department of Labor, Women's Bureau, Washington, DC; Document 39, Reel 11, PCSW.

43. Employment Standards Administration, Women's Bureau, *1975 Handbook on Women Workers*, 85.

44. Colonel Elizabeth Hoisington (WAC) testimony, "Enlisted Promotion Policy Review," Subcommittee on Enlisted Promotion Policy Review, House Armed Services Committee, October 5, 1967, 1307; Pre Public Law 90-130 Hearings Folder, Military Operations, Programs, and Organization, Marine Corps History and Museum Division; RG127; NACP. Holm, *Women in the Military*, 163.

45. Moskos, *The American Enlisted Man*, 52.

46. "Take Your Place Among the First Ladies of the Land . . . America's Finest!" advertisement, *New York Times*, April 24, 1952 (emphasis in original).

47. Bettie Morden (presumed author), handwritten document "Comparison of Grade Structure," early 1970s; Grade Structure Comparison Folder, Background—WAC; RG319; NACP.

48. Holm, *Women in the Military*, 193–94.

49. Holm, 193–94.

50. Judy Campbell interview with Tanya Roth, November 30, 2009.

51. Haarhaus interview.

52. "Monthly Basic Pay and Allowances," October 1, 1949, Defense Finance and Accounting Service.

53. "Biographic Information on Captain Robin Lindsay Catherine Quigley, United States Navy," 2. Biographical Data—Quigley, Robin (Capt) Folder, Box 1, BuPersooW, Naval Historical Center.

54. "Monthly Basic Pay and Allowances," October 1, 1967, Defense Finance and Accounting Service, https://www.dfas.mil/Portals/98/MilPayTable1967.pdf.

55. Ebbert and Hall, *Crossed Currents*, 39.

56. Morden, *The Women's Army Corps*, 126.

57. Statement of Brigadier General Jeanne M. Holm, Director-WAF, "Hearings before the Special Subcommittee on the Utilization of Manpower in the Military," Committee on Armed Services, House of Representatives, 92nd Congress, October 13 and 26, November 4 and 19, 1971, March 6, 1972, 12451–52; Hearings of the Subcommittee on the Utilization of Manpower Folder, Background—WAC; RG319; NACP.

Chapter 5

1. In her history of the WAC in World War II, Mattie Treadwell explains that mothers were not permitted in service in wartime either, nor had the Army Nurse Corps permitted pregnant women and mothers before the war. Treadwell particularly highlights the challenges around classifying pregnancy discharges. See Treadwell, *The Women's Army Corps*, 501–2.

2. Kessler-Harris, *In Pursuit of Equity*, 30.

3. Kessler-Harris, 31.

4. Historian Dorothy Sue Cobble cites economist Claudia Goldin's work, noting that up to 50 percent of all office workers at one point lost their jobs due to marriage, but the marriage bar in that area largely disappeared by the 1950s. Cobble, *The Other Women's Movement*, 74.

5. Holm, *Women in the Military*, 289–90. For history on marriage discharge policy in the Korean War, see Witt et al., "*A Defense Weapon Known to Be of Value,*" 2–3.

6. Joan (Eastwood) Neuswanger interview with Mary Jo Binker, 13 (File 331365); Women's Memorial Foundation Collection, Arlington, VA.

7. Polly Hazelwood interview with Tanya Roth, October 26, 2009.

8. Cheryl Bucy interview with Tanya Roth, July 6, 2010.

9. Carol Poynor interview with Tanya Roth, May 20, 2010.

10. Vuic explains that in the Army Nurse Corps, the policies were largely similar. Until the mid-1960s, nurses who married while on active service could seek discharge, no matter how much time was left in their service. Vuic, *Officer, Nurse, Woman*, 115.

11. Quoted in Kessler-Harris, *Out to Work*, 301.

12. May, *Homeward Bound*, xvii and charts in Introduction.

13. May argues that postwar Americans were obsessed with "nonmarital sexual behavior," and saw heterosexual marriage as representative of "mature" and "responsible" behavior. May, *Homeward Bound*, 82, 88.

14. Marge Menke interview with Tanya Roth, April 2010.

15. May, *Homeward Bound*, 149; "U.S. Working Women: A Chartbook," *U.S. Department of Labor, Bureau of Labor Statistics*, Bulletin 1880, 1975. Additionally, historian Jessica Weiss points out that "By 1963, 41 percent of American women 25 to 44 years old were in the labor force." Weiss, *To Have and to Hold*, 50. According to historian Stephanie Coontz, even during a period in which the stay-at-home mom was more valued than ever, "the social acceptability of women working also increased during the 1950s." Coontz, *A Strange Stirring*, 59.

16. Molnar, "'Has the Millennium Yet Dawned?': A History of Attitudes Toward Pregnant Workers in America," 170–71.

17. Rose Wuellner interview with Tanya Roth, March 11, 2010.

18. Mary Tener Davidson Hall interview with Ruth Stewart, undated; Mary Hall Collection (AFC/2001/001/42839), LOC VHP, http://lcweb2.loc.gov/diglib/vhp/story/loc.natlib.afc2001001.42839/transcript?ID=sr0001.

19. LaDonna Darks interview with Tanya Roth and Tori Verneau, March 2010; she did not recall the exact year, but said it was around 1967 or 1968.

20. Carol Deom interview with Emmy Huffman, October 30, 2003; Carol Deom Collection (AFC/2001/001/17598), LOC VHP, http://lcweb2.loc.gov/diglib/vhp/story/loc.natlib.afc2001001.17598/transcript?ID=sr0001.

21. House Armed Services Subcommittee Hearings on S.1641, February–March 1948, 5667; Publications of the U.S. Government, RG287; NAB.

22. May explains that government propaganda pushed women back into the home, in part for men to have jobs when they returned, but also to promote the idea of the nuclear family. Even so, 69 percent of working wives wanted to keep working after the war, and by 1946 75 percent of women who had jobs in war industries were still working, but most were making less money. Overall numbers of women workers did rise, but mostly due to older women entering the war. May, *Homeward Bound*, 65–66.

23. Amy Rutenberg's analysis of Cold War military manpower policy includes the World War II debates over draft deferments for fathers. Just as women's roles as wives and mothers were central to American ideology at mid-century, Rutenberg argues that married men's status as breadwinners and fathers was also "ingrained in American legal and political culture." Rutenberg, *Rough Draft*, 36; see also page 88 of her work for more discussion of fathers.

24. House Armed Services Subcommittee Hearings on S.1641, February–March 1948, 5666; RG287; NAB.

25. President Harry S. Truman, Executive Order 10240, April 27, 1951, "Regulations Governing the Separation from the Service of Certain Women Serving in the Regular Army, Navy, Marine Corps, or Air Force," John T. Woolley and Gerhard Peters, *The American Presidency Project*. Santa Barbara, CA, http://www.presidency.ucsb.edu/ws/index.php?pid=78393.

26. There were provisions, however, for women who gave up their parental duties. Army Special Regulation 140-175-1 carried out the provisions of Executive Order 10240, but allowed that "Women who have surrendered all rights to custody and control of such children or dependent (under 8 years of age) through formal adoption or final divorce proceedings will not be discharged under these provisions." Quoted by Alba Martinelli Thompson, "Armed Forces Reserve Act: Hearings before a Subcommittee of the Committee on Armed Services, United States Senate," (HR 5426) 82nd Congress, Second Session, May 1952, 20.

27. Witt et al., *"A Defense Weapon Known to Be of Value,"* 90.

28. "Fighting N.J. Woman Hails Reserve Action," *New York World Telegram and Sun*, June 28, 1952. Anna Rosenberg Bert Hartry 813 file; Women's Memorial Foundation Collection, Arlington, VA.

29. Anna Rosenberg correspondence with Alba Martinelli Thompson, quoted in "Armed Forces: A Woman Scorned," *Time* magazine, June 9, 1952.

30. Anna Rosenberg correspondence with Alba Martinelli Thompson, quoted in "Armed Forces: A Woman Scorned," 17.

31. "Armed Forces Reserve Act: Hearings before a Subcommittee of the Committee on Armed Services, United States Senate," (HR 5426) 82nd Congress, Second Session, May 1952, 16.

32. "Armed Forces Reserve Act," May 1952, 16.

33. "Armed Forces Reserve Act," May 1952, 19.

34. "Armed Forces Reserve Act," May 1952, 19.

35. "Armed Forces Reserve Act," May 1952, 19–20.

36. "Armed Forces Reserve Act," May 1952, 255.

37. "Armed Forces Reserve Act," May 1952, 253.

38. "Mothers in Uniform," newspaper unknown, Peoria, IL. Anna Rosenberg Bert Hartry 813 file; Women's Memorial Foundation Collection, Arlington, VA.

39. Witt et al. note that although the Senate passed the Armed Forces Reserve Act that year with an allowance for servicewomen to remain in the reserves after having children, the bill did not pass in the "more conservative House." Witt et al., *"A Defense Weapon Known to Be of Value,"* 91.

40. Thacker Lewis interview, Women Veterans Historical Collection, UNCG. Many women interviewed for the Women Veterans Historical Collection at UNC–Greensboro, the Women in Military Service for America Memorial (WIMSA), and the Library of Congress Veterans History Project also received discharges on pregnancy. From the UNC–Greensboro collection, see also Jane Heins Escher, Ruth Payne Brown. From WIMSA, see Jacquelyn Anderson, Janet Horton. In the Library of Congress Veterans History Project, see Shirley Eustis and Mary Tener Davidson Hall.

41. Jacquelyn Anderson oral history, 16; Women's Memorial Foundation Collection, Arlington, VA.

42. Mary Salmen Collection (AFC/2001/001/16237), Mary Salmen interview with Judith Rosenkoetter, LOC VHP, http://lcweb2.loc.gov/diglib/vhp/story/loc.natlib.afc2001001.16237/transcript?ID=sr0001. Navy policy documents also expressed that discharge should occur as early in a woman's pregnancy as possible. Memorandum, "Information on Policies for Women in the Navy," May 14, 1953. Reel 1, WAVES, Records for the Asst. Chief of Personnel for Women, 1942–1973, Scholarly Resources, Inc.

43. Ruth Virginia Payne Brown Papers, Ruth Payne Brown interview with Eric Elliott, 2000, WV0193.5.001; the Betty H. Carter Women Veterans Historical Project, Jackson Library, UNCG, http://library.uncg.edu/dp/wv/results5.aspx?i=2687&s=5&c=3. Brown married during her first WAC enlistment and divorced her husband for desertion and nonsupport after she left the military.

44. Ebbert and Hall, *Crossed Currents*, 155.

45. Joan E. Gerichten Papers, Joan Gerichten interview with Eric Elliott, October 29, 1999 (WV0109.5.001); The Betty H. Carter Women Veterans Historical Project, Jackson Library, UNCG, http://library.uncg.edu/dp/wv/results5.aspx?i=2628&s=5. Holm notes two additional examples from the Vietnam War era that demonstrate the alternate standards for men with children: one widowed sergeant received praise for going to Vietnam even after his wife's death left him in charge of his children, while a single male chaplain was lauded for adopting two Vietnamese children. Holm, *Women in the Military*, 293–94.

46. Gerichten interview.

47. Memo to Assistant Chief for Women, "Retention, upon pregnancy, of women officers and enlisted women; policy concerning," October 4, 1962, Dependency-Pregnancy Policy, 1962, 1970–1972 File, Box 3, BuPers00W, Naval Historical Center.

48. "Regulations Covering Discharge on Marriage, [Pregnancy], [Parenthood] (1942–1978)"; Discharge Policy Folder, Background—WAC; RG319; NACP.

49. Holm, *Women in the Military*, 292.

50. Ebbert and Hall, *Crossed Currents*, 196.

51. Letter to Chief of Naval Personnel, "Retention on Active Duty; request for," Correspondence, 1970–1989 File, Jordine Von Wantoch Papers, Naval Historical Center.

52. "Change of Command: Personnel Support Activity," July 8, 1982; Change of Command, 1982 File, Jordine Von Wantoch Papers, Naval Historical Center.

53. Chief of Naval Personnel to Jordine Von Wantoch, "Retention on Active Duty; information concerning," July 1970; Correspondence—Pregnancy Case, Jordine Von Wantoch Papers, Naval Historical Center.

54. Rebecca Ann Lloyd Papers, Rebecca Ann Lloyd interview with Beth Carmichael, 2006, WV0346.5.001; The Betty H. Carter Women Veterans Historical Project, Jackson Library, UNCG, http://library.uncg.edu/dp/wv/results5.aspx?i=2730&s=5&c=4.

55. "Woman Captain Files Suit Against USAF" *The Milwaukee Journal*, September 29, 1970, and "Air Force Allows Son His Mother," *Kingsport Post*, March 9, 1972.

56. "Discrimination in the Air Force," *Washington Post*, October 1, 1970, Reel 18, WAVES, Records for the Asst. Chief of Personnel for Women, 1942–1973, Scholarly Resources, Inc.

57. Ebbert and Hall, *Crossed Currents*, 199; notes that when Von Wantoch retired in 1986—after thirty years of service—her daughter was sixteen, a senior preparing for Johns Hopkins University.

58. Director—WAC General Mary E. Clarke, "Message from the Director," *WAC Journal* 1975; Director WAC Bios, Continued Folder, Background—WAC; RG319; NACP.

59. Director—WAC General Mary E. Clarke, "Message from the Director," *WAC Journal* 1975; Director WAC Bios, Continued Folder, Background—WAC; RG319; NACP.

60. Holm, *Women in the Military*, 300–303.

61. Morden, *The Women's Army Corps*, 16 and 138.

62. "President Overturns Pentagon Abortion Rule," Ken Clawson, *Washington Post*, April 3, 1971; Pregnancy and Abortion Folder, *Women Marines 1918–1973* files; Records of the USMC, RG 127; NACP.

63. "Memo for Colonel Milligan," undated; Training Center Folder, Records of the Director of the WAC 1949–1950; RG 319; NACP.

64. The Court decision addressed each trimester of pregnancy. In the first trimester, the Court ruled that the state could not prevent women from seeking or obtaining abortions and thus struck down laws that prohibited first-term abortions. During the second trimester, the Court allowed that states had some right to regulate abortion, but "could not deny a woman the right to terminate her pregnancy." In the third trimester, however, the Court allowed limits on abortion "except . . . to preserve the life or health of the mother." Mohr, *Abortion in America*, 248–49.

65. Memorandum for the Surgeons General of the Military Departments on "Termination of Pregnancies in Military Facilities," July 16, 1970; 1900 Separation Folder, *Women Marines 1918–1973* Files; Records of the USMC, RG 127; NACP.

66. Colonel Bettie Morden, Memorandum, "Policy Regarding Unmarried Pregnancy," July 6, 1972; Policy File DWAC Folder, Background—WAC; RG319; NACP.

67. Quoted in "President Overturns Pentagon Abortion Rule."

68. Memo, Art Quem to Phil Buchen "DOD Abortion Policies," May 14, 1975; Folder: Defense Department—Abortion Policy (1), Philip Buchen Files, 1974–1977; Ford Library.

69. "Policy on Abortions in Conflict, DoD Told," *Army Times*, July 16, 1975; Abortion and Family Planning Folder, Background—WAC; RG319; NACP.

70. "Abortion Rules Handed Services," in *Army Times*, October 8, 1975; Abortion and Family Planning Folder, Background—WAC; RG319; NACP. Another 1975 memo written by DOD Assistant General Counsel Jerome Nelson clarified that the 1970 and 1971 policies only permitted therapeutic abortions, and not elective ones. Memo, Nelson to Hoffmann, "Memorandum for Mr. Hoffmann on DOD Abortion Policies," August 4, 1975, 2; Folder: Defense Department—Abortion Policy (2), Philip Buchen Files, 1974–1977; Ford Library.

71. Rachel Benson Gold, "Lessons from Before Roe: Will Past be Prologue?," *Guttmacher Policy Review* 6, no. 1, March 1, 2003, https://www.guttmacher.org/gpr/2003/03/lessons-roe-will-past-be-prologue#. See box, "Legal Status of Abortion Throughout American History."

72. Patrick Sloyan, "WACs Get Abortions Despite Ban," *Newsday* (excerpt), May 11, 1975. Folder: Defense Department—Abortion Policy (1), Philip Buchen Files, 1974–1977; Ford Library, https://www.fordlibrarymuseum.gov/library/document/0019/4520504.pdf.

73. "Abortion Services and Military Medical Facilities—Background," *CRS Report 95-387*, January 9, 2013, https://www.everycrsreport.com/reports/95-387.html.

74. "Congress Finally Ok's FY80 Appropriations," *Army Times*, December 24, 1979; Abortion and Family Planning Folder, Background—WAC; RG319; NACP.

75. "New Army Abortion Policy," June 1979, source unknown; Abortion and Family Planning Folder, Background—WAC; RG319; NACP.

76. Lt. Col. Rhoda Messer with General Mildred Bailey, October 4, 1978 session, 8. U.S. Army Military History Institute Senior Officer Debriefing Program, Carlisle Barracks, PA. Copy held as File 005319, Women's Memorial Foundation Collection, Arlington, VA.

Chapter 6

1. "Sex Hygiene and Venereal Disease," War Department, September 30, 1942, online at https://collections.nlm.nih.gov/ext/dw/101641387/PDF/101641387.pdf.

2. The Signal Corps in Collaboration with the Surgeon General, *Sex Hygiene*. Filmed in 1941. YouTube video, 25:53. Posted November 24, 2017, https://youtu.be/3ViTCVkrcbM. For more details, see Audrey Amidon, "John Ford and the First

Battlefront of World War II, 'The Unwritten Record,'" National Archives, May 18, 2016, https://unwritten-record.blogs.archives.gov/tag/sex-hygiene/.

3. "Hygiene Educational Guide for Women Officers and Women Officer Candidates of the Armed Forces," (DA Pam 21–44, NAVMED P-5060, AFM 160–44), Departments of the Army, The Navy, and the Air Force, April 1958, 1, 3. Hygiene Educational Folder, Background—WAC; Records of the Army Staff, RG319; NACP.

4. "Hygiene Educational Guide for Women Officers," 18.

5. "Hygiene Educational Guide for Women Officers," 19.

6. "Hygiene Educational Guide for Women Officers," 17.

7. Chief Master Sergeant Sharon L. Masek interview with Hugh N. Ahmann, March 1988, 63; K239.0512-1792; AFHRA.

8. Meyer, *Creating G.I. Jane*, 149, 156.

9. For more on the World War II slander campaign against the WAC, see Meyer, *Creating G.I. Jane*, chap. 2; Holm, *Women in the Military*, 51–54; and Treadwell, *The Women's Army Corps*, 191–218.

10. Bérubé and D'Emilio, "The Military and Lesbians during the McCarthy Years," 761.

11. Quoted in Yellin, *Our Mothers' War*, 321; also discussed in Treadwell, *The Women's Army Corps*, 625.

12. Treadwell, 625.

13. Treadwell, 625.

14. Meyer argues that the wartime WAC created a system of sexual regulation that focused on behavior that would threaten the corps' existence; Meyer, *Creating G.I. Jane*, 150.

15. Bérubé, *Coming Out Under Fire*, 257, 259, 260.

16. Bérubé and D'Emilio, "The Military and Lesbians during the McCarthy Years," 764.

17. Bérubé and D'Emilio, 765–66.

18. Bérubé and D'Emilio, 768–69.

19. Colonel Mary Hallaren, "Letter to All Wacs," April 12, 1951, Mary Hallaren Collection, U.S. Army Women's Museum, Fort Lee, VA.

20. "Unit Commander's Discussion Supplement," Social Hygiene Training, circa 1961; Social Behavior Lessons for WACs Folder, Background—WAC; Records of the Army Staff, RG319; NACP.

21. Margot Canaday's work is central to understanding how military officials enacted policies that enforced citizenship according to a heterosexual norm. For more details, see Canaday, *The Straight State*, 174–213.

22. I have identified subjects of homosexuality discharge investigations by their initials, unless the individual pursued legal relief and entered the public record. "Psychiatric Examination in the Case of J., D.M., HMS (W) USN"; Discharge and Fraudulent Enlistments, 1949–1950 Folder, Reel 2; WAVES.

23. Canaday *The Straight State*, 175.

24. Canaday, 196–97n82.

25. For more details of these investigations, see Canaday, 196.

26. "Discharge of EW Under AR 600-443 and AR 615-365," May 17, 1951 case (Private B.P.), and "Separation of Homosexuals," May 12, 1951 case (Private C.P.); Discharge Files; Records of the Adjutant General's Office, RG407; NACP.

27. See Decimal File 220-8 Homosexuality files in boxes 3592, 3593, 3777, and 3778. Each case includes at least two women, with upwards of sixty-four women being accused in one investigation in March 1951 (Case 4-2582) and a Fort Lee case involving twenty Wacs the same month (File Number FGGN-39-159-351); Discharge Files; RG407; NACP.

28. See Case 4-2582; Discharge Files; RG407; NACP. Similar questions in other testimonies.

29. Canaday, *The Straight State*, 204.

30. "Discharge of EW Under AR 600-443 and AR 615-365," May 17, 1951; Discharge Files; Records of the Adjutant General's Office, RG407; NACP.

31. "Discharge of EW Under AR 600-443 and AR 615-365."

32. D'Emilio, *Coming Out Under Fire*, 45-46.

33. Shirley Ann Thacker Lewis Papers, S. Ann Thacker Lewis interview with Therese Strohmer, 2006, WV0405.5.001; The Betty H. Carter Women Veterans Historical Project, Jackson Library, UNCG, http://library.uncg.edu/dp/wv/results5.aspx?i=3840&s=5&c=4.

34. "WAC Enlisted Personnel Discharged Shortly After Entering the Army" c. 1962; Discharge Policy Folder, Background—WAC; RG319; NACP.

35. See chapter 10 discussion about the case involving the USS *Norton Sound* in 1979-80.

36. For more on the Lavender Scare, which ran parallel with the Red Scare and specifically ousted suspected homosexual employees from the State Department, see Johnson, *The Lavender Scare*.

37. "Meeting of WAF Staff Directors," March 19 and 20, 1959, 6 and 7; K141.33-1; AFHRA.

38. *The Crittenden Report*, 6, 4.

39. *The Crittenden Report*, 5.

40. *The Crittenden Report*, 43, 44.

41. *The Crittenden Report*, 43, 7 (emphasis in original).

42. *The Crittenden Report*, 71.

43. Letter from Unknown Servicewoman, February 15, 1951, in D'Emilio and Bérubé, "The Military and Lesbians during the McCarthy Years," 771-72.

44. Letter from Unknown Servicewoman, San Francisco, CA, March 16, 1951, Bérubé and D'Emilio, "The Military and Lesbians during the McCarthy Years," 774.

45. Letter from Staff Counsel, ACLU, April 4, 1951, Bérubé and D'Emilio, "The Military and Lesbians during the McCarthy Years," 774-75. While it is unclear whether this letter is a response to the February 1951 one, especially given the reference to the army and not the air force, it nonetheless demonstrates the ACLU's position.

46. *Fannie Mae Clackum v. United States*, 296 F.2d 226 (Ct. Cl. 1960), January 20, 1960, *Justia*, http://law.justia.com/cases/federal/appellate-courts/F2/296/226/131693/.

47. *Garner v. United States*, 161 Ct. Cl. 73, March 6, 1963, *Caselaw Access Project*, Harvard Law School, https://cite.case.law/ct-cl/161/73/.

48. Canaday, *The Straight State*, 200.

49. Humphrey, *My Country, My Right to Serve*, 12.

50. Bérubé, *Coming Out Under Fire*, 243, 139.

51. Humphrey, *My Country, My Right to Serve*, 18.

52. Quoted in 2004 *Military Education Initiative* included in file. She returned to active duty in 1994 after becoming a psychologist and served for five years under "Don't Ask, Don't Tell," until retirement in 1999. Dr. Galen Grant, Oral History File 176435; Women's Memorial Foundation Collection, Arlington, VA.

53. Winston Groom, "Lesbian Lieutenant Loses 1st Round to Air Force," *Washington Star-News*, October 4, 1974, 48; reprinted in DOD *Equal Opportunity: Current News* 60, October 10, 1974; DOD Publications, Box 35, Ford Library.

54. Press Release, DWAC Annual Historical Summaries Folder, Background—WAC; RG319; NACP.

55. "Female GI Fights Discharge," *Washington Star*, May 19, 1977; DWAC Annual Historical Summaries Folder, Background—WAC; RG319; NACP.

56. Philip Rawls, "Gender Expert Labels Former WAC Male," *The Montgomery Advertiser*, June 14, 1977.

57. "Army Woman Wed to Ex-Wac Called Good Soldier, but . . ." in *St. Petersburg Times*, June 8, 1977.

58. "WAC's Discharge Ruled for Her Marriage to Transsexual," *Independent Press-Telegram*, Long Beach, California, June 25, 1977.

59. Legally, Sode and Von Hoffburg were a married couple. After her discharge, Sode-Von Hoffburg pursued her case outside the military, when she "filed suit in a district court seeking a declaratory judgment that the Army regulation under which she was discharged is unconstitutionally vague and, as applied to her, is an unconstitutional abridgement of her rights to freedom of thought and association, privacy, substantive due process, freedom of religion, and freedom from cruel and unusual punishment." Sode-Von Hoffburg's suit further cited her discharge, termination of married housing benefits, and the military's refusal to recognize her spouse—along with her own discharge—as violations of the Fourth, Fifth, and Ninth Amendments. However, the court dismissed the case on the grounds that Sode-Von Hoffburg "had failed to exhaust her administrative remedies." In 1980, Sode-Von Hoffburg tried to appeal because "exhaustion of administrative remedies is futile in this case, and that the available administrative procedures and remedies are inadequate." 615 F.2d 633 (1980). The case was again dismissed.

Chapter 7

1. Adelaide Kingman, speech to the Los Angeles Chapter of the Daughters of the American Revolution (DAR), January 1958; Kingman, Mrs. Howard E. (Adelaide B.) Folders, DACOWITS Files; Records of the Office of the Secretary of Defense, RG330; NACP.

2. For information on the Office of Civilian Defense and women's World War II volunteer roles in the group, see Yellin, *Our Mothers' War*, chap. 6. Maureen Honey also discusses the Office of War Information and the Women's Advisory Committee to the War Manpower Commission in *Creating Rosie the Riveter*.

3. Judith Bellafaire argues that in selecting the membership demographic ideal, Marshall and Rosenberg invoked established, traditional methods of women's activism to support military recruitment. Marshall and Rosenberg believed Americans would respond positively to these women, "whose lives exemplified public service and volunteerism and who had risen to prominence in respected charitable organizations or in the caring professions." Bellafaire, "Public Service Role Models: The First Women of the Defense Advisory Committee on Women in the Services," 424.

4. Meyer, *Creating G.I. Jane*, 18.

5. Holm, *Women in the Military*, 204.

6. Cynthia Harrison analyzes the expansion of government roles for women in the Truman and Eisenhower presidencies, highlighting the tendency for these women to become "token" appointees. Harrison, *On Account of Sex*, chap. 4.

7. Members who served on both DACOWITS and the PCSW include Dr. Jeanne Noble, Dorothy Height, Katherine Peden, Margaret Hickey, and Elinor Guggenheimer.

8. "History of the Defense Advisory Committee on Women in the Services," c. early 1970s (author unknown), 2; DACOWITS Background Folder, Background—WAC; RG319; NACP.

9. "DOD Directive 5120.14," January 22, 1954, 3; DACOWITS Folder, Director-WAC Files, 1952–1959; RG319; NACP.

10. In late 1951, the organization had added subcommittees on Professional Services (focused on nurses and medical specialists) and Standards (to study what standards and qualifications the military should adapt to attract high-quality, career-oriented women). "History of the Defense Advisory Committee on Women in the Services," c. early 1970s (author unknown), 2; DACOWITS Background Folder, Background—WAC; RG319; NACP.

11. For example, a 1970 restructuring resulted in a five-subcommittee structure: Recruitment, Housing, Community Relations, Legislative Matters, and "Ad Hoc" Committees for Special Tasks. Aguilera, Donna C. "Status Report: Unmarried Housing Entitlements Issue," Unmarried Allowances DACOWITS Folder, Box 4, Commander of Naval Operations—Women Study Group, Naval Historical Center.

12. Kingman, speech to Women's Overseas Service League, Los Angeles Unit Meeting, March 3, 1958, 4; Kingman Folder, DACOWITS Files; RG319; NACP.

13. Despite DACOWITS' regular interactions with servicewomen, not every woman in the military knew of the group. Several factors affected the average servicewoman's familiarity with the organization, including rank, assignment location, and length of service. Although servicewomen could read of DACOWITS' activities in select military publications, at least by the 1970s, not every servicewoman may have read those materials. DACOWITS activity reports and other documents show that many members dedicated much time and effort to meeting

servicewomen, but servicewomen far outnumbered DACOWITS activists. For women who spent only two or three years in the services, it was possible to never encounter the group—or at least, not encounter them in any meaningful way. An informal survey of veterans, conducted through H-Minerva and personal e-mail correspondence with oral history contacts, generated uneven responses. While several respondents who served during the 1970s and after expressed familiarity with the organization, others who served from the 1950s through the 1980s noted they had never heard of the group. Author correspondence, December 2010.

14. From 1951–52, WAC Lt. Colonel Geneva F. McQuatters served in this capacity, followed by WAVE Commander Elinor Rich (1952–54), WAF Lt. Colonel Elizabeth Ray (1954–57; later Director of the WAF, 1961–65), WM Lt. Colonel Mary Hale (1957–60), and so on, rotating through the branches. Their names are listed in "Highlights of the 25th Anniversary of the Defense Advisory Committee on Women in the Services," History 1975–1976 Folder, Box 4, Records of the Bureau of Personnel Special Assistant for Women's Policy (PERS-00W), 1947–91, Naval Historical Center. See also "Operating Guide of the Defense Advisory Committee on Women in the Services," February 1954, 4–6; DACOWITS Folder, Files of the Director of the WAC, 1952–59; RG319; NACP.

15. "Highlights of The Defense Advisory Committee on Women in the Services," DACOWITS 35th Anniversary Meeting Program; Women in the Military Series, File 112, Sarah McClendon Papers, 1931–1992, State Historical Society of Missouri.

16. General Jeanne Holm, Panel Presentation by Line Directors, Women's Military Components, October 4, 1971, DACOWITS Fall 1971 Meeting Minutes, C-1-11; Minutes of the DACOWITS Fall Meeting—October 3–6, 1971 Folder, Background—WAC; RG319; NACP.

17. Document, Biography of Dr. Woods with additional DACOWITS information, "DACOWITS," Box 15, Papers of Clifford Clark, LBJ.

18. The "slander campaign" targeted women in the WAC in World War II with rumors that these women were "loose," "promiscuous," or lesbian. For detailed coverage of the World War II image problems, see chapter 11: "The Slander Campaign" in Treadwell, *The Women's Army Corps*, 191–218.

19. Kingman, speech to Women's Overseas Service League, Los Angeles Unit Meeting, March 3, 1958, 2; Kingman Folder, DACOWITS Files; RG 330; NACP.

20. See "Report of DACOWITS Activities." While it can be difficult to piece together DACOWITS member activities, there are two sources that provide insights. At the National Archives, RG 330 includes a twelve-box series on "DACOWITS Members and Correspondence," which holds files on select DACOWITS members who served between 1951 and 1959, including Kingman, Walker, and Blackwell. Schlesinger Library holds several "Activity Report" volumes from the late 1960s, which provide further detail on DACOWITS member efforts to promote women's military service. See RG 330, series "DACOWITS Members and Correspondence," NACP; Schlesinger Library, DACOWITS 1178-71-75, Box 1.

21. Ann Landers' Letters, "Girl Wants to Join Service; Parents Fret" in *The Washington Daily News*, October 16, 1963; DACOWITS Scrapbooks; RG330; NACP. Lederer served only a partial term from 1962 to 1963.

22. "Highlights of the 25th Anniversary of the Defense Advisory Committee on Women in the Services," 43; History 1975–1976 Folder, Box 4, Records of the Bureau of Personnel Special Assistant for Women's Policy (PERS-00W), 1947–91, Naval Historical Center. Information about Lockwood included in Bakken and Farrington, eds., *Encyclopedia of Women of the American West*, 190–93. The 1991 DACOWITS 40th Anniversary materials list the full names, city/state, and years of service for all members who served from 1951 to 1991. This document clarified many of the first names of early members, since previous rosters listed them under their husbands' names. *The Defense Advisory Committee on Women in the Services: 40th Anniversary, 1951–1991* (Washington, DC: DACOWITS Office, 1991); located in Sarah Newcomb McClendon Papers, 1931–92, State Historical Society of Missouri.

23. It is difficult to ascertain whether more African American or minority women served in DACOWITS during its first twenty-seven years. DACOWITS files at multiple presidential libraries and the National Archives do not contain much in the way of biographical materials. There are also few pictures of members or of the committee as a whole, and references to race or racial matters simply do not exist.

24. For thorough background on Dorothy Height, see her autobiography, *Open Wide the Freedom Gates: A Memoir*.

25. For background information on Zelma George, see Black Women Oral History Project interviews with Zelma George, 1974–76, Ruth Edmonds Hill, ed., *The Black Women Oral History Project, Volume 4*; and Walter Christmas, *Negros in Public Affairs and Government*, 50.

26. Dr. Woods's obituary available via *Los Angeles Times*, http://articles.latimes.com/2000/jan/05/news/mn-50930. Additional information on Dr. Woods in *Jet* magazine, 29 August 1963, 41.

27. Leslie, *The History of the National Association of Colored Women's Clubs, Inc.*, 171. Ollison is listed as the organization's eighteenth president. Additionally, Ollison received regular mention in *Jet* and other publications. For example, see *Jet*, December 21, 1967, 50.

28. "Mrs. George Pleased by Integration in Military," *The Cleveland Press*, February 24, 1955; DACOWITS Scrapbooks; RG330; NACP.

29. Black Women Oral History Project interviews with Dorothy Height, 1974–1976, Hill, ed., *The Black Women Oral History Project, Volume 5*, 121.

30. Schlesinger Library, DACOWITS 1178-71-75, Box 1, "Activities Report of the Defense Advisory Committee on Women in the Services," December 1967, 27.

31. Schlesinger Library, DACOWITS 1178-71-75, Box 1, "Activities Report of the Defense Advisory Committee on Women in the Services," December 1970, 67.

32. Few activity reports remain to account for individual members' activities each year, and annual recommendations do not include race-related issues. In chapter 4 of her analysis of activism inside the military, Mary Katzenstein also observes that DACOWITS did not take an interest in racial issues. Katzenstein, *Faithful and Fearless*.

33. Schlesinger Library, DACOWITS 1178-71-75, Box 2, "Historical Report Defense Advisory Committee on Women in the Services, September 1951–31 December 1952," Office of the Assistant Secretary of Defense, 2.

34. At the first DACOWITS meeting, WAC Colonel Mary Hallaren had told the women that the military needed to recruit a total of more than 70,000 women. Although the recruitment campaigns did generate enlistments, the efforts were considered "a failure" because the additions represented less than one-tenth of the goals sought by July 1952. Witt et al., *"A Defense Weapon Known to Be of Value,"* 80, 84.

35. Schlesinger Library, DACOWITS 1178-71-75, Box 2, "Historical Report Defense Advisory Committee on Women in the Services, September 1951–31 December 1952," Office of the Assistant Secretary of Defense, 2.

36. Schlesinger Library, DACOWITS 1178-71-75, Box 2, Miss Barbara J. Pendleton, "DACOWITS Briefing for New Members," A-2.

37. General Bailey, "Report on DACOWITS 1951–1971," DACOWITS Fall 1971 Meeting Minutes, D-1; Minutes of the DACOWITS Fall Meeting—October 3–6, 1971 Folder, Background—WAC; RG319; NACP.

38. Information on the resubmission of the recommendation to allow married women to live off-campus is included in Bailey's report (cited above), as well as *The Defense Advisory Committee on Women in the Services: 40th Anniversary, 1951–1991* (Washington, DC: DACOWITS Office, 1991); Sarah Newcomb McClendon Papers, 1931–1992, State Historical Society of Missouri. The 40th anniversary program also notes that the group began petitioning for BAQ for married servicewomen regularly in 1965.

39. General Bailey, "Report on DACOWITS 1951–1971," DACOWITS Fall 1971 Meeting Minutes, D-9; Minutes of the DACOWITS Fall Meeting—October 3–6, 1971 Folder, Background—WAC; RG319; NACP.

40. General Bailey, "Report on DACOWITS 1951–1971." The high demand for nursing professionals in the military likely accounts for the Army Nurse Corps' support of this idea. Additionally, as historian Charissa Threat explains, opening the Army Nurse Corps to male nurses in 1955 created uncertainty for many female nurses, and their interest in allowing mothers to remain in service may reflect such concerns. For more details on the role of nurses in civilian society and in the military, see Leighow, "An 'Obligation to Participate': Married Nurses' Labor Force Participation in the 1950s," in Meyerowitz, ed., *Not June Cleaver*; Threat, "Does the Sex of the Practitioner Matter? Nursing, Civil Rights, and Discrimination in the Army Nurse Corps, 1947–1955," in Bristol Jr. and Stur, eds., *Integrating the US Military*; and Vuic, *Officer, Nurse, Woman*.

41. Housing study outlined in May 1955 meeting minutes. DACOWITS Folder, Director of the WAC Files, 1952–1959; Records of the Army Staff, RG319; NACP.

42. In 1964, the organization conducted another housing study, and revisited the issue in 1966 and 1967, noting that "The DOD Directive No. 4165.47 of April 6, 1967, which established minimum standards for housing occupancy, is indicative of the continued interest by the DOD and members of DACOWITS to improve housing conditions for our military personnel." They kept pressuring DOD to apply their 1964 recommendations again in 1968, 1969, and 1970, but by that time it was about equalizing BAQ for married women. "History of the Defense Advisory Com-

mittee on Women in the Services," c. early 1970s (author unknown), 10, 23, 26, 31, 45, 56, and 68; DACOWITS Background Folder, Background—WAC; RG319; NACP.

43. DOD, "Enlisted Women in the Services: III. Some Satisfactions and Dissatisfactions of Service Life," Report 1356-347, April to May 1952, 4. Schlesinger Library, DACOWITS 1178-71-75, Box 2, Research Division, Office of Armed Forces Information and Education.

44. Letter to Major Harriet Moses from Dean Myrtle Austin, June 26, 1952; Austin, Dean Myrtle (1951) Folder, DACOWITS Files; RG330; NACP. Little evidence remains of ideas brought specifically by servicewomen to DACOWITS members. It seems to have been more common for DACOWITS to identify ideas during their visits to military installations, or through conversations with servicewomen in their communities.

45. "Minutes and Reports of the Defense Advisory Committee on Women in the Services Biannual Meeting, May 12–14, 1955, Washington, D.C.," 4; Director-WAC, 1952–1959 Files; RG319; NACP.

46. Holm mentions that she led a study in the mid-1950s regarding coeducational air force ROTC, but stresses that the test was unsuccessful. Holm, *Women in the Military*, 268.

47. Generals Bailey and Holm, "Report on DACOWITS 1951–1971," D-4.

48. Generals Bailey and Holm, "Report on DACOWITS 1951–1971," D-4 to D-5. The Women's Army Auxiliary Corps (WAAC) was a civilian auxiliary to the military. Women who served in the WAAC did not receive credit for military service in World War II prior to this act. The WAAC became the WAC in 1943, a recognized military service unit.

49. Generals Bailey and Holm, "Report on DACOWITS 1951–1971," D-7.

50. Navy Captain Robin Quigley, Panel Presentation by Line Directors, Women's Military Components, October 4, 1971, DACOWITS Fall 1971 Meeting, C-1-11; Minutes of the DACOWITS Fall Meeting—October 3–6, 1971 Folder, Background—WAC; RG319; NACP.

51. Generals Bailey and Holm, "Report on DACOWITS 1951–1971," D-16.

52. Margaret Eastman, "DACOWITS: A Nice Little Group That Doesn't Do Very Much" in *Family: The Magazine of the Army/Navy/Air Force/Times*, March 15, 1972; Background—WAC; RG319; NACP.

53. Gates et al. argued that these meetings should be open to the public according to federal law. The DOD disagreed on the basis that the leaders of the women's services often provided information that could potentially be of a sensitive nature. Ultimately, the court decided that the plaintiffs were correct and DACOWITS members expressed no concerns over the decision when the first outside visitor sat in that fall. U.S. District Court for the District of Columbia, 366 F. Supp. 797, October 10, 1973.

54. "Testimony by the National Organization for Women," DACOWITS Spring 1976 Meeting Minutes (25th Anniversary), G-2; Background—WAC; RG319; NACP.

55. "Memorandum for Lieutenant General Leo E. Benade on Continuation of Defense Advisory Committee on Women in the Services (DACOWITS)" from

Brigadier General Mildred C. Bailey, Director of the WAC, November 6, 1973; Background—WAC; RG319; NACP.

56. Brigadier General Jeanne Holm, "Panel Discussion by Line Directors, Women's Military Components," October 4, 1971, DACOWITS Fall 1971 Meeting, C-1-17; Minutes of the DACOWITS Fall Meeting—October 3–6, 1971 Folder, Background—WAC; RG319; NACP.

57. The organization exists today, although in much smaller form (and since the 1980s, with the inclusion of male members). For more information about DACOWITS today, visit the organization's official website: http://dacowits.defense.gov/.

Chapter 8

1. Generals Bailey and Holm, "Report on DACOWITS 1951–1971," DACOWITS Fall 1971 Meeting Minutes, D-7; Minutes of the DACOWITS Fall Meeting—October 3–6, 1971 Folder, Background—WAC; RG319; NACP.

2. For a full list of DACOWITS members from 1951–91, see *The Defense Advisory Committee on Women in the Services: 40th Anniversary, 1951–1991* (Washington, DC: DACOWITS Office, 1991); located in Sarah Newcomb McClendon Papers, 1931–92, State Historical Society of Missouri. For a list of all PCSW committee members, see Reel 2, PCSW.

3. "Final Report of the Federal Employment Policies and Practices Committee," August 1963, 49; President's Commission on the Status of Women, Reel 7, PCSW.

4. As DACOWITS members' backgrounds suggest, women's organizations had a long history in the United States, particularly as philanthropies and community service groups. In the 1950s, DACOWITS was perhaps the most significant example of government-related women's advocacy groups and was, in some ways, a precursor to the PCSW. Following PCSW came the development of the Citizens' Advisory Council on the Status of Women and the Interdepartmental Committee on the Status of Women. Similar local groups soon sprung up as well, in addition to the rise of feminist organizations like the National Organization of Women (NOW) beginning in 1966. For additional discussion of the legacy of the PCSW, see Harrison, *On Account of Sex*, and Stewart, *The Women's Movement in Community Politics in the U.S.*

5. "Final Report of the Federal Employment Policies and Practices Committee," August 1963, 49; President's Commission on the Status of Women, Reel 7, PCSW. For specifications on rank percentage limitations, see Holm, *Women in the Military*, 120.

6. "Final Report of the Federal Employment Policies and Practices Committee," August 1963, 49a, Reel 7, PCSW.

7. Holm, *Women in the Military*, 197.

8. Morden, *The Women's Army Corps*, 207–9.

9. For details of the process to secure what became Public Law 90-130, see Holm, *Women in the Military*, 192–203.

10. Technically, the navy did not have a Director–WAVES, because the WAVES as a unit ceased to exist after World War II. Still, the term "WAVES" persisted into the Cold War. The Assistant Chief of Naval Personnel for Women was the navy's equivalent of a Director–WAVES.

11. "Transcript Special Subcommittee on Enlisted Promotion Policy Page 1288 to 1878 Vol 33 dtd 5Oct67," Records of the USMC, Marine Corps History and Museum Division, Military Operations, Programs, and Organization, RG127; NACP.

12. Holm, *Women in the Military*, 200.

13. President Lyndon B. Johnson, "Remarks Upon Signing Bill Providing Equal Opportunity in Promotions for Women in the Armed Forces," November 8, 1967. John T. Woolley and Gerhard Peters, *The American Presidency Project*, Santa Barbara, CA, https://www.presidency.ucsb.edu/documents/remarks-upon-signing-bill-providing-equal-opportunity-promotions-for-women-the-armed.

14. Harrison, *On Account of Sex*, 176–80.

15. Kessler-Harris, *Out to Work*, 315; see also President Lyndon Johnson, "Executive Order 11375—Amending Executive Order No. 11246, Relating to Equal Employment Opportunity," October 13, 1967, https://www.presidency.ucsb.edu/documents/executive-order-11375-amending-executive-order-no-11246-relating-equal-employment.

16. Lieutenant John H. Wolf, JAGC, "Public Law 90–130: The Act Relating to Promotion and Tenure of Women Officers," in *JAG Journal*, May–June 1968, 121–22; PL90–130 Related Folder, Box 6, BuPers00W, Naval Historical Center.

17. According to Holm, by 1965 enlisted women held positions in just over half of the noncombat job groups. Women officers worked in nearly three-quarters of the open noncombat officer job groups, but all women—enlisted and commissioned—predominantly held positions in clerical, administrative, personnel, information, and desk jobs in general. See Holm, *Women in the Military*, 184.

18. Quigley and Brewer were the "youngest" of the 1970s directors, with commissioning dates in 1954 and 1952, respectively. Six of the remaining directors began their service in World War II; it is unclear when Bianca Trimeloni, the second-to-last WAF Director, began her military service, but it is likely that she also joined in the late 1940s or early 1950s at the latest.

19. "Equal Rights? The Waves Have Had 'em for Years!" undated, c. 1971. Records of the Bureau of Personnel, Special Assistant for Women's Policy (PERS-00W), Box 1, Biographical Data—Robin Quigley Folder, Naval Historical Center.

20. Brigadier General Mildred Bailey interview with Rhoda Messer, October 4, 1978, 17–18. United States Army Military History Institute Senior Officers Debriefing Program, Carlisle Barracks, PA. Copy held as Oral History File 005319, Women's Memorial Foundation Collection, Arlington, VA.

21. Mildred Bailey, "End of Tour Report: Memorandum for Secretary of the Army," July 28, 1975, 6; Bailey End of Tour Report Folder, Background—WAC; RG319; NACP.

22. Brigadier General Mildred C. Bailey, Director-WAC, "Memorandum for Lieutenant General Leo E. Benade on Continuation of Defense Advisory Committee on Women in the Services (DACOWITS)," November 6, 1973; DACOWITS Background Files Folder, Background—WAC; RG319; NACP.

23. Rita Lenihan, "Bulletin from the Assistant Chief of Naval Personnel for Women, Number 16," January 1, 1971, 2. Records of the Bureau of Personnel, Special Assistant for Women's Policy (PERS-00W), Box 8, PERS-K Bulletins Folder, Naval Historical Center.

24. Jeanette I. Sustad, "Memorandum #4: Woman Marine Matters," January 20, 1971, 2. Chief of Naval Operations Women Study Group, Box 1, Navy Correspondence/Memos, 1968–79, Naval Historical Center.

25. General Elizabeth Hoisington interview with Patricia Drugnan, date unknown, 5; Interview—General Hoisington Folder, Background—WAC; RG319; NACP.

26. General Elizabeth Hoisington interview with Patricia Drugnan, 12.

27. For perspective on ending the Women Marines, for example, see Report of Ad Hoc—1973 Folder, Stremlow WMs; Records of the USMC, RG127; NACP.

28. Letter from Captain Rita Lenihan in "Mail Call," *Navy Times*, November 1970. Chief of Naval Operations Women Study Group, Box 6, Clippings Folder, Naval Historical Center.

29. If the argument for the 1948 Women's Armed Services Integration Act centered, in part, around the contributions women had made in World War II, the 1970s directors embraced a similar notion wholeheartedly.

30. Major General Jeanne Holm interview with Mary Jo Binker; Jeanne Holm Collection (AFC/2001/001/4293), LOC VHP, http://lcweb2.loc.gov/diglib/vhp/story/loc.natlib.afc2001001.04293/.

31. Quoted in Margaret Eastman, "The Leading Ladies: Four Top Servicewomen Tell it Their Way" April 5, 1972, *Family* magazine, 9. Reel 18, Miscellaneous Press Clippings, 1971–1972 Folder, WAVES.

32. Quoted in Margaret Eastman, "The Leading Ladies: Four Top Servicewomen Tell It Their Way," 8.

33. Major General Clarke interview with Drugnan, 5; Interviews—Major General Clarke Folder, Background—WAC; RG319; NACP.

34. Gwen Austin, "Equality in the Army: 'A Long Way to Go,' Says Woman General," *Tampa Tribune-Times*, October 3, 1976.

35. Quoted in Eastman, "The Leading Ladies," 10.

36. Mildred Bailey, "Women in the Army," in *Commander's Digest: Women in Defense*, July 10, 1975, 7; Pepper Board 1964 Folder, Stremlow WMs; RG127; NACP.

37. "Proceedings of Utilization Subcommittee," DACOWITS Spring 1975 Meeting Minutes, F-6 and F-7; Background—WAC; RG319; NACP.

38. "Proceedings of Utilization Subcommittee."

39. "Briefing of DACOWITS," October 6, 1975; *Women Marines 1918–1973* Files (WM Files); Records of the USMC, RG127; NACP.

40. Eastman, "The Leading Ladies," 9.

41. Major General Jeanne Holm testimony, Women in the Military Hearings, House of Representatives, Subcommittee on Military Personnel, Committee on Armed Services, November 13, 1979, 11–12. Chief of Naval Operations Women Study Group, Box 3, Women in the Navy 1970–1979 Folder, Naval Historical Center.

42. Major General Jeanne Holm testimony, Women in the Military Hearings.

43. Holm went on to say that she interpreted combat widely, and although she would not immediately advocate putting women in the infantry—she noted that such a move should be done cautiously—she did not rule out any combat role for women. Major General Jeanne Holm testimony, Women in the Military Hearings.

44. In oral history interviews, veterans rarely discuss their attitudes toward feminism. Retired naval officer Judy Campbell emphasized that she did not become a feminist until after she had her children in the late 1970s and 1980s, well after she completed her military service. Judy Campbell interview with Tanya Roth, November 2009. WAC veteran Susie Stephens McArthur emphasized that she is not and has never been a feminist. Susie McArthur Papers, Susie (Stephens) McArthur interview with Hermann Trojanowski, 2001, WV0199.5.001; The Betty H. Carter Women Veterans Historical Project, Jackson Library, UNCG, http://library.uncg.edu/dp/wv/results5.aspx?i=2690&s=5.

45. Preface to Margaret Eastman, "You've Come a Long Way . . . Maybe," March 15, 1972, *Family: The Magazine of Army/Navy/Air Force/Times*; 1972 Articles Folder, Background—WAC; RG319; NACP.

46. Remarks at the White House by Major General Jeanne Holm, Special Assistant to President Ford, DACOWITS Fall 1976 meeting, O-10; Minutes: 25th Anniversary Meeting—November 14-18, 1976 Folder, Background—WAC; Records of the Army Staff, RG319; NACP.

47. Margaret Eastman, "The Woman in Uniform: How Liberated Can She Be? Part III" *Family* magazine, April 19, 1972, 24-25. Reel 18, Miscellaneous Press Clippings, 1971-1972 Folder, WAVES.

48. For information about the *Frontiero* decision, see *Frontiero v. Richardson*, 411 U.S. 677 (1973); Mayeri, "'When the Trouble Started': *Frontiero v. Richardson*"; Linda Kerber also discusses the case in *No Constitutional Right to Be Ladies*, 203, 230, 252, 276. In July 1973, Congress passed Public Law 93-64 to invalidate 37 U.S.C. 401, which had limited women's ability to declare dependents. Over that summer, the Comptroller General continued to evaluate the impact of the Supreme Court decision on military policies. Memorandum, "Entitlements of Female Members with Civilian Spouses," undated; BAQ Benefits Equality Issues Folder, Background—WAC; Records of the Army Staff, RG319; NACP.

49. Public Law 625 in *United States Statutes*, beginning on 361 and repeated in each Title of the law.

50. Memorandum Regarding H.R. 15127, "A Bill 'To Amend Titles 10 and 37, United States Code, to Provide Equality of Treatment for Married Female Members of the Uniformed Services,'" April 11, 1968, Married Women Equality Folder, Box 6, BuPersooW, Naval Historical Center.

51. J. Fred Buzhardt, Office of the Counsel of the DOD, Correspondence to Hon. John C. Stennis, Chairman, Senate Committee on Armed Services, October 30, 1970, 4, Married Women Equality Folder, Box 6, BuPersooW, Naval Historical Center.

52. Presentation on Current Legislation by Carole L. Frings, Office of the General Counsel, Office of the Secretary of Defense, DACOWITS Fall 1973 Meeting Minutes, E-1; Background—WAC; RG319; NACP.

53. Lt. Col. Rhoda Messer interview with Brigadier General Mildred Inez Bailey, October 4, 1978 session, 9-10. U.S. Army Military History Institute Senior Officer Debriefing Program, Carlisle Barracks, PA. Copy held as File 005319, Women's Memorial Foundation Collection, Arlington, VA.

54. E. Brouse, Captain and Director of Litigation and Claims Division, letter to Irving Jaffe, Chief, Court of Claims Section, regarding *Huber v. U.S.*; Letter from Assistant General Counsel Carpenter, General Accounting Office, to Honorable Edwin Weisl Jr., Assistant Attorney General, Civil Division, Department of Justice, regarding *Lieblich v. U.S.*, November 15, 1968; Chief of Naval Operations Women Study Group, Box 1, Navy Correspondence/Memos, 1968–1979, Naval Historical Center.

Chapter 9

1. For an overview of social activism in the 1960s, see Isserman and Kazin's *America Divided: The Civil War of the 1960s*; Kendrick, *The Wound Within: America in the Vietnam Wars*; and Farber and Bailey (with contributors), *The Columbia Guide to America in the 1960s*. See also Olson and Roberts, *Where the Domino Fell: America and Vietnam, 1945–2010*.

2. Spector, "The Vietnam War and the Army's Self-Image," in *Second Indochina War Symposium: Papers and Commentary*, 170.

3. Bailey, *America's Army*, 43. Bachman et al., *The All-Volunteer Force: A Study of Ideology in the Military*, 12. For analysis of the class divisions in the Vietnam-era army, see Appy, *Working-Class War*. Lawrence M. Baskir and William A. Strauss discuss draft-motivated enlistments in *Chance and Circumstance: The Draft, the War, and the Vietnam Generation*. For the service academies' difficulties in recruiting, see James Feron, "Education; West Point Goes Hunting for Recruits," May 7, 1985, *New York Times*, http://www.nytimes.com/1985/05/07/science/education-west-point-goes-hunting-for-recruits.html?&pagewanted=all.

4. Beth Bailey details many of the planning stages for eliminating the draft. Bernard Rostker, who participated in the draft-elimination research phases while working with the RAND Corporation in the early 1970s, also offers a thorough analysis of the transition to the All-Volunteer Force in Rostker, *I Want YOU! The Evolution of the All-Volunteer Force*. For AVF start date, see Bailey, *America's Army*, 3.

5. Historian Cynthia Harrison argues that most activists "shunned the label *feminist*" between the end of World War II and the middle of the 1960s. See Harrison, *On Account of Sex*, ix.

6. Berkeley, *The Women's Liberation Movement in America*, 47.

7. Technically, the term applies most appropriately to radical feminists who advocated that women should "liberate" themselves from the oppression of patriarchy. The term "women's libbers" also became a typically derogatory phrase to describe women activists in the 1970s. See Berkeley, *The Women's Liberation Movement in America*, 5.

8. For a thorough discussion of the three types of feminism, see Gatlin, *American Women Since 1945*, chapter 6, "The Politics of the Women's Movement," where she analyzes social, liberal, and radical feminism; the goals of each; and key influences. Berkeley also considers the differences between feminist groups; see 52. Alice Echols offers a study on radical feminism in *Daring to be Bad: Radical Feminism in America, 1967–1975*. Sara Evans further clarifies social and cultural feminism in *Tidal Wave:*

How Women Changed America at Century's End, 143. In addition, the rising popularity of the women's movement was reflected in the growth of groups like NOW, whose membership jumped from about 4,000 in 1970 to more than 20,000 within three years. Berkeley, *The Women's Liberation Movement in America*, 58.

9. For brief histories of the ERA, see Mansbridge, *Why We Lost the ERA*, and Berry, *Why ERA Failed*.

10. Harrison, *On Account of Sex*, 134.

11. Harrison, 191. Harrison describes the EEOC's stance toward sex discrimination problems as "half-hearted." Kessler-Harris provides the data on number of early sex discrimination complaints, noting that staff members "at first responded resentfully to the flood of complaints" in this area; see Kessler-Harris, *In Pursuit of Equity*, 247.

12. See Davis, *Moving the Mountain*, 49; and Mansbridge, *Why We Lost the ERA*, 10. According to Davis, prioritizing the ERA, along with fighting for the repeal of antiabortion laws, led to one of the first splits in the organization, resulting in the creation of the Women's Equity Action League (WEAL).

13. Mansbridge, *Why We Lost the ERA*, 10. She notes that union opposition to the ERA began to weaken after courts and the EEOC began to use Title VII to extend traditional protections to men, rather than remove them from women.

14. Frances Spatz Leighton, "New Stars in the Service," undated, publication unknown. Reel 18, Women's News File January 1970–January 1971 Folder, WAVES.

15. Myron Waldman, "Women Military Directors Silent on Lib," in *Virginian Pilot*, March 8, 1972, A9. Reel 18, Miscellaneous Press Clippings, 1971–1972 Folder, WAVES.

16. Bailey Testimony, "Hearings Before the Special Subcommittee on the Utilization of Manpower in the Military" [H.A.S.C. No. 92-51], 92nd Congress, First and Second Sessions, Committee on Armed Services, House of Representatives, March 6, 1972, 12466; Hearings Before the Special Subcommittee on the Utilization of Manpower in the Military Folder, Background—WAC; RG319; NACP.

17. Schlesinger Library, NOW Files, Box 193, Military 1971–1974 and 1983 Folder, NOW paper "The Equal Rights Amendment and the Draft," August 1971.

18. At the fall 1974 DACOWITS meeting, NOW representative Suzanne de Satrustegui noted that her San Antonio chapter of NOW was working to form a National Task Force on Women in the Armed Forces. Although later publications reference this task force, suggesting that it did in fact exist, the NOW records at the Schlesinger Library in Cambridge, Massachusetts, do not have any materials about this task force. In fact, information on NOW's efforts to support military women is incredibly sparse in their files, with the bulk of it coming in the early 1980s with the debates over registering women for selective service. The most direct evidence of second-wave feminist groups' involvement with the military comes with DACOWITS meeting records from the mid-1970s. In addition to de Satrustegui, the Women's Lobby, Inc., sent their Director of Military and Veteran's Affairs to speak, as did the Texas Women's Political Caucus. In spring 1975, Lorraine Underwood of NOW spoke at DACOWITS, along with the Women's Lobby Director of Military and Veterans' Affairs; Underwood specifically mentioned that the Committee

for Women in the Military had been created—she was chair of it. Minutes of the DACOWITS Fall Meeting—October 20–24, 1974 Folder and Minutes: DACOWITS Spring Meeting—April 6–10, 1975 Folder, Background—WAC; RG319; NACP.

19. Pat Leeper testimony, spring 1976 DACOWITS meeting, *Minutes: DACOWITS Spring Meeting*, April 21–25, 1976, G-2; Minutes: DACOWIT Spring Meeting—April 21–25, 1976 Folder, Background—WAC; RG319; NACP.

20. Merlene Cimons, "Now vs. U.S. Army in Admissions Policies," *Los Angeles Times*; reprinted in *New Orleans Times-Picayune*, October 22, 1975 and in DOD *Equal Opportunity: Current News*, no. 86, November 20, 1975; DOD Publications, Box 35, Ford Library.

21. Patricia Fagan letter to Assistant Secretary of the Navy, July 24, 1975. Records of the Bureau of Personnel, Special Assistant for Women's Policy (PERS-00W), Box 1, Correspondence 1972–1975 Folder, Naval Historical Center.

22. Amendment 1065, exempting women from the draft, failed by 72 to 18 and Amendment 1066, allowing Congress to make laws against women in combat, failed by 71 to 18. Congressional Record, March 21, 1972, CRS-9 and CRS-11, quoted in Library of Congress Congressional Research Services: Equal Rights Amendment—Selected Floor Debate and Votes. Patricia Lindh and Jeanne Holm Files, White House Public Liaison Files, Box 9, ERA General 2 Folder, Ford Library.

23. Congressional Record, March 21, 1972, CRS-1, quoted in Library of Congress Congressional Research Services: Equal Rights Amendment—Selected Floor Debate and Votes. Patricia Lindh and Jeanne Holm Files, White House Public Liaison Files, Box 9, ERA General 2 Folder, Ford Library.

24. Mansbridge, *Why We Lost the ERA*, 12.

25. Leslie Maitland, "US Amendment: What it Will Do," March 11, 1975, *New York Times*, 40.

26. For discussions of the impact of the ERA, both by advocates and those against the amendment, see: Women's Bureau, U.S. Department of Labor, "Women Workers in 1975: Issues," 6. Patricia Lindh and Jeanne Holm Files, White House Public Liaison Files, Box 2, March 25, 1975—Tuesday Meeting—EEO with Vice President Folder; Carolyn J. Jacobson, "ERA: Ratifying Equality," *AFL-CIO American Federationist*, January 1975, Patricia Lindh and Jeanne Holm Files, White House Public Liaison Files, Box 35, National Ad Hoc Committee for ERA Folder; Women Who Want to be Women (Texas Anti-ERA Group), "Ladies! Have You Heard?" Patricia Lindh and Jeanne Holm Files, White House Public Liaison Files, Box 9, ERA Printed Material 2 Folder; Stop ERA, "You Can't Fool Mother Nature" (brochure). Sheila Weidenfeld Files, Box 47, Women—ERA—General Folder, Ford Library. Barbara A. Brown, Thomas I. Emerson, Gail Falk, and Ann E. Freedman, "The Equal Rights Amendment: A Constitutional Basis for Equal Rights for Women," *The Yale Law Journal* 80, no. 5 (April 1971). Brown et al. consider a broad range of topics, including the question of rape laws and sexual assault. The authors expected that rape laws would likely be upheld or expanded to include men as victims of sexual assault.

27. Linda Kerber argues that "one of the major rocks on which the ERA debates foundered was the claim that proponents were flinging innocent young girls into the military machine—there to be treated as no better than men and to be brutal-

ized." For discussion of how the connection between military service and citizenship "remained a subtext" throughout both the ERA debates and the fight to ratify the ERA, see Kerber, *No Constitutional Right to be Ladies*, 283–87.

28. Brown et al., "The Equal Rights Amendment," 967.

29. Mansbridge suggests that Schlafly did not really make the draft and combat the central issues of her fight until 1980, although she did draw attention to the issue as early as 1972 and certainly addressed the draft in detail by 1975 in her regular Eagle Report. See "The Phyllis Schlafly Report," July 1975, Patricia Lindh and Jeanne Holm Files, White House Public Liaison Files, Box 9, ERA Printed Material 2 Folder, Ford Library. What is particularly interesting about the concerns over drafting women is that activists on both sides seemed to not realize that the topic had been broached at least twice before, during World War II and in the Korean War. For an account that discusses the early 1950s discussion of drafting women, see Witt et al., *"A Defense Weapon Known to Be of Value"*; Mansbridge, *Why We Lost the ERA*, 86, as well as chapter 8, note 45.

30. Brown et al., "The Equal Rights Amendment," 968.

31. Brown et al., 977.

32. Pamphlet, "The Promise of Equality: 'The Truth About the Equal Rights Amendment,'" District of Columbia Federation of Business and Professional Women's Clubs, 20–22. Patricia Lindh and Jeanne Holm Files, White House Public Liaison Files, Box 9, ERA Printed Material 1 Folder, Ford Library.

33. See also, for example, Leslie Maitland, "U.S. Amendment: What it Will Do," *New York Times*, March 11, 1975, 40; White Paper, "Q&A" (on ERA), May 5, 1976. Patricia Lindh and Jeanne Holm Files, White House Public Liaison Files, Boxes 9 and 35, Ford Library.

34. The National Federation of Business and Professional Women's Clubs, "Who Will Defend the Nation?" (brochure). Patricia Lindh and Jeanne Holm Files, White House Public Liaison Files, Box 9, ERA Printed Material 2 Folder, Ford Library.

35. Office of the Deputy Chief of Staff for Personnel, Department of the Army, Report of the Committee to Study the Proposed Equal Rights Amendment, December 1972, i; Study—"Impact of Passage of ERA on Women in the Army," December 1972 Folder, Background—WAC; RG319; NACP.

36. Office of the Deputy Chief of Staff for Personnel, Department of the Army, Report of the Committee to Study the Proposed Equal Rights Amendment, December 1972, iii.

37. Office of the Deputy Chief of Staff for Personnel, Department of the Army, Report of the Committee to Study the Proposed Equal Rights Amendment, December 1972, iii–iv.

38. Office of the Deputy Chief of Staff for Personnel, Department of the Army, Report of the Committee to Study the Proposed Equal Rights Amendment, December 1972, iv.

39. Office of the Deputy Chief of Staff for Personnel, Department of the Army, Report of the Committee to Study the Proposed Equal Rights Amendment, December 1972, vii.

40. Lt. General Bernard W. Rogers, "Utilization of Women in the Army," January 18, 1973, 2. Study—"Impact of Passage of ERA on Women in the Army," December 1972 Folder, Background—WAC; RG319; NACP.

41. Carole L. Frings, "The Effect of the Equal Rights Amendment on Women in the Military," *Minutes: DACOWITS Fall Meeting*, November 12–16, 1972, D-5. Patricia Lindh and Jeanne Holm Files, White House Public Liaison Files, Box 40, DACOWITS Folder, Ford Library.

42. Frings, "The Effect of the Equal Rights Amendment on Women in the Military," D-11.

43. Frings, D-15.

44. "The Phyllis Schlafly Report," July 1975, 1. Patricia Lindh and Jeanne Holm Files, White House Public Liaison Files, Box 9, ERA Printed Materials 2 Folder, Ford Library. Schlafly clarified that she believed this was dishonest at least of women old enough to remember that fathers up to the age of thirty-five were drafted in World War II.

45. "The Phyllis Schlafly Report," July 1975, 1.

46. "The Equal Rights Amendment: An Attack on Personal Freedoms," from January 1976 *Good News Broadcaster*, 3. Patricia Lindh and Jeanne Holm Files, White House Public Liaison Files, Box 9, ERA Printed Material 1 Folder, Ford Library. Additional publications also mentioned the draft and combat as problems, including "You Can't Fool Mother Nature," STOP ERA brochure and Jim Gallagher, ". . . then there's Schlafly," *Long Beach Independent Press-Telegram*, April 3, 1975. Both in Weidenfeld Files, Box 47, Women—ERA—General Folder, Ford Library. As late as 1981, Schlafly argued that the ERA had four specific implications for the military: drafting of women, women in combat, affirmative action to incorporate more women into the military, and equal recruitment of women to military academies. See "The Phyllis Schlafly Report," November 1981, http://www.eagleforum.org//era/psr/psrnov81.pdf.

47. Holm, *Women in the Military*, 203.

48. The Office of the Deputy Assistant Secretary of Defense (Equal Opportunity), "Women in the Armed Forces: A Statistical Fact Book," August 1, 1973, chart: Strength of Women in the Armed Forces. WAC Statistics Folder, Background—WAC; RG319; NACP. Office of the Assistant Secretary of Defense (Manpower, Reserve Affairs and Logistics), *America's Volunteers: A Report on the All-Volunteer Armed Forces*, 69; Records of the Bureau of Personnel, Special Assistant for Women's Policy (PERS-00W), Box 18, A Report on the All-Volunteer Armed Forces "America's Volunteers" 1978 Folder, Naval Historical Center.

49. Ed Gates, "Women in the Service," *The Retired Officer*, November 1977. Papers of Louise Wilde, Box 4, Sea Duty 1970s Folder, Naval Historical Center.

50. Holm, *Women in the Military*, 300.

51. "Hearings Before the Special Subcommittee on the Utilization of Manpower in the Military" [H.A.S.C. No. 92-51], 92nd Congress, First and Second Sessions, Committee on Armed Services, House of Representatives, March 6, 1972, 12439; Hearings Before the Special Subcommittee on the Utilization of Manpower in the Military Folder, Background—WAC; RG319; NACP.

52. "Hearings Before the Special Subcommittee on the Utilization of Manpower in the Military," 12440.

53. "Hearings Before the Special Subcommittee on the Utilization of Manpower in the Military," 12439.

54. "Hearings Before the Special Subcommittee on the Utilization of Manpower in the Military," 12440.

55. By 1970, the reenlistment rate in the navy had dropped from 35 percent to 9.5 percent after first tour of duty.

56. Zumwalt Jr., *On Watch: A Memoir*, 168. During his four years as Chief of Naval Operations, Zumwalt issued 121 "Z-Grams," which were either informational dispatches or policy changes. Z-66, "Equal Opportunity in the Navy" instituted his plan for working toward racial equal opportunity in the navy (December 17, 1970) and Z-116 addressed "Equal Rights and Opportunities for Women in the Navy" (August 7, 1972).

57. It is not quite evident why Zumwalt advocated limited numbers of women in all roles, but one possible reason may be that he saw slow expansion of women's opportunities as a way to allow women to prove they could perform the tasks effectively. Allowing small numbers of women to move into new job fields would also seem like less of a potential liability to those against the idea.

58. For discussion of Zumwalt's efforts to change women's status in the navy, see Zumwalt, *On Watch*, 261–62 and following. Full text of Z-116, https://www.history.navy.mil/research/library/online-reading-room/title-list-alphabetically/z/list-z-grams/z-gram-116.html.

59. Zumwalt, *On Watch*, 264–65.

60. Commander Catherine Leahey interview with Dave Winkler, January–February 2003, Naval Historical Foundation, 1 (Oral History File 053132); Women's Memorial Foundation Collection, Arlington, VA.

61. Commander Catherine Leahey interview with Dave Winkler, 3.

62. Leahey and another Lieutenant (JG), Judy Harrell, were the first two women assigned to the *USS Point Loma*. She served as Auxiliaries/Electrical Officer and then Operations Officer on that ship from August 9, 1979 to July 1, 1982. She spent eighteen years as a Surface Warfare Officer (SWO), the designation for officers qualified to serve at sea.

63. Her job was to learn to maintain and repair these card- and tape-punch machine systems. Essentially, she was in the electronic equipment maintenance field. Carol Wheeler interview with Tanya Roth, March 2010.

64. Carol Wheeler interview with Tanya Roth, March 2010.

65. Carol Wheeler interview with Tanya Roth, March 2010.

66. *Commander's Digest: Women in Defense Special Issue*, July 10, 1975 (vol. 18, no. 2), 2; Pepper Board 1964 Folder, Stremlow WMs; RG127; NACP.

67. Martin Binkin Address to DACOWITS, E-3; Minutes: DACOWITS Spring Meeting—April 17–20, 1977 Folder, Background—WAC; RG319; NACP.

68. Captain Robin Quigley, Pers-K Memorandum #5, February 23, 1972. Ellipses in original. Records of the Bureau of Personnel, Special Assistant for Women's

Policy (PERS-00W), Box 8, PERS-K Bulletins 1953–1972 Folder, Naval Historical Center.

69. "History of The Women in the Air Force, 1 July to 31 December 1975," (Director-WAF Report), 8; K141.33; AFHRA.

70. Morden, *The Women's Army Corps*, 397.

71. Technically, combat and combat support roles remained off limits. Rogers' comment does not say that women ARE integrating into the combat and combat service support branches, but rather that they are "progressing" toward that. Speech by General Bernard Rogers, Chief of Staff, U.S. Army, D-5; Minutes: DACOWITS Spring Meeting—April 17–20, 1977 Folder, Background—WAC; RG319; NACP.

72. Major General Jeanne Holm, "My Third Life," Speech to WAF Officers Reunion, November 6, 1976, 16. Patricia Lindh and Jeanne Holm Files, White House Public Liaison Files, Box 17, Holm Speech to WAF Officer Reunion 1976 Folder, Ford Library.

Chapter 10

1. "Who'll Fight for America?" *Time*, June 9, 1980.
2. Barbara Dolan, "West Point: The Coed Class of '80," *Time*, May 19, 1980.
3. Quoted in Martin Binkin, "Women's Rights and National Security," *Washington Post*, July 7, 1976, 15; Magazine and Newspaper Articles Folder, Background—WAC; RG319; NACP. For Sustad's opinions on the difference between men and women, see "Statement of Colonel Jeanette I. Sustad, U.S. Marine Corps . . . Before the Special Subcommittee on the Utilization of Manpower in the Military," undated; Reference of Women Marines Folder, Stremlow WMs; RG127; NACP.
4. General Elizabeth Hoisington interview with Bettie Morden, November 3, 1980, questions 52 and 55; Interview—General Hoisington Folder, Background—WAC; RG319; NACP.
5. For a list of significant alumni from these institutions, see: Notable Graduates, West Point, https://www.westpoint.edu/about/history-of-west-point/notable-graduates; Notable Graduates, U.S. Naval Academy, https://www.usna.edu/Notables/index.php; and Notable Grads, U.S. Air Force Academy, https://www.usafa.edu/notable-grads/.
6. Letter from Donald Quarles, Department of the Air Force, regarding SJ Res. 48, "To provide for the establishment of a United States Women's Armed Services Academy, and for other purposes," October 3, 1955; Academy 1955, 1972, 1973, 1955 Folder, Background—WAC; RG319; NACP.
7. HASC No. 94–9: "Hearings on HR 9832 to Eliminate Discrimination Based on Sex with Respect to the Appointment and Admission of Persons to the Service Academies and HR 10705, HR 11267, HR 11268, HR 11711, and HR 13729 to Insure That Each Admission to the Service Academies Shall Be Made without Regard to a Candidate's Sex, Race, Color, or Religious Beliefs," Subcommittee 2, House Armed Services Committee, 93rd Congress, 2nd session. May 29; June 4, 5, 12, 18, 19; July 16, 18; and August 8, 1974.

8. Letter to Senator Jacob Javits from James Johnson, Assistant Secretary of the Navy, September 30, 1971. PL90–130 Backup Folder, Box 6, BuPers00W, Naval Historical Center.

9. Letter to Senator Jacob Javits from James Johnson.

10. Testimony of Martin Hoffmann, "Hearings on HR 9832 . . . ." June 5, 1974, 68.

11. Schroeder also pointed out that Senators Stennis and Thurmond, among others, had voiced their support for women in the academies. Later, Admiral Mack, Superintendent of the Naval Academy, conceded that if the will of the people had changed, they probably needed to reevaluate and they hadn't done that yet. "Hearings on HR 9832 . . . ," June 5, 1974, 22 and 103.

12. "Hearings on HR 9832 . . . ," 228–29.

13. "Navy Keeps Academy All-Male but Opens R.O.T.C.," *New York Times*, February 8, 1972, and "Women Ruled Out for Annapolis; Congressional Sponsors Vow to Fight," *The Baltimore Sun*, February 9, 1972. Utilization of Women in the Services—Hearings Before Congress 1972 Folder, Box 13, BuPers00W, Naval Historical Center.

14. "Statement of Donald M. Fraser before the Subcommittee #2 of the Armed Services Committee on HR 10705, Concerning Admission of Women to the Service Academies," July 18, 1974, 1–2, Grace King Collection, Gift of Carolyn J. King (1009); Women's Memorial Foundation Collection, Arlington, VA.

15. Representative Stratton remarks, "Hearings on HR 9832 . . ." May 29, 1974, 43.

16. During the June 12 hearings, both Representative Charles Wilson (California) and Admiral Mack agreed that shifting some of the standards would be no big deal. Wilson repeated this belief during the June 19 sessions. "Hearings on HR 9832 . . . ," 111 and 191.

17. Admiral Mack comment during "Hearings on HR 9832 . . . ," June 19, 1974, 112.

18. Representative Charles Wilson comment, "Hearings on HR 9832 . . . ," June 19, 1974, 112.

19. General Clark comment during "Hearings on HR 9832 . . . ," June 18, 1974, 137. On July 16, Virginia Dondy of the Center of Women Policy Studies referenced women's participation on Olympic teams as evidence of women's physical ability, along with the growth of more equal physical education programs for boys and girls, both of which were allowing women the opportunity to "catch up" with men. "Hearings on HR 9832 . . . ," July 16, 1974, 220.

20. Janda, *Stronger Than Custom*, 21–22; see also House Congressional Record, 94th Congress, first session, 1974, 15449–456.

21. Janda, *Stronger than Custom*, 131 and 178–79.

22. See Jean Ebbert, "Women Midshipmen: A Report on the First Six Months," *Shipmate* magazine, March 1977. Sea Duty 1970s Folder, Box 4, Papers of Louise Wilde, Naval Historical Center. The Project Athena study chronicled the actions West Point took to integrate women. See "Report of the Admission of Women to the US Military Academy (Project Athena)," Gift of Alan Vitters (2003), Women's Memorial Foundation Collection, Arlington, VA.

23. "Report of the Admission of Women to the US Military Academy (Project Athena)," 24. Gift of Alan Vitters (2003), Women's Memorial Foundation Collection, Arlington, VA.

24. Cadet First Class Janet Libby interview with Majors Russell W. Mank and Major John E. Norvell, May 22, 1980, U.S. Air Force Oral History Program, 1–4; K239.0512-1315; AFHRA.

25. Cadet First Class June Van Horn interview with Major Russell W. Mank and Major John E. Norvell, April 29, 1980, U.S. Air Force Oral History Program, 7; K239.0512-1321; AFHRA.

26. Holm, *Women in the Military*, 382.

27. Quoted in Holm, 328.

28. Quoted in Holm, 329.

29. *Owens v. Brown*, 455 F. Supp. 291 (D.D.C. 1978), Justia, http://law.justia.com/cases/federal/district-courts/FSupp/455/291/1415795/.

30. Rear Admiral John J. O'Connor, Chief of Chaplains, "Memorandum for the Chief of Naval Personnel: Women at Sea," Box 14, BuPers00W, Naval Historical Center.

31. Karlyn Barker, "Women at Sea: Navy Traditions Being Rewritten," *The Washington Post*, February 25, 1979, Box 21, BuPers00W, Naval Historical Center.

32. Cooper, "Navy Women Deplore Life Aboard Warships," *San Diego Union*, September 4, 1978, Box 14, BuPers00W, Naval Historical Center.

33. Shilts, *Conduct Unbecoming*, 355.

34. Shilts, 354.

35. Ronald Yates, "Navy at Sea over 'Lust Boat' Scandal on Missile Ship," *Chicago Tribune*, August 31, 1980, 5.

36. "Lesbian Hearings Ended by Skipper," *The Bend Bulletin*, August 22, 1980, https://news.google.com/newspapers?nid=1243&dat=19800822&id=DdNYAAAAIBAJ&sjid=ufYDAAAAIBAJ&pg=6878,892723&hl=en.

37. Shilts, *Conduct Unbecoming*, 358.

38. Holm, *Women in the Military*, 337.

39. Holm, 381.

Conclusion

1. Brigadier General Mildred Bailey interview with Rhoda Messer, 4 October 4, 1978, Tape 8, side 1, 2–4. United States Army Military History Institute Senior Officers Debriefing Program, Carlisle Barracks, PA. Copy held as Oral History File 005319, Women's Memorial Foundation Collection, Arlington, VA.

2. See chapter 3 for more details. Stremlow, *A History of the Women Marines*, 30–31.

3. Holm, *Women in the Military*, 384.

4. Brigadier General Mildred Bailey interview with Rhoda Messer, 4 October 4, 1978, Tape 9, side 2, 29.

5. Holm, *Women in the Military*, 397.

6. Holm, 473.

7. Quoted in Holm, 470.

8. Iskra, *Women in the United States Armed Forces*, 107.

9. Donnelly, "Constructing the Co-Ed Military," *Duke Journal of Gender Law and Policy* 14 (2007): 815, 828.

10. Iskra, *Women in the United States Armed Forces*, 1.

11. Marina Koren, "The Combat Jobs Women Can Now Fight For," *The Atlantic*, December 3, 2015, https://www.theatlantic.com/national/archive/2015/12/women-in-the-military/418680/.

12. Andrew Swick and Emma Moore, "The (Mostly) Good News on Women in Combat," Center for a New American Security, April 19, 2018, https://www.cnas.org/publications/reports/an-update-on-the-status-of-women-in-combat.

13. Haring, "Meet the Quiet Trailblazers," *Army Times*, May 3, 2020, https://www.armytimes.com/opinion/commentary/2020/05/03/meet-the-quiet-trailblazers/.

14. Historian Nathaniel Frank asserts that in light of the numbers of women currently in the military, "without women . . . the military would simply not have enough bodies to complete its missions." In addition, Dr. John Nagl, president of the Center for a New American Security, a military research institution, argues that the U.S. military "literally could not have fought this war without women" (referring to the wars in Iraq/Afghanistan). Frank, *Unfriendly Fire*, 3. Nagl quoted in Lizette Alvarez, "G.I. Jane Breaks the Combat Barrier," *The New York Times*, August 15, 2009, http://www.nytimes.com/2009/08/16/us/16women.html?ref=women_at_arms.

15. Iskra, *Women in the United States Armed Forces*, 105.

16. Thomas Gibbons-Neff, "'On Parris Island, We Felt Isolated from the Rest of the World,'" *The New York Times Magazine*, January 11, 2019, https://www.nytimes.com/2019/01/11/magazine/marine-corps-integration-newsletter.html.

17. Andrew Dyer, "In Historic First, Women Begin Boot Camp at Marine Corps Recruit Depot San Diego," *The San Diego Union-Tribune*, February 9, 2021, https://www.sandiegouniontribune.com/news/military/story/2021-02-09/in-historic-first-women-begin-boot-camp-at-marine-corps-recruit-depot-san-diego.

18. Quoted in Gibbons-Neff, "The Marine Corps Battles for Its Identity, Over Women in Boot Camp," *The New York Times*, April 28, 2020, https://www.nytimes.com/2020/04/28/us/politics/marines-women.html.

19. Iskra, *Women in the United States Armed Forces*, 24.

20. Annual report 2019, Defense Advisory Committee on Women in the Services, https://dacowits.defense.gov/Portals/48/Documents/Reports/2019/Annual%20Report/DACOWITS%202019.pdf?ver=2020-03-27-095608-557.

21. Lt. Colonel Jessica Ruttenber (USAF) and Major Megan Biles (USAF), DACOWITS Open Comment Period re: Pregnancy Discrimination Concerns, March 3, 2020, https://dacowits.defense.gov/Portals/48/Documents/General%20Documents/RFI%20Docs/March2020/Lt%20Col%20Ruttenber.pdf?ver=2020-03-02-093455-923.

22. Anna Mulrine Grobe, "U.S. Military Draws a Line: No More Bias Against Pregnant Soldiers," *Christian Science Monitor*, September 16, 2020, https://www.csmonitor.com/USA/Military/2020/0916/US-military-draws-a-line-No-more-bias-against-pregnant-soldiers.

23. Philip Athey, "Marine Mothers Are Now Exempt from Fitness Tests, Weight Standards for One Year After Giving Birth," *The Marine Corps Times*, February 8, 2021, https://www.marinecorpstimes.com/news/your-marine-corps/2021/02/09/marine-mothers-now-have-1-year-after-giving-birth-to-pass-fitness-tests/.

24. Majors Sharon Sisbarro, Kerry Hogan, Sara Kirsten, and Captain Catherine Baniakas, "The DOD's Body Composition Standards Are Harming Female Service Members," *Military.com*, December 31, 2020, https://www.military.com/daily-news/opinions/2020/12/31/dods-body-composition-standards-are-harming-female-service-members.html.

25. Annual report 2019, Defense Advisory Committee on Women in the Services, https://dacowits.defense.gov/Portals/48/Documents/Reports/2019/Annual%20Report/DACOWITS%202019.pdf?ver=2020-03-27-095608-557.

26. 2008 study cited in Browder, *When Janey Comes Marching Home*, 133.

27. Marianne Lester, "Rape: A Report," *The Times Magazine*, January 26, 1976. Shirley Minge Collection (2096), Women's Memorial Foundation Collection, Arlington, VA. In his study of Don't Ask, Don't Tell, Nathaniel Frank notes that "fear of reprisal has been a serious problem in the American military," and the 2009 CBS piece points out that the military believes at least 80 percent of rapes remain unreported. Frank, *Unfriendly Fire*, 151.

28. Marianne Lester, "Rape: A Report." Shirley Minge Papers (2096), Women's Memorial Foundation Collection, Arlington, VA. For analysis on Tailhook, see the PBS "Debating Tailhook" resources, http://www.pbs.org/wgbh/pages/frontline/shows/navy/tailhook/debate.html.

29. Katie Couric, "Sexual Assault Permeates U.S. Armed Forces," CBS Evening News, March 17, 2009, http://www.cbsnews.com/stories/2009/03/17/eveningnews/main4872713.shtml.

30. Lisa Ferdinando, "DOD Releases Annual Report on Sexual Assault in Military," U.S. DOD, May 1, 2018, https://dod.defense.gov/News/Article/Article/1508127/dod-releases-annual-report-on-sexual-assault-in-military/.

31. Tara Copp, "Sexual Assault: Here Are the Bases Where Troops Are Most at Risk," *Military Times*, September 21, 2018, https://www.militarytimes.com/news/your-military/2018/09/21/sexual-assault-here-are-the-bases-where-troops-are-most-at-risk/.

32. Leo Shane III, "Defense Department to Make Sexual Harassment a Crime," *Military Times*, May 2, 2019, https://www.militarytimes.com/news/pentagon-congress/2019/05/02/defense-department-to-make-sexual-harassment-a-crime/.

33. Johnny Diaz, Maria Cramer, and Christina Morales, "What We Know About the Death of Vanessa Guillen," *New York Times*, August 14, 2020, https://www.nytimes.com/article/vanessa-guillen-fort-hood.html; Jennifer Steinhauer, "A #MeToo Moment Emerges for Military Women after Soldier's Killing," *New York Times*, July 11, 2020, https://www.nytimes.com/2020/07/11/us/politics/military-women-metoo-fort-hood.html.

34. Merrit Kennedy, "Congress Launches Investigation into Fort Hood Deaths," *National Public Radio*, September 8, 2020, https://www.npr.org/2020/09/08/910747947/congress-launches-investigation-into-fort-hood-deaths.

35. Sarah Mervosh and John Ismay, "Army Finds 'Major Flaws' at Fort Hood; 14 Officials Disciplined," *New York Times*, December 8, 2020, https://www.npr.org/2020/09/08/910747947/congress-launches-investigation-into-fort-hood-deaths.

36. Melissa del Bosque, "Fort Hood Soldiers Harbor Doubts About Army's Accountability Efforts," *The Intercept*, December 15, 2020, https://theintercept.com/2020/12/15/fort-hood-report-army/.

37. Peter W. Singer, "The Damning Paradox of 'Don't Ask, Don't Tell,'" Brookings Institute, June 2, 2009, https://www.brookings.edu/opinions/the-damning-paradox-of-dont-ask-dont-tell/.

38. Marisol Bellow, "'Don't Ask, Don't Tell' Affects Women, Minorities More," *USA Today*, May 27, 2010, http://www.usatoday.com/news/military/2010-05-26-dont-ask_N.htm; and Thom Shanker, "'Don't Ask, Don't Tell' Hits Women Much More," *The New York Times*, June 23, 2008, http://www.nytimes.com/2008/06/23/washington/23pentagon.html.

39. Air force nurse Major Margaret Witt's case offers one example of how the policy has been used to target those who serve while abiding by the "don't tell" element of the policy. As one journalist mentioned, in the final days of her trial Witt stressed that "she had never disclosed her sexual orientation to air force colleagues, nor had she ever engaged in homosexual relations on duty or on military grounds." To the contrary, she and her partner lived more than 200 miles from her military assignment location. Carol J. Williams, "Gay Air Force Flight Nurse Wins Reinstatement," *Los Angeles Times*, September 25, 2010, http://www.stltoday.com/news/national/article_69cbf90e-4d6b-5400-9b41-50f0361b4655.html.

40. Lolita C. Baldor, "Army Misses Recruiting Goal for First Time Since 2005," *Military Times*, September 21, 2018, https://www.military.com/daily-news/2018/09/21/army-misses-recruiting-goal-first-time-2005.html.

41. Claudia Grisales, "Trump's Attempted Ban of Transgender Military Service Remains Steeped in Confusion, Chaos," *Stars and Stripes*, July 25, 2018, https://www.stripes.com/news/us/trump-s-attempted-ban-of-transgender-military-service-remains-steeped-in-confusion-chaos-1.539500. "Transgender Military Service," *Human Rights Campaign*, March 2, 2020, https://www.hrc.org/resources/transgender-military-service.

42. "Executive Order 14004 of January 25, 2021, Enabling All Qualified Americans to Serve Their Country in Uniform," *Federal Register*, Volume 86, Number 17, Thursday, January 28, 2021, https://www.federalregister.gov/documents/2021/01/28/2021-02034/enabling-all-qualified-americans-to-serve-their-country-in-uniform.

43. "Table of Active Duty Females by Rank/Grade and Service," December 2020, DoD Personnel, Workforce Reports & Publications, Defense Manpower Data Center (DMDC), https://www.dmdc.osd.mil/appj/dwp/dwp_reports.jsp.

44. Quoted in Alvarez, "G.I. Jane Breaks the Combat Barrier," 3, http://www.nytimes.com/2009/08/16/us/16women.html?pagewanted=3&_r=1.

Bibliography

Archives

Air Force Historical Research Agency (Maxwell Air Force Base, AL)
Army Women's Museum (Fort Lee, VA)
Betty H. Carter Women Veterans Historical Project (Greensboro, NC)
Dwight D. Eisenhower Presidential Library (Abilene, KS)
Harry Truman Presidential Library (Independence, MO)
Gerald R. Ford Presidential Library (Ann Arbor, MI)
John F. Kennedy Presidential Library (Boston, MA)
Library of Congress (Washington, DC)
Lyndon B. Johnson Presidential Library (Austin, TX)
Marine Corps Archives (Quantico, VA)
National Archives (College Park, MD)
National Archives (Washington, DC)
Navy Operational Archives (Washington, DC)
Richard Nixon Presidential Library at National Archives (College Park, MD)
Schlesinger Library (Cambridge, MA)
State Historical Society of Missouri (Columbia, MO)
United States Army Historical Education Center (Carlisle Barracks, PA)
Women's Memorial Foundation Collection (Arlington, VA)

Sources

Adams-Ender, Clara L. *My Rise to the Stars: How a Sharecropper's Daughter Became an Army General*. Lake Ridge, VA: CAPE Associates, 2001.
Allen, E. Ann. "The WAC Mission: The Testing Time from Korea to Vietnam." Columbia: University of South Carolina, 1986.
Alonso, Harriet Hyman. *Peace as a Women's Issue: A History of the U.S. Movement for World Peace and Women's Rights*. Syracuse, NY: Syracuse University Press, 1993.
Anderson, Karen. *Wartime Women: Sex Roles, Family Relations, and the Status of Women During World War II*. Westport, CT: Greenwood Press, 1981.
Anderson, Kristi. "Working Women and Political Participation, 1952–1972." *American Journal of Political Science* 19, no. 3 (August 1975): 439–53.
Appy, Christian G. *Working-Class War: American Combat Soldiers and Vietnam*. Chapel Hill: University of North Carolina Press, 1993.
Bachman, Jerald G., John D. Blair, and David R. Segal. *The All-Volunteer Force: A Study of Ideology in the Military*. Ann Arbor: University of Michigan Press, 1977.

Bailey, Beth. *America's Army: Making the All-Volunteer Force*. Cambridge, MA: The Belknap Press of Harvard University Press, 2009.

Bakken, Gordon Morris, and Brenda Farrington, eds. *Encyclopedia of Women of the American West*. Thousand Oaks, CA: SAGE Publications, 2003.

Baker, Carrie N. "Race, Class, and Sexual Harassment in the 1970s." *Feminist Studies* 30, no. 1 (Spring 2004): 7–27.

Barakso, Maryann. *Governing NOW: Grassroots Activism in the National Organization for Women*. Ithaca, NY: Cornell University Press, 2004.

Barkalow, Carol. *In the Men's House: An Inside Account of Life in the Army by One of West Point's First Female Graduates*. New York: Poseidon Press, 1990.

Baron, Ava, ed. *Work Engendered: Toward a New History of American Labor*. Ithaca, NY: Cornell University Press, 1991.

Bartman, William. "Straight and Gay Servicewomen Battered in Wave of Witch Hunts." *Minerva's Bulletin Board*, no. 1989 (n.d.).

Baskir, Lawrence M., and William A. Strauss. *Chance and Circumstance: The Draft, the War, and the Vietnam Generation*. 1st ed. New York: Knopf, 1978.

Baxandall, Rosalyn, and Linda Gordon, eds. *Dear Sisters: Dispatches from the Women's Liberation Movement*. New York: Basic Books, 2000.

Beckett, Megan. *The Status of Gender Integration in the Military: Supporting Appendices*. Santa Monica, CA: Rand, 2002.

Belkin, Aaron, and Geoffrey Bateman, eds. *Don't Ask, Don't Tell: Debating the Gay Ban in the Military*. Boulder, CO: Lynne Rienner Publishers, 2003.

Bellafaire, Judith Lawrence. "Public Service Role Models: The First Women of the Defense Advisory Committee on Women in the Services." *Armed Forces and Society* 32, no. 3 (April 2006): 424–36.

Ben Shalom v. Secretary of the Army Alexander, May 20, 1980.

Berkeley, Kathleen C. *The Women's Liberation Movement in America*. Westport, CT: Greenwood Press, 1999.

Berry, Mary Frances. *Why ERA Failed: Politics, Women's Rights, and the Amending Process of the Constitution*. Bloomington: Indiana University Press, 1986.

Bérubé, Allan. *Coming Out Under Fire: The History of Gay Men and Women in World War Two*. New York: Free Press, 1990.

Binkin, Martin, and Alvin Schexnider. *Blacks and the Military*. Washington, DC: Brookings Institution, 1982.

Bordo, Susan. "The Body and the Reproduction of Femininity." In *Writing on the Body: Female Embodiment and Feminist Theory*, edited by Katie Conboy, Nadia Medina, and Sarah Stanbury, 90–111. New York: Columbia University Press, 1997.

———. *Unbearable Weight: Feminism, Western Culture, and the Body*. Berkeley: University of California Press, 1993.

Bowers, William T. *Black Soldier, White Army: The 24th Infantry Regiment in Korea*. Washington, DC: Center of Military History, U.S. Army, 1996.

Braudy, Leo. *From Chivalry to Terrorism: War and the Changing Nature of Masculinity*. New York: Alfred A. Knopf, 2003.

Breines, Wini. *The Trouble Between Us: An Uneasy History of White and Black Women in the Feminist Movement*. Oxford: Oxford University Press, 2006.

Bristol, Douglas Walter Jr., and Heather Marie Stur, eds. *Integrating the U.S. Military: Race, Gender, and Sexual Orientation Since World War II*. Baltimore, MD: Johns Hopkins University Press, 2017.

Browder, Laura. *Her Best Shot: Women and Guns in America*. Chapel Hill: University of North Carolina Press, 2006.

———. *When Janey Comes Marching Home: Portraits of Women Combat Veterans*. Chapel Hill: University of North Carolina Press, 2010.

Brownmiller, Susan. *Femininity*. New York: Linden Press/Simon & Schuster, 1984.

Canaday, Margot. *The Straight State: Sexuality and Citizenship in Twentieth Century America*. Princeton, NJ: Princeton University Press, 2009.

Cardona, Robert, and Elspeth Cameron Ritchie. "Psychological Screening of Recruits Prior to Accession in the US Military." In *Textbooks of Military Medicine: Recruit Medicine*, edited by Bernard L. DeKoning, 297–309. Washington, DC: Borden Institute, DOD, 2006. https://ke.army.mil/bordeninstitute/published_volumes/recruit_medicine/rm-ch16.pdf.

Chafe, William Henry. *The American Woman: Her Changing Social, Economic, and Political Roles, 1920–1970*. New York: Oxford University Press, 1972.

———. *The Paradox of Change: American Women in the 20th Century*. New York: Oxford University Press, 1991.

Chodorow, Nancy. *The Reproduction of Mothering: Psychoanalysis and the Sociology of Gender*. Berkeley: University of California Press, 1978.

Christmas, Walter. *Negros in Public Affairs and Government*. Yonkers, NY: Educational Heritage, 1966.

Clymer, Eleanor. *Modern American Career Women*. New York: Dodd, Mead, 1959.

Cobble, Dorothy Sue. *The Other Women's Movement: Workplace Justice and Social Rights in Modern America*. Princeton, NJ: Princeton University Press, 2004.

Cohen, Eliot A. *Citizens and Soldiers: The Dilemmas of Military Service*. Ithaca, NY: Cornell University Press, 1985.

Cohen, Elizabeth F. *Semi-Citizenship in Democratic Politics*. Cambridge: Cambridge University Press, 2009.

Collins, Winifred Quick. *More Than a Uniform: A Navy Woman in a Navy Man's World*. 1st ed. Denton: University of North Texas Press, 1997.

Conboy, Katie, Nadia Medina, and Sarah Stanbury, eds. *Writing on the Body: Female Embodiment and Feminist Theory*. New York: Columbia University Press, 1997.

Cooke, Miriam, and Angela Woollacott, eds. *Gendering War Talk*. Princeton, NJ: Princeton University Press, 1993.

Coontz, Stephanie. *A Strange Stirring: The* Feminine Mystique *and American Women at the Dawn of the 1960s*. New York: Basic Books, 2011.

Crawford, Vicki L., Jacqueline Anne Rouse, and Barbara Woods, eds. *Women in the Civil Rights Movement: Trailblazers and Torchbearers, 1941–1965*. Brooklyn, NY: Carlson Pub, 1990.

Cuordileone, K. A. "'Politics in an Age of Anxiety': Cold War Political Culture and the Crisis in American Masculinity, 1949–1960." *Journal of American History* 87, no. 2 (September 2000): 515–45.

Dalfiume, Richard M. *Desegregation of the U.S. Armed Forces; Fighting on Two Fronts, 1939–1953*. Columbia: University of Missouri Press, 1969.

D'Amico, Francine. "Citizen-Soldier? Class, Race, Gender, Sexuality, and the U.S. Military." In *States of Conflict: Gender, Violence, and Resistance*, edited by Susie Jacobs, Ruth Jacobson, and Jennifer Marchbank, 105–22. London: Zed, 2000.

D'Amico, Francine, and Laurie Weinstein, eds. *Gender Camouflage: Women and the U.S. Military*. New York: New York University Press, 1999.

Daniels, Cynthia R. *At Women's Expense: State Power and the Politics of Fetal Rights*. Cambridge, MA: Harvard University Press, 1993.

Davis, Flora. *Moving the Mountain: The Women's Movement in America Since 1960*. New York: Simon & Schuster, 1991.

De Groot, Gerard, ed. *A Soldier and a Woman: Sexual Integration in the Military*. Harlow, UK: Longman, 2000.

Deken, John. *Women of the Heartland: Tradition and Evolution in the Missouri Women's Movement*. University of Missouri-Columbia, 2009.

Delano, Page Dougherty. "Making Up for War: Sexuality and Citizenship in Wartime Culture." *Feminist Studies* 26, no. 1 (Spring 2000): 33–68.

DePauw, Linda Grant. *Battle Cries and Lullabies: Women in War from Prehistory to the Present*. Norman: University of Oklahoma Press, 1998.

Department of Veteran Affairs. "America's Wars Fact Sheet." Washington, DC, November 2019. https://www.va.gov/opa/publications/factsheets/fs_americas_wars.pdf.

D'Emilio, John. "The Homosexual Menace: The Politics of Sexuality in Cold War America." *Making Trouble: Essays on Gay History, Politics, and the University*. New York: Routledge, 1992.

D'Emilio, John, and Allan Bérubé. "The Military and Lesbians during the McCarthy Years." *Signs* 9, no. 4 (Summer 1984): 759–75.

Disher, Sharon Hanley. *First Class: Women Join the Ranks at the Naval Academy*. Annapolis, MD: Naval Institute Press, 1998.

Donnelly, Elaine. "Constructing the Co-Ed Military." *Duke Journal of Gender Law and Policy* 14 (2007): 815–952.

Dowling, Colette. *The Frailty Myth: Women Approaching Physical Equality*. 1st ed. New York: Random House, 2000.

Dunlap, Sabrina. "The Military Abortion Ban: How 10 U.S.C. Section 1093 Violates International Standards of Reproductive Health Care." *Berkeley Electronic Press* (Paper 1982). 2007. http://law.bepress.com/expresso/eps/1982.

Dyhouse, Carol. *Glamour: Women, History, Feminism*. London: Zed, 2010.

Ebbert, Jean, and Marie-Beth Hall. *Crossed Currents: Navy Women in a Century of Change*. 3rd ed. Washington, DC: Brassey's, 1999.

Echols, Alice. *Daring to Be Bad: Radical Feminism in America, 1967–1975*. Minneapolis: University of Minnesota Press, 1989.

Edwards, India. *Pulling No Punches: Memoirs of a Woman in Politics*. New York: Putnam, 1977.

Eisenhower, Dwight D. *Crusade in Europe*. Garden City, NY: Doubleday, 1948.

Eisenmann, Linda. *Higher Education for Women in Postwar America, 1945–1965*. Baltimore, MD: Johns Hopkins University Press, 2006.

Eisenstein, Hester, and Alice Jardine, eds. *The Future of Difference*. New Brunswick, NJ: Rutgers University Press, 1985.

Embser-Herbert, Melissa Sheridan. *The U.S. Military's "Don't Ask, Don't Tell" Policy: A Reference Handbook*. Westport, CT: Praeger Security International, 2007.

Enloe, Cynthia H. *Does Khaki Become You? The Militarization of Women's Lives*. London: Pandora, 1988.

Evans, Sara M. *Personal Politics: The Roots of Women's Liberation in the Civil Rights Movement and the New Left*. New York: Vintage Books, 1980.

———. *Tidal Wave: How Women Changed America at Century's End*. New York: Free Press, 2003.

Farber, David, and Beth Bailey (with contributors). *The Columbia Guide to America in the 1960s*. New York: Columbia University Press, 2001.

Farrell, Amy Erdman. *Yours in Sisterhood: Ms. Magazine and the Promise of Popular Feminism*. Chapel Hill: University of North Carolina Press, 1998.

Feaver, Peter D., and Richard H. Kohn, eds. *Soldiers and Civilians: The Civil-Military Gap and American National Security*. Cambridge, MA: MIT Press, 2001.

Feinman, Ilene Rose. *Citizenship Rites: Feminist Soldiers and Feminist Antimilitarists*. New York: New York University Press, 2000.

Feldstein, Ruth. *Motherhood in Black and White: Race and Sex in American Liberalism, 1930–1965*. Ithaca, NY: Cornell University Press, 2000.

Fenner, Lorry M. *Women in Combat: Civic Duty or Military Liability?* Washington, DC: Georgetown University Press, 2001.

Fisher, Ernest F. *Guardians of the Republic: A History of the Noncommissioned Officer Corps of the U.S. Army*. 1st ed. New York: Ballantine Books, 1994.

Foner, Philip Sheldon. *Women and the American Labor Movement: From World War I to the Present*. New York: Free Press, 1980.

Fowler, Stacy, and Deborah A. Deacon. *A Century in Uniform: Military Women in American Films*. Jefferson, NC: McFarland Press, 2020.

Frank, Nathaniel. *Unfriendly Fire: How the Gay Ban Undermines the Military and Weakens America*. 1st ed. New York: Thomas Dunne Books, 2009.

Freedman, Estelle B. *No Turning Back: The History of Feminism and the Future of Women*. 1st ed. New York: Ballantine, 2002.

Friedan, Betty. *The Feminine Mystique*. New York: W. W. Norton and Company, 2001.

Gabin, Nancy Felice. *Feminism in the Labor Movement: Women and the United Auto Workers, 1935–1975*. Ithaca, NY: Cornell University Press, 1990.

Gatlin, Rochelle. *American Women Since 1945*. Jackson: University Press of Mississippi, 1987.

Gerhard, Jane. *Desiring Revolution: Second-Wave Feminism and the Rewriting of American Sexual Thought, 1920 to 1982*. New York: Columbia University Press, 2001.

Gershick, Zsa. *Secret Service: Untold Stories of Lesbians in the Military*. 1st ed. Los Angeles, CA: Alyson Books, 2005.

Giardina, Carol. *Freedom for Women: Forging the Women's Liberation Movement, 1953–1970*. Gainesville: University Press of Florida, 2010.

Giddings, Paula. *When and Where I Enter: The Impact of Black Women on Race and Sex in America*. 1st ed. New York: Morrow, 1984.

Godson, Susan H. *Serving Proudly: A History of Women in the U.S. Navy*. Annapolis, MD: Naval Institute Press, 2001.

Goldfarb, Lynn. *Separated and Unequal: Discrimination Against Women Workers After World War II (The U.A.W. 1944–54)*. Silver Springs, MD: The Women's Work Project, 1976.

Goldin, Claudia Dale. *Understanding the Gender Gap: An Economic History of American Women*. New York: Oxford University Press, 1990.

Goodman, Jill Laurie. "Women, War, and Equality: An Examination of Sex Discrimination in the Military." *Women's Rights Law Reporter* 5, no. 4 (Summer 1979).

Grandstaff, Mark. "Making the Military American: Advertising, Reform, and the Demise of an Antistanding Military Tradition, 1945–1955." *Journal of Military History* 60, no. 2 (April 1996): 299–323.

Greenwald, Maurine Weiner. *Women, War, and Work: The Impact of World War I on Women Workers in the United States*. Westport, CT: Greenwood Press, 1980.

Griffith, Robert K. *The U.S. Army's Transition to the All-Volunteer Force, 1968–1974*. Washington, DC: Center of Military History, 1996.

Gropman, Alan. *The Air Force Integrates*. 2nd ed. Washington, DC: Smithsonian Institution Scholarly Press, 1998.

Gundle, Stephen. "Hollywood Glamour and Mass Consumption in Postwar Italy." *Journal of Cold War Studies* 4, no. 3 (Summer 2002): 95–118.

Harrison, Cynthia Ellen. *On Account of Sex: The Politics of Women's Issues, 1945–1968*. Berkeley: University of California Press, 1988.

Hartmann, Susan M. *From Margin to Mainstream: American Women and Politics Since 1960*. 1st ed. New York: Knopf, 1989.

Height, Dorothy I. *Open Wide the Freedom Gates: A Memoir*. 1st ed. New York: Public Affairs, 2003.

Heikkila, Kimberly Laina. "G.I. Gender: Vietnam War-Era Women Veterans and US Citizenship." PhD diss. University of Minnesota, Army Historical Research Center, Carlisle Barracks, 2002.

Helmer, John. *Bringing the War Home: The American Soldier in Vietnam and After*. New York: The Free Press, 1974.

Herbert, Melissa S. *Camouflage Isn't Only for Combat: Gender, Sexuality and Women in the Military*. New York: New York University Press, 1998.

Herek, Gregory M., Jared B. Jobe, and Ralph M. Carney, eds. *Out in Force: Sexual Orientation and the Military*. Chicago, IL: University of Chicago Press, 1996.

Hess, Gary R. *Vietnam: Explaining America's Lost War*. Malden, MA: Blackwell, 2009.

Higgonnet, Margaret et al., eds. *Behind the Lines: Gender and the Two World Wars*. New Haven, CT: Yale University Press, 1987.

Hill, Ruth Edmonds, ed. *The Black Women Oral History Project: From the Arthur and Elizabeth Schlesinger Library on the History of Women in America, Radcliffe College*. Westport, CT: Meckler, 1991.

Hillman, Elizabeth Lutes. *Defending America: Military Culture and the Cold War Court-Martial*. Princeton, NJ: Princeton University Press, 2005.

———. "Dressed to Kill: The Paradox of Military Women in Uniforms." In *Beyond Zero Tolerance*, edited by Mary Fainsod Katzenstein and Judith Reppy, 65–80. Lanham, MD: Rowman & Littlefield Publishers, 1999.

———. "The Female Shape of the All-Volunteer Force." In *Iraq and the Lessons of Vietnam, or, How Not to Learn from the Past*, edited by Lloyd C. Gardner and Marilyn B. Young. New York: New Press, 2007.

Hine, Darlene Clark. *Black Women in White: Racial Conflict and Cooperation in the Nursing Profession, 1890–1950*. Bloomington: Indiana University Press, 1989.

———. "Mabel K. Staupers and the Integration of Black Nurses into the Armed Forces." In *Black Leaders of the Twentieth Century*, edited by John Hope Franklin and August Meier, 241–57. Urbana: University of Illinois Press, 1982.

Hogan, David W., Jr., Arnold G. Fisch, Jr., and Robert K. Wright, Jr., eds. *The Story of the Noncommissioned Officer Corps: The Backbone of the Army*. Rev. ed. Washington, DC: Center of Military History, U.S. Army, 2009.

Holm, Jeanne. *Women in the Military, Revised Edition: An Unfinished Revolution*. Novato, CA: Presidio Press, 1993.

hooks, bell. *Feminist Theory: From Margin to Center*. Cambridge, MA: South End Press, 2000.

Horowitz, Daniel. *Betty Friedan and the Making of the Feminine Mystique: The American Left, the Cold War, and Modern Feminism*. Amherst: University of Massachusetts Press, 1998.

Humphrey, Mary Ann. *My Country, My Right to Serve: Experiences of Gay Men and Women in the Military, World War II to the Present*. 1st ed. New York: HarperCollins, 1990.

Huntington, Samuel P. *The Soldier and the State: The Theory and Politics of Civil-Military Relations*. New York: Vintage Books, 1957.

Iskra, Darlene M. *Women in the United States Armed Forces: A Guide to the Issues*. Santa Barbara, CA: Praeger, 2010.

Isserman, Maurice, and Michael Kazin. *America Divided: The Civil War of the 1960s*. 6th ed. Oxford: Oxford University Press, 2020.

James, Susan. "The Good-Enough Citizen: Female Citizenship and Independence." In *Beyond Equality and Difference: Citizenship, Feminist Politics, and Female Subjectivity*, edited by Gisela Bock and Susan James, 43–60. London: Routledge, 1992.

Janda, Lance. *Stronger Than Custom: West Point and the Admission of Women*. Westport, CT: Praeger, 2002.

Janowitz, Morris. *The Professional Soldier, a Social and Political Portrait*. Glencoe, IL: Free Press, 1960.

Jeffords, Susan. *The Remasculinization of America: Gender and the Vietnam War*. Bloomington: Indiana University Press, 1989.

Jensen, Kimberly. *Mobilizing Minerva: American Women in the First World War*. Urbana: University of Illinois Press, 2008.

Johnson, David K. *The Lavender Scare: The Cold War Persecution of Gays and Lesbians in the Federal Government*. Chicago: University of Chicago Press, 2004.

Johnson, Jesse J. *Black Women in the Armed Forces, 1942–1974*. Hampton, VA: Johnson, 1974.

Karpinski, Janis L. *One Woman's Army: The Commanding General of Abu Ghraib Tells Her Story*. 1st ed. New York: Miramax Books, 2005.

Katzenstein, Mary Fainsod. *Faithful and Fearless: Moving Feminist Protest inside the Church and Military*. Princeton, NJ: Princeton University Press, 1998.

Katzenstein, Mary Fainsod, and Judith Reppy, eds. *Beyond Zero Tolerance: Discrimination in Military Culture*. Lanham, MD: Rowman & Littlefield, 1999.

Kendrick, Alexander. *The Wound Within: America in the Vietnam Years, 1945–1974*. 1st ed. Boston: Little, Brown, 1974.

Kerber, Linda K. *No Constitutional Right to Be Ladies: Women and the Obligations of Citizenship*. 1st ed. New York: Hill and Wang, 1998.

Kessler-Harris, Alice. *In Pursuit of Equity: Women, Men, and the Quest for Economic Citizenship in 20th Century America*. Oxford: Oxford University Press, 2001.

———. *Out to Work: A History of Wage-Earning Women in the United States*. New York: Oxford University Press, 1982.

Krebs, Ronald R. *Fighting for Rights: Military Service and the Politics of Citizenship*. Ithaca, NY: Cornell University Press, 2006.

Langer, Cassandra L. *A Feminist Critique: How Feminism Has Changed American Society, Culture, and How We Live from the 1940s to the Present*. 1st ed. New York: IconEditions, 1996.

Laville, Helen. *Cold War Women: The International Activities of American Women's Organisations*. Manchester, UK: Manchester University Press, 2002.

Leslie, LaVonne. *The History of the National Association of Colored Women's Clubs, Inc.: A Legacy of Service*. Bloomington, IN: Xlibris, 2012.

Levine, Susan. *Degrees of Equality: The American Association of University Women and the Challenge of Twentieth-Century Feminism*. Philadelphia, PA: Temple University Press, 1995.

Lewis, Janet V., ed. *Women and Women's Issues in Congress: 1832–2000*. Huntington, NY: Nova Science Publishers, 2001.

Lundberg, Ferdinand. *Modern Woman: The Lost Sex*. New York: Harper & Brothers, 1947.

Lynn, John. *Battle: A History of Combat and Culture*. Boulder, CO: Westview Press, 2003.

Lynn, Susan. *Progressive Women in Conservative Times: Racial Justice, Peace, and Feminism, 1945 to the 1960s*. New Brunswick, NJ: Rutgers University Press, 1992.

MacGregor, Morris J. *Integration of the Armed Forces, 1940–1965*. Washington, DC: Center of Military History, 1985. http://www.history.army.mil/books/integration/IAF-fm.htm.

Mansbridge, Jane J. *Why We Lost the ERA*. Chicago: University of Chicago Press, 1986.

Marie von Hoffburg v. Clifford Alexander, April 14, 1980.

Martin, Janet M. *The Presidency and Women: Promise, Performance, & Illusion*. 1st ed. College Station: Texas A&M University Press, 2003.

Mathews, Donald G. *Sex, Gender, and the Politics of ERA: A State and the Nation*. New York: Oxford University Press, 1990.

May, Elaine Tyler. *Homeward Bound: American Families in the Cold War Era*. Rev. and updated ed. New York: Basic Books, 1999.

Mayeri, Serena, "'When the Trouble Started': *Frontiero v. Richardson*." In *Women and the Law: Stories*, edited by Elizabeth M. Schneider and Stephanie M. Wildman, 57–92. New York: Foundation Press, 2011.

McEnaney, Laura. *Civil Defense Begins at Home: Militarization Meets Everyday Life in the Fifties*. Princeton, NJ: Princeton University Press, 2000.

McEuen, Melissa A. *Making War, Making Women: Femininity and Duty on the American Home Front, 1941–1945*. Athens: University of Georgia Press, 2011.

Meeker, Martin. *Contacts Desired: Gay and Lesbian Communications and Community, 1940s–1970s*. Chicago: University of Chicago Press, 2006.

Mershon, Sherie. *Foxholes & Color Lines: Desegregating the U.S. Armed Forces*. Baltimore, MD: Johns Hopkins University Press, 1998.

Meyer, Leisa D. *Creating GI Jane: Sexuality and Power in the Women's Army Corps During World War II*. New York: Columbia University Press, 1996.

———. "The Myth of Lesbian (In)Visibility: World War II and the Current 'Gays in the Military' Debate." In *Modern American Queer History*, edited by Allida Black, 271–81. Philadelphia, PA: Temple University Press, 2001.

Meyerowitz, Joanne J. ed. *Not June Cleaver: Women and Gender in Postwar America, 1945–1960*. Philadelphia, PA: Temple University Press, 1994.

———. "Sex, Gender, and the Cold War Language of Reform." In *Rethinking Cold War Culture*, edited by Peter J. Kuznick and James Gilbert, 106–23. Washington: Smithsonian Institute Press, 2001.

Mifflin, Margot. *Looking for Miss America: Dreamers, Dissidents, Flappers, and Feminists—A Pageant's 100-Year Quest to Define Womanhood*. Berkeley, CA: Counterpoint Press, 2020.

Milkman, Ruth. *Gender at Work: The Dynamics of Job Segregation by Sex During World War II*. Urbana: University of Illinois Press, 1987.

Mitchell, Brian. *Women in the Military: Flirting with Disaster*. Washington, DC: Regnery, 1998.

Mohr, James. *Abortion in America: The Origins and Evolution of National Policy, 1800–1900*. New York: Oxford University Press, 1978.

Molnar, Courtni E. "'Has the Millennium Yet Dawned?': A History of Attitudes Toward Pregnant Workers in America." *Michigan Journal of Gender & Law* 12, no. 1 (2005): 163–87.

Moore, Brenda L. "African American Women in the US Military." *Armed Forces and Society* 17, no. 3 (Spring 1991).

———. *To Serve My Country, to Serve My Race: The Story of the Only African American WACS Stationed Overseas During World War II*. New York: New York University Press, 1996.

Morden, Bettie J., and Center of Military History. *The Women's Army Corps, 1945–1978*. Washington, DC: Center of Military History, U.S. Army, 1990.

Moskos, Charles C. *All That We Can Be: Black Leadership and Racial Integration the Army Way*. New York: Basic Books, 1996.

———. *The American Enlisted Man; the Rank and File in Today's Military*. New York: Russell Sage Foundation, 1970.

Mosse, George L. *The Image of Man: The Creation of Modern Masculinity*. New York: Oxford University Press, 1996.

Muir, Kate. *Arms and the Woman*. London: Sinclair-Stevenson, 1992.

Murnane, Linda Strite. "Legal Impediments to Service: Women in the Military and the Rule of Law." *Duke Journal of Gender Law and Policy* 14 (2007): 1061–96.

Myrdal, Gunnar. *An American Dilemma: The Negro Problem and Modern Democracy*. New Brunswick, NJ: Transaction Publishers, 1996.

National Defense Research Institute (U.S.), United States, and Rand Corporation. *Sexual Orientation and U.S. Military Personnel Policy: Options and Assessment*. Santa Monica, CA: Rand, 1993.

National Manpower Council (U.S.). *Womanpower: A Statement, with Chapters by the Council Staff*. New York: Columbia University Press, 1957.

Nelson, Anna. "Anna Rosenberg, an 'Honorary Man.'" *Journal of Military History* 68, no. 1 (January 2004): 133–61.

Olson, James S., and Randy Roberts. *Where the Domino Fell: America and Vietnam, 1945–2010*. West Sussex, UK: John Wiley & Sons Ltd, 2014.

Pateman, Carol. "Equality, Difference, Subordination: The Politics of Motherhood and Women's Citizenship." In *Beyond Equality and Difference: Citizenship, Feminist Politics and Female Subjectivity*, edited by Gisela Bock and Susan James, 14–27. New York: Routledge, 1992.

Phillips, Anne. *Feminism and Equality*. New York: New York University Press, 1987.

Putney, Martha S. *When the Nation Was in Need: Blacks in the Women's Army Corps during World War II*. Metuchen, NJ: Scarecrow Press, 1992.

Reagan, Leslie J. *Dangerous Pregnancies: Mothers, Disabilities, and Abortion in Modern America*. Berkeley: University of California Press, 2010.

Rimmerman, Craig, ed. *Gay Rights, Military Wrongs: Political Perspectives on Lesbians and Gays in the Military*. New York: Garland, 1996.

Rishell, Lyle. *With a Black Platoon in Combat: A Year in Korea*. 1st ed. College Station: Texas A&M University Press, 1993.

Rogan, Helen. *Mixed Company: Women in the Modern Army*. New York: Putnam, 1981.

Rosen, Ruth. "The Day They Buried Traditional Womanhood: Women and the Vietnam Experience." In *The Legacy: The Vietnam War in American Imagination*, edited by D. Michael Shafer, 233–61. Boston: Beacon Press, 1990.

Rostker, Bernard. *I Want You!: The Evolution of the All-Volunteer Force.* Santa Monica, CA: RAND, 2006.

Ruddick, Sarah. "Pacifying the Forces: Drafting Women in the Interests of Peace." *Signs* 8, no. 3 (Spring 1983): 471–89.

Rupp, Leila J. *Survival in the Doldrums: The American Women's Rights Movement, 1945 to the 1960s.* New York: Oxford University Press, 1987.

Rustad, Michael. *Women in Khaki: The American Enlisted Woman.* New York, NY: Praeger, 1982.

Rutenberg, Amy. *Rough Draft: Cold War Military Manpower Policy and the Origins of Vietnam-Era Draft Resistance.* Ithaca, NY: Cornell University Press, 2019.

Rymph, Catherine E. *Republican Women: Feminism and Conservatism from Suffrage through the Rise of the New Right.* Chapel Hill: University of North Carolina Press, 2006.

Scharf, Lois, and Joan Jensen, eds. *Decades of Discontent: The Women's Movement, 1920–1940.* Westport, CT: Greenwood Press, 1983.

Schofield, Mary Anne. "Miss America, Rosie the Riveter, and World War II." In *"There She Is, Miss America": The Politics of Sex, Beauty, and Race in America's Most Famous Pageant,* edited by Elwood Watson and Darcy Martin. New York: Palgrave Macmillan, 2004.

Scott, Wilbur J., and Sandra Carson Stanley, eds. *Gays and Lesbians in the Military: Issues, Concerns, and Contrasts.* New York: Aldine de Gruyter, 1994.

Segal, David R. *Recruiting for Uncle Sam: Citizenship and Military Manpower Policy.* Lawrence: University Press of Kansas, 1989.

Sherman, Janann. "'They Either Need These Women Or They Do Not': Margaret Chase Smith and the Fight for Regular Status for Women in the Military." *Journal of Military History* 54, no. 1 (January 1990): 47–78.

———. *No Place for a Woman: A Life of Senator Margaret Chase Smith.* New Brunswick, NJ: Rutgers University Press, 2000.

Sherry, Michael S. *In the Shadow of War: The United States Since the 1930s.* New Haven, CT: Yale University Press, 1995.

Shilts, Randy. *Conduct Unbecoming: Gays and Lesbians in the U.S. Military.* New York: St. Martin's Griffin, 2005.

Skaine, Rosemarie. *Women at War: Gender Issues of Americans in Combat.* Jefferson, NC: McFarland, 1999.

Smith, Jessie Carney, ed. *Notable Black American Women, Book II.* New York: Gale Research, 1996.

Smith, Margaret Chase. *Declaration of Conscience.* 1st ed. New York: Doubleday, 1972.

Smith-Daugherty, Rhonda. *Jacqueline Cochran: Biography of a Pioneer Aviator.* Jefferson, NC: McFarland, 2012.

Snyder, Thomas D., ed. *120 Years of American Education: A Statistical Portrait.* Center for Education Statistics. https://nces.ed.gov/pubs93/93442.pdf.

Solaro, Erin. *Women in the Line of Fire: What You Should Know About Women in the Military.* Emeryville, CA: Seal Press, 2006.

Solinger, Rickie. *Wake up Little Susie: Single Pregnancy and Race Before Roe v. Wade*. New York: Routledge, 1992.

Sparrow, John C. *History of Personnel Demobilization in the U.S. Army*. Pamphlet No. 20-210. Washington, DC: Department of the Army, 1952. http://www.history.army.mil/html/books/104/104-8/CMH_Pub_104-8.pdf.

Spector, Ronald. "The Vietnam War and the Army's Self Image." In *Second Indochina War Symposium: Papers and Commentary*, edited by John Schlight, 169–86. Washington, DC: Center of Military History, 1986.

Steiner, Gilbert Y. *Constitutional Inequality: The Political Fortunes of the Equal Rights Amendment*. Washington, DC: Brookings Institution, 1985.

Stewart, Debra W. *The Women's Movement in Community Politics in the U.S.: The Role of Local Commissions on the Status of Women*. New York: Pergamon Press, 1980.

Stiehm, Judith. *Arms and the Enlisted Woman*. Philadelphia, PA: Temple University Press, 1989.

———. *Bring Me Men and Women: Mandated Change at the U.S. Air Force Academy*. Berkeley: University of California Press, 1981.

———. "The Generations of U.S. Enlisted Women." *Signs* 11, no. 1 (Autumn 1985).

———, ed. *It's Our Military, Too!: Women and the U.S. Military*. Philadelphia, PA: Temple University Press, 1996.

Stremlow, Colonel Mary V. *A History of the Women Marines 1946–1977*. Washington, DC: History and Museums Division, Headquarters, U.S. Marine Corps, 1986.

Stur, Heather. *Beyond Combat: Women and Gender in the Vietnam War Era*. Cambridge: Cambridge University Press, 2011.

Swerdlow, Amy. *Women Strike for Peace: Traditional Motherhood and Radical Politics in the 1960s*. Chicago: University of Chicago Press, 1993.

Thistle, Susan. *From Marriage to the Market: The Transformation of Women's Lives and Work*. Berkeley: University of California Press, 2006.

Threat, Charissa J. *Nursing Civil Rights: Gender and Race in the Army Nurse Corps*. Urbana: University of Illinois Press, 2015.

Treadwell, Mattie E. *The Women's Army Corps: United States Army in World War II*. Washington, DC: Office of the Chief of Military History, Department of the Army, 1954.

United States Department of Defense. *Black Americans in Defense of Our Nation*. Washington, DC: Office of the Deputy Assistant Secretary of Defense for Civilian Personnel Policy/Equal Opportunity, 1991.

Valk, Anne M. *Radical Sisters: Second-Wave Feminism and Black Liberation in Washington, D.C.* Urbana: University of Illinois Press, 2008.

Vuic, Kara Dixon. "'I'm Afraid We're Going to Have to Just Change Our Ways': Marriage, Pregnancy, and Motherhood in the Army Nurse Corps during the Vietnam War." *Signs* 32, no. 4 (2007): 997–1022.

———. *Officer, Nurse, Woman: The Army Nurse Corps in the Vietnam War*. Baltimore: Johns Hopkins University Press, 2010.

———, ed. *The Routledge History of Gender, War, and the U.S. Military*. London: Routledge, 2018.

Wallace, Patricia Ward. *Politics of Conscience: A Biography of Margaret Chase Smith*. Westport, CT: Praeger, 1995.

Watson, Elwood, and Darcy Martin, eds. *"There She Is, Miss America": The Politics of Sex, Beauty, and Race in America's Most Famous Pageant*. New York: Palgrave Macmillan, 2004.

Webber, Winni S. *Lesbians in the Military Speak Out*. Northboro, MA: Madwoman Press, 1993.

Weiner, Lynn. *From Working Girl to Working Mother: The Female Labor Force in the United States, 1820–1980*. Chapel Hill: The University of North Carolina Press, 1985.

Weiss, Jessica. *To Have and to Hold: Marriage, the Baby Boom, and Social Change*. Chicago: University of Chicago Press, 2000.

Weitz, Rose, ed. *The Politics of Women's Bodies: Sexuality, Appearance, and Behavior*. 3rd ed. New York: Oxford University Press, 2010.

Wells-Petry, Melissa. *Exclusion: Homosexuals and the Right to Serve*. Washington, DC: Regnery Gateway, 1993.

Williams, Colin J. *Homosexuals and the Military: A Study of Less Than Honorable Discharge*. 1st ed. New York: Harper & Row, 1971.

Witt, Linda, Judith Bellafaire, Britta Granrud, and Mary Jo Binker. *"A Defense Weapon Known to Be of Value": Servicewomen of the Korean War Era*. London: University Press of New England, 2005.

Zumwalt, Elmo R. *On Watch: A Memoir*. New York: Quadrangle/New York Times Book Co, 1976.

Index

#MeToo, 223
80th Congress, 24, 211

abortion, 114, 115, 185, 265n12; legalization of, 115; military policies on, 115, 116
affirmative action, 164, 268n46
All-Volunteer Force (AVF), 84, 155, 157, 180, 199, 214, 225; impact on servicewomen, 157, 214; transition to, 180
America's Finest Women, 42, 61, 117, 138
American Association of University Women, 33, 147
American Civil Liberties Union (ACLU), 116, 132–33, 135–36, 156, 176, 213, 253n45
Anderson, Constance, 89
Anderson, Jacquelyn, 108
antiwar movement, 179, 183
appearances: concerns about, 41, 122
Army Nurse Corps, 8; director promoted to general, 183, 192; made permanent, 25; and mothers in service, 151; training of nurses, 62
Army-Navy Nurse Act, 15
Aspin regulations, 217
Assistant Chief of Naval Personnel for Women, 60, 98, 163, 168; creation of, 36, 236n56; elimination of, 169, 196; on homosexuality, 130; rank limitations on, 36–37. *See also* Hancock, Captain Joy; Lenihan, Captain Rita; Quigley, Captain Robin; Wilde, Captain Louise; Women Accepted for Volunteer Emergency Service in the Navy (WAVES)
assumptions, 198, 207, 208, 209, 216, 224, 225; impact of Equal Rights Amendment on, 188–89; about motherhood, 106; about sexuality, 122, 127, 131; gender-based service structures founded on, 36, 99, 116, 168, 170; challenges to policies based on, 118, 217
attrition: women's, 94, 96, 101

Bailey, Mildred: access to dependent benefits, 98, 177; Equal Rights Amendment and, 188; expansion of women's military opportunities, 166, 173; integrating men into WAC Center and, 215; military career, 81–82, 85, 95, 96, 167; and recruiting Black women, 54; views on DACOWITS, 154, 157, 158; views on equality, 166, 167, 216; views on motherhood and military career impact, 117; views on women in combat, 174, 183. *See also* Black women, recruiting of
basic allowance for quarters (BAQ), 98, 150, 177. *See also* benefits, dependent; *Frontiero v. Richardson*
benefits: dependent, 14, 38, 136, 143, 170, 176, 177; equal, 31. *See also* basic allowance for quarters (BAQ); *Frontiero v. Richardson*
Biden, Joseph, 225
Big Picture (series), 54, 64, 69
Bishop, Colonel Barbara, 72, 163, 245n32
Black women, 13, 69, 73, 90, 213; DACOWITS and, 148–49; recruitment of, 13, 54–56; representation of, 45, 53, 56, 68, 71, 74; strength of, 12, 54–55, 232n24

Bobbitt, Colonel Billie, 166
Boyce, Colonel Westray Battle, 23
Bradley, General Omar, 31, 61
Brewer, General Margaret, 166, 238n20
Brown, Ruth Payne, 108, 249n43
Bucy, Cheryl, 101

capabilities: assumptions about, 2, 3, 117, 118, 207; equality based on, 174, 175; service academies and, 206, 208; utilization according to, 7, 14, 38, 99, 143; women's, 161, 212
career fields: criteria for, 86; limits on, 14, 86, 217; open to women, 25, 54, 88–89, 91, 93, 181, 195, 201
careers, 37, 117, 121, 145, 221; military service as, 84, 141, 186, 202, 225; length of women's military, 13, 81–82, 94–95, 101, 110, 112; rank limitations on women's, 36, 96–97, 159–60, 201, 211, 218
Carnegie, Hattie, 64
Carter, Secretary of Defense Ash, 218, 224
citizenship, 5, 62, 67, 71, 72, 82, 85; based on heterosexuality, 56, 125, 138; conceptions of women's, 35, 100, 125, 152; martial, 42; military service as training for, 49, 82, 144, 266–67n27
Civil Rights Act of 1964, 164, 182
civil rights movement, 56, 179
Clackum, Fannie Mae, 133–34, 138
Clarke, General Mary, 113–14, 166, 172
class: military service and, 13, 43–44, 53–54, 67, 74, 102, 224
coast guard, 15, 55
Coller, Loretta, 134
combat: as central to military service, 174, 191, 201, 211, 225; connected to leadership roles, 160, 165, 202, 203, 204, 208, 209; definition of, 173–74; exclusion of women from, 156, 179, 193, 196, 198, 200, 209; gender and, 191, 198, 202, 221, 222; resistance to women in, 204–5, 207; women directors' views on, 174, 183, 201, 202; women unsuitable for, 173. *See also* combat exclusion
combat exclusion: gender-based, 86, 173, 196, 201, 202, 208, 210; Equal Rights Amendment impact on, 184, 186–87, 189, 190; removal of gender-based, 156, 192, 194, 197, 217–18, 219, 220
combat leadership: service academies' mission focused on, 173, 202, 203, 208, 209
communism, 7, 22
concerns: about negative perception of servicewomen, 50, 55
Cook, Lieutenant Janet E., 135
Crittenden Report, 57, 130, 131, 132, 224

Darks, LaDonna, 103
Daughters of the American Revolution, 33, 141
Defense Advisory Committee on Women in the Services (DACOWITS): as advisory body, 16, 141, 142, 144; criticism toward, 155; membership in, 142, 146–47, 148; mission of, 141, 143; and the President's Committee on the Status of Women (PCSW), 160–62, 163; race in, 148–49; recommendations from, 144, 150, 151, 153; recommendation on rank ceilings, 159–60; recommendation on combat, 173–74; recommendations on women's bodies, 221, 222; recruiting and, 143, 147, 149–50; and ROTC, 152, 153; as servicewomen's advocates, 142, 145, 154, 156–59, 163, 165, 217
deferments, 84, 104, 180, 188
demobilization, 22, 23
Democratic National Committee, 142, 147
Deom, Carol, 103
Department of Defense: abortion and, 114–16; authorization of DACOWITS, 16, 143–44; creation of, 28; elimination of pregnancy discharge, 114, 192;

family policies, 176, 177, 221; homosexuality policies, 51, 57, 224; pressured to change women's military roles, 159, 162, 169, 174, 219; reactions to DACOWITS recommendations, 142, 145, 149, 150–54, 156–57, 160, 173; sexual assault reporting, 222–23; standards pertaining to women, 221–22; use of civilian women as advisors, 143, 158; on women in combat, 173, 204

dependents: abortion access for, 116; limits on servicewomen claiming, 38, 98, 170, 176–77; women under 21 as, 37, 46. *See also Frontiero v. Richardson*; motherhood; pregnancy

desegregation, 10, 11–13; in women's services, 54

desire for highly-qualified women, 25, 49, 50, 121

détente, 135, 200

discrimination, 10; against mothers, 105, 111, 113; Civil Rights Act and, 164; Equal Employment Opportunity Commission and, 181–82; Equal Rights Amendment and, 185, 188; racial, 10, 11, 13, 71, 164, 182, 194; sex, 176, 184, 193, 212, 220, 224, 225, 226; women directors' views on, 172–73, 202

Don't Ask, Don't Tell, 224, 254n52

draft, 29, 42, 84, 94, 183; dissatisfaction with, 45, 179, 180; elimination of, 155, 178, 179, 180, 193, 198, 200, 201; Equal Rights Amendment and, 183–84, 186–90, 191; fathers and, 104; postwar continuation of, 21, 34, 44–47, 50, 69, 83, 93; ROTC as alternative to, 152; and women, 17, 143, 155, 189, 190, 191, 267n29

Dulinsky, Barbara, 92

Eastman, Margaret, 155, 262n31, 262n32, 263n47

economic citizenship, 5, 82

education: DACOWITS and, 143, 150, 152; on sex, 119, 120; race and, 13, 54;

and service academies, 203, 208; standards for enlistment, 45, 50, 53, 170, 175, 242n25; as service benefit, 45, 48, 55, 59, 69, 76, 82, 88; trends in, 13

Edwards, India, 142, 147

effective utilization, 85, 88, 143, 157, 161, 189, 220

Eisenhower, Dwight D., 7, 21, 35, 202; view on womanpower, 21–23, 25, 30, 34, 35, 85; testimony to Congress, 21, 27, 29

employment: discrimination in, 164, 177, 181, 182; military service as, 6, 30, 186; mothers and, 101, 103; President's Commission on the Status of Women and, 160–61; women's, 93, 181. *See also* career, military service as

enlistment standards, 37, 38, 45, 46, 55, 81, 186, 225; and education, 50, 54, 170, 175, 242n25

Equal Employment Opportunity Commission, 164, 181

equal opportunity, 14, 191, 203, 204; and effective utilization, 10; General Bailey on, 216; DACOWITS interest in, 156–57, 158; definition of, 192; Department of Defense commitment to, 16, 182; Executive order 11375 and, 164; military movement toward, 161, 162, 194, 196; pregnancy and, 221; President Johnson on, 164; women in ROTC as, 153, 195; and women in the service academies, 204–7. *See also* Public Law 90-130; Zumwalt, Elmo

equality: battle for, 159, 168, 175, 184, 201, 205, 225; definition of, 16, 31, 38, 53, 77, 99, 138, 192; limitations on, 14, 36, 38, 97, 100; negotiating, 14, 117; obstacles to, 118, 174, 216, 226; policies to create, 5, 37, 164–65, 174, 194; servicewomen and, 82, 131, 191, 219; women directors' views on, 1, 166–67, 170–73, 182, 202; women's, 6, 35, 150

Index 293

equal pay, 5, 14, 38, 82, 85; based on rank, 97, 165; for nurses, 234n17; military commitment to, 85, 169, 195; in the private sector, 6, 84; second-wave feminism and, 84, 166

equal rights: changing conceptions of, 177, 187; DACOWITS and, 157–58, 161, 173; national defense and, 183; second-wave feminism and, 181

Equal Rights Amendment (ERA): failure of, 191; history of, 181–82; impact of 186–90, 193–94, 200, 203, 205, 207; opposition to, 155, 181, 185, 190–91; passage of, 155, 184; ratification process of, 178, 192

Executive Order 10240, 105, 110

Executive Order 11375, 164. *See* equal opportunity

Executive Order 14004, 225

Executive Order 9981, 11, 54, 70

expansion of women's roles and opportunities, 32, 162, 174, 182, 187, 196, 201, 218, 269n57

Feminine Mystique, 3. *See also* Friedan, Betty

femininity: end of, 208, 221; and military service, 43, 53, 55, 59, 70, 73, 74; in recruiting, 41, 56; in training, 62, 64, 65, 72, 75, 77; white, middle-class conception of, 13, 44, 54, 67, 68, 76

feminism: women's leaders views on, 166, 178, 183. *See also* second-wave feminism

feminists: negative connotation of. *See* second-wave feminism

The First Ladies of the Land . . . America's Finest, 52

first women promoted to general, 183, 192

Ford, John, 119

Forrestal, James, 24, 30

Fort Hood Investigation, 223

Franklin, Janet, 91

Friedan, Betty, 3, 5
Frontiero, Sharron, 176, 178
Frontiero v. Richardson, 176–77

Garner, Grace, 133–34, 138
gender difference philosophy, 6, 7, 16, 100, 165; as foundation for equality in the military, 38, 77, 106, 118, 138, 216; movement away from, 6, 14, 163, 179, 192, 208
gender ideals, 9, 62, 76, 86
gender sameness philosophy, 2, 6, 8, 14, 16
Gerichten, Joan, 110, 117
G.I. Bill, 53, 102
Ginsberg, Ruth Bader, 176
glamour: military service associated with, 40, 41, 42, 43, 60, 73, 76
Glynn, General James, 220
Gordon, Gale, 93
Gorman, Colonel Emily, 162–63
Gragg, Rosa, 148, 161
Graham, Annie, 71
Grant, Galen, 135
Guillen, Vanessa, 223

Haarhaus, MaryAnne, 88–89, 97, 101
hairstyles, 51, 52, 64, 68, 69, 74, 75, 208
Hall, Mary Tener Davidson, 103, 108
Hallaren, Colonel Mary, 23, 24, 124; on mothers in uniform, 104–5, 107, 108, 117, 124; on utilization of woman-power, 25–26, 28; Women's Armed Services Integration Act and, 27, 33, 34, 37, 38
Hamerlinck, Winnifred, 111. *See also* pregnancy; waiver system
Hancock, Captain Joy Bright, 23, 60, 85
Harrison, Cynthia, 142, 164
Hays, General Anna, 183, 192
Hazard, Rear Admiral Roberta, 82
Hazelwood, Polly, 101
Height, Dorothy, 147, 148, 160
heterosexuality: importance in military service, 56, 102, 120, 138

294 Index

Hobby, Colonel Oveta Culp, 23, 62, 122, 141, 142, 147
Hoisington, General Elizabeth, 92; on equality, 168, 169; on removing barriers, 171, 201, 202; on women's reenlistment rates, 94; promotion to general, 183, 192; rank ceilings, 162–63
Holm, Major General Jeanne, 214, 216; on DACOWITS, 145, 153–54, 158; on equality, 1, 5, 6–7, 174–75, 198, 209; on standards, 50; on women's exclusion, 99; rank ceilings, 163, 165; views on directors, 170, 171
homosexuality, 123; ACLU and, 133; attitudes toward, 122, 123; defining and identifying, 57, 127, 131; discharges for, 128, 129, 133–34, 135–36, 138, 159, 165, 184, 213; efforts to control, 51, 57, 122, 129, 213, 214, 224; hygiene education and, 119; in the women's service components, 129, 134, 135; investigations into, 122, 125–28, 136; Kinsey findings on, 102; military leaders' concerns over, 121, 124, 129, 130, 132; recruit training on, 122, 123; World War II slander campaign associated with, 122. *See also* Crittenden Report; Don't Ask, Don't Tell; lesbianism; lesbians; USS *Norton Sound*; witch hunts
Horton, Joan, 108
House Armed Services Committee, 27–28, 32–33, 106, 156, 174, 177, 207
housing, 57, 98, 102, 136, 143, 150, 153, 188; concerns about, 88; standards, 144, 145, 151, 177
Huber, Katherine, 177
hygiene education, 119, 130, 131. *See also* "Sex Hygiene"

image of servicewomen, 72, 221
integration, 171, 172; of marine boot camp, 71; postwar efforts, 23–35, 39; racial, 10, 11, 12, 54, 56, 70, 148; women's, 130, 168, 197, 208, 214, 216

Johnson, Clara Christine "Chris," 90–91
Johnson, Assistant Secretary of the Navy James, 204
Johnson, Lyndon B.: effort to promote women officers, 162, 164; Executive Order 11375 and, 164; Public Law 90-130 and, 163; views on equal opportunity, 164–65; Women's Armed Services Integration Act and, 32, 34
Johnson, Mayrell, 33
Junior League, 33, 146

Keesler Air Force Base, 129, 132
Kennan, George, 22
Kennedy, John F., 156, 160
King, Lieutenant Colonel Grace, 205
Kingman, Adelaide, 141, 143, 144, 146, 147
Kinsey, Alfred, 102
Korean War, 106, 108; creation of DACOWITS during, 141; decline in Black servicewomen after, 55; discussion on drafting women, 267n29; marriage discharge suspended, 101; manpower needs, 141; numbers of women in service, 44, 55; recruiting failures, 45

labor union women, 6, 84
Lackland Air Force Base, 69, 88, 89, 113, 129
ladies: as problematic construction, 77, 208; servicewomen as, 43, 51, 59, 60, 62–63, 216; training to create, 52, 64, 73, 76, 121
Lamb, Ann, 71
Leahey, Commander Catherine, 195
legislation: to admit women to service academies, 204, 207; coast guard and womanpower, 15; dependent benefits, 154, 176–77; desegregation and lack of, 10; to eliminate Section 6015, 174, 210; and the Equal Rights Amendment, 184, 186, 190, 194; to make womanpower permanent, 15, 23–25,

Index   295

legislation (cont.)
27–29, 32, 34, 39; prohibiting federal funds for abortion, 116; protective labor, 100, 164, 181–82; proposed for drafting women, 17; to remove rank limitations, 162–64, 165; for reserve status only, 32, 34; used to control military size, 160; wartime women's services, 23, 28. *See also* Don't Ask, Don't Tell; Equal Rights Amendment; protective labor legislation; *specific entries under* Public Law; Section 6015; Women's Armed Services Integration Act

Lenihan, Captain Rita, 163, 166, 168, 169, 176

lesbianism: defining and identifying, 122, 125, 126, 127, 129, 131; fears of military service as encouraging, 43

lesbians: in the military, 129, 134, 135; stereotype of servicewomen as, 121; unsuitable for military service, 16, 50, 53, 57–59, 121–22, 124–25; discharge of, 126, 129, 131, 138, 164, 213; World War II and, 122. *See also* homosexuality

Lewis, Ann Thacker, 108, 129

liberal feminists. *See* second-wave feminists

limitations: gender-based, 2, 3, 6, 157, 168, 211, 224–25; impact on womanpower, 94, 107, 150, 161, 169; on combat, 179, 202; on rank, 96, 162; removal of, 143, 153, 158, 162–63, 165, 172, 207; as legal, 99; on utilization, 101, 117; Women's Armed Services Integration Act and, 36, 38; women's efforts to negotiate, 6, 9, 16, 105, 114, 159. *See also* Public Law 90–130; pregnancy discharge; protective labor legislation; rank

Lord, Mary Pillsbury, 141, 142, 147; on women's integration, 28

Lucas, Carmen, 92

Lucas, Colonel Ruth, 55

MacArthur, General Douglas, 202

Mack, Vice Admiral William, 203, 207

male, military as default, 8, 11, 206

manpower, 106, 180, 199; needs, 25, 28, 31 34, 45, 92, 200, 215; shortages, 29, 44, 108, 214; utilization, 193

marriage, 48, 55, 57, 105, 117, 124, 136–38, 152; age at, 3; bars to women's employment, 101; discharge policies, 101–2, 103, 121; and military service, 76, 94, 95, 61, 72, 103, 104; policies on, 94, 189; sex within, 102, 120–21

Marshall, George, 142

Marshall Plan, 34

martial citizenship, 42

martial masculinity, 44

masculine: military as, 39, 46, 62, 120, 165, 186, 197, 219

masculinizing: fear of military service as, 43, 55, 63, 76

Masek, Sharon, 89, 121, 124

McArthur, Susie, 90, 92

McCarthy, Joseph, 129

McClendon, Sarah, 148, 155

Menke, Marge, 103

military academies. *See* service academies

military occupational specialties: open to women, 86–87, 196, 216

military service: as career opportunity, 16, 44, 95, 117, 124, 225; as citizenship obligation, 42; as preparation for future, 48, 49, 53, 64, 65, 121, 123

Miss America, 40–42, 43, 60, 68

Monroe, Marilyn, 40–42

Morden, Bettie, 95, 99

motherhood, 104, 114, 117, 124, 138; discharge, 105–8, 109, 112, 114, 115; and military service, 103, 113, 152, 221; regulations on, 16, 94, 103, 105, 110, 117, 159; waiver system, 111, 112. *See also* mothers; pregnancy; Thompson, Alba Martinelli

296   Index

mothers: retention of, 117; stay-at-home, 3, 146, 191; women as potential, 100–101; working, 102–3, 109, 110, 112, 113, 114, 248n22. *See also* motherhood; waiver system
Muller vs. Oregon, 100–101

National Association of Colored Women's Clubs, 148–49, 161
national defense, 56, 131, 134, 158, 200, 218, 225; acceptance of women in, 171, 172, 182, 196, 219, 220, 226; Americans' understanding of, 43, 69, 143; benefits of women in, 10, 23, 41; combat as central to, 44, 174; importance of men in, 44, 46, 209, 226; percentage of women in, 179, 218; postwar vision of, 22, 35, 85. *See also* masculine
National Organization for Women, 142, 177, 181; and DACOWITS, 156–57; efforts to support servicewomen, 156–57, 183; and Equal Rights Amendment, 182, 184, 187, 192
naval vessels, women on. *See* women in ships
Navy Nurse Corps, 15, 25
Neller, General Robert, 220
Neuswanger, Joan, 101
Never Wave at a Wac, 60–61, 63, 66, 70
Nixon, Richard, 115–16, 180, 194
Noble, Dr. Jeanne, 148, 160
noncombatant, 35–36; women defined as, 2, 31, 35, 37, 203, 204, 209

O'Connor, John, 211–12
O'Connor, Sandra Day, 148, 173
obligation: military service as, 35, 42, 83, 84, 186, 191
Ollison, Myrtle, 148, 149
Owens v. Brown, 210. *See also* Section 6015

paid employment: women's participation in, 93, 103, 185
Pan American Airways, 72

parental permission, 37, 44, 46, 238n22
Paul, Lieutenant General Willard S., 23–24, 26, 27
pay, 37, 98, 150, 159; combat, 98; equity, 31, 38, 67, 97, 133–34, 177, 216; officers in World War II, 81, 234n17. *See also* equal pay
perception of servicewomen: as equals, 224; as inferiors, 219, 224, 226; as mannish, 55; negative, 50; as sexual objects, 222
postwar occupation, 7, 22
Poynor, Carol, 81–82, 92, 102
pregnancy, 123, 138, 189; DACOWITS and, 151, 221–22; discharge policies, 50, 94, 102–5, 108–11, 113, 129, 184; discrimination due to, 114, 221; enlistment policies related to, 38; impact on careers, 95, 101, 111, 159, 165; removal of discharge policies, 114, 170. *See also* abortion; Executive Order 10240; motherhood; Thompson, Alba Martinelli; Von Wantoch, Captain Jordine; waiver system
preparedness, 21–24, 27, 28, 30, 31
President's Commission on the Status of Women (PCSW), 142, 183; DACOWITS and, 156, 160, 161–62; goals of, 142; protective labor legislation and, 164, 181; rank limitations and, 161–62, 165; recommendations of, 161–62
President's Committee on Civil Rights, 10
promotion, 67, 97–98, 167, 183, 189–90, 194, 218; equal, 168; removal of restrictions, 160, 161–63, 202, 211; restrictions on women, 86, 95, 96, 159, 201, 216
propaganda, 41, 183; use of children in, 46; World War II, 43, 248n22
protective labor legislation, 3, 164, 181, 182, 185
Proud Parents, 46, 47
Public Law 90-130, 163–64
publicity, 40, 42, 51, 61, 69, 71, 143–47, 153, 213, 237n14

Index   297

Quigley, Captain Robin, 166; career progression, 98; elimination of Assistant Chief of Naval Personnel for Women, 169, 196–97; on DACOWITS, 154; on equality, 166, 169, 172

race, 90, 149, 194, 226; and challenges to recruiting Black women, 54; and enlistment standards, 54; and military integration, 11, 12, 13, 53–54, 58, 70, 71; in recruiting materials, 53, 56; in training materials, 73. *See also* whiteness
Ranger School, 218
rank: equal, 82, 95, 97; military system of, 97–98
rank ceilings: removal of, 14, 143, 158, 162–63, 165, 172, 192; on women, 36, 94, 96, 159, 161
recruiting, 25, 31–32, 143, 146, 150, 153, 180, 199; of Black women, 12, 13, 53, 54–56; campaigns, 40, 41, 44, 54, 58, 60, 61, 145, 149; emphasis on quality in, 48, 50, 51; lack of success in, 45, 148, 216; limits on married women in, 38, 46; minimum age, 45; physical examinations in, 49–50; and sexual morality, 43, 50, 53; use of race and class in, 43, 44, 54, 55, 56
recruiting materials: appeal to parents in, 37, 40, 44, 46–47, 48, 49, 58, 72, 147; depiction of uniforms in, 44, 51–52, 64, 76; educational opportunities, 48, 53; and heterosexuality, 50, 53, 56–57; images of men and women in, 57; and race, 71; themes in, 48, 76, 150; and whiteness, 53, 57, 58
regular vs. reserve debate, 30–34
restrictions. *See* limitations
retention: problems with, 150, 151, 153, 194
Riley, Colonel Emma, 130
Roberts, Lieutenant Colonel Mary Juanita D., 162
Roe v. Wade, 115, 116

Rogers, Bernard, 190, 197
Roosevelt, Eleanor, 142, 147
Rosenberg, Anna, 106, 107, 108, 117, 141, 142, 145
Reserve Officers Training Corps (ROTC), 152, 155; admission of women to air force ROTC, 152–53, 192, 203; declining enrollments, 180; proposed opening to women, 152, 189; women in, 195, 203, 206

Salmen, Mary, 109
Schlafly, Phyllis, 185, 186, 190–91
Schoon, Carol, 93
second-wave feminism, 1, 5, 6, 14: and DACOWITS, 156; and combat, 156, 183; equal pay and, 84; and the Equal Rights Amendment, 181; influence on womanpower, 3; rise of, 142, 177, 179; and servicewomen, 184; success of, 180; varieties within, 181
Section 6015: efforts to repeal, 173–74, 210–11. *See also Owens v. Brown*
Section Eight Discharges, 134
segregation: racial, 10, 13, 39, 54, 148; of womanpower, 39, 69, 71, 182, 197, 198, 201, 220. *See also* desegregation
Selective Service, 22, 46, 50, 104
Senate Armed Services Committee, 24, 25, 27, 34
service academies: accommodations for women, 208; admission of women, 14, 16, 192, 207; call to admit women, 156, 157, 173; connection to leadership, 84, 202, 203, 208; declining enrollments, 180; Equal Rights Amendment and, 203, 207; male cadet attitudes toward women, 209, 214; physical standards, 206; sexual integration, 203, 209; women's athletics, 208
servicewomen: acceptance of, 171, 172, 182, 196, 219, 220, 226; Equal Rights Amendment impact on, 184, 185–88, 190, 191, 193, 196; and feminism,

166, 169, 170, 172, 175, 182–83; as liaisons with DACOWITS, 144–46, 152, 154, 163; moral standards for, 51, 120, 138
sex: education, 119; discrimination, 113, 172, 176, 181–82, 184, 188, 193, 225
"Sex Hygiene," 119
sexual assault, 219, 222–24, 226
sexual harassment, 223, 226
Share Service for Freedom, 42, 149, 150
Sirica, Judge John, 210–11
Skirts Ahoy!, 60–61, 64, 66, 75
slander campaign: World War II, 121, 237n14, 256n18
Smith, Margaret Chase, 32–33, 34
Smith, Captain Tommie Sue, 113
Sode, Marie, 136–38
Somebody Special, 49, 51, 52, 53, 87
standards: good character, 50, 51, 52, 120; health, 206, 208, 222; postpartum, 222; for servicewomen, 28, 72, 170, 219; women's ability to meet, 12, 13, 42, 48, 54
statistics: abortion, 115; education, 13; homosexuality, 57, 130, 131; income, 84–85; Black servicewomen, 12, 54–55, 71; sexual assault, 223–24, 226; women's service, 12, 91, 92, 95
Stecher, Beatrice, 91
STOP ERA, 185, 192
Stratton, Samuel, 206, 207
Streeter, Colonel Ruth, 23
Strictly Personal, 65, 66, 71, 75
Sustad, Colonel Jeanette, 166, 168

Tailhook Scandal, 223
temporary: women's military service as, 4, 60, 81, 97, 159
Thompson, Alba Martinelli, 105–8, 109, 111, 112, 175,
Towle, Colonel Katherine, 85
traditional gender roles. *See* gender ideals
training: as a means to make ladies, 56, 59, 61, 64, 65, 74, 77, 121; basic training and boot camp, 69, 219, 220; character and image development in, 66–67, 72–73, 75, 76, 120, 121, 123; citizenship improvement and, 67, 72; race and, 13, 54, 70, 90; weapons and women's, 63, 70, 71, 189, 190, 192; whiteness in, 13; women excluded from advanced opportunities, 96, 99, 186, 203–4; World War II, 62
transgender servicemembers, 17, 25, 136, 137, 224–25. *See also* Executive Order 14004; Sode, Marie; Von Hoffburg, Kristian
Treadwell, Mattie, 62, 122
Trimeloni, Colonel Bianca, 166
Truman, Harry, 22, 27, 35, 54, 70, 105, 109, 142
Truman Doctrine, 34

Uncle Sam, 21, 81, 82, 120, 121
Universal Military Training, 34, 46
U.S. Air Force Academy, 202, 203, 205–7, 209
U.S. Military Academy. *See* West Point
U.S. Naval Academy, 202, 203, 204, 205, 208, 210
USS *Norton Sound*: lesbian witch hunt on board, 212–14
USS *Sanctuary*, 210
USS *Vulcan*, 212
utilization, 85, 189, 220; inconsistencies in, 88, 165, 193, 214; of women, 86, 117, 157, 161, 169, 188, 198, 215

Van Horn, Cadet June, 209
Vietnam War, 9, 45, 72, 92–93, 101, 110–11, 180, 194
Vinson, Carl, 30, 104
Von Hoffburg, Kristian, 136–138. *See also* Sode, Marie; transgender service members
Von Wantoch, Captain Jordine, 111, 112, 113, 114, 117, 221

The Wac is a Soldier, Too, 64, 71
waiver system, 111–14, 189. *See also* Hamerlinck, Winnifred; pregnancy; Smith, Tommie Sue; Von Wantoch, Jordine
War Department, 24, 28, 119, 122, 141
War Manpower Commission, 141
weapons training, 189, 190, 192, 208; excluded from WAF training, 63; for men, 69; in naval training, 62; *Never Wave at a WAC* depiction of, 70
West Point, 189, 190, 202, 203, 209; Class of 1980, 200, 208
Wheeler, Carol, 195
White House Conference on Effective Uses of Womanpower, 102
whiteness: in recruiting materials, 53, 56; in training materials, 68; used to structure women's service, 13, 43, 57, 67, 75, 102
Wilde, Captain Louise, 72
witch hunts, 122, 126, 129–30, 132, 135, 138, 213, 224
womanhood: ideas of American, 41, 43–44, 53, 56–57, 65, 117, 142, 147, 152
Womanpause, 217
womanpower, 50, 51, 62, 120, 144–47, 198, 200, 225–26; Equal Rights Amendment impact on, 184, 188, 192, 193, 198; expansion of, 32, 211, 216; femininity and, 41, 53–57, 75, 76, 77; impact on modern defense, 21, 29, 35, 150, 225; postwar retention of, 24, 25, 27, 28, 30, 34; reassessment of, 141, 145, 163, 165, 175, 180, 205, 214, 219; race and, 13, 55, 149; utilization of, 23, 26, 31, 86, 102, 103, 162, 178
Women Accepted for Volunteer Emergency Service in the Navy (WAVES), 36, 45, 60, 62, 68, 166, 210; Director of, 23, 36, 53, 98, 130, 163, 166, 182, 196, 197, 236n56; homosexuality in, 123, 125–26, 129; racial integration of, 12, 70, 242n30. *See also* Assistant Chief of Naval Personnel for Women; Hancock, Captain Joy; Lenihan, Captain Rita; Quigley, Captain Robin; Wilde, Captain Louise; Zumwalt, Admiral Elmo
women at sea, 211, 212
Women in the Air Force (WAF), 36, 44, 45, 50, 63, 92, 197, 203; Director of, 37, 53, 130, 145, 163, 166, 170, 171, 182; homosexuality in, 132–35; instructional guidebooks, 67–68, 73; racial integration of, 13, 55, 70. *See also* Bobbitt, Colonel Billie; Holm, Major General Jeanne; Riley, Colonel Emma; Trimeloni, Colonel Bianca
Women Marines (WM): Director of, 23, 37, 85, 130, 163, 166, 168, 197; racial integration of, 12, 13, 24, 55, 69, 71, 72, 197. *See also* Bishop, Colonel Barbara; Brewer, General Margaret; Sustad, Colonel Jeanette
Women's Armed Services Academy, 203
Women's Armed Services Integration Act, 11, 14, 15, 27, 28, 35, 36; provisions of, 35–39; rank limitations in, 36–38; women's components created, 36, 39
Women's Army Auxiliary Corps (WAAC), 62, 81, 197
Women's Army Corps (WAC): Black women in, 12, 13, 54, 55, 71; Director of, 23, 36, 97, 166, 168, 172, 188–89, 215; homosexuality in, 122, 124, 126–29; training, 63, 65–66, 70, 74–76; in World War II, 23, 27, 28, 43, 62. *See also* Bailey, General Mildred; Clarke, General Mary; Gorman, Colonel Emily; Hallaren, Colonel Mary; Hoisington, General Elizabeth; Women's Army Auxiliary Corps
women's bodies: regulations of, 117, 118. *See also* pregnancy; homosexuality
women's jobs: nontraditional, 14, 92, 93, 94, 213, 214; similarity to civilian jobs, 62, 89, 91, 186, 216; traditional,

300 Index

88, 91, 92, 209, 210, 214, 216. *See also* careers

women's liberation movement. *See* second-wave feminism

women's Lobby, 156, 265

women's service components: elimination of, 116, 196, 197, 217

women's sexual behavior: concerns over, 117, 121, 126, 213

Woods, Dr. Geraldine, 148, 149

World War I, 119, 234n17

Wright-Patterson Air Force Base, 129, 132

Wuellner, Rose, 103

Zumwalt, Admiral Elmo, 194, 195, 196, 210; and Z-gram, 116; "Equal Rights and Opportunities for Women in the Navy," 210, 269n56